The Economics of Consumption

ECONOMICS OF DECISION MAKING IN THE HOUSEHOLD

The Economics of Consumption

ECONOMICS OF DECISION MAKING IN THE HOUSEHOLD

WILLARD W. COCHRANE
Department of Agricultural Economics
University of Minnesota

CAROLYN SHAW BELL
Department of Economics
Wellesley College

McGRAW-HILL BOOK COMPANY, INC.
New York · Toronto · London · 1956

THE ECONOMICS OF CONSUMPTION

Library of Congress Catalog Card Number 55-9537

Preface

In the hazy and ill-defined land of consumption economics, we find numerous volumes focusing on personal finances, consumer education, and various aspects of buymanship but few that concentrate on the economics of consumption. As teachers in the applied field of consumption economics, we have felt the need of a text that grows out of the main stream of economic thinking, that employs analytical methods from modern economics, and that deals with problems amenable to solutions by economic analyses. In more general terms, we have felt the need of a text that describes and analyzes the decision making of households within the frame of reference provided by modern economics. *And it has been our purpose in writing this volume to develop a text that meets this need.* It is further our hope that this volume will contribute to the organization of a field of study and inquiry that concentrates on the economics of decision making in the household: demonstrates that there is, in fact, such a field, and provides some guides for those who seek to explore it.

In developing this text, the authors have assumed that student users will have completed a conventional course in the principles of economics. The analytical portions of this volume begin in all cases at an elementary level and proceed step by step. Thus the student who has not had or may have forgotten his principles of economics can follow the reasoning. But whether the analyses can, without a "principles" background, be placed in a proper and meaningful perspective is another question. In the view of the authors, this volume is best suited for use in a course that builds on the principles of economics and develops one of its many applied fields, namely, the economics of consumption. The course we have in mind is thus comparable in level and coverage with a first course in money and banking, international trade, or labor economics.

But certain basic and practical questions arise at this point: "Why do we need a course and text of the types outlined here?" "What good is a course and text which describe and analyze the decision making of consumers?" "Why not tell the consumer which automobile or hot-water heater is the best buy and let it go at that?" The negative answers are easy. In the first place, there is no one best buy in automobiles or anything else for all consumers in all situations. In the second place, information of the best-buy type quickly gets out of date.

The positive answer is more difficult. The fundamental question is: "Why do we concentrate on developing an understanding of the decision-making processes in consumption rather than the provision of information for use in decision making?" Certainly the latter activity is important. It is the view of the authors, however, that, in a rigorous course of study to be taken only once in a lifetime, the emphasis should be on gaining an understanding of the processes involved. This view is based on one compelling reason: If we understand the nature of an operation or a process, we are then in a position to work with it, modify it, or control it, if we so desire. Understanding is power, whether it be with respect to the operation of a gasoline motor or the consumption process. If we understand the nature of the consumption process—the decision making and behavior involved—we are better able to appraise and refine our own behavior, as well as join with others in the formulation of policies bearing on consumption.

Understanding the behavior of individuals and groups in their consumption activities comes hard. Thus, in this volume, we have sought to organize and present the available research and thinking in this field to provide a basis for understanding the behavior of individuals and groups in their consumption activities.

Since ideas and concepts rarely jump full-blown from the mind of man, most of the ideas and concepts presented in this volume were acquired and assimilated by the authors from their teachers and other workers in the field. Where ideas or concepts are taken directly from the work of others, this has been acknowledged or noted in the text or in footnotes. The greater part of the text, however, represents the authors' formulation or treatment of ideas and concepts now current or gaining currency in the field. Shortcomings in this book and errors of fact, judgment, or logic are, thus, the responsibility of the authors alone.

WILLARD W. COCHRANE
CAROLYN SHAW BELL

Contents

PART ONE

Introduction

The following four chapters are designed to introduce the student and interested persons to the general area known as the economics of consumption. Chapter 1 is concerned with delineating the field—describing and defining the subject matter to be studied. Chapter 2 presents in definitional form some important and regularly employed concepts in an effort (1) to familiarize the student with these concepts, (2) to minimize those problems and difficulties which are primarily terminological, and (3) to enhance the precision of discussions in this area. Chapter 3 attempts in a few brief pages to describe the economy in which we live—to set forth its general purpose, organization, and performance in the United States of the 1950s. Chapter 4 describes the position of the consumer in the economy of the United States—describes the financial status, income allocations, and material well-being of the average consumer.

To some, much of the material presented in Part I will be old stuff; hence those individuals will want to hurry through this part. To others, some of the introductory ideas will appear difficult and confusing, since the full implications of these ideas rest upon their development in later parts of the volume. These individuals will have to worry along with the introductory ideas for the present and seek their fuller meaning in later sections. But all readers will want to give careful consideration to Chapter 1, for the conceptual design of this volume and the authors' conception of the general area known as the *economics of consumption* are laid down in that brief chapter.

1. What Is Consumption Economics?

Consumption involves a broad slice of human activity. It is concerned with all phases of the using up of goods and services in living. Thus, we may be said to be consuming when we are eating food, sleeping on a bed, visiting the dentist, or going to school. But there are other aspects to consumption. The choosing, or selecting, of a particular bill of goods and services is a part of the consumption process. This in turn involves acquiring information, participating in transactions, making decisions, and so on. Then it may be suggested that production involves consumption: a metal press is gradually used up in stamping out automobile fenders; many pencils were consumed, used up, in the production of this book; the laborer eating his lunch is consuming in order to acquire the energy to continue with his production activity. And the college football player would seem to be producing a service and consuming recreational equipment at one and the same time. Thus, it would appear that consumption and production are intermixed and that consumption permeates most, if not all, human activities.

THE CONCEPT OF CONSUMPTION

Part of our difficulty arises out of the fact that we have not determined as yet what precisely is meant by (1) *consumption* and (2) *production.* Let us, therefore, develop some definitions and see if those definitions do not help to bring some order into a chaotic world of fact and ideas. By production we generally mean the *combination* and *use* of various inputs—units of land, labor, capital, and management—to yield (or produce) some product or service. In this definition, there is an element of selection—the choice of inputs; there is an element of "using up"—in the use of inputs; and there is the element of obtaining something—the output of so many units of a product. Now it is also the case that each of these elements is a part of consumption. There is an element of selection in consumption—the selection of a particular set of goods and services. There is an element of "using up" in consumption—the using up of different goods and services in living. And there is an element of obtaining something in consumption—this output we call satisfaction (or utility). Goods and services are "used up" in consumption to "produce" satisfaction (or utility) for the consumer. Thus we might define consumption as the combination and use of goods and services to produce satisfaction for the consumer.

In this view, consumption is analogous to production—only the nature of the product is different. The output of a productive activity is so many units of a physical good or service (e.g., washing machines, haircuts); the output of consumption is so many units of satisfaction (or utiles). Thus an activity which combines and uses up units of labor, leather, textiles, machines, and such services as storage, transportation, and selling to place a number of units of shoes in stores throughout the United States is *production,* and an activity which combines and uses up units of food, music, and floor space for dancing to yield so many units of satisfaction to a young couple in love is *consumption.* It may be difficult on occasion to determine whether a particular activity is in fact consumption, or some other category of human activity, but at least the concept is clear.

INTRODUCING ECONOMICS

But everything that is consumption is not economics. Or, stated more precisely, the term economics of consumption is not a synonym for consumption. What, then, do we mean by consumption economics? In the first place, it is a narrower idea than consumption; it is limited to the economic, or perhaps the socioeconomic, aspects of consumption. Generally speaking, the economist working in the field of consumption will not be concerned with the technological and physiological aspects of consumption. He will not investigate, but will take as given, such things as the wearing qualities of linoleum, the tensile strength of rayon, the physical process of transforming animal protein into human cell tissue, and so on. This is not to suggest that these aspects of consumption are unimportant. On the contrary, they may be very important. But, in the division of labor that has developed in the sciences, these aspects fall outside the province of economics, hence outside the province of the economics of consumption.

In the second place, and in a more positive vein, consumption economics is concerned with the problem of choice: how choice decisions are made. Why does the consumer choose one particular combination of goods and services (a combination involving so many units of commodity X, so many units of commodity Y, and so on), and what would happen if he were to choose some other combination? But the economist is interested in this problem of choice only in one special, although almost universal, case, namely, where the means of satisfying wants are scarce relative to those wants. In other words, the choice problem becomes an economic problem only where the number and extent of wants exceed the means of satisfying those wants and a *choice* must be made with respect to the wants to be satisfied. To the individual, the economic problem of consumption takes the form of limited income and unlimited wants; hence, the individual must make a choice with respect to the goods and services to be consumed to satisfy those wants. Thus, some economists would be inclined to define consumption economics as a field of study which explains the choice-making process of consumers where the number and extent of wants exceed the means of satisfying them.

This definition yields a rather narrow field of study for consumption economics. The field so delimited would comprise two principal areas of work, (1) the development of a theory of consumer behavior which explains the choice-making process and (2) the development of measures of the degree of satisfaction associated with different choice patterns (i.e., the derivation of utility functions). In large measure, the field of consumption economics as developed by economists has been limited to the first of these two areas—the development of a *theory* of consumer choice. Proceeding on the assumption that each consumer seeks to maximize his total satisfaction, economists have formulated an elaborate and, we shall argue, a plausible, although not very useful, theory of choice. This theory generally excludes the technological aspects of consumption; it excludes, for example, the nutritional implication of the consumption of a particular type of food or the wearing qualities of wool versus nylon. It also takes as given such things as consumer tastes, buymanship, and information. It would not investigate such questions as how tastes and preferences are formed or whether in some sense those tastes are good or bad; and again it would not investigate ways of informing the consumer or enhancing his ability to bargain. In this sense, the theory is narrow; it excludes most of what the layman would consider to be consumption economics.[1]

[1] For examples see Tibor Scitovsky, *Welfare and Competition,* Irwin Series in Economics, Richard D. Irwin, Inc., Homewood, Ill., 1951, pp. 29–30; and George Stigler, *The Theory of Price,* rev. ed., The Macmillan Company, New York, 1952, pp. 68–74.

Where the theoretical area of study has been circumscribed by economists out of "choice," the second area is circumscribed by the hard facts of the world. The measurement of human satisfaction (utility functions) associated with different choice patterns has been technically impossible. We say "has been," since some progress in measuring the utility of money has been made in recent years, but the measurement problem remains extremely difficult.[2] Not much has been done in this direction, nor have we reason to expect much in the way of results for some time to come. Thus, the field of work growing out of the definition of consumption economics suggested above is narrower than the beginning student might reasonably have expected. The thing being maximized, satisfaction, turns out to be nonmeasurable, and in the development of a theory of consumer choice economists have, for all practicable purposes, excluded the "facts" of consumption from it.

Because of the conceptual strait jacket imposed by the definition of consumption economics given above, some economists, including the authors of this volume, are inclined to broaden that definition somewhat. An expanded concept, but one still growing out of the choice-making process, might be stated as follows: *Consumption economics is the study of decision making by households with respect to the choice of goods and services used in living, together with the relationships growing out of, and the activities surrounding, that decision making.* Implicit in this definition is the idea of scarce means—the fact that all wants of all consumers cannot be satisfied with the available means of production. Thus, the central problem of choice remains. Further, this definition would, as would the previous one, exclude from the field the technological aspects of consumption. We should leave, for example, such considerations as the nutritive content of a pound of beefsteak to the nutritionists and the wearing qualities of different fabrics to the textile people.

But where the previous definition focuses exclusively on the theory of choice, the latter definition suggests that the consequences of particular choices might be traced, described, and analyzed. It suggests, also, that we need not take as given such things as tastes and preference and information. The implications of creating or modifying tastes may with some logic be included in the field, as may also a consideration of different levels of information on consumer behavior. And the nature of institutional arrangements under which choices are made (e.g., the structure of retail

[2] Frederich Mosteller and Philip Nogee, "An Experimental Measurement of Utility," *Journal of Political Economy*, October, 1951.

markets, merchandising practices, and legal restraints) would seem to comprise a rich and fruitful area of investigation. In this view, then, the problem of choice retains the leading role, but it does not comprise the entire play. The other members of the cast, as well as the story itself, give meaning and substance to the performance (consumption economics), which are not conveyed by the leading actor alone (the central problem of choice).

THE FIELD OF CONSUMPTION ECONOMICS

We gain a better appreciation of the field of consumption economics growing out of the second definition, which we shall take as a working definition, from a review of the areas of work that are implied in that definition. The two areas of work growing out of the previous definition would be included here, also. Thus in our concept of consumption economics the development of a theory of consumer choice might be designated as the first area of study, and the measurement of satisfaction (utility functions) associated with choice patterns the second. And these are important areas of work. The received theory of consumer behavior is stilted and formal, centering in the maximizing acts of the individual; it is badly in need of development to make it applicable in more real world situations. But no theory can grow and become useful in application where measurement is not possible. Hence, more work concerned with the measurement of the psychological product, satisfaction, is imperative.

A third area of work which is implied by our definition is the formulation of and measurement of economic relations that emerge from particular choice patterns. A good example of what we have in mind here is the Marshallian concept of demand: the relation of price of product to quantity taken. But other concepts of demand may be formulated and measured; such relations as size of income to quantity taken, net worth to quantity taken, and size of family to quantity taken come to mind. The relation of different combinations of goods and services consumed (i.e., kinds and quantities) to significant independent, or causative, variables would seem to comprise a fruitful area of study within the field of consumption economics.

A fourth area would include a study of the implications of the above relations for the rest, or other segments, of the economy. In other words, what are the implications for a particular industry, or the economy, of a given level of product demand, and what are the implications of a change in that demand? To take a concrete case, the impact on prices, quantities consumed, and returns to producers of the shift in consumer preference from fresh oranges for juice to quick-frozen orange concentrate might be investigated. Other people might be interested in this impact also—the fruit- and vegetable-marketing man for example. But there is room for more than one approach to such a problem, and certainly consumption economics has reason to consider the *consequences* of a change in the pattern of consumer behavior as manifested in a change in demand.

At quite a different level, the allocation of income by consumers between spending and saving cannot be ignored. What all consumers do in the way of spending and saving determines in part the general level of economic activity—whether the economy experiences prosperity or depression. Hence, a consideration of the implications of consumer income-expenditure relations becomes a vital area of consumption economics.

A fifth area of study would be concerned with the structure of wants: how they are formed and how they are modified. Economists are divided on the question of whether this is an appropriate area for economic study and investigation. Many will argue that this area properly belongs to the fields of anthropology, psychology, and sociology. But if this is the case, how, for example, are we to treat advertising? Is the economist to pretend that it does not exist where it is undertaken at a *cost* with the expressed purpose of manipulating and creating wants? And the agricultural economist who has ignored the influence of nutrition education on the structure of the demand for food over the past two decades would have a difficult time explaining some of the things that have happened there—the changed position of citrus fruit and apples, for example. In this area, the economist probably needs to join forces with the anthropologists and psychologists to fully describe and explain the various aspects of want creation. But the economist can hardly overlook this area of work, and it seems to fall more nearly within the field of consumption economics than any other.

A sixth area of work would include a consideration of the varied problems surrounding consumption adjustments (i.e., purposive changes in consumption). Thinking in terms of the individual, what basis exists for recommending a particular change or adjustment in consumer behavior? On what grounds is the economist or consumption specialist to recommend a changed pattern of consumption where, because personal satisfaction is not measurable, the person making the recommendation cannot know what it means to the consumer involved? If the consumption specialist knew that every consumer derived the same amount of satisfaction from each kind and quantity of consumption as he did, the problem would be easy. But he does not know this, and he should recognize that he does not know it. In fact, he knows nothing about interpersonal utility comparisons. How then is the specialist to help the consumer make wise choices? This is a problem that has plagued thoughtful home advisors for a long time, and it is one that must be faced and dealt with.

And where adjustments in consumption are effected, on whatever grounds, what are the welfare consequences of such adjustments to all persons involved? For example, when the government provides goods or services for consumption, such as public education or public assistance to the needy, two sets of consumers are affected. The taxpayer's consumption is different from what it would be in the absence of such measures, and the consumer receiving benefits is also in a changed position. Has the total satisfaction of all consumers, or their welfare, been increased or lessened? A consideration of such problems, whether concerned with consumption adjustments of the individual or society, would seem to fall within the province of consumption economics.

A seventh area would include a study of markets and the marketing system in which the consumer makes selections and becomes a party to transactions. One market is not like every other market; the typical consumer trades in varied and many differently structured markets. In some, he is a price taker; in others, he is expected to bargain. In some, price competition is important; in others, product competition plays the dominant role. And in these varied markets the consumer encounters all kinds of merchandising practices, regulations, and customary procedures. All these institutional arrangements (i.e., arrangements made by man operating in a society) condition and influence the consumer in his choice and selection of goods and services. Hence, a study of the institutional arrangements that influence the decision making of consumers becomes an integral part of consumption economics.

An eighth area for study is concerned with the information problem. But here we must be careful not to include the universe. Consumption economics cannot itself cover the curriculum of a school of home economics, and individual teaching efforts will be wasted which concentrate on the "best buys" of the day or the season. In other words, we should not expect to find in consumption economics, possibly in some new, mysterious form, a presentation of the vast and diverse knowledge developed in schools of home economics with respect to goods and services used in living. And neither should we expect to find a text in this field to take the form of a shoppers' guide, packed with information which quickly gets out of date. But consumption economics can and should deal with several basic problems which pertain to information: (1) How does the nonspecialized buyer of many, many lines (i.e., the consumer) keep informed? (2) How and to what extent does lack of information impair the consumer's position, the workings of the market, the use of resources? (3) What is the relation of consumer protection to the information problem? These are some interesting and profound aspects of information which may be studied within the field of consumption economics without attempting to present the end product of consumer information, namely: Which is the best buy of meat today? The dissemination of this latter type of information is more properly the subject of a field which might be called consumer education.

CONSUMPTION ECONOMICS RECONSIDERED

A reconsideration of the definitional and classificational problems discussed in this chapter makes it clear that the field of consumption economics does not have fixed limits. Neither is it, however, just what your authors might wish to make it. It would prove difficult to convince students that consumption economics should comprise, for example, a study of the reproduction rates of fireflies or an account of the Third Crusade. It must first of all be concerned with some aspects of (1) consumption and (2) economics. Second, it must *persuade* students and interested persons that those aspects of consumption and economics designated as comprising the field of consumption economics lead to something *useful* by some criteria. And a reasonable criterion would seem to be the ability of this field of ideas to explain *the economics of decision making in the household.*

But sporadic attempts in the past to delimit and develop a field of consumption economics have not been too persuasive—that is, generally successful. Despite the great amount of work that has been done with respect to the consumer in the economy, a field of work which makes the decision making of the household the central point of inquiry has not emerged. Consumer purchase (or budget) studies have for the most part developed in a world unto themselves; the theory of consumer behavior has been incorporated directly into economic theory; and so-called practical efforts have most often degenerated into the dissemination of shopping-type information. In short, nothing akin to the fields of production economics or labor economics has yet developed in the area which we have delineated as consumption economics, or the economics of consumption. The explanation for this lack of development, although there are recent signs of an awakening,[3] is not hard to find; workers in this field have not persuaded students and interested parties on a widespread basis that a useful purpose is served in developing a discipline, or field of work, which takes as its central core the decision making of the household.

It is hoped that the ideas presented in this chapter will help breathe some life into the idea that a field of consumption economics exists, and that the development in this volume of the eight areas of work within the delineated field will persuade students and interested persons that, in fact, such a field exists. In the organization of this volume, the eight areas of study are developed in Parts II to IV, but not in the order outlined in this chapter. Part I, including this chapter, is designed to provide the student with sufficient background and perspective to enable him to grasp the significance and fuller meanings of the analyses that follow. Part V moves out of the realm of decision making by individual consumers or consuming units and deals briefly and in an exploratory way with collective decision making and collective consumption.

An answer to the question "What is consumption economics?" has been sketched. But individuals with varied backgrounds and experience no doubt have already begun to infer substance and meaning to this sketch which vary in the extreme. It, thus, becomes the task of this volume to develop the substance and meaning of this sketch and thereby provide a complete and integrated picture of the field of consumption economics.

Questions and Points for Discussion

1. What is meant by consumption? How do the processes of consumption and production differ?
2. What at this preliminary stage does the term economics of consumption mean to you?
3. Make a list of the areas to be studied within the field of consumption economics.

[3] See the essay by Ruth P. Mack, "Economics of Consumption," in Bernard F. Haley (ed.), *A Survey of Contemporary Economics*, Richard D. Irwin, Inc., Homewood, Ill., 1952, vol. II.

References

Mack, Ruth P.: "Economics of Consumption," in Bernard F. Haley (ed.), *A Survey of Contemporary Economics,* Richard D. Irwin, Inc., Homewood, Ill., 1952, vol. II.

Scitovsky, Tibor: *Welfare and Competition: The Economics of a Fully Employed Economy,* Irwin Series in Economics, Richard D. Irwin, Inc., Homewood, Ill., 1951, chap. III.

Waite, Warren C., and Ralph Cassady: *The Consumer and the Economic Order,* McGraw-Hill Book Company, Inc., New York, 1949, chap. I.

2. *Some Basic Concepts*

Since the main outlines of the field of consumption economics have been drawn, it would seem appropriate at this point to begin to study some aspects of it. And in a way we do. But in a somewhat formal and not too exciting way. It is difficult to make progress in a field where the meanings of words and concepts are either unknown or ambiguous. Thus, it would seem advisable to spend some time now learning the technical meaning of certain everyday words, such as income, and to grasp the import of certain basic concepts, to avoid some difficult times later on. For if we all talk the same language (i.e., are in agreement on the meaning of things), the problem of communication is reduced many-fold.

DECISION-MAKING UNITS OF THE HOUSEHOLD

We employ the term *household* throughout this volume in a generic or inclusive sense to describe all sorts of decision-making units engaged in consumption. More precisely, any unit noncollective in form that makes choices with respect to the goods and services used in living is a household. Thus, the unit *household* on the consumption side of the economy is comparable with the unit *firm* on the production side. But now let us explore more thoroughly the form and composition of decision-making units engaged in consumption.

In everyday usage, and in technical usage too, the consumer is taken to be an individual human being. It is the individual who consumes, in the sense of "using up" inputs of goods and services, to produce satisfaction (utility); hence, the individual is called a *consumer*. There is a temptation, then, to conclude that the individual is the primary decision-making unit on the consumption side of the economy; and this, in fact, is what has often been done in economics. But each individual does not consume in the sense of choosing (or selecting) the combination of goods and services "used up" by him in the production of satisfaction. In fact, very few individuals are completely free to choose as they please among alternative goods and services. Clearly, babies do not make their own choices, children generally make their selections under some form of supervision, and husbands and wives make important choices about the household unilaterally at their own peril (consultation usually proves wiser). Thus, it would appear that the family is an important type of household unit and a convenient unit of analysis. The choice of goods and services to be consumed is often made within the family unit, and individual members consume in accordance with that choice pattern.

But is the family unit an ideal unit of inquiry for all purposes? It appears not. For example, there may be more than one decision-making unit in a particular family. A family with a grown son working, but living at home, will be likely to have two decision-making points: the son making decisions with respect to the use of his funds, and the rest of the family (husband, wife, and remaining children) making decisions with respect to their pool of funds. On the other hand, we often find the case where both husband and wife work, but pool their incomes, and make their selections jointly from a common pool of income. And then, of course, there are many single consumers who do not live in families.

Because the family unit and the decision-making unit do not parallel in all cases, a unit of inquiry has been developed which is called a *consuming unit* (or *spending unit*). This is a unit whose members pool their funds (or income) and where decisions with respect to the use of those funds are made as a unit.[1] In other words, the decision making is centered at some point in the unit, and the choice of goods and services made at that decision-making point determines what goods and services individual members will "consume." In this formulation, a single person working and living alone is a consuming unit; a family where most or all of the income is pooled is a consuming unit. But a family in which the income is not pooled will have as many consuming units as there are pools of income (i.e., decision-making units).

For many, if not most, types of work in consumption economics, the consuming unit turns out to be an ideal unit of inquiry. It focuses attention on the key problem of choice; the unit is defined by the pool of funds and decisions as to its use. The using up of a particular set of goods and services after it has been selected moves quickly out of the realm of economics. But occasions arise, particularly in the field of food consumption, where it is useful to measure the *size* of a consuming unit in

[1] For a general discussion see *Family Spending and Saving in Wartime*, U.S. Department of Labor Bulletin 822, 1945, pp. 11–12.

terms of the amount of the item consumed. In such cases, it is customary to make some representative individual, say an adult male, equal to 1 unit and express other individuals as some percentage of that whole unit. Thus, for example, in the consumption of fats and oils an active adult man might equal 1 unit, an active adult woman 0.8 unit, children thirteen years and over 0.9 unit, children ten to twelve years 0.7 unit, children seven to nine years 0.4 unit, and so on down the age ladder. In this scheme of things, each consumer is reduced to a common unit of measure—an adult equivalent. And the size of a family or consuming unit may be expressed in terms of adult equivalents by adding up the specific measures assigned to each member of the family.

To illustrate, since the fat intake of an adult male is considerably greater than that of a small child or even an adult woman, we might not want to measure the size of family with respect to fat consumption (or any other food item for that matter) simply in terms of the number of persons in it. In an effort to be precise, we might want to measure the size of family with respect to fat consumption in terms of adult equivalents.[2] In such a case, a family of four adults composed of two men and two women would equal 3.6 units, a family with two very small children would equal 2.2 units, and so on for families of other age and sex distributions.

Our unit of inquiry thus depends upon the nature of the inquiry. For most types of economic analyses, the consuming unit provides a useful and meaningful concept with which to work. In some cases, the family unit proves most useful, and, in more specialized cases, the conversion of different classes of consumers into adult equivalents aids in the drawing of relevant comparisons. In other words, the composition and even the concept of the decision-making unit in consumption may vary. *But our unit of inquiry is always the decision-making unit, and each decision-making unit is defined as a household.*

MEASURES OF LIVING AND CONSUMPTION

We need a set of concepts which permit us to describe (1) what people are consuming or how they are living and (2) what people think they should be consuming or how they should be living. Such a set of concepts becomes indispensable where we wish to compare the con-

[2] See *Family Food Consumption in the United States,* U.S. Department of Agriculture Miscellaneous Publication 550, 1942, p. 137.

sumption or living of a particular group through time or differences in the consumption or living among groups at any particular time. And anyone who reflects for a moment on how consumption patterns have changed for his family or community over the last decade will be impressed by the extent of that change and the need to measure this change in some way. The same can be said for those who have traveled north or south in the United States or perhaps to some foreign country; patterns of consumption and living are highly varied.

Table 2-1 presents a set of concepts which are useful in describing the consumption or living of a given group and in distinguishing between different aspects of that consumption and living. In the first place, consumption and living are distinguished from one another: *consumption* includes only those goods and services acquired in the market, whereas *living* includes nonmarketable goods, services, and conditions. And *standards* are distinguished in turn from *planes* and *levels:* the former are goals toward which consumers strive, whereas the latter are concerned with what has been achieved. The concepts of plane and level, too, are distinguished: plane refers to a complete listing of items; level refers to a composite or aggregate value of the items comprising the plane.

To summarize these ideas, plane of (or level of) living is a more inclusive concept than plane of (or level of) consumption. But in either case plane and level refer to items actually consumed. Similarly, standard of living is a broader concept than standard of consumption; but in either case standard refers to some desired performance. A standard of living may be viewed as a level of living which people feel belongs to them. Thus, actual choices, which convert into levels of living, are conditioned in large measure by the accepted standard of living. In this connection, it should be noted that a given standard of living is not the best of all possible worlds but rather a way of living that people strive to achieve—a way of living which if not attained leaves them dissatisfied. The standard of living of a people may be viewed as the social product of those people, and to the individual in the group the standard appears as something imposed upon him by the group.

PRICES AND PRICE LEVEL

The concept of *price* is so familiar to most of us that we are inclined to feel that the meaning of this term is perfectly clear. And in a general way most of us do know what we mean by price. The price of a given

Table 2-1. Concepts of Planes, Levels, and Standards of Consumption and Living

Consumption	*Living*
Plane of Consumption is described by the list of goods and services acquired in the market and actually consumed. It is an objective concept in that it considers the goods and services actually consumed rather than the satisfaction derived from them. It is descriptive in that it refers to *actual* consumption. It is limited to goods and services acquired in the market.	*Plane of Living* is described by the list of all goods, services, and conditions actually consumed or experienced. It is objective in that it lists goods, services, and conditions actually consumed or experienced rather than the satisfaction derived from them. It is an inclusive concept in that it includes all things consumed or experienced in living: goods and services acquired in the market plus such things as the use of public facilities (e.g., parks, police protection, public schools), working conditions, freedom to choose occupations and location of residence, etc. But it remains a descriptive concept, since it simply lists all that is consumed or experienced in living.
Level of Consumption is described by a composite or aggregate of the list of goods and services acquired in the market and actually consumed. In contrast to the plane of consumption it is expressed in one number; it thus provides a convenient means for ranking different planes of consumption.	*Level of Living* is described by a composite or aggregate of all items which comprise the plane of living. It is an expression of the plane of living in one number or value. Thus it remains objective and descriptive.
Standard of Consumption is described by the list of goods and services that may be acquired in the market which people *think* they should consume. It is a normative concept in that it refers to "what ought to be" rather than what is, as in the case of plane or level.	*Standard of Living* is described by the list of goods, services, and conditions which the individual or group strives to attain, to maintain if once attained, and to regain if lost. It is a normative concept describing how the individual or group believes he or it ought to be living.

SOURCE: Adapted from Adolf Kozlik, "Concepts of Plane, Standard, Level and Satisfaction of Consumption and Living," *Journal of Marketing*, July, 1944, pp. 55–57; see also J. S. Davis, "Standards and Content of Living," *American Economic Review*, March, 1945.

commodity *X* is measured by the amount of money that must be given up in exchange for commodity *X*. In the United States, price is measured in dollars and cents; the price of commodity *X* is measured by the number of dollars and cents paid in exchange for that commodity. In colonial Virginia, prices were reckoned in "hands" of tobacco (the accepted unit of exchange—money—was tobacco); the price of $1 in foreign exchange is 35 grams of fine gold, and, in prison camps during World War II, the standard unit of exchange in which prices were reckoned was the cigarette.[3] Outside of primitive barter economies, then, the price of one commodity is always measured in terms (or units) of another commodity—a commodity (e.g., paper, gold, tobacco, cigarettes) that is acceptable as a unit of exchange, hence serves as money. But what precisely is this thing price which is measured in terms of some commodity serving in the role of money?

Price turns out to be a ratio: the ratio that one unit of the commodity in question exchanges for units of money. Thus, one Ford exchanged for $2,000 in the United States in 1952; one loaf of bread exchanged for 40 cigarettes in a German prison camp in 1945. In both these cases, we have a ratio—a ratio which describes the terms on which the good exchanges for money. The name for this ratio is price. And since money may be exchanged for all kinds of commodities, the price of a given commodity, say X, describes the terms (the ratio) on which this commodity exchanges for all other commodities.

Price level. Very often we like to refer to what is happening over time to the prices of a group of related commodities; hence, we speak of the price level of this group of commodities or that. In the everyday reading of a newspaper, for example, one comes across references to the general price level, the farm price level, the retail price level, and so on. There are, in fact, as many different price levels as there are groupings of commodities for which people are interested. But this idea of a price level is a bit more sophisticated than that of a single price. First of all, the concept is concerned with describing what is happening to the prices of a group of commodities that are related by some criterion of classification (e.g., all food, wholesale prices, etc.). Second, the concept is concerned with what happens to those prices over time; we may, for example, be interested in how the general price level has changed since 1940 or since the end of World War II.

In this respect, the word *level* is suggestive. The price level for all goods and services purchased at retail, at any one time, may be obtained by summating the prices of all items purchased at retail at that particular time. Now if the price of each item falls by one-half over a year's time, the retail price level will have fallen by one-half. Conversely, if the price of each commodity purchased at retail doubles over a year's time, the

[3] R. A. Radford, "The Economic Organization of a P.O.W. Camp," *Economica*, November, 1945, reprinted with certain changes in *Basic Economics: A Book of Readings*, Prentice-Hall, Inc., New York, 1951, pp. 77–90.

retail price level will have doubled. The problem of measurement, of course, becomes more complicated where some prices are falling and some are rising through time. Further, the measurement of price levels in a completely accurate sense is made impossible by (1) the introduction of new items (e.g., TV sets, frozen foods), (2) the elimination of old items (buggy whips), and (3) changes in the proportions sold of each commodity in a commodity grouping. But economists do the best they can, and price-level series of all types and descriptions are published regularly by different agencies—public and private.

The device used to measure price levels, and changes in price levels, is the index number. Index numbers may be used to measure phenomena other than prices—the index of industrial production, for example [4]—but their common use is in connection with prices. There are many different types of index numbers or methods of constructing index numbers. But we shall not inquire into the different types and methods of construction, since we are not concerned primarily with the methodology of index numbers. We are concerned with the concept of price level, however, and since that concept takes on substance only in the form of an index number, we shall look at the construction of a simple, but commonly used, type, to gain a better appreciation of the concept of a price level.

The index number that we shall consider is called a *ratio of aggregates.* Now let us suppose that our problem is that of measuring changes in the retail price level of food, over a three-year period, and the decision has been made to use the method known as a ratio of aggregates. To keep the problem simple, we assume that there are only three different food commodities involved, *X*, *Y*, and *Z* (the newcomer to index numbers may wish to conceptualize commodities *X*, *Y*, and *Z* in the more realistic terms of sugar, bread, and meat; he should also recognize that in fact 50 to 100 commodities might be involved and still not be all-inclusive). And price information is given for each commodity for each of the three years. These price data are as shown in the table on page 20. The index values were computed in the following fashion: Sum the price data for each year, next divide those sums by the sum for the base year, which in this case is taken to be year 1, and then multiply each quotient by 100. Any one of the three years could have been selected for a base (or some other year for which the information is given might have been selected), but it is common to make the first year, or first group of years.

[4] Published regularly in the *Federal Reserve Bulletin.*

Kind of product	Price per pound		
	Year 1	Year 2	Year 3
X	$0.10	$0.15	$0.15
Y	0.15	0.20	0.15
Z	0.65	0.75	0.50
Total...............	$0.90	$1.10	$0.80
Index value.........	100	122.2	88.8

the base in index-number construction. In this case, where year 1 is taken as the base year, the index value for year 1 is 100 ($0.90 \div 0.90 = 1 \times 100 = 100$), the value for year 2 is 122, and the value for year 3 is 89. In other words, the retail price level for food in this illustration rose 22 points between years 1 and 2 and fell 33 points between years 2 and 3.

The index number just computed is also known as an *unweighted* index number. Thus its full and correct name is an "unweighted ratio of aggregates." Generally speaking, this type of index number will not provide desirable results, and, technically speaking, it is not truly unweighted. More precisely, it is not weighted in accordance with any specific purpose; it is weighted in an accidental fashion by the value of the commodity prices involved. For example, commodity Z has more influence in the above construction than X and Y since it is larger and its absolute price changes are greater.

But it may well be that Z is a little-used commodity, whereas X is a much-used commodity. If this is the case, it would seem reasonable to give more weight in the index to commodity X, even though its price per pound is low, and less weight to commodity Z. This would have the result of causing the index as a measure of the retail price level of food to move in a new pattern and more nearly in harmony with commodity X. And we can calculate such an index number—a ratio of weighted aggregates—where certain quantity information is given to the problem. Where we know the pounds consumed by the community for each commodity, the index number is weighted with that quantity information by multiplying the price of a commodity for any given year by the quantity consumed (e.g., the datum for commodity X, year $1 = 0.10 \times$

60 = 6.00; the datum for commodity Y, year 1 = $0.15 \times 30 = 4.50$). The weighted price data and index values are given in the accompanying table. These index values rise more rapidly between years 1 and 2 and fall less

Kind of product	Weights (total pounds consumed in millions)	Price for each year × constant weights		
		Year 1	Year 2	Year 3
X	60	$ 6.00	$ 9.00	$ 9.00
Y	30	4.50	6.00	4.50
Z	10	6.50	7.50	5.00
Total........		$17.00	$22.50	$18.50
Index value..		100	132.4	108.8

between years 2 and 3 than in the unweighted case. As such, they provide a more representative description of changes in the retail price level for food, since this pattern of movement is more nearly in harmony with the dominant commodity of the index, namely, *X*.

In the world of reality, single commodity items are not likely to dominate an index so completely as do commodity *Z* in the unweighted calculation and commodity *X* in the weighted calculation. The Wholesale Price Index published by the U.S. Bureau of Labor Statistics is, for example, a weighted aggregate index made up of nearly 800 items each of which is priced regularly and weighted into the index by the quantity sold during a historical period. In this and other indices, the values assigned to the weights are of great importance, for the values assigned to the weights, in fact, determine the index values, hence the measure of price level. But single items, or even a few items, are not likely to dominate an index which includes some 800 items.

Cost of living. This is a particular price level that excites the interest of consumers and has important political implications. The consumer is concerned because it measures the cost to him (the price) of those items consumed in living. Thus, the cost of living may be said to rise when the prices of goods *regularly* (or normally) bought by the consumer rise, and the cost of living falls when the prices of goods *regularly* bought by the consumer fall. The idea is simple enough. But the problems begin and never end when it comes to measuring this particular price level.

The Consumer Price Index published by the U.S. Bureau of Labor Statistics is commonly used to measure the cost of living in the United States. As in the measurement of any price level, this index prices a specific set of goods and services over time. But a problem arises as to what set of goods and services are to be priced—as to whose cost of living is to be measured. Is the list of goods and services to include blue-denim shirts and overalls or white shirts and woolen suits, hard-top convertibles or pickup trucks, fishing poles or golf clubs, and so on ad infinitum? The set of goods and services included and priced in the index may measure perfectly the cost of living of white-collar workers and do a poor job for hard-handed laborers, or conversely. Or, depending upon the items included, it might accurately measure the cost of living of urban people and not rural people. In point of fact, the Consumer Price Index refers to the consumption of wage earners and clerical workers living in cities of the United States. In 1952, these "index" families, with an average income *after taxes* of $4,160 per year, represented about 40 per cent of the families in the United States and about two-thirds of all city families. It is clear, then, that the Consumer Price Index does not purport to measure the cost of living for families living in rural areas, or for families with higher incomes, whose consumption patterns may differ.[5]

Next, there is the problem of keeping the cost-of-living index up to date. In order to keep the index up to date (i.e., measure the true cost of living at any one time) where tastes and preferences change, new items must be introduced into the index through time and obsolete items dropped out. Thus the question arises: "When are TV sets to be introduced into the index and radios to be dropped out?" This example is somewhat extreme; in the usual case, the problem is one of adjusting the weights—giving more importance to items increasing in use and reducing in importance items declining in use.

But when new items are introduced, obsolete items are dropped, or in the more usual case the weights of items included in the index are adjusted, the comparative value of the index is reduced. As the items included in the cost-of-living index change along with the weights of the items involved, *the index in fact changes:* the same bill of goods is not being compared over time. Those persons responsible for measuring the cost of living are thus confronted with a dilemma: if the index is not kept up to date, it cannot accurately measure the cost of living of any group,

[5] Further information is given in *The Consumer Price Index: A Layman's Guide*, U.S. Department of Labor Bulletin 1140, 1953.

but keeping it up to date reduces its value for gauging changes in costs over time. A compromise is called for, and that is generally what happens. New items are introduced slowly, obsolete items are dropped out slowly, and weights are adjusted haltingly in an effort to maintain a continuity in the index, hence facilitate comparisons in the cost of living through time.

INCOME CONCEPTS

Consumer incomes. Income to the individual may take one of three forms:

1. Money income
2. Real income
3. Psychic income

The concept to which we are most accustomed is money income. But even here we want to be sure of our working concepts. By money income, we mean money receipts over a *period of time*. The money income of a family for a year is all the money receipts of that family during the year. The one idea we want to keep straight with respect to money income, as with all income concepts, is that the concept refers to a *period of time* —a week, or a month, or a year.

An often-used, but more difficult, concept is that of real income. By real income, we mean the goods and services which a person, or consuming unit, has to consume over a period of time. Thus, real income comprises the bill of goods and services available for consumption over a period of time; hence, it becomes a good measure of the material well-being of individuals. And we are particularly interested in the real-income concept since it is similar to the idea of consumption level; the two terms may in most cases be used interchangeably. Both are concerned with actual goods and services that are consumed.

It is when we come to measuring real incomes that the difficulties arise. To accurately describe the real income of an individual, or consuming unit, it would be necessary to make a complete inventory of the goods and services available for consumption by the unit involved over a period of time. The compilation of such inventory lists for any large number of individuals or groups would be costly and time-consuming, hence prohibitive on any large scale. But even if cost were not a factor, how could the inventory list of any one consumer be compared meaningfully over time or the inventory lists of different individuals or groups be compared at any particular period in time? The comparison of different inventory lists comprised of varied and diverse items would indicate little as to comparative real incomes. Not until these lists are reduced to some common denominator (e.g., pounds, money value) do they yield useful measures of real income for comparative purposes. Thus, we are led back to some type of index-number construction to obtain a useful measure of real income.

One solution might be to price each item in each inventory list by a set of constant prices and compare the aggregate values over time or between individuals. But this again would involve the costly inventory process, hence prove to be an impossible task if a large number of consuming units were involved. A rough measure of real income may, however, be derived by deflating (dividing) an index of money income by the relevant index of prices. By this procedure, if the index of prices rises by the same amount as the index of money incomes, real incomes remain unchanged, for consumers can buy neither more nor less with their money incomes. Where prices rise more rapidly than money incomes, real incomes fall, and conversely. As an illustration (see the accompanying table), let us deflate an index of money incomes derived from the Survey of Consumer Finance[6] by the Consumer Price Index, for the period 1946 to

	1946	1947	1948	1949	1950	1951	1952
Index of money incomes....	85.5	94.1	105.6	100.4	111.5	119.0	127.1
Consumer Price Index......	83.4	95.5	102.8	101.8	102.8	111.0	113.5
Index of real incomes.......	102.5	98.5	102.7	98.6	108.5	107.2	112.0

1952, to see what happened to the real incomes of consumers.[7] It will be observed that the index values of real income as computed in the table rise more slowly than do the index values of money incomes, since the level of consumer prices is also rising over the period involved.

Perhaps a more familiar way of measuring real income is that of expressing money incomes in terms of constant dollars (or prices). This

[6] The index values of money income are derived from the median money income, before taxes, of spending units (all persons living in the same dwelling and related by blood, marriage, or adoption, who pooled their incomes for their major items of expense) as determined by the yearly "Surveys of Consumer Finances," *Federal Reserve Bulletin,* 1946–1953.

[7] All indices are on a 1947–1949 base.

is achieved by dividing money incomes in current dollars by the relevant price index. Using the data described above, a measure of real income is derived for the period 1946 to 1952 by dividing the median money income of consuming units for each year by the Consumer Price Index value of the same year. These measures of income—money income in current dollars and real income in constant dollars—are given in the accompanying table. Both methods of computing real incomes show that,

	1946	1947	1948	1949	1950	1951	1952
Current dollars.........	$2,300	$2,530	$2,840	$2,700	$3,000	$3,200	$3,420
Constant 1947–1949 dollars..............	2,758	2,649	2,763	2,652	2,918	2,883	3,013

although the median money incomes of consuming units rose some 50 per cent between 1946 and 1952, the increase in real income was much smaller. In both 1947 and 1949, real income declined from the previous years. But, in 1947, the decline resulted from price rises alone; in 1949, there was a substantial decline in money income.

The third concept of income to the individual is *psychic income:* the flow of satisfactions received by the individual over a period of time. But, to date, no unit has been developed for measuring satisfactions received; hence, we know very little about the psychic income of individuals, families, or consuming units. We do not know that the satisfaction received from a particular good or service is the same to all individuals, nor can we measure the difference (if this exists) in satisfactions received by different people. The concept may help explain why college professors stick to teaching even though their money incomes are low (they are thought to receive a psychic income from working with ideas). But, in the main, the concept of psychic income is not very useful.

Estimates of national income. The money incomes of consuming units arise out of the payments received by income earners of those units for factors of production (e.g., land, labor, and capital) offered by them for hire or use. The sum of all payments received by income earners in a given period for the nation as a whole may be termed, not too precisely at this point, the national income. The national income is an aggregative concept; it is an aggregate of all income payments received in the national economy. Hence, estimates of national income provide useful measures of the size of the national economy as well as changes in the size of the national economy.

Since the income payments to factors of production in any period grow out of the receipts obtained from the sale of the goods and services produced by those factors, it turns out that estimates of national income and national product are the same—identical. This conclusion [8]

> . . . is suggested by observation of the operations of a typical business firm. On the one hand, such a firm produces and sells a flow of product values. On the other hand, it pays out (or retains) incomes that accrue in the course of its operations. This double aspect of the activities of the single business firm suggests that the measurement of national output can be approached in a twofold manner, either by summing product values or by summing income flows. It will be seen that the measure of national output in terms of product flows which is obtained by pursuing this approach is the gross national product and that the corresponding measure in terms of income flows is the national income.

The key concept in national income accounting is the Gross National Product. The GNP may be defined as the market value of the total output of goods and services produced by the nation's economy. A measure of GNP is derived by adding the values of all final products produced in a given period and omitting all intermediate products. For example, the GNP includes the value of each loaf of bread sold, but not the value of the intermediate product flour.

From the aggregate Gross National Product, numerous other product and income measures may be derived. In broad terms, the Gross National Product less various capital depletion items equals Net National Product; the Net National Product less indirect business taxes equals national income; national income plus and minus various and sundry transfer payments equals personal income; personal income less various personal taxes equals disposable personal income. And this latter concept is an important one for consumption economics, for it describes and measures that income which consuming units are free to dispose of as they see fit—are free to spend on whatever they choose or to save.

These various national-income and product concepts are given substance in Table 2-2. Each is derived precisely and in logical order in that table. A full discussion of these concepts involving definitions, logical content, and practical uses is to be found in Chapter 14.

[8] *National Income and Product of the United States, 1929–1950,* U.S. Department of Commerce, National Income Division, 1951, p. 21.

Table 2-2. Relation of Gross National Product, National Income, Personal Income, and Disposable Income, 1952
(In millions of dollars)

Gross national product			$346,095
Less:	Capital consumption allowances		25,304
	Depreciation charges	$ 22,456	
	Accidental damage to fixed capital	677	
	Capital outlays charged to current expense	2,171	
Equals:	Net national product		320,791
Plus:	Subsidies minus current surplus of government enterprises		−229
Less:	Indirect business tax and nontax liability		28,049
	Business transfer payments		999
	Statistical discrepancy		555
Equals:	National income		290,959
Less:	Undistributed corporate profits		8,081
	Corporate profits tax liability		19,965
	Corporate inventory valuation adjustment		981
	Contributions for social insurance		8,685
	Excess of wage accruals over disbursements		−29
Plus:	Net interest paid by government		4,876
	Government transfer payments		12,091
	Business transfer payments		999
Equals:	Personal income		271,242
	Wage and salary disbursements	185,068	
	Other labor income	5,510	
	Proprietors' and rental income	49,939	
	Dividends	9,128	
	Personal interest income	12,318	
	Transfer payments	13,090	
	Less: personal contributions for social insurance	3,811	
Less:	Personal tax and nontax payments		34,373
	Federal	31,143	
	State and local	3,230	
Equals:	Disposable personal income		236,869
Less:	Personal consumption expenditures		218,424
Equals:	Personal saving		18,445

SOURCE: Adapted from U.S. Department of Commerce, *Survey of Current Business*, July, 1954, Tables 3 and 4, p. 5, published in *National Income Supplement* for 1954.

SAVINGS

One of the choices open to consuming units in the use of their limited incomes is that of not spending. This use of income (i.e., not spending) we describe as saving. A working definition flows directly from this concept: savings is equal to income less consumption expenditures. A measure of personal savings computed by the above working definition for the national economy is presented in Table 2-2; disposable personal income of $236,869 million less personal consumption expenditures of $218,424 million equals personal savings of $18,445 million in 1952.

Although the above definition is conceptually clear and lends itself readily to measurement, it casts savings in the role of a residual. For some consuming units, this may be a proper characterization—particularly those units which do little or no saving. But, for most consuming units which save regularly, the act of saving represents a conscious, deliberate choice. Consuming units are motivated to save for a variety of reasons: to obtain a fund for contingencies, for old age, for speculation, for a trip around the world, and so on. In all these instances, however, a conscious choice in the use of income is involved. Further, we observe that savings in many instances represent deferred consumption: savings are effected out of current income to permit a wanted form of consumption in some later period.

Thus, it is probably not inappropriate to view savings as a sort of special type of consumption expenditure. Choice is exercised in a current period; the "using up" of the funds, or what the funds are used to acquire, to produce consumer satisfaction occurs in some later period.

PRODUCTION AND UTILITY FUNCTIONS

Production functions. A production function describes a relation between the output variable and the various (one or more) input variables. Thus, an older term for a production function is input-output relation. The word *function* is used here, as it is in mathematics, to describe a relation—a relation between one variable and one or more other variables. To illustrate, we say that the height of children is a function of, is related to, age; or the yield of corn is a function of, is related to, rainfall, fertilizer, and labor inputs. In the former case, we have a simple functional relationship between height and age, in the latter case a more complex production functional relationship between yield and rainfall, fertilizer, and labor inputs.

Now, the precise way in which output is related to inputs (i.e., the conceptualization and measurement of production functions) is the subject matter of production economics. Hence, this is an area of study that we can skip over lightly in consumption economics; the problems of the firm in combining inputs to yield some output which maximizes the profit of the firm reside outside the province of consumption economics. But we need to be aware that a set of relations exist on the production side (in the theory and practice of the firm) which have their exact counterparts on the consumption side (in the theory of the household). These input-output relations (i.e., production functions) of the firm take three principal forms, (1) total relations, (2) average relations, and (3) marginal relations. In other words, we have a relation which states how total output varies with different input combinations, how average output varies with different input combinations, and how marginal output varies with different input combinations. And when prices are attached to the various inputs used, the cost of producing a unit of output at various input combinations may be derived. The cost functions of a firm are computed from the production functions, when the prices of inputs are given.

In this highly abstract review of production functions, one more important idea needs to be brought out. The marginal production function of the firm, when converted into a cost function, becomes the short-run supply function of the firm. The marginal cost function describes what price must be offered to the firm in order to induce it to produce one more unit of output; hence, it may be described as a supply function. It describes how much the firm stands ready to produce at varying prices. In the case of any commodity, say pork, the summation of all these firm supply functions yields the well-known market supply function found in all elementary texts in economics. So, in a very general way, we know where the market supply curve under competitive conditions comes from, and we know further, perhaps with a sense of relief, that we shall not investigate these kinds of problems in this volume.

Utility functions. We have some idea now of what is meant by a function; in mathematical parlance, function is a synonym for relation. Hence, we could substitute the term *utility relation* for *utility function* if we desired. The word utility has a long history; it was introduced into economics by the English utilitarian philosophers of the early nineteenth century. Bentham, one of the foremost of the utilitarians, held that "Nature has placed mankind under the governance of two sovereign masters *pain* and *pleasure*." Pain yields disutility, pleasure yields utility, and man will follow whichever line of action yields the greatest utility. In other words, man will *choose* whichever line of action (combination of goods) yields the greatest pleasure or satisfaction or utility. Rational man seeks to maximize his satisfaction, utility, and will make those decisions which maximize his total satisfaction.

When English utilitarianism went out of style as a philosophical base, the idea of utility ceased to be fashionable in economics. The economist who held to the concept of utility in the 1930s was considered to be an old fuddy-duddy. But, important from our point of view, the loss of the utility base meant the loss of an economic rationale of consumer behavior. If consumers in their decision making were not to maximize utility, what were they to maximize? What principle could be said to govern consumers in their decision making? Some economists tried to slip out of the impasse by substituting the word satisfaction for utility—a not too helpful approach. The more sophisticated turned to a concept of utility which did not imply the measurability of utility and to an analytical approach—the indifference approach—which seemed to avoid the need for any concept of utility.

But, since World War II, the concept of utility seems to be gaining a measure of respectability again. This would seem to be the case for several reasons: (1) Call it what you will (satisfaction or utility), the only theory of consumer behavior which we have which commands any respect requires that some entity be maximized. (2) It has been recognized that the indifference approach really does not avoid the conceptual requirement of utility. (3) There have been recent and modestly successful experiments in measuring utility. So we shall boldly deal with utility functions, since they are indispensable to the theory of consumer behavior that will be presented in Part II.

Utility is the output of the household and varies with the consumption of different input combinations (combinations of goods and services). Thus, a functional relation may be said to exist between utility and the consumption of different combinations of goods and services. It may be extremely difficult (in the past, it has been impossible) to measure these relations. But this does not mean that they are nonexistent; an appeal to personal experience strongly suggests some relation between consumption and satisfaction. And we can, as in production, conceptualize these functional relations in three forms, (1) total relations, (2) average relations, and (3) marginal relations.

Much of the remainder of this volume will be devoted to the conceptualization of these utility functions. But it would perhaps help at this point to indicate that the marginal utility function for the individual may be converted into a demand schedule for the individual for the commodity involved. And, as in the case of supply, these individual demand schedules may be summated into the demand schedule for the commodity in question. Thus, we see in grand outline the source of the twin concepts of demand and supply which dominate market behavior in a competitive economy. We see, further, those aspects of this market behavior with which we shall be concerned. We shall concentrate on problems of the household which arise out of its efforts to maximize utility.

Questions and Points for Discussion

1. What is the difference between a consuming (or spending) unit and a family unit?

2. What do we mean by cost of living? What problems are encountered in constructing an index of cost of living?

3. Measure the change in the cost of living between year 1 and year 10 where we have three commodities involved, *X*, *Y*, and *Z*, and the data in the accompanying table are given.

Units of—	Prices in year 1	Prices in year 10	Pounds of items consumed by community in year 1
X	$0.10	$0.20	50,000
Y	0.15	0.15	30,000
Z	0.30	0.25	20,000

4. What is meant by real income? How are changes in real income measured over time?

5. Take the estimates of national income and product published by the U.S. Department of Commerce for any recent year other than 1952, and construct a table similar to Table 2-2.

6. What is a production function? What is a utility function? What problems are associated with estimating the utility functions of consumers?

7. Compare plane of consumption with standard of consumption. Compare standard of consumption with standard of living.

References

The Consumer Price Index: A Layman's Guide, U.S. Department of Labor Bulletin 1140, 1953.

Davis, J. S.: "Standards and Content of Living," *American Economic Review*, March, 1945.

National Income and Product of the United States, 1929–1950, U.S. Department of Commerce, National Income Division, 1951.

Waite, Warren C., and Ralph Cassady: *The Consumer and the Economic Order*, McGraw-Hill Book Company, Inc., 1949, chaps. IV–V.

3. The Economic System: Purpose, Organization, and Performance

Most people have a tendency to take the economy for granted. Each person knows that small portion of the economy of which he is an integral part; each is familiar with prices, wages, profits, production methods, consumption patterns, and government regulations in his immediate realm of experience. But, beyond that experience, the economy may be likened to the universe: it is always there; it is infinitely complex; and the man in the street has all sorts of "theories" and opinions concerning its behavior.

A great deal of work has been done in the past 100 years in the way of measuring, describing, and explaining the economy of this nation and others. A tremendous amount of information dealing with the performance of the economy has been collected by government and other institutions. And a wide area of agreement has been reached with regard to the operating behavior of the economy; areas of disagreement develop and widen in large measure with respect to what *ought to be done* about certain problems of the economy. Thus, we shall make use of the accumulated information and understanding of the past century to present an over-all picture of the operating economy in this chapter. This picture, along with that to be developed in the following chapter, provides a setting or background against which to analyze and appraise the economic decision making of households.

PURPOSE OF THE ECONOMY

The economies of nations or social groups are complex things comprised of many different decision-making units, practices, and institutions. And the structure and organization of economies vary greatly among nations or social groups. But economies of all nations or social groups must meet and solve the same basic, or central, problems. In this sense, economic systems have purpose.

Basic problems of every economic society. Each and every society—whether it be a primitive type as in the case of the American Plains Indians, or a totalitarian state as in the case of the U.S.S.R., or a mixed-enterprise, capitalistic nation as in the case of the United States, or a simple Robinson Crusoe economy—must meet and solve in some way three fundamental economic problems. These problems are: [1]

1. *What* commodities shall be produced and in what quantities? That is, how much and which of many alternative goods and services shall be produced?
2. *How* shall goods be produced? That is, by whom and with what resources and in what technological manner are they to be produced?
3. *For whom* are goods to be produced? That is, who is to enjoy and get the benefits of the goods and services provided? Or to put the same thing in another way: How is the national product to be distributed among different individuals and families?

Different economic societies solve these problems in different ways. Primitive societies typically solve them through custom—immemorial custom. In other words, the choice of commodities, the choice of resources and technical methods, and the distribution of the total social product are determined at any given time among primitive people by patterns of behavior established beyond memory or record. In a totalitarian state of the Russian variety, the method of solution is altogether different. Planning boards or commissions make the decisions with respect to "what commodities with what resources and for whom." And, in the Russian experience, free choice with respect to consumer goods and occupation has been conspicuously absent; all resources, human and material, are fitted together in the master plan involving a solution to the above three problems.

In the mixed-enterprise, capitalistic economy of the United States of the 1950s, the three-sided problem of *what, how,* and *for whom* goods and services shall be produced is solved through the workings of the price system in a set of related and relatively free markets. In other words, the choice of commodities, the use of resources and technical methods, and the distribution of the total national product in the United States as of 1955 are determined through a pattern of prices in a set of markets where producers seek to maximize revenue and consumers seek to maximize satisfaction and choice is relatively free. How does all this occur? How does the price system yield a solution to the three basic economic problems in

[1] Paul A. Samuelson, *Economics: An Introductory Analysis,* 2d ed., McGraw-Hill Book Company, Inc., New York, 1951, pp. 13–14.

the mixed-enterprise, capitalistic economy of the United States? It is to a formulation of such an explanation that we now turn.

But let us digress for a moment on the meaning of the term *mixed-enterprise, capitalistic economy*. By "mixed-enterprise" we mean that the economy is comprised in part of private enterprise and in part of government actions and activities. In what proportions these parts are "mixed" in the economy of the United States, as of 1955, we cannot say with precision; the private part would, however, seem to dominate the scene. By "capitalistic" we mean that capital goods are used generally and intensively in production processes. But perhaps the key word in the term is "enterprise." Since the founding of the Republic, the dominant theme has been enterprise—that is, the combining of resources in new ways to produce new products and to increase output. Thus, we say that the economy of the United States is a mixed-enterprise, capitalistic economy.

How the basic problems are solved in the economy of the United States. The pricing system works to achieve a solution of the three basic problems along the following lines: First, each and every product, service, and factor of production has a price: bread has a price, refrigerators have a price, haircuts have a price, automobile parking space has a price, the services of labor have prices in the form of wage rates, the services of land have a price in the form of rents, and so on through the economy. How these prices are set we shall ignore for now. Second, each and every individual receives money for what he sells, and in turn he uses that money to buy goods, services, or factors of production. Now, suppose that consumers want more of some good or service—say more television repair service. Orders for service pile up in repair shops, since the existing supply of repairmen cannot meet the increased demands for service. The cost of repair service now rises, and before long the wages of television repairmen also rise. Increased wages induce new workers to move into this field, first from closely allied fields (e.g., radio and electricity) and second from unrelated fields (e.g., farming and school teaching). And when there are enough new workers to satisfy the demand, wage rates stop rising. Finally, then, *assuming other things are equal,*[2] an equilibrium is reached where

[2] This is a poorly understood and much abused phrase. Economists who use it, including the present authors, do not mean that all processes in the economy other than the one under consideration actually hold constant. They simply *assume* that other processes hold constant in order to reason logically through to a conclusion with respect to the process under consideration. This assumption is comparable to the laboratory controls of the chemist or physicist.

the price of repair work, wage rates to repairmen, and human resources stop moving.

In the determination of the price of television repair work, a solution has been achieved for this little sector of the economy with respect to the three basic economic problems. First, the quantity of repair work was determined. Second, the volume of resources, labor and other factors, was determined. Third, the wages to laborers and payments to other factors were determined. And all this occurred automatically in this case. The final solution was not planned or arrived at by following a blueprint. Self-interest—profit maximization on the production side and satisfaction maximization on the consumption side—motivated the shifts described and the price solutions reached. The working of the price system guided the process to a solution of the three basic problems.

Now, visualize the process described above repeated over and over again in all parts of the economy for each type and class of goods, services, and productive factors, and what emerges is a picture of the over-all economy in operation. In short, the economy is a vast system of trial and error wherein solutions to the three basic economic problems take place simultaneously. For each good, service, and factor, the movement toward equilibrium occurs through trial and error—by successive approximation. A high price for a product causes buyers to drop out and suppliers to come into the market; a low price has the opposite effect. And the quantities demanded and supplied in each product, service, or factor line continue to be adjusted—changed—until a point is reached where neither price nor quantity shows any tendency to move.

At this point, final equilibrium is realized; at this point, a full and complete solution to the problems

1. What commodities shall be produced in what quantities
2. How shall goods be produced
3. For whom are goods to be produced

is simultaneously achieved. Actually, of course, such a final equilibrium solution is never reached in the world in which we live. Something new is always coming along to upset a particular process of successive approximations before a full and complete solution is reached. But the economy of the United States, comprised of a multitude of parts and processes, is always tending in the direction of a complete and final solution of the three basic problems under the "guidance" of the price system.

The fact that a final solution is never reached rests on two causal elements:

1. There is a continuous introduction of new wants and new methods of satisfying wants.

2. Resource shifts do not occur so automatically as may have been implied in the foregoing discussion.

Thus, the economy, like the dog chasing a rabbit, is always chasing equilibrium but rarely if ever catches it. The rabbit (price) always zooms off in a new direction just as the dog (resource adjustment) is about to pounce on it. And the larger, awkward dog falls down taking the sharp corner (an illustration of the difficulties involved in resource adjustment). Hence, the race begins all over again, with price taking a new course.

We should not get the idea that the self-regulating, self-motivating process that we have been describing works smoothly and perfectly, because it does not. There are all kinds of forces, which economists call "frictions," at work in the economy to impede, or deter, or halt the automatic resource adjustments and price movements described above. Resource shifts, particularly human resource shifts, are often impeded by rules passed by trade associations and trade unions, legal barriers enacted by governments, and uncertainty or lack of knowledge in the minds of the individuals involved. These forces act to restrict entry into fields of production, hence obstruct resource adjustments.

Further, individual members of the economy do not always like the specific price-resource solutions that emerge in the automatic process. Such individuals or groups generally ask government to enact legislation designed to regulate prices, control production, prohibit the consumption of certain items, and so on. Action on the part of government to achieve any of these purposes means, of course, that the police power of government has been used to influence the solution of the three basic economic problems. And we see the power of government used in this way on all sides of us: the tariff and trade control structure, farm price supports, price ceilings in wartime, income tax laws, minimum-wage legislation, state and local licensing provisions, and countless other governmental actions, controls, and interventions in the economy. It is this proliferation of governmental activities in the economy which causes us to describe it as a mixed-enterprise economy.

We do not suggest that governmental action in the economy is bad per se. The consequences of each action are different, and each must be traced and appraised before any meaningful judgment can be made with respect to them. Further, each action was undertaken, in all probability, at the behest of some group dissatisfied with the working of the automatic system, and we assume through democratic processes. But whatever one's views are on the desirability of this governmental action or that, there is no blinking the fact that such actions by government do lead to different solutions from those in the case of an economy free of direct governmental intervention.[3]

ORGANIZATION OF THE ECONOMY

The economy which we have been describing is organized into a system of markets. The vast system of trial and error working toward an equilibrium of prices and quantities (i.e., the economy) takes place in a system of markets. The right amounts of labor, machines, and raw materials are combined in a multitude of different processes to produce the kinds and quantities of goods and services wanted by consumers under the direction of the pricing system *through continuous adjustments among markets.* Producers obtain input factors first in one market and then another, always seeking the lowest price and best quality; sellers of finished products and services offer supplies first in one market and then the next, always seeking a combination of high prices and large volume; consumers try the goods and services of first one store and then the next, or one shopping area and then the next, in an effort to gain the greatest total satisfaction from their limited incomes. This continuous adjustment process, having some influence on the price in each market, is the process whereby the kinds and quantities of goods and services that consumers want get produced and placed in the spots at the times that consumers want them. This ubiquitous process is called the *substitution process.* And it is this substitution process which relates or integrates individual markets into a meaningful whole.

The concept of markets. The question now arises: "What is a market?" A market may be said to exist wherever transactions occur. The essential elements of any market are buyers and sellers with facilities for trading. The scope of any market is limited by the number of buyers and sellers who are in close communication with one another and who handle a *similar* commodity. Sellers may be said to handle similar commodities

[3] What is or is not direct governmental intervention is difficult to define. Generally we would say that price controls and trade restrictions represent direct governmental action, whereas the operation of the courts and school systems only supplements the operation of the free economy. But a law stating that minors must attend school until they are eighteen certainly affects the economy directly.

when, from the viewpoint of buyers, their respective commodities are closely substitutable. If, on the other hand, commodities handled by different sellers are not considered close substitutes by buyers, then the commodities are not similar and the sellers are in separate markets.

We may distinguish one market from another by a break or gap in the chain of substitution. For example, one seller may have automobiles to sell and another offer typewriters. Since it is unlikely that the products of these two sellers would be considered to be close substitutes by buyers, we would say that these sellers operate in different markets. But by a similar reasoning two sellers, one of Fords and the other of Chevrolets, would belong to the same market.

In the development of a generalized explanation of the workings of a free-enterprise economy, economists have formulated the concept of a *perfect market.* And a system of perfect markets is described as a *perfectly competitive system.* The nature of "perfect competition" is summarized in three conditions:

1. Each buyer (household) and seller (firm) is so small relative to the market that the influence of each buyer and seller on price is imperceptible.
2. Prices and resource mobility are not restricted in any way.
3. All buyers and sellers have complete information.

The beauty of a perfectly competitive system, and its value in logical reasoning, rests in the fact that, where the above three conditions are satisfied in full, the vast system of trial and error, which we call the economy, moves smoothly and directly to an equilibrium of prices and production. The difficulty with the concept rests in the fact that probably no market ever satisfied the above three conditions in full and most markets in the United States have developed along very different lines. In other words, buyers and sellers in actual markets have taken and continue to take all kinds of actions which make those markets "imperfect" (i.e., create conditions which violate one or all of the three conditions of perfect competition). Illustrations of such actions include setting price floors and price ceilings with the aid of government, establishment of legal restrictions to entry, amalgamation to achieve large-scale production, price leadership and follower relations, market sharing, and tacit and overt price collusion.

And why have such actions been taken over and over again in real markets? Not because the persons involved were necessarily evil or bad and not because they sought to violate the concept of a perfect market invented by economists. Buyers and sellers in markets have taken actions which violate the perfect-competition criteria, time and time again, because it was to their best interests to do so. Hence, we need to ask and answer the following question: "In what sense is a perfect market perfect?" Certainly it is not perfect in the sense that operators think of a market of this structure as being *ideal*. If buyers and sellers generally held the view that the ideal market involved

1. Many buyers and sellers no one of whom influenced price
2. No restriction to mobility
3. Perfect or complete information

the headlong flight from markets approaching this structure would not have occurred during the past 100 years. Further, fewer and fewer economists subscribe to the view that perfect competition represents the ideal form of economic organization. Very few economists would trade the mass-production mass-consumption economy of today for the atomistic organization of perfect competition.

Perfect competition involving a system of perfect markets, then, is not to be considered a norm; but it does provide a useful purpose as a bench mark or standard of comparison. A perfect market may be likened to sea level in the measurement of elevations. We do not wish to reduce all land forms to sea level; on the contrary, man is generally engaged in trying to control the natural forces at work eroding and washing the land. But sea level does provide a useful bench mark in measuring the height of various land forms on the earth's surface. So with the abstract concept of the perfect market. It turns out to be a useful standard of comparison in describing and analyzing markets. But the drawing of comparisons with the standard does not mean that all markets should be converted to the structure of a "perfect market." A "perfect market" in this volume simply refers to a market which satisfies three rigorous conditions.

Given the perfect market as a standard of comparison—sea level for economics—let us review the principal classes of markets, classified according to their structure on the selling side. In other words, until the focus of this analysis shifts explicitly to the buying side, we shall assume that there are many buyers in all markets and consider only the changing structural characteristics on the selling side. This procedure is not too unrealistic for at least two reasons: (1) Product markets at retail typically do have many buyers. (2) Once we see the influence of numbers in the market from the selling side, it is not difficult to infer in a general way the influence of numbers on the buying side.

Free competition. This type of market situation most nearly resembles the abstract concept of perfect competition. The essential structural characteristics of this type of market are (1) many sellers and (2) a homogeneous product (i.e., the many sellers all handle an identical product). A market which has so many sellers that no one seller has a perceptible or significant influence on the price of the homogeneous commodity handled may be defined as a freely competitive market. Information, however, can never be complete and perfect in real situations. Some operators by luck or diligence or chicanery will have better information than others. Hence, a freely competitive market differs from a perfectly competitive market first because the complete information condition is not satisfied in this class of markets (or in any other real market situation for that matter). Second, various forms of restriction to entry—restraints to mobility—will commonly be found in freely competitive markets. In short, a freely competitive market is a perfectly competitive market where the mobility and information conditions are not fully satisfied—where the facts of life are forced upon the abstract concept.

Markets of this type are not commonly found in retail shopping areas; a shopping area will typically have only a *few* grocery stores, or shoe stores, or furniture stores, or department stores. In fact, freely competitive markets are not too common in any part of the economy. About the only places where markets approaching this structure are to be found are in the terminal markets for agricultural commodities. The cash and "futures" wheat markets in Minneapolis, Kansas City, and Chicago are examples to be noted. Similarly structured markets are also to be found in certain cotton markets and in numerous large city fruit and vegetable markets. But markets of this type have given way in most instances to markets of different structure—to markets where operators exercise more control over the price and quality aspects of the commodities involved.

It is a characteristic of freely competitive markets that prices move up or down readily—are flexible. This flexibility arises out of the fact that changes in demand and supply conditions are readily observed and directly felt by operators in these markets. The decisions of individual operators to buy or sell turn on their interpretations as to what such changes in demand or supply will mean in terms of a change in price; the small operator among many "plays" against price, not against the actions of his rivals.

Hence, price varies directly and readily with changes in demand or supply via the decisions made with respect to it and how it is expected to move.

It is also a characteristic of freely competitive markets that profits are at a minimum. Excessive profits are competed away. For this reason, freely competitive markets are often considered to be advantageous to consumers. But where small firms are the rule, it is also generally the case that handling and fabrication techniques are underdeveloped or backward. Small firms typically cannot afford to develop new techniques and are often slow to adopt them once developed. Thus, it is not possible to generalize with respect to the desirability of freely competitive markets. If they are modern and advanced with respect to facilities and production methods, they will be advantageous to consumers, but if antiquated and inefficient, they will not.

Monopolistic competition. In this market situation, we continue to find *many sellers*, but each seller handles a commodity different in some respect from that of every other competitor. The product of each seller is *differentiated* from that handled by every other competitor. This differentiation may be achieved through the use of a brand name or a trade-mark or the creation of a distinct physical appearance or quality. Thus each seller has a monopoly over the specific commodity handled; no other seller has a commodity quite like the one in question. But each seller is in competition with every other seller in the market since the commodities in question are close substitutes (i.e., each of the differentiated products may be used to satisfy the same specific want). With elements of monopoly and competition both present, then, this market situation is called monopolistic competition.

Information is generally imperfect in such markets. Buyers or consumers generally do not know what the quality difference existing between the commodity substitutes may be. Who knows, for example, what exactly are the quality differences existing between the many brands of cigarettes to be found on the market—except perhaps the color and design of the packages? And, of course, any distinction achieved through the use of patent rights, trade-marks, or brand names is not open to competitors. Hence, restriction to entry is an important idea here; a competitor is prohibited by law, custom, or force from entering into the production and sale of a product exactly like that of the firm in question.

Examples of this type of market situation are not hard to find. The many producers and sellers of women's apparel are a case in point. The many different bars and eating places found in large cities fit this market situation. And the many different brands of cigars, canned peas, and candy bars are also examples of monopolistic competition.

Differentiated-product prices tend to be more stable than homogeneous-product prices. The producer-seller of, say, a line of women's hats *sets* the price of those hats at what he believes to be the maximum revenue price and then leaves the price alone until he knows that he is wrong. Then he resets it. These are administered prices—administered by the seller—and they sometimes hold constant for long periods of time. Excess profits are, however, generally wiped out in this market situation through the competition of the many sellers for increased sales. Thus we have a situation characterized by monopoly prices and competitive profits. The consumer benefits in this type of market situation from the variety of products offered and the continuous innovation with respect to the commodities. He is at a disadvantage, however, in that firms typically do not operate at maximum efficiency (or minimum cost): firms operating in this type of situation are more concerned with catching the eye of the consumer than producing at minimum cost. And the consumer is always handicapped in this market situation by a lack of reliable information.

Imperfect oligopoly. This market situation is characterized by few sellers and product differentiation. In this class of markets, we find so few sellers that the action of any one has a direct influence on the operations of each of his rivals; this is what the word *oligopoly* means—"few sellers." The word *imperfect* precedes oligopoly to indicate that the sellers involved do not handle a homogeneous product. Each seller's product is differentiated from that of his rivals. The important consideration in this type of market is, then, *rivalry*.

Sellers are so few in number that each seller has a clear picture of the competitive behavior of each of his rivals: the price policy of his rivals, the production methods employed, and the product competition involved. Hence, any one seller clearly recognizes what the competitive behavior of a rival (or rivals) means in terms of his operation. In this type of market, rivalry becomes *personal*, and this in turn leads to various forms of competition: from an unaggressive live-and-let-live form at one end of the scale to the bitterest dog-eat-dog form at the other.

This type of market situation is commonly found in the area of consumer durables. This is what we find in the market for automobiles, electric appliances, television sets, rugs, mattresses, farm machinery, power tools, and soap. In short, this is perhaps the most common type of market situation encountered by consumers. And it will be recognized at once that the products involved in this class of markets are all mass-produced. This type of market seems to develop wherever the output of mass production is consumer goods.

Prices are characteristically stable in this type of market. Prices of automobiles, for example, generally change once a year with the new model, and the prices of television sets, electric appliances, rugs, and mattresses change only at infrequent intervals. Price competition is not important in these markets; the unflattering term "price chiseler" is used to describe firms that engage in price cutting. Competition generally takes the form of product competition. Each producer-seller tries to produce a better or more eye-catching product; thus models change at frequent or regular intervals, and a great deal of time and effort is spent in developing new products. The benefits to consumers from this type of market situation take the form of better products; product competition leads to technological development and this to improved products. The lack of price competition, however, leads in many cases to excessive profits and always a sluggishness in the reduction of product prices.

Perfect oligopoly. This market situation is similar to the previous one in that few sellers are involved. But in this case each seller handles the same product; we say that the product is homogeneous. Since few sellers are involved, personal rivalry emerges as the dominant consideration. The view of producer-sellers in this class of markets might be described as follows: "What my rival does has a direct and perhaps all-important effect on my operations." This is particularly true with respect to price cutting. Since the product of each producer is identical with that of all other producers, any producer-seller who cuts his price will immediately capture the market. Hence, price cutting by any one firm must lead to a price war. But where firms have tremendous investments in plant and equipment, price wars are to be avoided like the plague. Reasoning by analogy, poker players may like to gamble for low stakes, but not, say, when their lives are involved. Thus, all manner of live-and-let-live pricing policies emerge in this situation. The most common is that of price leadership; by tacit (or perhaps overt) agreement, one firm is established as the price leader, and all others follow this firm to avoid a price war.

The classic example of this market situation, which is rarely found at the consumer level, is that of steel production. But the situation exists also for such commodities as cement, sulphur, and bakery flour. Clearly, market structures which we describe as perfect oligopolies develop most commonly in the raw materials.

Prices are administered in perfectly oligopolistic markets—that is, price is set by the leader, or by agreement, at a level which is optimum, by some criteria, to the firms involved. But prices do not tend to be so stable as in those cases where products are differentiated and each firm has a partial monopoly. Through substitution, changes in demand and supply conditions are reflected more directly and forcibly in raw-materials markets than in consumer-durable markets; hence, raw-materials prices are more flexible than durable-goods prices. In other words, users of raw materials (i.e., producers of other goods) watch the prices of raw materials closely and substitute one for another, in so far as technically possible, when one material becomes lower-priced than others. Thus, we tend to get price competition *between* products and industries, but not *among* firms within an industry producing the identical product.

Pure monopoly. This market situation involves a single seller. But the question arises immediately as to what is meant by a single seller. In the cases of both monopolistic competition and imperfect oligopoly, each seller in the market handles a product that is different from that of his competitors. Each seller in such markets is in a sense a single seller, hence a monopolist. In speaking of a pure monopoly, then, we must have something else in mind. By pure monopoly we mean a situation involving a single seller of a product *which does not have close substitutes.* In this situation, the seller sets that price which maximizes his net revenue, and he does this without taking into account the action of rivals. There may be some not too distant product substitutes to be considered in setting the price of his product, but the nagging question of what his rivals may do no longer needs to be considered. The question is not relevant since the rivals are nonexistent.

Monopolies are rather difficult to find in pure form (i.e., with only distant substitutes). For many years, the Aluminum Company of America existed as the classic case of a monopoly, but this monopoly was broken during World War II. Perhaps the best examples of monopolies are to be found in the public utilities field. In most communities, electricity, gas, and public transportation are furnished by single sellers, which hence may be described as monopolies. And sometimes, in small towns, we find a single barber or store that assumes a monopolistic position in the community. But with the widespread use of the automobile these local monopolies are not so important as they once were.

With no rivals to consider, the single seller will always set that price which maximizes his profits. For this reason, uncontrolled monopolies rarely work in favor of consumers. Confronted with this situation, consumers have typically banded together and sought the aid of government in controlling prices or rate structures of single sellers. Hence, public utility rates are typically set, or at least reviewed, by public commissions established to protect the interests of the consuming public. As the result of the development of this type of public policy, the completely free, unrestrained monopolist has, along with the passenger pigeon, become extinct.

Market structures on the buying side. To this point, all variations in market structure have been considered from the selling side. If only markets at the retail level were to be considered, we could, perhaps, drop the discussion at this point, for in most retail markets we find many buyers. This is the typical market structure with respect to numbers on the buying side at the retail level. But, at the wholesale or producer level, we find most of the structural variations described above on the buying side, too. Thus, we shall consider briefly the nature and implications of different structural characteristics on the buying side of the market.

At the wholesale level, markets comprised of several or a few buyers are commonly found. In some cases, few buyers are confronted by many sellers (e.g., the meat packers in terminal livestock markets); in other cases, a few buyers are confronted by a few sellers (e.g., automobile manufacturers purchasing tires); and, in still other cases, a few buyers are confronted by a single seller (e.g., several milk distributors purchasing fluid milk from a farmers cooperative bargaining association). Where a few buyers confront many sellers, the price will be set by the buyers at a level most acceptable to them. Typically, the price leader sets the price, and the available supplies are shared by the purchasers in accordance with some tacit or overt agreement. In such market situations, excessive profits for buyers are common, and prices to sellers are lower than they would be if free competition existed on both sides of the market.

In those cases where few buyers confront either a few sellers or a single seller, trading activities across the market take the form of *bargaining*. Price is determined in accordance with the economic strength and finesse of the opposing parties or groups. Actually such market situations tend to develop into bilateral monopolies, where there is in fact, if not in name, only one buyer and one seller and prices and quantities are determined through bargaining.[4]

Market situations involving a single buyer are not uncommon. Agriculture is replete with examples of a single buyer confronting many sellers, although it is probably true that this market situation was more common in the past than it is today. The history of agricultural cooperation in the United States is largely one of many small sellers banding together to enhance their bargaining power in dealing with the one or few buyers to be found in a local market. In labor markets, too, the single buyer is often found. This buyer of labor service is often a large manufacturer or processor. At one time in American history, labor markets often took the form of one or a few buyers (business firms) and many small sellers of labor service (individual laborers). But laborers banded together in unions, as farmers did into cooperatives, and labor markets of the 1950s commonly take the form of one seller (the union) and one or several buyers (business firms). Thus, the structure of labor markets in the United States is often one of a bilateral monopoly. In this market situation, price (or the wage rate) is determined by the strength and finesse of the bargaining parties.

In sum, there are many different classes or categories of markets, when we consider all the different possible structures on both sides of the market. In some markets—freely competitive markets—price is determined in a completely *unconscious* manner: it is formed and discovered out of the higgling in markets comprised of so many individuals that no one has any perceptible influence on the final price outcome. On the other hand, we have some markets—bilateral monopolies—where price is determined in a completely *conscious* manner: it is formed and discovered through a bargaining process involving two contending parties. And, between these two extremes, we find markets of varying structures, where prices are formed and discovered in varying ways. But all these prices are tied together—related—through the process of substitution. Consumers substitute one commodity for another in an effort to maximize their well-being; producers substitute one factor for another in an effort to maximize their net return. In some cases, this process of substitution may work slowly and haltingly—but always it is at work, guided by and

[4] This concept has been called "countervailing power" in a recent exposition emphasizing its importance to the economy as a whole. J. K. Galbraith, *American Capitalism*, Houghton Mifflin Company, Boston, 1952.

influencing in turn the price system. In this way—through the working of all the markets described—we obtain a simultaneous solution to the three basic problems:

1. What commodities in what quantities?

2. How shall those commodities be produced—with what resources and by what methods?

3. For whom shall those goods be produced?

PERFORMANCE OF THE ECONOMY

The economy of the United States has developed and grown beyond the wildest expectations of the founding fathers. And it continues to grow in a spectacular fashion. The rate of growth of almost every segment of the economy since World War II has astonished most observers. One of the important underpinnings of the growth of the American economy has been population growth. We have had to build vast numbers of houses, stores, schools, and hospitals to shelter a rapidly increasing population. A second important basis of economic growth has been territorial expansion. As we explored and occupied a major part of the continent of North America, we had to build roads, canals, fences, barns, factories, and warehouses as a part of that occupation process. A third basis of economic growth has been technological advance—the development of new methods and the adoption of these new methods in factories and on farms. Americans have a profound faith in technological advance; they are willing to spend time and money on the development of new methods; and always a daring few are willing to give the new methods a trial. Hence, technological advance has resulted in extensive and intensive capital formation in most industries.

It would be wrong, however, to visualize the American economy as growing steadily and smoothly. The economy has grown in spurts. And these spurts have been associated with important areas of capital formation. The prolonged period of prosperity, running from the 1840s into the 1870s, is associated with railroad building; the next great period of growth, running from 1900 to 1929, is associated with the rise of the electrical and automobile industries. The latest period of growth, from 1946 to 1956, is associated with a general expansion in plant and equipment and residential construction. But, between these periods of growth and development, we find the nemesis of the American economy—business depressions, or slumps. Some of these have lasted as long as twenty-five years (e.g., the period 1875 to 1900). Some have been of shorter duration, but perhaps more severe in terms of the amount of unemployment, number of business failures, and low income (e.g., the period 1929 to 1940). Thus the nagging fear of "economic bust" seems always to be with us—even in periods of great economic prosperity and growth.

We cannot, however, review the performance of the economy of the United States from 1790 to the present.[5] Hence, we shall concentrate on the development of the economy from 1929 to 1953. In this review, we shall consider first production, then prices, and finally incomes.

Production, 1929 to 1953.[6] The total output of the national economy, measured in terms of the prices of the products sold and defined as the Gross National Product (GNP), is shown by the solid line in Figure 3-1.

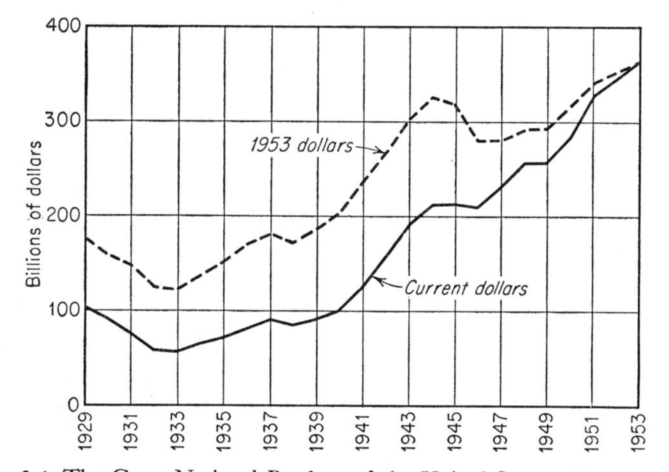

FIG. 3-1. The Gross National Product of the United States, 1929 to 1953.

We observe that the total output of the economy measured in current dollars declines following 1929 and does not regain that level until 1940. This was the Great Depression of the 1930s. It was a period of low physical production and low prices, and these conditions produce the hollow in GNP between 1929 and 1940. Following 1940, the GNP begins to climb, and it maintains a general upward trend through 1953.

[5] For an excellent discussion of this subject see Harold F. Williamson (ed.), *The Growth of the American Economy*, Prentice-Hall, Inc., New York, 1951. See particularly chaps. 5, 17, 34, and 48.

[6] For a discussion of later periods see recent issues of *The Economic Report of the President* together with *Report to the President, The Annual Economic Review by the Council of Economic Advisors.*

One slight dip is to be observed in 1946 and one brief plateau between 1948 and 1949; but these are only lapses from a general upward movement. This upsurge in GNP grows out of increased physical productivity and rising prices.

The dashed line in Figure 3-1 describes the movement in GNP where it is assumed that prices were constant at the 1953 level over the entire period. Describing the GNP in terms of constant 1953 dollars removes the influence of *changes in prices* from the value aggregates and indicates what happened to physical production alone. And we see that removing the influence of price changes does change the total-output picture somewhat. The hollow in the 1930s is of shorter duration, and the rate of increase following 1940 is less sustained. An important decline in physical production took place following World War II which is obscured by a compensating price change in the current dollars estimates of GNP.

The allocation of the total output of the economy among major uses —consumption, domestic investment, foreign investment, and government—may be seen by absolute values and percentages in Table 3-1. The principal category of expenditure in the 1930s was personal consumption —running at the level of 75 to 85 per cent of the total. Government expenditures (with all the WPA's, PWA's, and AAA's) and private investment were relatively unimportant in this period—running at a level of 5 to 15 per cent, respectively. But government expenditures increased dramatically during World War II. In 1943 and 1944, government expenditures accounted for nearly half the Gross National Product. Following World War II, domestic investment expenditures increased importantly as the economy embarked upon a housing and plant and equipment boom. Thus, in the early 1950s, expenditures by government and private investors account for nearly 40 per cent of the GNP.

Another way of looking at production in the United States is in terms of employment. The employment picture over the period 1929 to 1953 is summarized in Table 3-2. One point that emerges from even a cursory review of these data is the extent of unemployment in the 1930s. Some 12 million persons were officially unemployed in 1932 and 1933; this constituted almost 25 per cent of the total civilian labor force. We observe also that the total labor force grows rapidly when it needs to grow. The civilian labor force declined almost not at all between 1940 and 1944 when 11 million men were taken out of civilian employment and put in the armed forces. A lot of people must have entered the labor force during this five-year period who did not consider themselves in the labor

Table 3-1. *Gross National Product and Expenditure, 1929–1953*
(Dollar figures in billions)

Period	Gross national product *	Personal consumption expenditures		Gross private domestic investment		Net foreign investment		Government purchases of goods and services	
	Amount	Amount	Per cent of total	Amount	Per cent of total	Amount	Per cent of total	Amount	Per cent of total
1929	$104.4	$ 78.0	75.7	$16.2	15.5	$ 0.8	0.8	$ 8.5	8.1
1930	91.1	71.0	77.9	10.3	11.3	0.7	0.8	9.2	10.1
1931	76.3	61.3	80.3	5.5	7.2	0.2	0.3	9.2	12.1
1932	58.5	49.3	84.3	0.9	1.5	0.2	0.3	8.1	13.8
1933	56.0	46.4	82.9	1.4	2.5	0.2	0.4	8.0	14.3
1934	65.0	51.9	79.8	2.9	4.5	0.4	0.6	9.8	15.1
1935	72.5	56.3	77.7	6.3	8.7	−0.1	−0.1	10.0	13.8
1936	82.7	62.6	75.7	8.4	10.2	−0.1	−0.1	11.8	14.3
1937	90.8	67.3	74.1	11.7	12.9	0.1	0.1	11.7	12.9
1938	85.2	64.6	75.8	6.7	7.9	1.1	1.3	12.8	15.0
1939	91.1	67.6	74.2	9.3	10.2	0.9	1.0	13.3	14.6
1940	100.6	71.9	71.5	13.2	13.1	1.5	1.5	14.1	14.0
1941	125.8	81.9	65.1	18.1	14.4	1.1	0.9	24.8	19.7
1942	159.1	89.7	56.4	9.9	6.2	−0.2	−0.1	59.7	37.5
1943	192.5	100.5	52.2	5.6	2.9	−2.2	−1.1	88.6	46.0
1944	211.4	109.8	51.9	7.1	3.4	−2.1	−1.0	96.5	45.6
1945	213.6	121.7	57.0	10.4	4.9	−1.4	−0.7	82.9	38.8
1946	209.2	146.6	70.1	27.1	13.0	4.6	2.2	30.9	14.8
1947	232.2	165.0	71.1	29.7	12.8	8.9	3.8	28.6	12.3
1948	257.3	177.6	69.0	41.2	16.0	2.0	0.8	36.6	14.2
1949	257.3	180.6	70.2	32.5	12.6	0.5	0.2	43.6	16.9
1950	285.1	194.0	68.0	51.2	18.0	−2.2	−0.8	42.0	14.7
1951	328.2	208.3	63.5	56.9	17.3	0.2	0.1	62.8	19.1
1952	346.1	218.4	63.1	50.7	14.6	−0.2	−0.1	77.2	22.3
1953	364.9	230.1	63.1	51.4	14.1	−1.9	−0.5	85.2	23.3

* Due to rounding, the expenditure components do not exactly equal the GNP.
SOURCE: U.S. Department of Commerce, *Survey of Current Business*, July, 1954, Table 2, p. 4.

force prior to 1940. In short, the aged, the infirm, and the housewife join the labor force when the job opportunities are there and leave it when the job opportunities become scarce. We observe further that the civilian labor force declined immediately after World War II (in 1945) but expanded once again with the postwar boom.

Two more points need to be made with respect to Table 3-2. First, we observe that the number of persons engaged in agriculture declined steadily from 1935 and that this decline became particularly sharp follow-

Table 3-2. *Civilian Labor Force, Employment, and Unemployment, 1929–1953*
(Thousands of persons 14 years of age and over)

Period	Total	Employment *			Unemployment	Unemployment as per cent of civilian labor force
		Total	Agricultural	Nonagricultural		
1929	49,180	47,630	10,450	37,180	1,550	3.2
1930	49,820	45,480	10,340	35,140	4,340	8.7
1931	50,420	42,400	10,290	32,110	8,020	15.9
1932	51,000	38,940	10,170	28,770	12,060	23.6
1933	51,590	38,760	10,090	28,670	12,830	24.9
1934	52,230	40,890	9,900	30,990	11,340	21.7
1935	52,870	42,260	10,110	32,150	10,610	20.1
1936	53,440	44,410	10,000	34,410	9,030	16.9
1937	54,000	46,300	9,820	36,480	7,700	14.3
1938	54,610	44,220	9,690	34,530	10,390	19.0
1939	55,230	45,750	9,610	36,140	9,480	17.2
1940	55,640	47,520	9,540	37,980	8,120	14.6
1941	55,910	50,350	9,100	41,250	5,560	9.9
1942	56,410	53,750	9,250	44,500	2,660	4.7
1943	55,540	54,470	9,080	45,390	1,070	1.9
1944	54,630	53,960	8,950	45,010	670	1.2
1945	53,860	52,820	8,580	44,240	1,040	1.9
1946	57,520	55,251	8,320	46,930	2,273	4.0
1947	60,168	58,027	8,266	49,761	2,142	3.6
1948	61,442	59,378	7,973	51,405	2,064	3.4
1949	62,105	58,710	8,026	50,684	3,395	5.5
1950	63,099	59,957	7,507	52,450	3,142	5.0
1951	62,884	61,005	7,054	53,951	1,879	3.0
1952	62,966	61,293	6,805	54,488	1,673	2.7
1953 †	63,417	61,894	6,528	55,366	1,523	2.4

* Includes part-time workers and those who had jobs but were not at work for such reasons as vacation, illness, bad weather, temporary layoff, and industrial disputes.

† Preliminary.

SOURCE: *Economic Report of the President*, January, 1954, p. 182.

ing 1949. Between 1935 and 1953, the number of persons employed in agriculture declined from 10.1 million to 6.5 million. Second, we observe that unemployment was held to 2 or 3 per cent of the civilian labor force in most years following World War II.

The indices of production presented in Figure 3-2 summarize the

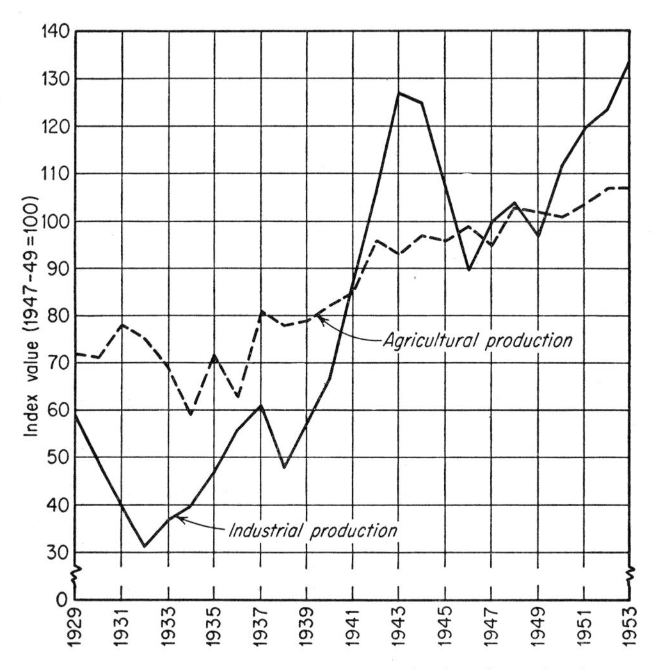

FIG. 3-2. Indices of industrial and agricultural production.

changes in physical production—variability and growth—in the United States since 1929. *Industrial production* has varied greatly. It was cut in half between 1929 and 1932, and it quadrupled between 1932 and 1943. Since 1943, the year-to-year variations have been relatively large. *Agricultural production* exhibits a less pronounced tendency to vary from year to year. The widest swings are associated with the severe droughts of 1934 and 1936. We observe, however, a general upward movement over the entire period 1929 to 1953, with the most rapid advance coming in the period 1936 to 1942.

Prices, 1929 to 1953. The movement of wholesale prices since 1929 has the same general configuration as that of industrial production (compare Figures 3-2 and 3-3). This might at first appear strange. We are generally told that increased supplies lead to falling prices, and conversely. And this is generally true with respect to single or individual commodities. But it is not true with respect to the economy *as a whole*. In periods of business depression, production and prices fall together, and, in periods of prosperity, production and prices rise together. With general increases in the demand for all factors to increase production, the incomes of all factors rise, with the consequence that all commodity prices rise along with factor prices and production.

We do observe, however, some rather important differences between the behavior of farm and nonfarm prices. Nonfarm prices are more sluggish than farm prices. Nonfarm prices are not so quick to fall and they do not fall so far as do farm prices: witness the periods 1929 to 1932 and

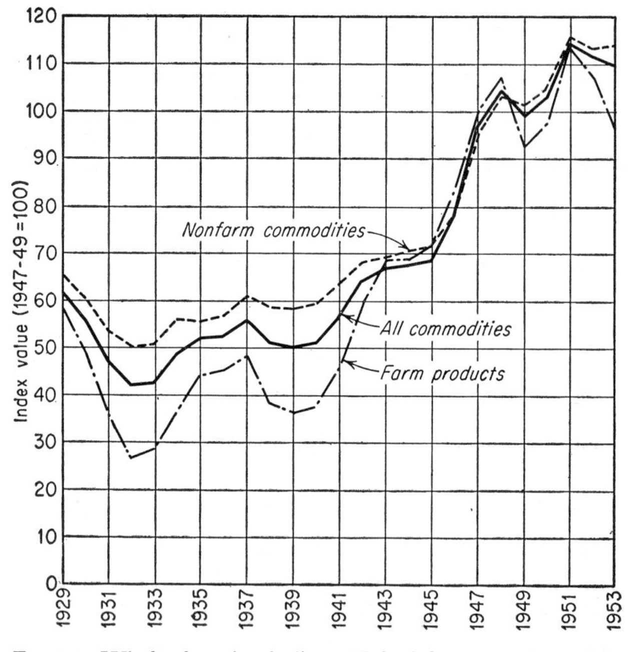

FIG. 3-3. Wholesale price indices, United States, 1929 to 1953.

1951 to 1953. This difference in price behavior is to be explained by the fact that most farm prices are *made* in markets approaching a freely competitive structure, whereas nonfarm prices are more typically made in markets of a monopolistic structure. For example, prices of wheat, cotton, feed grains, and eggs vary immediately and directly with each change in the conditions of demand or supply. This is always the case in markets where there are so many buyers and sellers that no single unit can influence or control price. Such is not the case, however, with steel, textiles, farm machinery, and cement: in the oligopolistic markets in which these items are sold, prices are administered by sellers and are changed only after sellers have experienced for some time the changed conditions of demand or supply. In nonfarm industries, adjustments are more frequently made in production than prices (compare Figures 3-2 and 3-3). The different patterns of price and production behavior between farm and nonfarm commodities are thus to be explained by the different structure of markets to be found in these different segments of the economy.

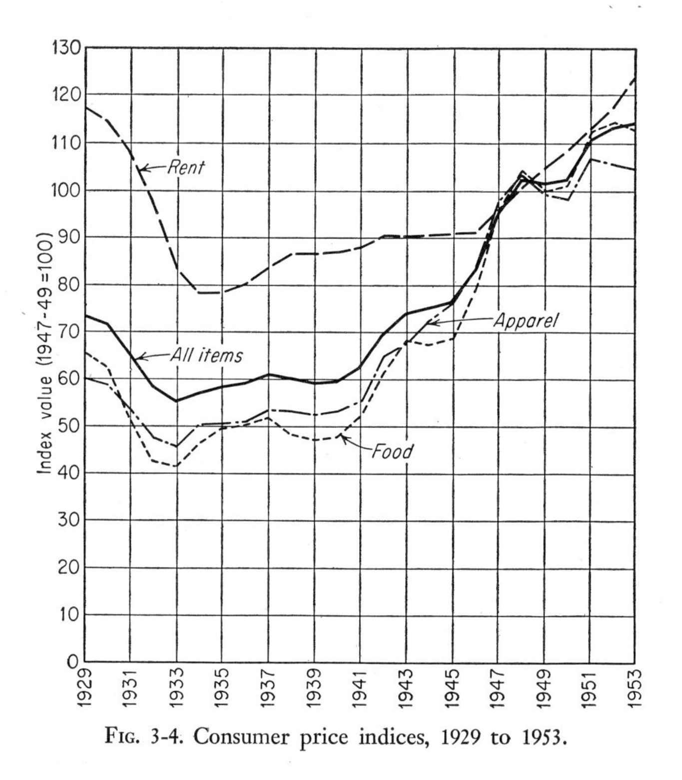

FIG. 3-4. Consumer price indices, 1929 to 1953.

Prices at retail tend to be modestly more stable than prices at wholesale (compare the "all commodities" line in Figure 3-3 with the "all items" line in Figure 3-4). And we observe a peculiar steplike movement in the over-all level of consumer prices over the period 1929 to 1953 (see the "all items" line in Figure 3-4). Consumer prices moved up importantly in 1941 to 1943, held relatively constant during 1943 to 1945, shot skyward in 1946 to 1948, remained constant again in 1948 to 1950, and then took another upward hop in 1951. This stair-step movement is associated first with war, then with the efforts of the Office of Price Administration, then with the removal of OPA, then with the peak of a boom, then with a hot phase of a cold war, and finally with a second effort at price control. In general, however, consumer prices follow the same major pattern as do wholesale prices. And this is reasonable, since the price movements at both levels were generated by the same set of forces—the forces that gave rise to prosperity and depression.[7] Only in the case of retail prices, government acting in the interests of consumers attempted at various times to hold a lid on prices, and these attempts, involving holding the lid on, taking it off, and putting it back on, produced a steplike movement of prices at retail.

The behavior patterns of the individual components of the consumer price index presented in Figure 3-4 are too varied to trace through time. But several generalizations can be drawn from the presentation in the figure. First, food prices are the least stable. Second, apparel prices have been quick to exhibit a weakness in boom periods. Third, rents do not follow the general level of consumer prices: uncontrolled rents exhibit a tendency to remain high relative to other consumer items.

Personal incomes, 1929 to 1953. The total amount of income received by individuals—total personal income—is given in Table 3-3 by years, together with sources of that income. It is apparent at once that the receipt of income follows the same general pattern over time as that for production and prices. Production, prices, and incomes follow the contours, or describe the contours, of general business activity. It is important to note, however, that salaries and wages account for between 60 and 70 per cent of the income received. In short, most of the income received in the United States takes the form of salaries and wages. In contrast, the amount of income received from interest and dividends has fallen to less than 10 per cent in recent years.

The disposition of personal income by all consuming units is described in Table 3-4. Since 1943, personal income taxes have accounted for almost 20 per cent of the personal income received. Personal disposable income (personal income less personal taxes) can be used in two ways, (1) consumption expenditures and (2) savings. We observe that by far the largest

[7] An explanation of business fluctuations is presented in Chaps. 14 and 15.

Table 3-3. Personal Income, 1929–1953
(Dollar figures in billions)

Period	Total personal income *	Salaries, wages, and other labor income		Proprietors' and rental income		Dividends and personal interest income		Transfer payments	
	Amount	Amount	Per cent of total	Amount	Per cent of total	Amount	Per cent of total	Amount	Per cent of total
1929	$ 85.8	$ 51.0	59.4	$20.2	23.5	$13.2	15.4	$ 1.5	1.7
1930	76.9	46.7	60.7	16.3	21.2	12.4	16.1	1.5	2.0
1931	65.7	39.6	60.3	12.5	19.0	11.0	16.7	2.7	4.1
1932	50.1	30.9	61.7	8.0	16.0	9.1	18.2	2.2	4.4
1933	47.2	29.4	62.3	7.6	16.1	8.3	17.6	2.1	4.4
1934	53.6	34.1	63.6	8.7	16.2	8.7	16.2	2.2	4.1
1935	60.2	37.2	61.8	12.0	19.9	8.8	14.6	2.4	4.0
1936	68.5	42.5	62.0	12.3	18.0	10.4	15.2	3.5	5.1
1937	73.9	46.7	63.2	14.8	20.0	10.6	14.3	2.4	3.2
1938	68.6	43.6	63.6	13.7	20.0	9.0	13.1	2.8	4.1
1939	72.9	46.6	63.9	14.4	19.8	9.6	13.2	3.0	4.1
1940	78.9	50.5	64.0	15.9	20.2	9.8	12.4	3.1	3.9
1941	96.3	62.8	65.2	20.9	21.7	10.3	10.7	3.1	3.2
1942	123.5	83.0	67.2	28.5	23.1	10.1	8.2	3.1	2.5
1943	151.4	106.7	70.5	33.3	22.0	10.3	6.8	3.0	2.0
1944	165.7	118.5	71.5	35.0	21.1	10.8	6.5	3.6	2.2
1945	171.2	119.4	69.7	36.5	21.3	11.6	6.8	6.2	3.6
1946	178.0	113.8	63.9	41.5	23.3	13.4	7.5	11.4	6.4
1947	190.5	125.2	65.7	40.9	21.5	14.7	7.7	11.8	6.2
1948	208.7	137.9	66.1	45.6	21.8	16.2	7.8	11.3	5.4
1949	206.8	137.4	66.4	42.0	20.3	17.2	8.3	12.4	6.0
1950	227.1	150.3	66.2	44.6	19.6	19.8	8.7	15.1	6.6
1951	255.3	175.6	68.8	49.9	19.5	20.7	8.1	12.6	4.9
1952	271.2	190.6	70.3	49.9	18.4	21.4	7.9	13.1	4.8
1953	286.1	204.4	71.4	49.0	17.1	22.8	8.0	13.8	4.8

* Due to rounding, the sources of personal income do not exactly equal total personal income.
SOURCE: U.S. Department of Commerce, *Survey of Current Business*, July, 1954, Table 3, p. 6.

proportion of total disposable income is allocated to consumption expenditures. The proportion varies from year to year, but only rarely does it fall below 80 per cent, and that in wartime. Or, looking at the allocation of disposable income from the savings side, the per cent saved varied from —1.3 in 1933 to 25 in 1944. The United States is sometimes characterized as a high-savings economy, but in more normal peacetime years the allocation of total disposable income by consumer units to savings falls between 5 and 10 per cent.

Table 3-4. Disposition of Personal Income, 1929–1953
(Dollar figures in billions)

Period	Personal income	Less personal tax and nontax payments	Equals disposable personal income	Less personal consumption expenditures	Equals personal net saving	Net saving as per cent of disposable personal income
1929	$ 85.8	$ 2.6	$ 83.1	$ 79.0	$ 4.2	5.1
1930	76.9	2.5	74.4	71.0	3.4	4.6
1931	65.7	1.9	63.8	61.3	2.5	3.9
1932	50.1	1.5	48.7	49.3	−0.6	−1.2
1933	47.2	1.5	45.7	46.4	−0.6	−1.3
1934	53.6	1.6	52.0	51.9	0.1	0.2
1935	60.2	1.9	58.3	56.3	2.0	3.4
1936	68.5	2.3	66.2	62.6	3.6	5.4
1937	73.9	2.9	71.0	67.3	3.7	5.2
1938	68.6	2.9	65.7	64.6	1.1	1.7
1939	72.9	2.4	70.4	67.6	2.9	4.1
1940	78.9	2.6	76.1	71.9	4.2	5.5
1941	96.3	3.3	93.0	81.9	11.1	11.9
1942	123.5	6.0	117.5	89.7	27.8	23.7
1943	151.4	17.8	133.5	100.5	33.0	24.7
1944	165.7	18.9	146.8	109.8	36.9	25.1
1945	171.2	20.9	150.4	121.7	28.7	19.1
1946	178.0	18.8	159.2	146.6	12.6	7.9
1947	190.5	21.5	169.0	165.0	4.0	2.4
1948	208.7	21.1	187.6	177.6	10.0	5.3
1949	206.8	18.7	188.2	180.6	7.6	4.0
1950	227.1	20.9	206.1	194.0	12.1	5.9
1951	255.3	29.3	226.1	208.3	17.7	7.8
1952	271.2	34.4	236.9	218.4	18.4	7.8
1953	286.1	36.0	250.1	230.1	20.0	8.0

SOURCE: U.S. Department of Commerce, *Survey of Current Business*, July, 1954, Table 3, p. 6.

Questions and Points for Discussion

1. What are the basic problems of every economic society? How are these problems solved in the economy of the United States?
2. What do economists mean by a "perfect market"? Are all markets in the United States perfect? If not, what or how do "imperfections" arise?
3. Indicate some of the ways in which the structure of markets may vary. What are some of the implications of differently structured markets for consumers?
4. Compare farm prices and production over time with nonfarm prices and production.
5. What proportion of total personal income comes from salaries and wages? What proportion from dividends and interest?
6. How has the Gross National Product in the United States varied since 1929? How much of this variation is explained by changes in physical output?

References

Bain, Joe S., *Price Theory*, Henry Holt and Company, Inc., New York, 1952, chaps. 4–7.

Economic Report of the President, recent issues.

Samuelson, Paul A.: *Economics: An Introductory Analysis*, 2d ed., McGraw-Hill Book Company, Inc., New York, 1951, chaps. 2 and 3.

Williamson, Harold F. (ed.): *The Growth of the American Economy*, Prentice-Hall, Inc., New York, 1951, chaps. 17, 34, 45, and 48.

4. *The Consumer in the Economy*

There are two principal classes of decision makers in the economy: businessmen and consumers. The decision making of businessmen is concerned with the choice and use of resources in firms; the decision making of consumers is concerned with the choice and use of resources in households. This entire volume deals with the many and diverse implications of decision making by consumers, and Part II concentrates on a presentation of an explanation, or rationale, of the decision-making process of consumers. Thus, we shall not attempt to develop and present an explanation (i.e., a hypothesis) of consumer decision making in this chapter.

We want to do two things in this chapter, (1) set forth the economic position of households in the American economy and (2) describe in terms of level and content of consumption the results of past decisions of consumers. The first type of information provides a background against which to analyze consumer behavior—provides a description of the economic base from which decisions are made. The second type of information enables us, after the fact, to study the form and content of consumer decision making—enables us to see what, in fact, consumers did. In other words, we shall try in this chapter, first, to set forth those important elements, fixed in the short run (e.g., family income), which consumers must take into consideration in making choices and, second, to observe the results of past decision making by consumers.

THE DISTRIBUTION OF INCOME

The distribution of income among consumers may be considered in numerous ways. The distribution of consuming units by income classes is one way; the distribution of total income received by income classes is another. The distribution of income may also be described by occupational groupings or other distinguishing characteristics. Finally, income received may be considered before or after income taxation.

In this discussion we shall consider the distribution of income first by income classes: by consuming units and total income received within income classes. And the discussion will be conducted in terms of income before taxation, except where comparisons with income after taxation are appropriate and *possible*. Lastly, the discussion will turn to the distribution of income by occupations.

The distribution of income by income classes. The distribution of consuming units by income classes for the years 1946 and 1951 to 1953 is shown in Table 4-1. The distribution of incomes received by consuming

Table 4-1. *Percentage Distribution of Consuming Units and Total Money Income by Income Classes before Income Taxes, 1946–1953*

Money income before taxes	1953		1952		1951		1946	
	Consuming units	Total money income	Consuming units	Total money income	Consuming units	Total money income	Consuming units	Total money income
Under $1,000	10	1	11	1	13	1	17	3
$1,000–$1,999	13	4	14	5	15	6	23	12
2,000– 2,999	14	8	16	10	18	12	25	21
3,000– 3,999	16	12	18	15	18	16	17	20
4,000– 4,999	16	15	15	16	15	17	8	13
5,000– 7,499	21	27	17	25	14	22	6	11
7,500– 9,999	5	10	5	10	4	26	4	20
$10,000 and over	5	23	4	18	3			
All cases	100	100	100	100	100	100	100	100
Median income	$3,780		$3,420		$3,200		$2,300	
Mean income	4,570		4,070		3,820		2,870	

SOURCE: "1953 Survey of Consumer Finances," *Federal Reserve Bulletin*, June, 1953 and "1954 Survey of Consumer Finances," *Federal Reserve Bulletin*, July, 1954. Income data for each year are based on interviews during January, February, and early March of the following year.

units is seriously distorted in 1946. Some 17 per cent of all consuming units fall in the income class $1,000 and under, and fewer than 4 per cent fall in the top income classes of $7,500 and over. And the modal income class (i.e., the class with the greatest frequency) is not the middle one (or ones) —it is third from the bottom of the scale. In statistical terms, the distribution of incomes in 1946 is highly skewed; it fails to fall into a normal bell-shaped curve. This means that the earning power of consuming units was so distributed in 1946 that a very few received very high incomes and a large number received very low incomes.

It will be observed, however, that the distribution of consuming units by income classes becomes less skewed in 1951 and 1952. In 1952, the number of consuming units in the lowest income class falls to 11 per cent, the number in the top income classes of $7,500 and over rises to 9 per cent, and the modal income class moves up one class from 1946. And, except for the growing bulge in income class $5,000–$7,499, the distribution of consuming units by income classes fits a normal curve fairly well in 1953. In short, there has been some tendency for incomes received to become more normally distributed since the end of World War II.

To this point, all references to Table 4-1 have been concerned with the distribution of consuming units by income classes. We have as yet said nothing about the degree of equality, or inequality, of incomes. And we should be clear that a normal distribution of incomes does not mean equal incomes; a normal distribution implies only that the greatest concentration of incomes occurs over the middle range of incomes and that relatively few consuming units fall in the very low- and very high-income classes.

The degree to which consumer incomes are unequal in the United States may be ascertained in a rough fashion by relating the data on consuming units to the data on total money income in Table 4-1. In 1946, for example, the 17 per cent of all consuming units falling in the income class $1,000 and under received 3 per cent of the total money income, whereas the 4 per cent of all consuming units falling in the income classes $7,500 and above received 20 per cent of the total money income. Less dramatic but more significant, the 82 per cent of all consuming units falling in the bottom four income classes in 1946 received 56 per cent of the total money income; the 18 per cent of all consuming units falling in the upper four income classes received 44 per cent of the total money income. These data indicate that consumer incomes in 1946 were decidedly unequal.

From changes in the distribution of consuming units by income classes between 1946 and 1953, it might be guessed that some tendency existed for incomes to become more equally distributed over the period. In 1953, for example, 53 per cent of the consuming units fall in the bottom four income classes, as compared with 82 per cent in 1946. But these data tell us little about the degree of income equality, or inequality, until they are related to the data on the distribution of total money income by income classes. And we observe that the 53 per cent of all consuming units falling in the bottom four income classes in 1953 received only 25 per cent of the total money income, whereas the 47 per cent of all consuming units falling in the top four income classes received 75 per cent of the total money income.

The continued income inequality over the period 1946 to 1953 is brought out more clearly in Figure 4-1. The Lorenz curves in Figure 4-1 showing the cumulative percentage of total money income received as related to the cumulative percentage of consuming units for both 1946 and 1953 do not indicate that there was any significant shift either toward or away from a greater equality of incomes for the period involved,

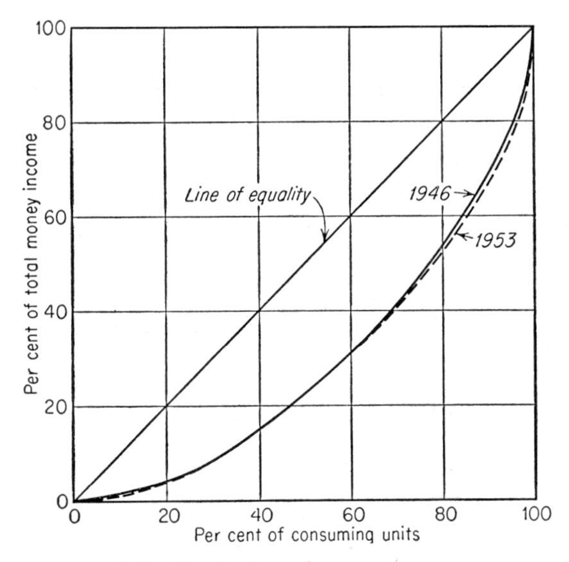

FIG. 4-1. Lorenz curves of the distribution of money income among consuming units, United States, 1946 and 1953.

although if any change is to be observed it is toward greater inequality. As compared with the line of income equality, however, the Lorenz curves for both 1946 and 1953 describe income distributions that are markedly unequal.

The absolute level of the average money income of consuming units for the years involved should be noted (see Table 4-1). The median, or exact middle, income stood at $2,300 in 1946 and rises to $3,780 in 1953. This is a substantial increase for the period involved. But many people will be surprised to learn that the income of the consuming unit falling in the exact middle of the income range was as low as it was for the period 1946 to 1953.

The influence of Federal income taxes on the distribution of consuming units and total money income by income classes may be seen in Table 4-2.

Comparing the data on the distribution of consuming units for the year 1953 in Tables 4-1 and 4-2, we see that Federal income taxes had two effects, (1) that of reducing the number of consuming units falling in the classes $5,000 and above and (2) producing a greater concentration of consuming units in the income class $3,000–$3,999. In short, the over-all influence of Federal income taxation is that of yielding a more normal (i.e., less skewed) distribution of consumer incomes.

Federal income taxation also influences the degree of income equality; it tends to make disposable incomes more equal. Relating the data on the distribution of consuming units to total money income received before and after Federal income taxation makes this tendency clear. The ratios [1] of the percentage of total money income received to the percentage of consuming units in the bottom four income classes for the years 1951 to 1953 are as shown in the accompanying table. The ratios may be inter-

Year	Before taxes	After taxes
1951	0.547	0.643
1952	0.525	0.621
1953	0.472	0.574

preted in the following way: If incomes were distributed equally each ratio would equal 1; thus, the actual value of any one ratio is the percentage of the *total money income* that consuming units in the four income classes involved would need to receive to make all consuming-unit incomes equal. In 1951, then, consuming units falling in the bottom four income classes received before taxes only 55 per cent as much total money income as would be required to make their incomes equal to all others, but after taxes the percentage increases to 64. In 1953, the percentage before taxes is 47 and after taxes is 57. During the period 1951 to 1953, then, Federal income taxes had the effect of making consuming-unit incomes more equal in any given year, *but over the three-year period incomes were becoming increasingly unequal.*

Another view of the degree of income inequality in the United States and the influence of Federal income taxation on this inequality is pre-

[1] The ratio for 1951 before taxes is computed as follows: 35 per cent ÷ 64 per cent = 0.547 where the percentage of total money income received = 35 per cent and the percentage of consuming units in the bottom four income classes = 64 per cent.

Table 4-2. Percentage Distribution of Consuming Units and Total Money Income by Income Classes after Income Taxes, 1952 and 1953

Disposable income	1953		1952	
	Consuming units	Total disposable money income	Consuming units	Total disposable money income
Under $1,000	10	1	11	1
$1,000–$1,999	15	6	16	7
2,000– 2,999	16	11	20	14
3,000– 3,999	20	17	19	19
4,000– 4,999	16	19	15	18
5,000– 7,499	16	24	13	22
$7,500 and over	7	22	6	19
All cases	100	100	100	100
Median disposable income	$3,460		$3,150	
Mean disposable income	3,920		3,570	

SOURCE: "1954 Survey of Consumer Finances," *Federal Reserve Bulletin*, July, 1954.

sented in Table 4-3. Once again, the degree of income inequality in the United States is made clear. Before Federal income taxes, 10 per cent of all consuming units in the top bracket received about 30 per cent of the total money income over the years 1949 to 1951, whereas the 10 per cent of all consuming units in the lowest bracket received only 1 per cent of the total money income. Federal income taxation changes the picture modestly in the direction of greater income equality, but the basic condition of inequality remains unchanged.

The distribution of income by occupations. The income received by each consuming unit must come from some source. It is interesting to classify consuming units by the occupation of the head of the consuming unit and observe the influence of occupation on consumer incomes. Such a classification is presented in Table 4-4. Occupation would seem to have an important influence on size of income. In all years for which data are available, the subcategory "Managerial" heads the list of average incomes received; managers, not too surprisingly, hold the preferred income po-

Table 4-3. *Percentage of Total Money Income Received by Each Tenth of the Nation's Consuming Units, Ranked by Size of Income, 1949–1951*

Consuming units	Money income before Federal income tax			Money income after Federal income tax (disposable income)		
	1951	1950	1949	1951	1950	1949
Highest tenth....	31	29	30	28	27	28
Second..........	15	15	15	15	15	15
Third...........	12	13	12	13	13	13
Fourth..........	10	11	11	11	11	11
Fifth............	9	9	9	9	10	9
Sixth............	8	8	8	8	8	8
Seventh.........	6	6	6	7	7	7
Eighth..........	5	5	5	5	5	5
Ninth...........	3	3	3	3	3	3
Lowest tenth.....	1	1	1	1	1	1
All cases.........	100	100	100	100	100	100

SOURCE: "1952 Survey of Consumer Finances," *Federal Reserve Bulletin*, September, 1952.

Table 4-4. *Median Incomes within Occupational Groups*

Occupation of head of consuming unit	Median income			
	1953	1952	1951	1946
All consuming units.............	$3,780	$3,420	$3,200	$2,300
Professional and semiprofessional..	5,540	5,310	4,500	4,000
Managerial and self-employed:				
Managerial..................	6,610	5,500	5,350	*
Self-employed................	5,000	4,730	4,180	*
Clerical and sales...............	4,100	3,850	3,410	2,600
Skilled and semiskilled..........	4,400	4,000	3,800	2,700
Unskilled and service............	2,530	2,470	2,100	1,600
Farm operator..................	2,060	2,190	1,880	1,300

* Data not available.

SOURCE: "1953 Survey of Consumer Finances," *Federal Reserve Bulletin*, June, 1953; and "1954 Survey of Consumer Finances," *Federal Reserve Bulletin*, July, 1954.

sition. But the incomes of professional and semiprofessional workers are consistently near the top of the range of average incomes received. Since the salaries of teachers could hardly have put the professional group in this position, we must infer that the earnings of medical doctors and lawyers were sufficiently high to do so.

The incomes of clerical workers tend to fall more closely to median consuming-unit incomes than those for any other occupation. At the bottom of the list are to be found farm operators. Incredible as it may seem, the average annual net income of farm operators in 1952 was $2,190. We recognize, of course, that this value, along with all others discussed in this section, is an average and that many farm operators had higher net incomes; but many could have higher incomes only in so far as many had lower incomes.

NET WORTH OF CONSUMING UNITS

The net worth of a consuming unit is equal to the sum of its assets less total debt. The net worth of a consuming unit describes the accumulated wealth of that unit. And we are interested in the net worth of consumers for two reasons: (1) the net worth position of a consuming unit together with the composition of its assets and debts should influence the decision making of the unit; (2) the net worth position of consuming units becomes a useful measure of the material well-being of those units. Thus, we shall review the net worth position of consuming units in the United States, first, to provide background for analysis and, second, to provide standards for current comparisons.

Size of net worth. In 1953, most consuming units owned assets in excess of their debts (i.e., the net worth of most consuming units was positive). This we see in Table 4-5. Only 11 per cent of all consuming units owed debts in excess of assets (i.e., had negative net worth positions). And nearly half the consuming units were worth $5,000 or more. At the top of the wealth-accumulation scale, some 11 per cent of all consuming units were worth $25,000 or more. It is interesting to observe from Table 4-5 that the proportion of consumers with large net worth ($25,000 and over) increased between 1950 and 1953, as also did the proportion with debts in excess of reported assets (i.e., those with negative net worth). In short, the ownership of wealth was becoming more unequally distributed during this period of prosperity.

As might be expected, these net worth data are correlated with age.

Table 4-5. Percentage Distribution of Net Worth of Consuming Units

Amount	1953	1950
Negative	11	8
0– $ 499	14	27
$ 500– 999	6	
1,000– 2,999	14	24
3,000– 4,999	9	
5,000– 9,999	17	33
10,000– 24,999	18	
25,000– 49,999	7	8
$50,000 and over	4	
All cases	100	100
Median	$ 4,100	*
Mean	11,900	*

* Data not available.
SOURCE: "1953 Survey of Consumer Finances," *Federal Reserve Bulletin*, September, 1953.

The net worth of consumers between the ages of 18 and 24 years averaged $300. The net worth of consuming units reaches a maximum of $8,500 for the age bracket 55 to 64 years and then declines for ages 65 and over.

Composition of net worth. The ownership of different types of assets varies greatly among consumers (see Table 4-6). The most widely held asset in 1953 was liquid assets—United States government securities and savings and checking accounts. Some 71 per cent of all consuming units held liquid assets in 1953, but the percentage of consuming units holding such assets varied importantly by size of income. High-income consuming units most frequently held liquid assets, and conversely. Large proportions of consumers owned homes and automobiles—about 40 per cent and 60 per cent, respectively. Interestingly, investments in farms were most frequent at the lower end of the income scale, and investments in nonfarm businesses and corporate stock were most frequent at the upper end of the income scale.

Some 62 per cent of all consuming units owed debt in 1953. And consumer debts were found most frequently in the income class $5,000–$7,499 (see Table 4-6).

The composition of net worth changes substantially with the amount

Table 4-6. Percentage Ownership of Assets and Debt Liability by Income Groups, 1953

Item	All consuming units	1952 money income before taxes			
		Under $3,000	$3,000–$4,999	$5,000–$7,499	$7,500 and over
Assets:					
Liquid	71	52	76	93	98
Automobile	61	36	70	84	92
Owner-occupied nonfarm home	43	32	43	57	65
Owner-occupied farm	5	9	4	3	3
Other real estate	14	11	11	19	31
Business interest *	7	3	6	8	22
Corporate stock	7	4	5	10	28
Money loaned out	12	12	11	14	17
Debt owed	62	51	68	75	63

* Includes unincorporated nonfarm business and owner-operated privately held corporations.

SOURCE: "1953 Survey of Consumer Finances," *Federal Reserve Bulletin*, September, 1953.

of resources (i.e., net worth) and with age (see Table 4-7). As net worth increases, the ratio of business and investment assets to net worth rises sharply, whereas the ratios of consumer capital goods and fixed-value assets (e.g., liquid assets) to net worth decline substantially. In other words, as consumers become wealthier, the composition of that wealth changes. It will also be noted that the ratio of debt to net worth declines as net worth increases, indicating the stronger personal finance position of consuming units with large net worth.

Important changes in the composition of net worth also accompany increases in the age of consumers (see Table 4-7). The net worth of consumers less than thirty-five years of age reflects primarily the ownership of consumer capital goods, which are financed to a large extent by borrowing. As age increases, both consumer capital goods and debt decline in relation to net worth.

In other words, the younger families attempt to acquire in relatively short periods the large stock of consumer capital and durable goods that are a part of the American standard of living. To finance these outlays for

Table 4-7. Assets and Debt as Percentage of Net Worth, Early 1953

Group characteristic	Net worth	Variable-value assets		Fixed-value assets ‡	Total assets	Debt §
		Consumer capital goods *	Business and investment assets †			
All spending units	100	45	51	17	113	13
Age of head of spending unit:						
18–34	100	70	48	17	135	35
35–54	100	47	52	15	114	14
55 and over	100	35	52	18	105	5
Net worth:						
$ 0–$ 999	100	140	9	50	199	99
1,000– 4,999	100	103	13	31	147	47
5,000– 24,999	100	73	28	19	120	20
$25,000 and over	100	23	67	15	105	5
Aggregate dollar valuation, in billions	$641	$288	$328	$109	$725	$84

* Includes automobiles and owner-occupied nonfarm homes.

† Includes owner-occupied farms, farm machinery, livestock, crops, interests in unincorporated businesses and privately held corporations, real estate other than home or farm on which owner is living, and corporate stock.

‡ Includes liquid assets and loans made by spending units.

§ Includes mortgages and other real estate debt, installment and other short-term debt.

SOURCE: "1953 Survey of Consumer Finances," *Federal Reserve Bulletin*, September, 1953.

automobiles, houses, and major household appliances, the younger consuming units need and have been willing to use installment credit. Hence, the frequency and size of debt is high among this class of families.

PERSONAL CONSUMPTION EXPENDITURES

Patterns of consumer expenditure do not on the average change greatly from year to year. This basic stability in consumer expenditure data, hence in the use of income by consumers, is established in Table 4-8. In the early 1950s, all consumers allocated about 35 per cent of their total outlays to food, tobacco, and alcoholic beverages, 12 per cent to clothing, accessories, and jewelry, 11 per cent to housing (i.e., the provision of shelter), 13 per cent to household operation (e.g., expenditures for furniture, lights and fuel, rugs and washing machines, and so on), 5 per cent to medical care and death expenses, 10 per cent to transportation, 6 per cent to recreation, and some 8 per cent to all other items (e.g., religious activities, education, personal care). Now, reviewing the entire period 1929 to 1953, we observe that these percentage allocations do not change importantly over the years. The percentage of expenditure outlays allocated to food, tobacco, and alcoholic beverages increases somewhat over the period as consumers have purchased more and more services (e.g., packaging, processing, and eating out) with their food. And the percentage allocations to clothing and housing have declined moderately. But in the other categories, and in the main, the percentage allocations to different product lines and services have remained remarkably stable.

Although the percentage allocations of expenditure outlays among different consumption categories hold relatively stable from year to year, *total money expenditures do not.* Following the contours of general business activity, total consumption expenditures decline from $78.8 billion in 1929 to $46.3 billion in 1933 and then rise persistently, although not smoothly, to 1953—reaching a high of $229.9 billion in that year. With this great increase in dollar expenditures, one question immediately comes to mind: "How much of this dollar increase represents an increase in the consumption of goods and services?" In other words, how much did the real level of consumption increase between 1929 and 1953?

LEVELS OF CONSUMPTION

By removing the influence of changing prices from consumer expenditure data (i.e., stating expenditure data in constant prices), expenditure data are made to describe changes in *quantities* consumed. This is what has been done in Table 4-9, where personal consumption expenditures are broken into three categories—durable goods, nondurable goods, and services—and are presented in constant 1939 prices. These expenditure data are in real terms, hence describe changes in quantities consumed.

It will be observed that total consumption expenditures expressed in constant 1939 prices almost doubled between 1929 and 1953. In other words, the actual quantities of goods and services consumed by all consumers almost doubled between 1929 and 1953. Interestingly enough, the increase in real consumption over the same period is nearly the same in

Table 4-8. Personal Consumption Expenditures by Type of Product or Service, 1929–1953

(Dollar figures in billions)

Year	Food and tobacco *		Clothing, accessories, and jewelry		Personal care		Housing		Household operation		Medical care and death expenses	
	Amount	Per cent of total	Amount	Per cent of total	Amount	Per cent of total	Amount	Per cent of total	Amount	Per cent of total	Amount	Per cent of total
1929	$21.4	27.1	$11.0	14.0	$1.1	1.4	$11.4	14.5	$10.5	13.3	$ 3.6	4.6
1933	12.8	27.6	5.4	11.6	0.7	1.4	7.8	16.9	6.4	13.8	2.4	5.2
1935	17.7	31.5	6.9	12.3	0.8	1.4	7.6	13.5	7.6	13.5	2.8	4.9
1937	21.6	32.2	8.0	11.9	1.0	1.4	8.4	12.5	9.3	13.9	3.2	4.8
1939	21.1	31.2	8.3	12.3	1.0	1.5	8.9	13.3	9.5	14.0	3.4	5.0
1940	22.6	31.4	8.8	12.2	1.1	1.5	9.2	12.8	10.3	14.3	3.6	5.0
1941	26.5	32.2	10.5	12.7	1.2	1.5	9.9	12.0	11.7	14.3	4.0	4.8
1942	32.8	36.0	13.1	14.4	1.4	1.5	10.6	11.6	12.3	13.5	4.5	4.9
1943	37.9	37.1	16.3	15.9	1.7	1.7	11.1	10.9	12.7	12.4	5.0	4.9
1944	41.5	37.2	18.1	16.2	1.9	1.7	11.7	10.5	13.5	12.1	5.6	5.0
1945	45.9	37.3	20.2	16.5	2.1	1.7	12.2	9.9	14.9	12.1	5.9	4.8
1946	53.7	36.6	22.4	15.2	2.2	1.5	13.0	8.8	19.0	12.9	7.0	4.8
1947	60.5	36.5	23.1	13.9	2.3	1.4	14.6	8.8	22.7	13.7	7.8	4.7
1948	63.9	35.9	24.2	13.6	2.2	1.2	16.5	9.3	24.5	13.8	8.5	4.8
1949	63.1	35.0	23.0	12.7	2.2	1.2	18.1	10.0	23.5	13.0	8.9	4.9
1950	65.6	33.7	23.1	11.9	2.3	1.2	20.2	10.4	26.4	13.6	9.5	4.9
1951	73.7	35.4	24.6	11.8	2.4	1.2	21.9	10.5	27.3	13.1	10.2	4.9
1952	77.8	35.6	25.2	11.6	2.5	1.6	24.0	11.0	27.6	12.7	10.9	5.0

* Expenditures for alcoholic beverages included.

Table 4-8. *Personal Consumption Expenditures by Type of Product or Service, 1929–1953* (*Cont.*)
(Dollar figures in billions)

Year	Personal business		Transportation		Recreation		Private education and research		Religious and welfare activities		Foreign travel and remittances		Total consumption expenditures	
	Amount	Per cent of total	Amount	Per cent of total	Amount	Per cent of total	Amount	Per cent of total	Amount	Per cent of total	Amount	Per cent of total	Amount	Per cent of total
1929	$ 5.2	6.6	$ 7.5	9.5	$ 4.3	5.5	$0.7	0.8	$1.2	1.5	$0.8	1.0	$ 78.8	100
1933	3.1	6.6	3.9	8.5	2.2	4.7	0.5	1.0	0.9	1.9	0.4	0.8	46.3	100
1935	3.3	5.9	5.2	9.2	2.6	4.7	0.5	0.9	0.9	1.5	0.4	0.6	56.2	100
1937	3.9	5.8	6.4	9.6	3.4	5.0	0.6	0.9	0.9	1.3	0.5	0.7	67.1	100
1939	3.7	5.5	6.3	9.3	3.4	5.1	0.6	0.9	0.9	1.4	0.3	0.5	67.5	100
1940	3.8	5.3	7.0	9.7	3.7	5.2	0.6	0.9	1.0	1.4	0.2	0.3	72.1	100
1941	4.1	5.0	8.2	10.0	4.2	5.1	0.7	0.8	1.0	1.2	0.3	0.3	82.3	100
1942	4.0	4.4	5.4	5.9	4.7	5.2	0.8	0.9	1.2	1.3	0.3	0.3	91.2	100
1943	4.1	4.0	5.6	5.5	4.9	4.8	1.0	0.9	1.4	1.3	0.6	0.5	102.2	100
1944	4.4	4.0	5.9	5.3	5.6	5.0	0.9	0.8	1.6	1.4	1.0	0.9	111.6	100
1945	4.8	3.9	6.7	5.4	6.3	5.1	0.9	0.7	1.6	1.3	1.6	1.3	123.1	100
1946	5.5	3.7	11.6	7.9	8.9	6.1	1.0	0.7	1.6	1.1	0.7	0.5	146.9	100
1947	6.2	3.7	14.9	9.0	9.7	5.9	1.3	0.8	1.6	1.0	0.8	0.5	165.6	100
1948	7.0	3.9	16.9	9.5	10.0	5.6	1.5	0.8	1.7	1.0	1.0	0.6	177.9	100
1949	7.6	4.2	19.3	10.7	10.3	5.7	1.7	0.9	1.8	1.0	1.2	0.6	180.6	100
1950	8.7	4.5	22.6	11.6	11.3	5.8	1.8	0.9	1.9	1.0	1.2	0.6	194.6	100
1951	9.2	4.4	22.1	10.6	11.3	5.5	2.0	1.0	2.0	0.9	1.4	0.7	208.1	100
1952	10.0	4.6	22.5	10.3	11.7	5.4	2.2	1.0	2.1	1.0	1.7	0.8	218.1	100

SOURCE: *The Economic Almanac 1953–1954*, Thomas Y. Crowell Company, New York, p. 433, as adapted from U.S. Department of Commerce, *National Income and Expenditure Data*. Personal consumption expenditures consist of the market value of purchases of goods and services by individuals and nonprofit institutions and the value of food, clothing, housing, and financial services received by them as income in kind. It includes the rental value of owner-occupied houses but does not include purchases of dwellings which are classified as capital goods.

Table 4-9. *Personal Consumption Expenditures in 1939 Prices, 1929–1953*
(In billions of dollars)

Period	Total	Durable goods	Nondurable goods	Services
1929	$ 62.2	$ 8.0	$29.1	$25.1
1930	58.6	6.4	27.7	24.5
1931	56.6	5.3	27.5	23.9
1932	51.8	3.9	25.2	22.7
1933	51.1	3.8	24.9	22.4
1934	54.0	4.4	27.0	22.6
1935	57.2	5.4	28.6	23.2
1936	62.8	6.6	31.8	24.4
1937	65.0	7.0	32.9	25.1
1938	63.9	5.7	33.4	24.8
1939	67.5	6.7	35.3	25.5
1940	71.3	7.7	37.1	26.5
1941	76.6	8.9	40.1	27.6
1942	75.8	5.7	41.3	28.8
1943	78.0	5.0	42.6	30.4
1944	81.1	4.6	44.5	32.0
1945	86.3	5.3	47.9	33.2
1946	95.7	10.4	50.2	35.2
1947	98.3	12.3	49.5	36.4
1948	100.3	12.6	49.7	38.0
1949	103.2	12.9	50.7	39.6
1950	108.9	15.5	51.7	41.7
1951	108.5	13.4	52.4	42.6
1952	111.4	12.9	54.5	44.0
1953 *	115.9	14.4	55.9	45.6

* Estimate based on incomplete data; by Council of Economic Advisers.
SOURCE: *Economic Report of the President*, January, 1954, p. 170. Detail will not necessarily add to totals because of rounding.

each major category of consumption: 80 per cent for durable goods, 92 per cent for nondurables, and 82 per cent for services. Actually, the category of consumption which many people might have guessed to have increased most—consumer durables—increased least. And the consumption of soft goods (e.g., foods, clothing, and camera supplies) increased most.

But one thing is abundantly clear: consumers on the average enjoy a much higher level of consumption in 1953 than they did in 1929. The level of consumption in all major lines has increased importantly—almost doubled. This is a point that is often forgotten in discussions concerned with the influences of war, taxes, and inflation. Of course, all consumers have not benefited equally in this great increase in material well-being. But where in the history of the world have so many people increased their consumption of real goods and services so much in so short a period?

Questions and Points for Discussion

1. Construct a vertical bar chart of the distribution of consuming units by income classes for the most recent year that data are available. Is this distribution normally distributed?

2. What can you say about the equality of incomes from the chart constructed under (1) above? What additional data are useful in apprais-ing the equality of incomes? How equal or unequal are incomes in the year under consideration?

3. How does the Federal income tax influence the (*a*) distribution of incomes and (*b*) the equality of incomes?

4. Does occupation have any influence on the size of incomes?

5. What do we mean by net worth? What factors seem to influence size of net worth?

6. How does the composition of net worth change with (*a*) size of net worth and (*b*) age?

7. Have there been any important changes in the allocation of consumer expenditures among categories of expenditure since 1929?

8. What has happened to the real level of consumption by categories since 1929? Since 1946?

References

"Annual Survey of Consumer Finances," relevant issues of the *Federal Reserve Bulletin*.

The Economic Almanac, 1953–1954, Thomas Y. Crowell Company, New York, 1953, sec. XVIII, "Consumption and the Standard of Living"; see also later editions.

Katona, George: *Psychological Analysis of Economic Behavior,* McGraw-Hill Book Company, Inc., New York, 1951, chap. 8.

Samuelson, Paul A.: *Economics: An Introductory Analysis,* 2d ed., McGraw-Hill Book Company, Inc., New York, 1951, chap. 4.

PART TWO

The Theory of Consumer Behavior

A theory of consumer behavior has been developed within the main stream of economic theory which focuses on the actions of individuals in their efforts to maximize utility. This theory is often criticized as being cold and formal, which indeed it is; but it is basic to a general understanding of consumer behavior. It is to an understanding of consumer behavior as magnetic north is to navigation. Not everyone wants to travel north, but the concept of north and its measure by the magnetic pole assist all of us in our travels. Thus, the received theory of consumer behavior is presented in Part II in as complete, yet readable, form as the authors can achieve. The basic problem confronting the consumer is set forth in Chapter 5, and theoretical solutions to that problem are presented, first, in direct utility terms and, second, by the indifference approach in Chapters 6 and 7.

It is important also that students understand the implications of the received theory of consumer behavior. Thus the concern of Chapter 8 is, first, with the uses to which the theory may be put and, second, with its obvious and inner weaknesses. But criticism should and does entail the obligation to present something in the way of alternatives for the audience to appraise—in this case, alternative or modified theoretical formulations of consumer behavior. This is done in Chapters 9 and 10. Several recent developments having for their purpose the improvement, modification, or circumvention of the received theory of consumer behavior are reviewed in Chapter 9. Finally, a direct-action approach is suggested in Chapter 10.

5. *The Central Problem of Choice*

We come now to the heart of consumption economics. The consumer is endlessly confronted with the problem: "How shall I use my limited funds? What combination of goods and services shall I choose?" And the economist is confronted with a problem: "How, or by what process, does the consumer select the combination of goods and services that he does?" The two problems are not identical, but a solution to the second, more general problem provides insights and perhaps predictive value with respect to the more specific problem confronting the individual.

But the question may be asked: "In what sense is the consumer confronted with a problem?" The answer to that is twofold. First, the making of a choice from among different alternatives always constitutes a problem to the person involved; this we take as a truism. Second, the necessity of making choices is forced upon the consumer; he cannot escape choice decisions. And it is the logic and implications of this second aspect of the problem that we shall now develop.

THE NATURE OF THE CHOICE PROBLEM

For the individual consuming unit. The conditions which force the individual consuming unit to make choices with respect to the kinds and quantities of goods and services that it consumes may be given as follows:

1. Each consuming unit has a limited (finite) income.
2. Each consuming unit has varied and unlimited (infinite) wants to be satisfied.
3. Each good or service to be consumed to satisfy a want may be acquired only at a price (a nonzero price).

Given these conditions, which we recognize to be all too common in the real world, the consuming unit cannot purchase all the goods and services (in variety and quantity) to satisfy all of its wants. Therefore, it must select some specific combination of goods and services from all those available (each at a nonzero price). And we assume that the consuming unit will select that combination of goods and services which maximizes the total satisfactions of the individuals comprising it. Without entering into a discussion of the appropriateness of this maximizing assumpton at this point, its importance to the ideas under development becomes readily apparent. If we can assume that the consumer (i.e., the decision maker of the consuming unit) seeks to maximize the total satisfactions of the unit, and this does not seem too unreasonable, then we can predict in every situation which choice the consumer will make; he will make the selection which yields the greatest satisfaction. Thus, in a highly abstract sense, we can predict the unique combination of goods and services that the consumer will select.

The point might be made that a millionaire with an income of a million or two per year represents an exception to the first condition of limited income; hence, this consumer is not forced to make a choice with respect to wants to be satisfied. In a sense, this is correct, although there are not many consumers in this situation. But, in a more general sense, this millionaire faces a limitation, too—the limitation of time. If he attends the races, he cannot at the same time be playing golf. He can afford to do both in terms of money, but he cannot be in two places at the same time. Thus he must make a choice. Most of us would like to be in the position of having to make the type of decision involved here, but nonetheless a choice must be made. The rich man does not have the time to do all the things that his income will permit; hence, he must make a choice with respect to which wants he will satisfy. In this sense, he is no different from the middle-income earner choosing between a fishing trip and a new jacket or a beggar choosing between a good meal and a drink of whisky. The millionaire is limited by time alone, the latter two by income and possibly time. But all are limited; hence, all are forced to choose between alternative means of satisfying wants.

For the economy as a whole. We have stated the central problem of choice in terms of the individual consuming unit, but an analogous problem exists for the economy as a whole. And we have already come across this idea; it was discussed in Chapter 3. The question posed there was the following: "What resources shall be combined in what ways to produce what goods and services for whom?" Implied in this sequence of questions is the idea that there are insufficient resources to produce all the goods and services wanted by individuals comprising the economy. If this was not made explicit earlier, it needs to be now. There are insufficient resources to produce all the hospitals, schools, roads, military supplies, durable goods, food, clothing, housing, and recreation that all citizens of the United States want. This is all too obvious for the underdeveloped economies (e.g., Iraq and India), but it is also the case for the United States and Canada. This should not come as a surprise, for if each consuming unit comprising the whole is unable to satisfy all its wants, it would be strange indeed if the problem were solved when all consumers were added together into a unit known as society.

There are good reasons for believing that division of labor, specialization, and exchange lead to increases in real income, but this is not the point at question here. The real income benefits of division of labor, specialization, and exchange are and have been a part of the United States and Canadian economies for many decades; the realization of an interdependent economy has not, however, lifted individual consuming units of these economies into a world of free goods where choice is unnecessary. Thus, a consideration of the problem of choice from the aggregative point of view in no way changes the fundamental problem.

The outward form of the problem is, however, changed somewhat: for the consuming unit, the problem of choice comes down to a choice from among goods and services already produced; for the economy as a whole, the choice problem takes the form of deciding which resources will be used in what combinations to produce the goods and services wanted by consumers. All economies are confronted with this problem, for the same reason that each member of every economy since the beginning of time has been confronted with this problem. The reason in its crudest, but most meaningful, form is that—there is not enough of everything to go round.

Decisions with respect to the use of resources are made in different ways in different types of economies. In Western Europe during the Middle Ages, resources were employed in exactly the same way for several centuries—the choice decisions were dictated by immemorial custom. In a frontier society such as California during the Gold Rush, where the individual is unencumbered by family, church, or state, the automatic pricing system reigns supreme—scarce resources move readily into those employments where prices are highest.

In the United States in the decade of the 1950s, the price system plays an important role, perhaps a dominant role, but not an exclusive role in directing the use of resources to produce the goods and services wanted by members of society. Many decisions with respect to the use of resources are made through government in political markets. We make collective decisions to produce armaments, school systems, and roads, and we tax ourselves in one way or another to pay for the resources employed in producing these collective goods. Thus, as we have already observed, the economy of the United States is a mixed-enterprise economy: some decisions with respect to the use of resources, hence with respect to which goods are to be produced, are registered through the market via the price indicator; other decisions are made collectively through government.

Although the choice problem confronting the economy as a whole is basically the same as that confronting the individual, we shall deal here with the problems in terms of the individual or household, for several reasons. First, and most important, the analytical task of describing how the economy arrives at a solution to the sequence of questions, "What resources combined in what ways to produce what commodities?" is extremely difficult; such an approach would require the writing of a general treatise in economics, and this is not the time or place to attempt that. Second, technically a solution to the choice problem in terms of the economy of the whole leads outside the province of consumption economics and into the difficult land of supply. Third, where time is limited, we too must make a choice, and we believe that we can probe the choice problem more thoroughly by conducting the analysis in terms of the decision making of households than by attempting to deal with the total economy.

Major steps in the analysis of the choice problem. Basically the entire volume is concerned with the choice problem: how choices are made and the implications of these choices for the consumer and the economy. But it should prove advantageous to set forth the general procedural steps of this analysis at this point. These steps are:

1. Present a generalized explanation of the process whereby the consuming unit chooses a combination of goods and services that maximizes its satisfaction. The limitations of this body of theory, as well as possible avenues of improvement, are also presented. Chapters 6 to 10 are concerned with this step.

2. Observe and describe the actual behavior of households in the choosing or selecting of goods and services used in living. Chapters 11 to 13 are concerned with this step.

3. Analyze the influence of consumer choices on the operating economy —on the level of employment, the allocation of resources, and consumer well-being. Chapters 14 and 15 and all of Part IV are concerned with this step.

4. Recognize that the consumer does not or may not always want to

act independently but prefers on occasion to make decisions as a member of a group—usually through government. This collective decision making by consumers creates all sorts of analytical difficulties, but it cannot be ignored. Parts of Chapters 8, 10, 15, and 23 and all of Chapters 24 and 25 are concerned with this step.

THE INCOME LIMITATION

A review of consumer incomes in recent years brings out clearly the limiting aspects of these incomes. The median income per consuming unit before taxes in the United States was $3,000 in 1950, $3,200 in 1951, and $3,420 in 1952. After taxes, average income is, of course, lower; the median disposable income per consuming unit was $2,850 in 1950 and $2,970 in 1951. Consuming units with incomes falling in the middle brackets are narrowly circumscribed with respect to the use of these incomes. To take an extreme example, the decision by a consuming unit with a median income to buy a Cadillac would take all its income for one year and then some. Obviously, such a choice is out of the question for such a consuming unit; if the unit were to choose a Cadillac, it would have nothing left for the purchase of food, clothing, and shelter.

But let us take a more realistic example and see how much freedom the average consuming unit enjoys in its selection of goods and services. The income of families living in Denver, Colorado, averaged $4,107 in 1948;[1] the number of persons per family approximated 3. The average Denver family allocated its income as follows:

$1,153 to food
$618 to housing, fuel, and light
$499 to clothing
$448 to automobile
$358 to taxes of all kinds

Allocations to these five basic items amounted to $3,076, which means that just about $1,000 remained to cover all other items (home furnishings and equipment, medical care, personal care, recreation, education, gifts, church, insurance, and savings). And, breaking down the largest item, food, we see that food purchases averaged less than $100 per month. It is clear that the average family did not dine out regularly or effect large

[1] This average is for the approximate 95 per cent of families that had incomes of $10,000 or less. See *Family Income, Expenditures and Savings in 10 Cities*, U.S. Department of Labor Bulletin 1065, 1952, p. 19.

savings; in point of fact, the savings of the average family were negative (–$55).

This is not to suggest that individuals living in families with average incomes, in 1948, or 1950, or now, are suffering serious deprivations; they are not. Nonetheless, they had and have income problems. Most of them think long and hard before making the decision to purchase a new washing machine, a new suit of clothes, or a life insurance policy, for if they choose one of the above items, for example, they may be giving up a two-week vacation, a new living-room chair, or a chance to trade for a good "used" car. These are the types of choice patterns forced upon families with average incomes or lower. And families with incomes ranging up to $10,000 are confronted with analogous choice decisions: should the family increase its insurance program or buy a new car—expand its rate of saving for retirement or college educations for the children or purchase a cottage at a lake or beach? Income limitations force all but the very rich to choose—to choose a particular combination of goods and services for consumption from among a multitude of alternatives. And even the very rich are not entirely free; time imposes a limitation on them. They must budget that precious item time, where income does not limit. Thus the rich and the poor and those in between are forced by the limitations of income or time or both to make choices in their use of income or time or both, for none have enough of both to consume all the things they might want.

VARIED AND UNLIMITED WANTS

The subject of human wants and want creation is a complex one—one wherein the economist is prone to erect some amateurish or bad psychology and then stumble over it in his meanderings through this poorly charted field. This is particularly true when the economist attempts to develop "explanations" of human wants (i.e., theories of their origin and growth). Inquiries of a fundamental nature with the object of "explaining" wants should perhaps be undertaken by teams comprised of anthropologists, psychologists, physiologists, and economists. Unfortunately, such interdisciplinary studies have rarely, if ever, been undertaken, and in the meantime the economist working in the consumption area feels compelled to consider the problem of human wants and their creation. Consequently, there has been a great deal of work done in the way of describing and classifying human wants by persons interested in consumption economics.[2]

Some of this work of classification and description may contain some psychological pitfalls, but it is useful to the beginner in this field. The better discussions portray the wide diversity of wants, suggest the relative potentiality or intensity of different wants, and perhaps in some cases lead to an appraisal of one's own structure of wants. Thus, the following classification and discussion of human wants is presented not as a final or definitive scheme but rather to provide some insights into the bases and motivations of consumer behavior.

Classification of human wants

I. Individual physiological requirements and inborn tendencies which take the form of wants for:
   A. Food
   B. Protection against the elements as in the case of:
      1. Shelter (e.g., housing)
      2. Body covering (e.g., clothing)
   C. Sex and family
   D. Communal or social activities

II. Social, or group-created, wants classified according to the form of social, or group, behavior
   A. Custom-made wants
   B. Conspicuous consumption
   C. Fashion-made wants
   D. Imitative wants
   E. Producer-made wants
      1. Advertising
      2. Technological advance

If human wants were limited to those arising out of physiological requirements and inborn tendencies, human wants would be relatively simple. All the wants indicated under group I are satisfied in primitive societies [e.g., the American Plains Indians of 200 years ago, the Thai (Siamese) farmer of the 1950s]. And classes *A*, *B*, and *D* under group I

[2] See Leland J. Gordon, *Economics for Consumers,* American Book Company, New York, 1944, part II; Paul S. Nystrom, *Economic Principles of Consumption,* The Ronald Press Company, New York, 1929, chap. IV; C. S. Wyand, *The Economics of Consumption,* The Macmillan Company, New York, 1937, part III.

are adequately satisfied in the barracks society of the military. It is with the introduction of social, or group-created, wants under group II that the doors are opened wide to a variety of wants.

It should be noted that the criteria of classification change from group I to group II. Hence, the classes of wants under the two principal groups are not mutually exclusive. The classes of wants under group I are substantive (i.e., suggest the types of things that consumers may want), whereas the classes of wants listed under group II are more concerned with the form that substantive things take and variations in these forms. And we reason that the form which consumption takes and variations in that form result in the main from group and social actions. Thus, the criterion of classification under group II is that of the type or nature of the group or social action leading to want creation.

To illustrate, in twentieth-century America we eat food to satisfy a physiological requirement as have men from the beginning of time, but we also want that food served on a table, eaten from individual plates with knives, forks, and spoons. These latter demands are group-imposed and will vary from society to society. Nonetheless, these particular eating forms imposed by group action are important to individuals, and individuals in our society want to satisfy them if they can. And in most cases they can; only bums in the "jungle" fail to satisfy these group-imposed eating forms in twentieth-century America. But again they (the bums) develop their own group eating forms which they *want* to satisfy.

Social, or group-created, wants provide a society with its distinctiveness, variety, and color. And since it is these group-created wants which make individual want structures limitless, hence assure us of a problem to study in consumption economics, we shall consider the import of each class of social, or group, behavior under group II briefly.

Custom-made wants. One of the most important forces influencing individual wants is custom. As a form of social control, the power of custom is tremendous, but its influence is so commonplace and so widespread that most people are not conscious of it. In this area of consumption, custom may be defined as a tendency on the part of a *group* to consume according to a fixed pattern; this is in contrast to a habit which may be thought of as a tendency on the part of an individual to consume according to a fixed pattern. Custom might be described as a group habit. Thus it may be said, for example, that a certain individual has a smoking habit; but it is a custom among certain groups to smoke after dinner.

It is reasonable to suppose that most customs had their origin in some act of producing utility. A group which initiates a food or clothing custom probably does so to provide greater satisfaction *given the conditions of the times*. But once a custom becomes established, it may continue long after the original justification for it has disappeared. The dead hand of the past achieves an effective control over current wants and choice decisions through the social instrument of custom. And the institution of family plays a key role in the continuation of customs. Customs are painlessly transmitted by example and precept in the family.

The power of custom seems to be stronger in man's consuming activities than in his producing activities. The reason for this would seem to rest in the fact that subjective tests and personal emotions tend to be relatively important as guides in consumption, whereas objective tests and the logic of income maximization provide the principal guides in production. The pioneer in production is a hero; the pioneer in consumption is peculiar. And since most of us dislike being regarded as peculiar, and this can be avoided by conforming to custom, that in fact is what we do. Thus group customs play a ubiquitous role in controlling and molding individual wants, hence in influencing choice decisions.

Conspicuous consumption. Among the many forces influencing individual choice is that curious, but significant, urge to consume for the sake of display. Thorstein Veblen in his celebrated work *The Theory of the Leisure Class*[3] gave to this form of social behavior the expressive, but disparaging, name of *conspicuous consumption*. It may be defined as the consumption of goods and services on a grand scale for the purpose of demonstrating pecuniary power rather than that of providing utility through use. The very essence of conspicuous consumption is waste; utility is produced for the consumer through extravagance and waste rather than use.

In primitive tribal life, conspicuous consumption takes the form of class distinction based on physical power and prowess rather than pecuniary power. The braves reserve for themselves certain forms of consumption which are denied to lesser men and to women. Only those who have achieved distinction in the hunt and on the battlefield are permitted to enjoy certain luxuries; the choicest morsels of food, the most desirable skins, and the most beautiful feathers are designated for their exclusive use.

The ingenuity of modern men has created new and no less effective means of conspicuous consumption. Foreign travel is an effective means

[3] Modern Library, Inc., New York, 1934.

amounts of leisure time. Forces opposing fashion include inertia or dislike of change, religious and secret societies, and sumptuary laws (e.g., laws prescribing the amount of material that may be used in a skirt or a pair of trousers).

But it would be a mistake to view fashion as progressive. Leaders in fashion may introduce a new style or simply reintroduce old styles. Further, fashions in clothes seem to go in cycles, with the old being reintroduced after convenient lapses in time—convenient with respect to loss of memory or increasing nostalgia. Then again, it may be fashionable to wear pieces of clothing which certainly cannot contribute to personal comfort—celluloid collars and high-heeled shoes, for example.

The questions are often asked: "How and where are fashions controlled?" "Who controls fashions?" It would seem that no group does; fashion would seem to be best explained in terms of herd, or mob, psychology. Producers and advertisers help spread new fashions, but they seem unable to initiate or stop them. Consumers in general seem to exercise a veto power over fashion. Some consumers are more important than others in setting fashions. Royalty once enjoyed considerable power over fashions, but today wealthy individuals and other persons of prominence who seek the public eye and possess something of a competitive spirit are leaders of fashion. Many participate in the fashion parade, some lead, some follow; but it is difficult to locate the point of leadership, if, indeed, such a point exists.

The short clothes fashion cycle of modern times is difficult to explain. Mass production and mass communication make it possible—but what generates the cycle? Where does the impetus to rapid changes in clothing styles originate? Some suggest that fashion changes in clothing can be explained as an attempt on the part of members of each sex to win favor with the opposite sex. Others find the explanation in the desire to consume conspicuously. Fashion is regarded by some as a means of escape from drab routine, while others associate it with seasonal changes. A composite explanation of fashions in dress, then, recognizes the sex factor and the restless search for beauty and harmony; it includes curiosity, efforts to escape boredom, imitativeness, and seasonality.

Imitative consumption. The tendency to imitate is common to all age groups and social strata. And it is not a form of social behavior that need necessarily be frowned upon. The copying of new ideas with respect to types of foods, ways of preparing food, clothing materials, styles of architecture, house furnishings and equipment can be beneficial to all concerned. But, regardless of the moral judgments involved, copying, or imitating, is a tremendously potent force in the disseminating of new ideas with respect to consumer goods, hence in expanding and intensifying the structure of human wants.

Imitation in a materialistic society such as ours converts with a seductive subtlety into emulation. And by emulation we mean the tendency for individuals to wish to equal or excel others in some field of activity (e.g., consumption). Emulative consumption is thus a close cousin to conspicuous consumption. The motives are similar if not identical, but the form of consumption may vary importantly. In conspicuous consumption, the accent is on display; in emulative consumption, the goal is somewhat more prosaic–simply a bigger and better consumer good. But, in either case, the motive leads to competitive consumption.

Competition in buying now assumes a new significance. Instead of a rivalry in which buyers compete with one another to get the best bargain, the rivalry becomes one of seeing who can get the biggest and most gadgets (e.g., the widest television screen, the car with the most horsepower, the washing machine with the most automatic features). The popular conception of competitive consumption is expressed in the phrase "keeping up with the Joneses." While the breadwinner schemes and struggles to equal or excel Mr. Jones in the size of his pay check, the housewife schemes and struggles with equal determination to equal or excel Mrs. Jones in the grandeur of her expenditures.

Competitive consumption thus drives in the direction of more varied and more intense want creation. Each consuming unit wants something like that of its neighbor's, but a newer model. This *neighborhood effect*, or what Duesenberry has called the *demonstration effect*,[4] provides a built-in mechanism for creating wants. Competitive consumption causes consumption standards to rise along with, but always ahead of, rising productivity. We are assured that individual want structures will outdistance productive capacity where each consumer wants something bigger and better than the last item acquired by his neighbor.

Producer-made wants: advertising. A good argument can be made for advertising from the consumer point of view. Points to be made in favor of advertising are (1) that consumers are provided with information concerning the availability of goods, prices, discovery of new products, and

[4] *Income, Saving and the Theory of Consumer Behavior*, Harvard University Press, Cambridge, Mass., 1949, pp. 25–32.

discovery of new uses for old products; (2) that through the use of this information competition is made more effective; and (3) that advertising, by increasing sales, results in large-scale production with consequent economies which are passed on to consumers in the form of lower prices, better products, or both. There are perhaps better ways of informing the consumer than through advertising, but he must be informed, and to the extent that advertising provides accurate and descriptive information, it provides a useful service. The second point is more debatable. The third point is perhaps the most powerful. Mass production, and the economies which flow from it, *requires* a mass market, and this advertising assures. Mass production in consumer-durable industries is to an important degree dependent upon effective advertising.

An equally strong, and perhaps more persuasive, argument can be made against advertising. Much advertising is wasteful because it is useless as a source of information and is competitive in nature. This is perhaps the most damaging argument to be made against advertising; from an economic viewpoint, much of it represents a sheer waste of resources. No case whatever can be made for the competitive advertising that we witness for soaps and cigarettes. And we know from personal experience how misleading the claims of advertisers can be at times. From an aesthetic point of view, much advertising represents a misuse or a repugnant use of art and natural resources, and even more of it represents an insult to the intelligence of human beings. Finally, from the social point of view, it may be argued that advertising degrades and corrupts values and exploits and commercializes intimate personal situations and relations.

But the point to keep in mind here is that advertising is an important creator and manipulator of wants. *And, distinct from other social or group actions investigated here which create (or control) wants, advertising is purposive.* It is used with a purpose to create wants. And producers have found that it works. Thus, we may expect producers to keep on using it, and on a broad scale, as a means of creating and manipulating consumer wants.

Producer-made wants: technological advance. In the long run, this force may have more influence in shaping and formulating individual wants than any other, with the possible exception of custom. Prior to the twentieth century, such a statement would have had to be qualified to include only Western cultures. But today the whole world seeks material gains based upon technological advance.

Generally speaking, technological advance does not influence consumer wants directly. The influence of this modern force is felt through the other forces which we have examined: advertising, imitation and emulation, conspicuous consumption, and fashion. But we need only look round us to perceive the force of technological advance in molding human wants. Try to get along without the telephone, modern plumbing, central-heating systems, the automobile, electric lights, and refrigeration—try, and discover how badly you *want* these modern material things which are the fruits of technological advance. The entire structure of human wants in America in the 1950s is conditioned by the technological advance of the past fifty years, and we may anticipate an even greater rate of technological advance, hence want modification, in the next fifty years than in the last.

Viewing in retrospect the various classes of social-behavior patterns which influence the wants of consumers, there would appear to be two opposing long-run forces. Custom is the conserving force, powerful and ubiquitous, working to maintain the *status quo* in human wants. Technological advance is the innovating force, becoming increasingly powerful in modern society, working to create a new world with a new structure of human wants. Advertising, competitive consumption, conspicuous consumption, and perhaps fashion are forces working on the side of technological advance. This latter group of forces provides the means, the vehicles, through which technological advance modifies old wants and creates new ones. And, in twentieth-century America, it would appear that technological advance with its shorter-run allies have the upper hand in creating (or controlling) wants.

THE CHOICE PROBLEM RESTATED

The various classes of social, or group, behavior under group II of the classification of human wants, working through the few fundamental drives of group I, have produced an infinity of wants in the typical American consumer of the 1950s; social and group actions have created for the average consumer a structure of wants varied and intense beyond all measure. But the income of the average consuming unit is not sufficient to acquire goods and services to satisfy more than a minute fraction of these wants. Thus the consuming unit is endlessly confronted with the problem of how it will use its limited income. It must determine which wants are to be satisfied and to what degree; then it must select a specific combination of goods and services to satisfy these wants. This process we call the central problem of choice.

Basically the central problem of choice consists of two steps: *first*, choice decisions with respect to which and to what degree each want is to be satisfied; *second*, choice decisions with respect to the combination of goods and services to be acquired to satisfy the pattern of wants already determined. Since choice decisions with respect to which wants are to be satisfied cannot be measured objectively, and since it is also probably the case that decision making at this subjective level never becomes firm or explicit, economists typically make the assumption that each consumer is rational (i.e., each consumer selects that combination of goods and services which *best* satisfies the want pattern already determined). Use of this assumption permits the economist to ignore step 1 and concentrate on step 2—the combination of tangible goods and services selected. In this frame of reference, the central problem of choice reduces to the selection of a specific bill of goods and services from among all those goods and services available.

Whether such an assumption violates reality is open to debate. Many persons concerned with the choice problem feel that it is inadmissible; they argue with considerable logic that many or most of us do not know the best ways of consuming to satisfy certain wants (e.g., the best way of satisfying certain nutrient requirements of the human body). In this view, there is room for educational programs and other types of social action designed to help the consumer select that combination of goods and services under step 2 which best satisfies the pattern of wants selected under step 1.

In any event, it is important to recognize that the central problem of choice consists of two separate and distinct steps, for we shall at a later time make use of this distinction. This opening wedge between step 1 and step 2 we shall try to enlarge and in so doing expand and develop the theory and practice of consumer behavior. But in the following two chapters we shall make the conventional assumption that choice decisions under step 2 in fact satisfy the choice decisions under step 1. In other words, it is assumed that the problem of choice exists at only one level and the combination of goods and services selected may be taken as an objective measure of that pattern of choices.

Questions and Points for Discussion

1. What conditions give rise to the choice problem? How does the choice problem of the individual consuming unit differ from, and in what respects is it similar to, that for the economy as a whole? State as succinctly as possible what is meant by the central problem of choice.

2. Can you improve on the classification of human wants presented in this chapter? How would your classification differ?

3. List and discuss those forces at work in the economy which mold and control human wants.

4. Describe and discuss the two steps in the process of consumer choice.

References

Duesenberry, James S.: *Income, Saving and the Theory of Consumer Behavior,* Harvard University Press, Cambridge, Mass., 1949, chaps. II and III.

Gordon, Leland J.: *Economics for Consumers,* American Book Company, New York, 1944, part 2.

Norris, Ruby Turner: *The Theory of Consumer's Behavior,* Yale University Press, New Haven, Conn., 1941, chap. IV.

Veblen, Thorstein: *The Theory of the Leisure Class,* Modern Library, Inc., New York, 1934.

6. *The Utility Solution*

As suggested earlier, the consuming unit or household may be likened to a firm. Like a firm, it buys inputs and transforms them into a final product. The final product of the consuming unit, however, is not some physical product that can be seen or tasted or handled. It is a psychological product to which we give the name *utility*, and units of this final product, utility, may be conveniently called *utiles*. Where the firm (the producing unit) buys land, labor, capital, and raw materials and transforms them into a physical product, the consuming unit buys food, clothing, shelter, and recreation and transforms them into satisfaction, or utility. In this view, utility is the ultimate product of human activity; all physical goods, even consumer goods, are intermediate products and have value only because they have the capacity to produce an ultimate product, utility.

The term consuming unit is used above to imply that the decision-making unit in consumption generally is composed of several individuals—very often it is the family. But in the discussion that follows it will be convenient to treat the consuming unit as if it were composed of only one person. Granted this simplification, the utility functions of the individual are identical with those of the consuming unit, whereas, if we were to assume somewhat more realistically that the consuming unit is composed of three or four individuals, it would become necessary to add the utility functions of the individuals involved at each point in the analysis, hence work with an aggregative utility function. We can avoid these mechanical difficulties by working with a single individual consuming unit, which is what we shall do.

UTILITY FUNCTIONS

The utility data. If utility were measurable, we could and would obtain utility data—the number of utiles associated with different input combinations—from experiments. Experiments could be designed and conducted to measure the utility derived by the individual from varying quantities of a particular good or service. In these experiments, the consumption of all other goods and services would be held constant, for we are interested only and exclusively in the effect that varying quantities of the good in question have on the total utility of the individual. With the aid of our imaginations, then, we can visualize an experiment involving some sort of apparatus for measuring utility, in which the total utility received by the individual is registered as he consumes different quantities of a particular good, but his consumption of all other goods is held constant.

But utility is not measurable, or has not been up until very recently. And the successes achieved in measuring the utility of money have not as yet been duplicated for individual commodities.[1] What then should we do? Wait until utility can be measured? Or proceed with illustrative material that enables us to present a theory of consumer behavior the latter of which may be verified later? We shall follow the latter course of action. Thus, the total utility schedule presented in Table 6-1 is hypothetical.

Table 6-1. *Utility Schedules of a Hungry Man for Candy Bars*

Data from hypothetical experiments		Derived relations	
No. of candy bars (1)	Total utility, utiles (2)	Average utility, utiles (3)	Marginal utility, utiles (4)
0	0	0	0
1	10	10	10
2	40	20	30
3	60	20	20
4	72	18	12
5	80	16	8
6	84	14	4
7	84	12	0
8	72	9	−12
9	54	6	−18

The absolute size of the values presented in column 2 of Table 6-1 is unimportant, for the calibration on a measuring stick can be of

[1] These experiments in measuring the utility of money are discussed in an appendix to this chapter.

any size. In other words, a given distance when measured by different units of measure (e.g., inches, feet, miles) will be found to have different values, but the actual distance remains the same. But the relation of one magnitude to the next in the total utility column is important. And, in these "playlike" data, that relation has been established by what we think we know about consumer behavior.

The utility schedules. The utility data from a series of hypothetical experiments are given in Table 6-1. The total utility schedule of column 2 shows how the total utility of a hungry man changes as he consumes varying numbers of candy bars. When this man eats one candy bar, the total utility registered is 10 utiles; when he consumes two candy bars, total utility is 40 utiles; and so on. Actually, of course, these experiments were never conducted since we are unable at the present time to measure the utility associated with actual consumption. But we shall pretend that these experiments were conducted and that these data were obtained. In this illustration, we use candy bars since the units are small and it is realistic to consider a man eating different numbers of candy bars at one sitting.[2] But this hypothetical experiment might have employed apples, bottles of beer, pairs of shoes, hats, catcher's mitts, or electric toasters.

The hypothetical data of Table 6-1 suggest that total utility increases rapidly with the first few candy bars consumed (through the second one); that total utility continues to increase with the consumption of additional

[2] The question might be asked: "Will not the time period involved influence the values attained in the utility schedules? In other words, may not the utility schedules of the hungry man be different depending on whether he were required to eat the candy bars in one hour or one day?" And the answer is "Yes," because the state of hunger of the man involved would change with the passage of time. The point to be made, however, is not that the time periods are different, but rather that the conditions of the problem change with the passage of time. For where the conditions of the problem change (i.e., the state of the individual or the combination of goods and services consumed changes), the utility schedules cannot describe what they are supposed to describe, namely, how the utility of the individual varies in response to, *and only in response to,* changes in the quantities consumed of the good in question. On the other hand, where the state of the individual and the combination of goods and services consumed by him do not change significantly over time, the experiments yielding the utility data may with propriety, and realism, occur over time. The addition, then, of pairs of shoes or nylon hose in an experiment designed to yield utility schedules might be visualized as occurring over a year's time where the wardrobe and the state of the person involved did not change significantly. Again, it is not the length of run which is critical; it is that changes in the quantities of the item consumed take place where the basic conditions surrounding the experiment do not change.

candy bars (candy bars 3 to 7), but the rate of increase is now declining; and that, with candy bar 8, total utility falls absolutely. Presumably candy bar 8 made our human guinea pig sick.

From the total utility data obtained from experimentation (in this case, a hypothetical series of experiments), two important and interesting relations may be derived. The *average utility* per candy bar is derived by dividing total utility by the number of candy bars eaten; these average data are presented in column 3. It will be observed that average utility rises, levels off, and then declines. The *marginal utility* per candy bar is derived by subtracting from the total utility associated with the last bar eaten the total utility associated with the previous bar eaten (e.g., the marginal utility of the fifth candy bar in column 4 of Table 6-1 is computed as follows: the 80 total utiles associated with the fifth candy bar *less* the 72 total utiles associated with the fourth candy bar *equals* 8 utiles). The schedule of marginal utilities in column 4 of Table 6-1 thus describes the *additional* units of satisfaction, utiles, associated with each *additional* candy bar consumed by the hungry man. And we see that the term marginal utility refers to the units of satisfaction associated with the additional, or final, or marginal unit consumed.

It will be observed that marginal utility rises sharply through the second candy bar, declines from candy bar 3 to 7, and becomes negative with candy bar 8. It will also be observed that the three different phases of the marginal schedule correspond to, or have their counterpart in, the total utility schedule. In a mathematical sense, this parallel relationship grows out of the fact that the marginal schedule is a derivative of the total; but, in a substantive sense, this parallel action grows out of the fact that the behavior of the individual at the margin determines the configuration of all his utility functions. These relations are portrayed graphically in Figure 6-1.

Diminishing marginal utility. The data in column 4 of Table 6-1 indicate that a point is reached in the consumption of candy bars where the utility associated with an additional bar, the marginal bar, begins to decline. In this case, the utility (20 utiles) gained from eating bar 3 is less than that gained (30 utiles) from eating bar 2. And as additional bars are eaten, the utility from successive bars declines until a point is reached where the consumption of the seventh bar adds no utility over that of the sixth bar and the eighth bar yields a negative utility—possibly in the form of a stomach ache. In other words, where successive units of a particular good are consumed *and the consumption of all other goods and*

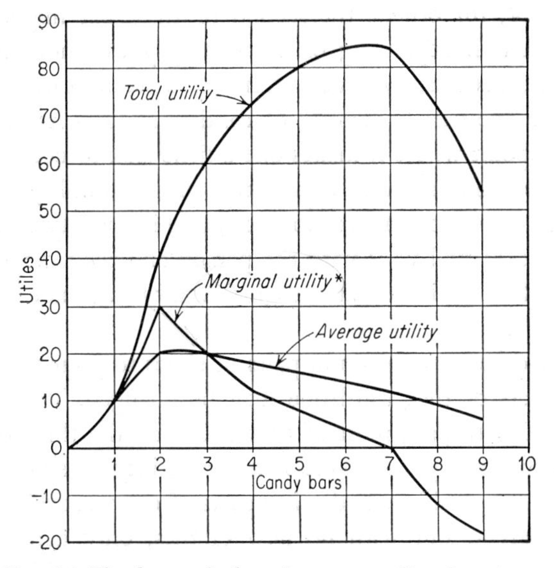

FIG. 6-1. Total, marginal, and average utility functions.

* A note on graphics: the marginal utility curve should cut the average curve at the highest point of the latter (somewhere between the 2d and 3d candy bars), and the marginal utility curve should cut the zero axis at the highest point of the total curve (somewhere between the 6th and 7th candy bars). But because discrete series are used, mathematical correctness is not achieved in the graph. This correctness may be approximated in all cases by plotting the marginal curve ½ unit to the left along the horizontal axis.

services is held constant, a point is reached where the utility associated with each successive unit of the good consumed begins to diminish. This we know as the principle of *eventually diminishing marginal utility*. Now the data from Table 6-1 do not establish or prove this principle of diminishing marginal utility either for candy bars or for commodities in general. But these data do illustrate the principle, and it is of crucial importance that we grasp the concept involved. The workings of this principle are central to most theories of consumer behavior, as it would seem to be to man in all his consuming activities.

There are several reasons for believing that the marginal utility of a commodity eventually falls as the quantity of that commodity consumed increases. The first, and perhaps most cogent, reason rests on an appeal to personal experience. Let each reader think back to the candy-bar example and review the possibilities of that experiment in terms of his own experience. For some, the first bar might taste the best, hence provide the most utility; for others, the second or third bar might provide the greatest satisfaction depending on how hungry the individual might be or his preference for candy bars. But, in any case, most of us can visualize a point where one particular kind of candy bar loses its delicious flavor and a further point where it makes one a little sick to contemplate eating any more. The points at which diminishing marginal utility sets in (second bar in Figure 6-1) and absolute total diminishing utility sets in (seventh bar in Figure 6-1) will vary with the person and the time and the place. But it is hard to believe that marginal utility will not eventually diminish.

Consider another example—add pairs of shoes to your wardrobe where no other aspects of that wardrobe may be changed. With the addition of a third or fourth pair, most of us would find the thrill of a new pair of shoes getting pretty weak—the marginal utility of shoes would begin to diminish. If we could expand other parts of our wardrobe, the situation might be different. But with no new clothes, only additional pairs of shoes, the satisfaction derived from additional pairs would certainly begin to fall after some point. And when shoes started to fall on your head every time you opened the closet door, the point of absolute total diminishing utility would have been reached.

Personal experience with automobiles would seem to lead in the same direction—toward the workings of the principle of diminishing marginal utility. Most families could use a second car effectively, hence derive a great deal of satisfaction from a second car. Perhaps it would prove difficult to know whether the utility derived from a second car was more or less than that of the first. But for many, if not most, families, a third or fourth car would provide little in the way of additional pleasure. In fact, a third or fourth car might begin to be a nuisance—the disutility of parking and maintenance might outweigh the additional utility provided. In short, experience with individual commodities does not provide many, if any, examples where marginal utility increases with successive units consumed; on the contrary, the great pleasure provided by earlier units typically gives way to disgust, nausea, or annoyance as more units are consumed. Personal experience suggests that eventually diminishing marginal utility is the norm.

Diminishing marginal utility has a basis in logic as well as in human experience. The first of these logical propositions is that commodities are not perfect substitutes for one another. Commodities are typically used for one thing (e.g., shoes to wear on the feet, food to eat); further, most commodities tend to be consumed in certain approximate proportions. Now, the acquisition of more and more units of a commodity which can be used to satisfy only one kind of want (e.g., shoes) where that commodity is consumed in certain approximate proportions with other commodities (e.g., suits, shirts, hats, overcoats) can mean only that the utility associated with additional units of the commodity in question will fall, and fall rapidly, after some point. Take, for example, a man living in Minnesota during January who needs an overcoat but keeps acquiring shoes under the terms of this experiment. The tenth pair of shoes will not make him very happy when he needs an overcoat to protect him against the cold. Shoes cannot be used (substituted) for an overcoat. In this situation, he would be better off with five pairs of shoes and one overcoat than with ten pairs of shoes and no overcoat. Since he lacks an overcoat, the marginal utility of the eighth, ninth, and tenth pair of shoes would probably be pretty low for this consumer.

Looking at this problem from the opposite pole, consider the state of things if some commodity were a perfect substitute for all other commodities. The marginal utility of this perfect substitute is not likely to fall as the consumer gets additional units of it. If the marginal utility of this perfect substitute begins to fall as a food, the consumer can substitute it for whatever else he may need. He can wear it on his head or his feet or travel in it. In this fairy story, the Minnesota consumer, finding that he had a disproportionate amount of footwear, would simply convert some of this wondrous commodity into an overcoat and use it to keep warm. The marginal utility of a commodity which could be used for all things (was a perfect substitute) would not decline until the consumer began to get too much of everything. Since money can be exchanged for almost any commodity or service, it comes close to this category of perfect substitutes, and as we shall see in a minute, this gives rise to certain exceptional cases.

A second logical basis of diminishing marginal utility is that no *particular* want is unsatiable. If salt were a free good, for example, individuals would not consume an infinite amount of it. The consumption of salt and many other commodities by individuals never goes above a fixed amount —the point of satiety. This point of satiety in consumption is the point where total utility begins to decline and marginal utility equals zero. And since the consumption of quantities prior to the point of satiety yielded some utility, it must be the case that marginal utility is declining between those quantities where marginal utility is positive and utility is zero.

Somewhat as a digression, but important to our understanding of the concept of marginal utility, it needs to be pointed out that an important exception to the principle of diminishing marginal utility may exist with respect to money. Friedman and Savage argue that the choice patterns of individuals in certain situations are not consistent with diminishing marginal utility of money; [3] individual choice patterns in certain situations suggest that the marginal utility of money may be increasing for these individuals in these situations. The situations involved are risk or chance situations wherein individuals may gamble or buy insurance. The behavior pattern involved is the willingness of many individuals to buy lottery tickets and take other "long shots" where the chances of a large gain are small and the chances of a small loss are great. Individuals willing to take this sort of gamble, and there are many, must take somewhat the following view of money: "With my small income, the loss of a few dollars will not hurt me much (the decline in utility is not proportionate to the decline in money), but should I win, there are many wondrous things I can do with that money (the increase in utility is more than proportionate to the increase in money)." The graphic configuration of such a total utility function is just the opposite of that presented in Figure 6-1; the total utility curve in Figure 6-1 is concave to the abscissa—the candy-bar axis. The curve of the gambler noted above must be convex to the abscissa. This line of reasoning has prompted Friedman and Savage to set forth the following hypothesis with regard to the total utility function of consumer wants: [4]

5. The function describing the utility of money income had in general the following properties:

a. Utility rises with income, i.e., marginal utility of money income everywhere positive;

b. It is convex from above below some income, concave between that income and some larger income, and convex for all higher incomes, i.e., diminishing marginal utility of money income for incomes below some income, increasing marginal utility of money income for incomes between that income and some larger income, and diminishing marginal utility of money income for all higher incomes;

6. Most consumer units tend to have incomes that place them in the seg-

[3] Milton Friedman and L. J. Savage, "The Utility Analysis of Choice Involving Risk," *Journal of Political Economy*, vol. 56, pp. 279–304, 1948, and reprinted in *Readings in Price Theory*, Richard D. Irwin, Inc., Homewood, Ill., 1952.

[4] *Ibid.*, p. 95.

ments of the utility function for which marginal utility of money income diminishes.

But even if these economists are correct, the principle of diminishing marginal utility has not been relegated to an unimportant role. Increasing marginal utility for money need not lead to increasing marginal utility for individual commodities. Indeed, it could not where individual commodities are imperfect substitutes. And, with respect to the marginal utility of money, the general case would seem to be one of decreasing returns.

Division of Expenditure

Now that we have some notion of the principle of diminishing marginal utility, let us try to formulate a general principle governing the division of expenditure by consuming units.[5] What we seek is a principle which indicates the "best" division of a given expenditure among the many alternative uses open to a consuming unit. In the solution of this problem, we continue to assume that utility is measurable. We also make use of the principle of diminishing marginal utility.

Granted the measurability of utility, it seems reasonable to expect that each consuming unit will allocate its funds in each line of expenditure to that point where the utility received is equal in each line of expenditure. We would expect each consuming unit to adjust its spending within each line of expenditure (e.g., food, clothing, travel, recreation) until the utility received from the last unit of expenditure (say $1) is equal in each line. This must be the case where it is assumed that each consuming unit seeks to maximize the utility received from any given expenditure. Consider the implications of marginal utilities not being equal in each line of expenditure; let us assume that the last $1 spent for food yields 100 utiles but the last $1 spent for recreation yields 150 utiles. This cannot be a final, stable situation for the consumer. He can increase his total utility by taking dollars out of food expenditure and using them for purchasing recreation. And this he will do until the utilities received from the last unit of expenditure are equal in each line.

Weighted marginal utility. Unfortunately, the world is not so simply organized as is implied in the above statement. Prices and units of commodities vary in the world of reality; the consumer does not buy items

[5] A good discussion of this problem is to be found in Kenneth E. Boulding, *Economic Analysis,* rev. ed., Harper & Brothers, New York, 1948, chap. 29.

in convenient expenditure units of $1. An expenditure of $1 for jelly beans would flood the typical consumer of jelly beans, whereas an expenditure of $1 on a fur coat would not add up to a down payment. Thus, where commodity prices and units vary, economists have devised a measure called *weighted marginal utility* which is useful in making comparisons. The weighted marginal utility of a commodity is equal to the number of utiles obtained from the marginal unit of that commodity divided by the price of that commodity. In effect, this procedure provides a measure of the utility associated with a unit change in expenditure. In other words, the concept of weighted marginal utility permits us to compare utilities resulting from marginal units of expenditure (e.g., $1 in the United States) where prices and units of the commodities involved vary.

Let us illustrate the concept of weighted marginal utility with an arithmetic example. Suppose some individual A consumes only two commodities *X* and *Y*. The relevant data for commodity *X* are:

Utiles derived from the last unit of *X* consumed	= 20
Price of commodity *X*	= $0.20

The weighted marginal utility of commodity *X* for Consumer A is $20 \div 0.20 = 100$. Thus we can say that the W.M.U. of commodity *X* to Consumer A is 100 utiles per $1. This is perhaps more easily seen from the fact that $1 spent for commodity *X* would purchase 5 units of commodity *X* when its price is 20 cents; now, 5 units × 20 utiles per unit = 100 utiles per $1.

The relevant data for commodity *Y* are:

Utiles derived from the last unit of *Y* consumed	= 15
Price of commodity *Y*	= $0.10

In this case the W.M.U. of *Y* equals $15 \div 0.10$, or 150 utiles per $1. When these two commodities are expressed in common units, utiles per $1, which the concept of weighted marginal utility makes possible, they may be compared directly. And we observe, for Consumer A, that commodity *Y* is more desirable than *X*; commodity *Y* provides Consumer A with more utiles at the margin than *X*. Thus, we would expect Consumer

A to withdraw dollars from expenditure on X and use them to acquire more units of Y. By this action, Consumer A would increase his total utility. And we would expect this type of substitution to go on until the W.M.U.'s in each of the two lines of expenditure, X and Y, were equal. And if there were more than two lines of expenditure, which seems likely, the process of substitution and adjustment would go on among the various lines until the W.M.U.'s in all lines of expenditure were equal. In this way, the best division of expenditure is achieved.

The key role of diminishing marginal utility. But the question may be asked: "Why should the weighted marginal utilities in different lines of expenditure ever become equal? Why in the illustration presented above would not Consumer A keep substituting Y for X indefinitely? Why should not this consumer allocate all his funds to the purchase of Y and none to X?" The answer as to why this consumer would not al-

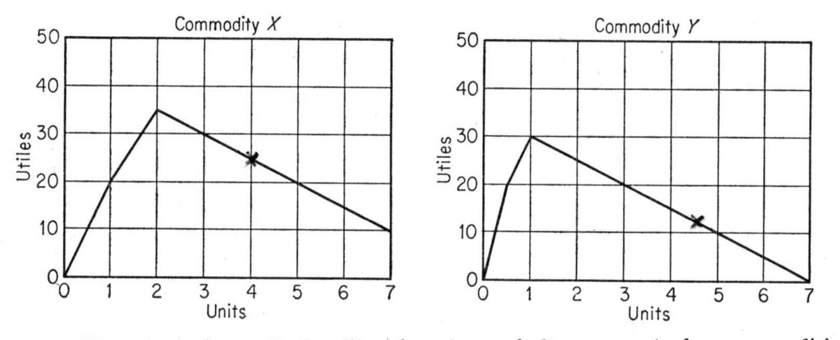

FIG. 6-2. Hypothetical marginal utility functions of Consumer A for commodities X and Y.

locate all his funds to commodity Y grows out of the workings of the principle of diminishing marginal utility. The marginal utility of Y must fall as more of Y is consumed, and the marginal utility of X must rise as less of it is consumed. This double relationship is illustrated in Figure 6-2. The datum, 20 utiles, for commodity X is associated with the 5th unit of X; as fewer units are consumed, the marginal utility of X rises, reaching a maximum with the 2d unit. On the other hand, the datum, 15 utiles, for Y is associated with the 4th unit of Y, and the marginal utility of Y falls as more units are consumed, reaching zero at the 7th unit. Where these relationships hold, it follows that a point must be reached where the weighted marginal utilities are equal.

The best division of expenditure for Consumer A can now be developed in terms of commodities X and Y. In the earlier situation, the W.M.U.'s were 100 for commodity X and 150 for commodity Y for Consumer A; in this situation, Consumer A increases his purchases of Y and decreases his acquisitions of X. As a result, the marginal utility of X rises, and that for Y falls. Assuming no change in the prices of X and Y, a new situation may be presented as follows:

Commodity X:

Utiles derived from the last unit of X	= 25
Price of commodity X	= \$0.20
W.M.U. (25 ÷ .20)	= 125

Commodity Y:

Utiles derived from the last unit of Y	= 12.5
Price of commodity Y	= \$0.10
W.M.U. (12.5 ÷ .10)	= 125

The weighted marginal utilities are now equal for Consumer A with respect to X and Y. Given the above prices for X and Y, this equality occurs with 4 units of X and 4½ units of Y (see Figure 6-2; it will be noted that the marginal utilities of X and Y are not equal at this combination, but with price $X = 0.20$ and price $Y = 0.10$, the W.M.U.'s are equal). Any movement away from this combination of X and Y would reduce the total utility received by Consumer A. If Consumer A were to increase his expenditure on Y and decrease his expenditure on X, the W.M.U. of Y would decline and that for X rise; so it would be to his advantage to return to combination $4X$ and $4½Y$. And should he increase his expenditure on X and decrease his expenditure on Y, the W.M.U. of Y would rise and that for X would fall; so again it would be to his advantage to return to combination $4X$ and $4½Y$.

The combination $4X$, $4½Y$ is thus defined as the *equilibrium* combination of X and Y for Consumer A. At this combination, the total satisfaction of A is maximized with respect to these two commodities. In the above illustration, however, the total expenditure for X and Y does not hold constant as Y is substituted for X. Total expenditure declines by 20 cents, or the price of one unit of X, and increases by 5 cents, or the price of a half unit of Y, yielding a net decline in total expenditure for X and Y of 15 cents. But we *assume* here that this 15 cent gain is used to acquire more units of other products S, T, and U whose weighted marginal utilities were, as in the case of *Y*, greater than 125. And we assume, further, that the increased acquisitions of products *S*, *T*, and *U* by Consumer A just reduce his W.M.U.'s for each of these products to 125. By this convenient assumption, then, we avoid a complex solution with respect to *X* and *Y* where the 15 cents must be fed back into fractional increases in *X* and *Y*, and we arrive at a final equilibrium solution for Consumer A with respect to the allocation of a *fixed* total expenditure where the W.M.U.'s are equal in each line of expenditure (i.e., for all product lines *S*, *T*, *U*, *X*, and *Y*).

This is a principle of great importance; we call it the equimarginal principle. In general terms, it runs as follows: In dividing a fixed quantity of funds among a number of alternative uses, that amount will be apportioned to each use so that the gain in utility involved from transferring a unit of expenditure into one use is just equal to the loss in utility involved in the use from which the unit of expenditure is withdrawn. And, of course, the principle applies no matter how many lines of expenditure the fixed quantity of funds may be apportioned among.

Limitations of the equimarginal principle. Like most useful concepts, the equimarginal principle has certain limitations. Foremost among these limitations is one that plagues many aspects of economics—namely, the indivisibility of goods. The concept is most meaningful when applied to items such as food or clothing which are readily divisible, hence may be purchased in small units. Individuals build up experience with respect to items which they buy regularly and in varying combinations. They learn from experience what a small change in the proportions consumed means in terms of their total satisfaction. But the purchase of a house is a different story. Here is an indivisible item that is purchased only a few times in a lifetime. There is little chance to experiment with this type of purchase; hence, the individual has no idea what satisfaction will or can be derived from the acquisition of a particular house. The investment of funds in a house is usually so large that the value systems of the individuals involved—the want structure of the consuming unit—are permanently modified. One can conceptualize the utility function for pieces of pie, pairs of shoes, or even pieces of furniture, but not for houses or trips to Europe. These items are too large, too important, to consider from the point of view of the additional utility provided by a second unit. In the acquisition of large, expensive, indivisible items, consumers do not move along well-defined utility functions such as are illustrated in Figure 6-2; such purchases shift, change, and modify old utility functions in unknown and unpredictable ways. In short, the purchase of large, one-shot items does not fit the theory.

Another difficulty with the equimarginal principle grows out of the fact that the consumption of many items (most goods except foods) does not coincide with the budget period (i.e., the period for which the size of total expenditure is fixed). Implicit in the discussion of the equimarginal principle has been the idea that goods and services are consumed within the period for which the total fund to be expended is fixed. But this is not the way we find things in the real world. Many things that are purchased in one budget period are used throughout subsequent budget periods (e.g., cars, house furnishings, houses). In making a decision whether or not to buy a new dining-room suite, for example, the consuming unit must not only consider current gains and losses in utility but compare the utility to be received through time from this dining-room suite with the losses in utility over time involved in giving up certain other items. Thus accurate comparisons between different alternative lines of expenditure often require an "accounting" of the potential utility-producing capacity of those alternatives in future periods. This time problem does not invalidate the equimarginal principle: it simply makes it more complicated in concept than one might at first be inclined to think.

SIZE OF TOTAL EXPENDITURE

The equimarginal principle provides, with certain limitations, a useful explanation of how a consuming unit divides a fixed quantity of financial resources (i.e., total expenditure) among alternative uses. But, as developed to this point, it does not "explain" in any sense how the size of the total expenditure may vary; on the contrary, it has been rigidly assumed that the size of the total expenditure is constant. A complete theory of consumer behavior must provide not only a solution to the problem of the best division of a fixed expenditure but some explanation as to the size of the total fund to be expended.

The problem of determining the size of the consuming unit's total expenditure for any given period would seem to break down into two component parts. First, how is the size of money income determined for any given period? Second, how is that money income distributed between consumption and savings? Given the training and capacity of the income earner(s) of a consuming unit, the basic problem in determining the size of money earnings is that of determining the distribution of the time of the individual(s) between *work* and *leisure*. Time is the limiting element here. Each worker has twenty-four hours to *spend* each day between work and leisure, and how the individual spends that time will determine in large measure the size of his money income. The problem is analogous to that of the division of expenditure; hence, a *general* application of the equimarginal principle should provide a formal solution.

With freedom to choose between work and leisure, each individual will divide his time between those uses in such a way as maximizes his total utility. This is achieved, it will be recalled, when his distribution of time is such that the gain in utility resulting from a small increase in one is exactly balanced by the loss in utility resulting from a similar decrease in the other. For instance, if an individual spends 8 hours at work and 16 hours at leisure, and if with this distribution of time the marginal utility of time spent on work were 10 utiles per minute and the marginal utility of time spent on leisure were 12 utiles per minute, it would be to the advantage of this individual (i.e., would increase his total utility) to withdraw time from work and transfer that time to leisure. It would be advantageous to effect such a transfer of time until the falling marginal utility of time spent at leisure met the rising marginal utility of time spent at work and the marginal utilities of time spent in these two uses thus became equal. Where the training and capacity of the income earner are given, the money earnings of the individual are thus determined by the number of hours worked in the division of the day between work and leisure.

We have assumed in the above discussion (1) that work may be undertaken in convenient, divisible units and (2) that all income is received in the form of wages for work performed. This, of course, is an oversimplification. The simple choice between a little more work and a little less leisure, or conversely, is rarely open to the income earner. And most consuming units receive a part of their income in the form of interest, rents, or profits. But these realities do not invalidate the equimarginal principle: they only limit its applicability.

In determining the size of the total expenditure in any one period, there remains the problem of determining how the consuming unit allocates its money income between spending and saving. This problem, too, can be solved in formal terms through the application of the equimarginal principle. But several important questions remain: "Why do people save at all?" "What utility does saving provide, and may this utility be conceptualized as we have done for candy bars?" Frankly, economists do not have firm answers to these questions. Some economists feel that they have the answers, but there is little agreement among economists with respect to these answers. We can, however, list several factors which appear to influence savings. In utility parlance, these factors have some influence on the utility of savings, hence influence consumer decisions with respect to the division of income between spending and saving. They include (1) size of present incomes, (2) size and certainty of future incomes, (3) time preference (i.e., the tendency to live in the present in contrast to the carefulness with which the future is anticipated), and (4) interest rates. Some economists would place exclusive emphasis on points 1 and 2, others exclusive emphasis on points 3 and 4, and still others on some combination of all four.[6] But the conclusion remains that economists do not have anything very useful to say in the way of providing an explanation as to how consuming units divide their money incomes between spending and saving. We shall discover, however, as we go along that some useful empirical relations exist between money income and spending and saving.

Appendix to Chapter 6

The Measurement of Utility

In 1951, two economists, Frederik Mosteller and Philip Nogee, reported on a series of experiments conducted by them in the measurement of utility.[7] More specifically, the experiments were designed to measure the utility of money for some 15 men who were subjected to experimentation. It would be wrong, however, to imagine that these men had an elaborate apparatus in the form of a utility thermometer or galvanometer attached to them in some way. This is not the case. The experiments which led to specific measures of utility for each man took the form of a series of games of chance, where measures of the value of money (i.e., the utility of money) to each player (gambler) were

[6] An appreciation of the problems and complications connected with the savings questions can be gained from A. G. Hart, *Money Debt and Economic Activity*, Prentice-Hall, Inc., New York, 1948, chaps. V–VIII, and Lester V. Chandler, *The Economics of Money and Banking*, rev. ed., Harper & Brothers, New York, 1953, chaps. 22–26.

[7] "An Experimental Measurement of Utility," *Journal of Political Economy*, October, 1951, pp. 371–404.

ascertained from the willingness of the players to take a chance of loss or gain in situations of varying riskiness. In other words, the degree to which a man valued money (real money, and his money) was ascertained from a series of experiments in which the man was subjected to varying chance situations which could lead to either money gains or money losses for him; how these players used their money in these situations thus provided patterns of behavior which were converted into measures of the utility of money.

Some appreciation of the nature of these experiments and the results obtained can be gained from a few passages from the Mosteller-Nogee report: [8]

> . . . With this information at hand, an experimental plan to measure utility was evolved which has four main steps: (*a*) to have subjects participate in a game with opportunities to take or refuse certain gambles or risks entailing use of *real money;* (*b*) from behavior in the game to construct a utility curve for each subject; (*c*) to make predictions from the utility curves about future individual behavior toward other and more complicated risks; and (*d*) to test the predictions by examining subsequent behavior toward more complex risks. It was hoped that this experimental sequence would show whether it was indeed possible to construct utility curves for individuals and, if so, whether these curves could be used to predict future behavior of the same individuals.

Following the presentation of certain theoretical formulations, the authors developed these ideas in terms of their own problem, thus:

> To bring this discussion back to the experiment, consider the objects A, B, and C . . . as
>
> Object A: receipt of 25 cents,
>
> Object B: neither receipt nor loss of money,
>
> Object C: loss of 5 cents.
>
> Most individuals will prefer A to B, and B to C. Statement 3 of the quotation suggests that, if these preferences hold and the utility rationalization for behavior is correct, there will be some probability combination of A and C such that an individual is indifferent between the A–C combination and B. Writing $U(X)$ for the utility of X, this means there must exist some probability p such that
>
> $$pU(A) + (1 - p)U(C) = U(B),$$
>
> or, to use our monetary example,

[8] *Ibid.*, pp. 373–374, 383–386.

$$pU(25¢) + (1 - p)U(-5¢) = U(0¢).$$

This equation suggests that three money values be chosen in an experiment and that p then be varied until the indifference point is reached. However, the experimenters preferred to fix two money values—B and C—and the probability p, and search for an A that would bring a balance. This is done partly in deference to the view that most people are more familiar with amounts of money than with probabilities. Thus, for a particular fixed probability p_o, it is necessary to find an A such that, for a given individual,

$$p_oU(A) + (1 - p_o)U(-5¢) = U(0¢).$$

An operational definition must be set up for "indifference" or the "=" of the above equation. Let D be the object composed of a p_o chance of A and a $1 - p_o$ chance of C (losing 5 cents). Then when an A is found such that B and D are chosen *equally often*, i.e., each chosen in half of their simultaneous presentations, the individual is said to be indifferent between B and D, and the utility of B is said to be equal to the utility of D for him.

In other words, a value for A in the last equation must be attained from experimentation, which, given the probability p_o, makes the left-hand side of the equation equal to the right. In the language of Mosteller and Nogee, $D = p_o$ chance of $A + 1 - p$ chance of $C = 0$, since the value of $B = 0$. This was the measurement problem confronting the experimenters—to obtain measures of A for individuals (players) in situations of varying riskiness.

In deriving the utility function of players, the A values thus provide the observations along the horizontal axis (i.e., the abscissa). The coördinate values in utiles to be plotted along the vertical axis were derived as follows:

. . . Since "the loss of 5 cents" and "neither winning nor losing" are the two anchoring points in the fundamental equation, it is convenient to assign them the following utilities:

$$U(0¢) = 0 \text{ utile}, \qquad U(-5¢) = -1 \text{ utile},$$

where "utile" is the arbitrary name of the unit of measurement. Substituting these evaluations in the indifference equation and solving for $U(A)$, we see that, if B and D are found to be indifferent (equal),

$$U(A) = \frac{1 - p_o}{p_o} \quad \text{utiles.}$$

For any known probability p_o of winning A, the utility of A is known from the start from the equation just given; but A must be determined experimentally. In other words, the individual by participating in the experiment tells how much a certain number of utiles is worth to him in money. The utility scale has been assigned, and the money scale must be tied to it at different points.

The money values of A to be related to the utile values in constructing the utility function of players were derived empirically as follows:

As the first step in the analysis of the data, it was necessary to find the "indifference offer" to each subject on every hand. For each hand a range of offers had been made (see Table 6-2 [9]). The proportion of times the subject elected to play each offer was calculated (see example for subject B-1 in Table 6-3), and these points were plotted on ordinary arithmetic graph paper with vertical axis as per cent participation and horizontal axis as amount of offer in cents (see Fig. 6-3). A freehand curve or a broken-line curve was then fitted to the points.

Table 6-2. The Range of Monetary Offers Made in the Course of the Experiment for Each Group and Each Hand

(Subject puts up 5 cents)

Hand	Group A	Group B	Group C
44321	\$0.01–\$0.07	\$0.01–\$ 0.07	\$0.01–\$0.07
66431	0.03– 0.10	0.03– 0.10	0.03– 0.10
55221	0.07– 0.16	0.05– 0.16	0.03– 0.16
22263	0.19– 0.43	0.13– 0.43	0.10– 0.43
55562	0.39– 0.72	0.28– 0.72	0.11– 0.72
22255	0.79– 1.42	0.79– 1.63	0.23– 1.42
44441	4.00– 8.00	4.00– 10.00	0.25– 8.00

The abscissa value of the point where this curve crossed the 50 per cent participation line gave in cents the subject's indifference offer for that hand. In other words, for that hand this calculation yielded an interpolated offer which the subject would be equally likely to accept or reject if given the opportunity.

[9] The table and figure numbers have been changed in this quotation to correspond to the numbering of tables and figures in this chapter.

The procedure for calculating the A values both in cents and the number of utiles associated with each A value is now set forth. The experimenters thus proceed to calculate these values for subject (player) B-1.

Since the probability p of winning is fixed for a given hand, the utility of the indifference offer is just $(1 - p)/p$, as described in Section II. For example, the data of Figure 6-3 yield an indifference offer of 10.6 cents. Hand 55221 has a probability of 0.332 of being beaten. Therefore the utility is about 2 utiles and the utility curve of subject B-1 will pass through the point (10.6, 2).

Table 6-3. Basic Information Required for Subject B-1 and Hand 55221 to Estimate His Indifference Point

Offer, cents	No. of times presented	No. of times played	Per cent (times played ÷ times presented)
16	14	14	100
12	14	13	92.9
11	14	9	64.3
10	14	4	28.6
9	14	1	7.1
7	14	0	0
5	11	0	0

The complete schedule of data out of which to construct the total utility function for money for subject B-1 is given as follows:

Situations of varying riskiness	Money in cents (the indifference offer)	Money in *utiles*
0	0	0
1	4.8	0.5
2	5.0	1.0
3	10.6	2.0
4	28.5	5.0
5	60.0	10.0
6	163.0	20.0

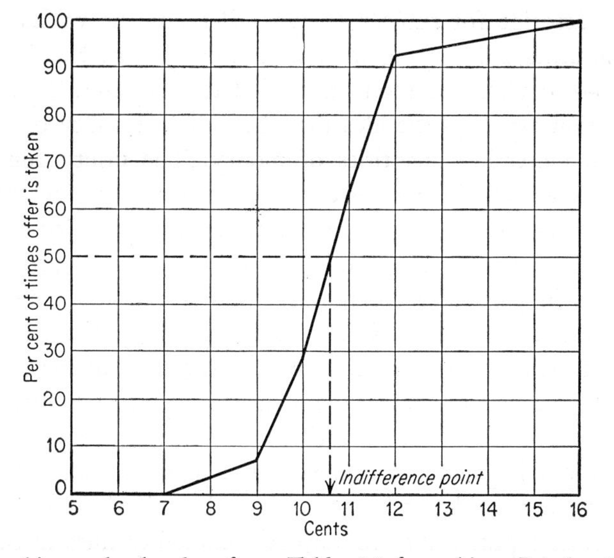

FIG. 6-3. In this graph, the data from Table 6-3 for subject *B*-1, hand 55221, are plotted to show how the indifference point is actually obtained. (All aspects of this figure are reproduced in facsimile from "An Experimental Measurement of Utility," *Journal of Political Economy*, October, 1951, p. 385.)

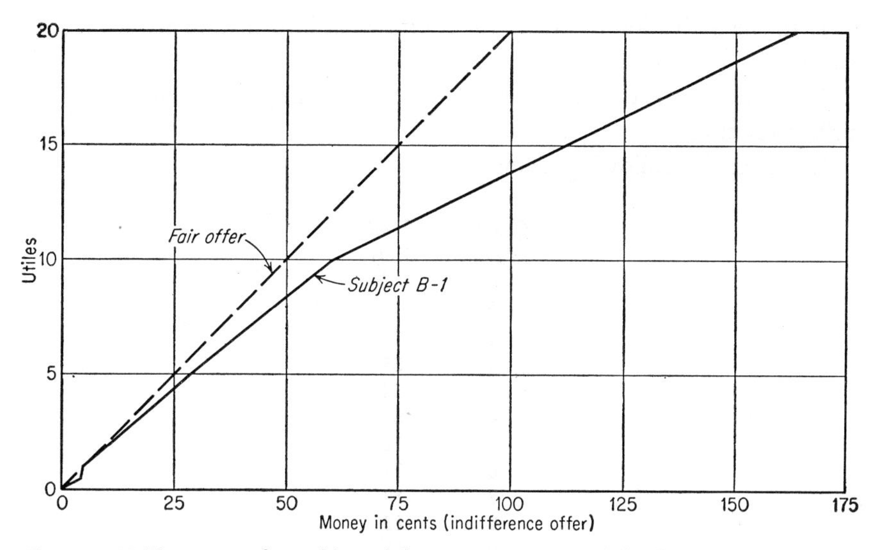

FIG. 6-4. Utility curve for subject (player) *B*-1, and straight line showing mathematically fair offer.

These data describe for subject (player) *B*-1 how he values money, as measured in utiles, for varying amounts of money. These data are plotted in Figure 6-4 to yield the total utility function for *B*-1. This particular utility function expresses the idea that the marginal utility of money decreases with increasing quantities of money. The utility functions for all players, however, do not show the decreasing marginal utility pattern of Figure 6-3; some players registered increasing utility curves.

Whether similar types of gambling experiments would produce meaningful results in particular commodity lines is extremely doubtful. Individuals are not used to gambling for hamburgers or chicken dinners, and it would be next to impossible to hold the state of hunger constant during an experiment or from experiment to experiment. But it is often the case in science that, once a tough experimental problem is cracked, sufficient insight is gained to deal with the problem more efficiently in diverse ways. It would not be surprising, then, if the measurement of utility becomes a practicality in various commodity lines in the not too distant future.

Questions and Points for Discussion

1. In the derivation of utility functions, what information are we trying to isolate? What difficulties do we encounter?

2. Define total utility function, average utility function, marginal utility function.

3. Given the following data:

Quantity of food, lb	*Total utility, utiles*
0	0
1	10
2	35
3	50
4	62
5	72
6	79
7	83
8	83
9	79

Derive the average and marginal utility data, and plot these data in functional form in a graph (i.e., present in graph form the total, average, and marginal utility functions).

4. What evidence do we have that marginal utility eventually declines?

5. What is the equimarginal principle? What is weighted marginal utility?

6. How is the principle of diminishing marginal utility basic to the workings of the equimarginal principle? Develop an arithmetic example illustrating the workings of the equimarginal principle.

7. Into what two component parts does the determination of the size of the total expenditure break? What role does the equimarginal principle play here? What factors are said to influence savings?

References

Boulding, Kenneth E.: *Economic Analysis*, rev. ed., Harper & Brothers, New York, 1948, chap. 29.

Marshall, Alfred: *Principles of Economics*, 8th ed., The Macmillan Company, New York, 1936, book III, pp. 83–101.

Samuelson, Paul A.: *Economics: An Introductory Analysis*, 2d ed., McGraw-Hill Book Company, Inc., New York, 1951, pp. 476–479.

7. *The Indifference Solution*

The assumption that utility is measurable is highly irritating to some people. This is more "make-believe" than they will permit themselves. Generally, such critics do not object to some formulation of the concept of diminishing marginal utility—perhaps with a substitution of the word satisfaction for utility. This is fortunate for them and the world, for the world would be a strange place indeed if some principle akin to diminishing marginal utility were not at work. Imagine the state of affairs that would exist if for each consumer the satisfaction derived from a second unit were greater than from the first, that from a third unit greater than from the second, and so on. Consumer behavior would be highly explosive; the consumer would have no motive to stop consuming any particular good or service. The baby who got started on milk would not be interested in *anything* else, for he could always increase his total satisfaction by having another bottle. Or imagine the plight of the individual who, for whatever reason, got started drinking beer.

No, the criticism is not, and cannot be, of the general concept of diminishing marginal utility (satisfaction). The quarrel is at a different level; the critics of the utility approach argue that it is wrong to construct a theory of consumer behavior which makes use of measured units of utility, where in fact the psychological product, utility, is not measurable. They ask: "Cannot the behavior of consumers be described in a general and vigorous way without making use of the idea that utility is measurable?" The answer is: "Yes—via the indifference approach."[1] The indifference approach does not, however, deny the concept of utility (i.e., that individuals derive some psychological product from the consumption of goods and services): it simply circumvents the need for measuring *how much* satisfaction is derived from the consumption of a

[1] This approach was first given a general and systematic treatment, in English at least, by J. R. Hicks in his monumental volume *Value and Capital*, Oxford University Press, New York, 1939, part I.

particular combination of goods. And this is all that critics of the utility approach require, for they, too, do not deny the concept of utility.

THE INDIFFERENCE MAP

The assumptions involved. The choice decisions of any consumer with respect to two commodities, say *Y* and *X*, can be converted into an indifference map for that consumer (see Figure 7-1, for example). But before we explore the intricacies of the indifference map and how it is constructed, let us consider the assumptions that lie back of it (i.e., the conditions which must be satisfied in order that an indifference map may be constructed). The first assumption to be considered is that commodities *X* and *Y* are substitutes for one another. Most commodities are substitutes to some degree: orange juice and tomato juice are probably close substitutes; bicycles and automobiles would seem less close; and piano lessons and bread probably enter into a substitutive relationship only rarely. But there are some items which do not act as substitutes—which combine only in fixed proportions. Left and right shoes are a good example. In such cases, there is no decision problem with respect to the best combination: one left shoe combines with one right shoe; the items are complementary. It is only where items may be substituted for one another that a decision problem arises. And it is only where commodities substitute for one another that it is possible to arrive at two different combinations which please the consumer equally well, hence to which he is indifferent.

The second assumption to be considered is that the consumer can tell the investigator which combination he prefers and to which combinations he is indifferent (i.e., which combinations provide him with equal satisfaction). Implied in this second assumption is the further idea that the commodities are highly divisible. For if the commodities are not highly divisible, it may prove impossible to formulate specific combinations to which the consumer is indifferent. The problem is analogous to that of the child playing with blocks: it is easier to make two equal-sized block columns out of unequal-sized blocks where there are many small pieces than where there are only a few large pieces. And, to continue this analogy, we assume that the individual, the consumer, can on observation correctly state which pile is the higher if that is the case or whether they are equally high if that is the case. Product divisibility bears on the assumption that the consumer can tell which combination he prefers

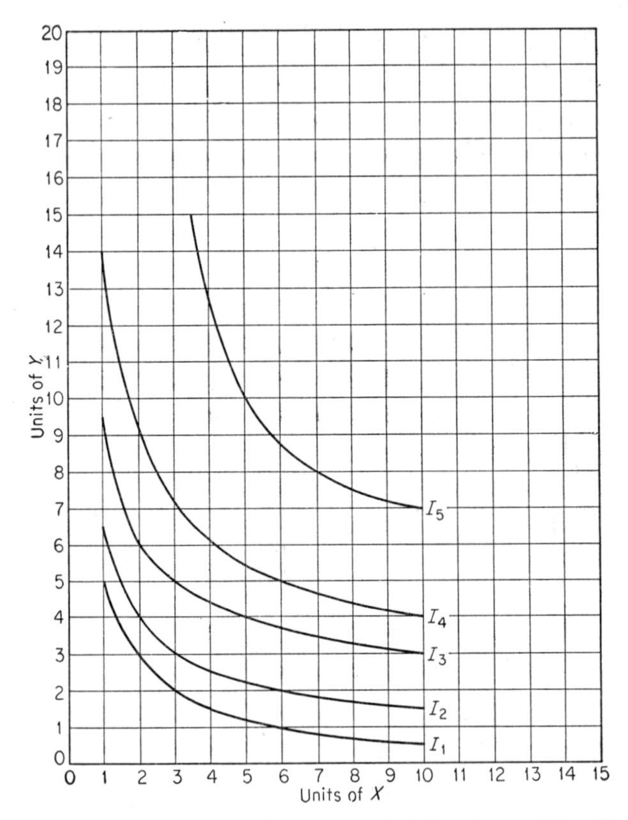

FIG. 7-1. The indifference map for Consumer B for commodities Y and X.

and to which he is indifferent in two ways, (1) products must be divisible in order to formulate combinations to which the consumer is indifferent and (2) products must be divisible in order that consumers may gain sufficient experience with them to correctly appraise their capacity to produce satisfaction.

The contour data. The indifference map of a consumer is composed of individual contour lines (see Figure 7-1), where each contour line describes a series of combinations involving two commodities to which the consumer is indifferent (i.e., each combination of commodities in the series is equally desirable). The problem, thus, becomes that of obtaining the data out of which to draw in these indifference-contour lines.

But how is the economist to obtain these data? The obvious answer would seem to be: Go out and ask consumers. And if our imaginations are sufficiently vivid, we might visualize a survey-type research project where the economist goes out with a schedule, sits down with a consumer, and asks him questions regarding his preferences with respect to different combinations of two commodity substitutes. The nature of this questioning might run as follows: "Do you prefer combination 1 composed of 3 apples and 6 bananas to combination 2 composed of 4 apples and 5 bananas?" And should the respondent answer, "I like them equally well," the economist has hit the jack pot: he has two points on a particular indifference curve. He may now ask the next question: "Do you prefer combination 2 composed of 4 apples and 5 bananas to combination 3 composed of 5 apples and 2 bananas?" And so on ad infinitum. Now, theoretically, this type of questioning should yield the contour data out of which to construct the consumer indifference map. If the consumer can distinguish between combinations, and can state which he prefers, then it should be possible to design experiments which in fact yield the preference data needed to construct the indifference map. This was the great selling point of this approach in its period of popularization; this was the dream of the 1930s.

The consumer did not need to know anything about the amount of satisfaction provided by particular combinations (i.e., the number of utiles per combination). All he had to be able to do was register his preferences, and the measurement problem in consumer behavior was licked. The fact that economists or psychologists did not know how to measure utility no longer need prove a stumbling block to quantifying consumer behavior; that stumbling block could now be circumvented. But this is not the way things have worked out. Empirically derived indifference maps are as scarce as empirically derived utility functions. The few experiments conducted to derive contour data have not provided descriptive measures that have expanded our knowledge with respect to consumer behavior in specific commodity lines or provided the less detailed type of information needed to illustrate the indifference method in a volume such as this.

Why this is the case is not readily understandable. But a tentative explanation may be offered. The areas in which the indifference approach is most adaptable (where commodities are close substitutes and are highly divisible), as in the apple-banana illustration, tend to be areas so trivial that investigator and respondent alike quickly lose interest, if it ever existed. And in the more important areas (where commodities are not close substitutes and are not readily divisible), as with such combinations as washing machines and draperies or automobiles and life insurance policies, the consumer does not have sufficient experience to decide which are preferred combinations and which are not. The whole thing becomes unreal to the consumer, hence impossible experimentally.

But we should not get the idea that the indifference approach is worthless, because it, too, fails the measurement test. This is not the case; as an expository or teaching device, it is superior to the utility approach. If students do not black out at the first sight of a slightly complicated graph, a clearer and more incisive view of the theory of consumer behavior may be gained by means of the indifference approach than by the more old-fashioned utility approach. So let us concoct some "playlike" contour data, as we did in the utility case, to illustrate the analysis.

Let us begin by deriving the hypothetical data out of which to draw in the contour line (or indifference curve) for a Consumer B for commodities *Y* and *X*. Needless to say, we assume these commodities to be close substitutes and readily divisible. As an anchoring point in the derivation of these hypothetical contour data, we describe the first combination to B; it is composed of 5*Y* and 1*X*. The first question might then be: "Do you prefer this first combination or a second combination composed of 4*Y* and 2*X*?" To this question, Consumer B might respond by saying, "I prefer the second combination." Now the investigator knows that combination 2 is on a different, higher contour line than combination 1. But the questioning goes on until the investigator obtains a particular combination of *Y* and *X* to which Consumer B is indifferent as between it and combination 1. Now the investigator has a second point on the same contour line (indifference curve) as combination 1. And assuming that the questioning is successful, a series of combinations of *Y* and *X* may be obtained each of which Consumer B likes equally well. The data which yield one contour line (indifference curve) are given as in the accompanying table.

Y, units	*X, units*
5	1
3	2
2	3
1	6
½	10

If to any one of the combinations in this table more of *Y* is added and *X* is held constant, then Consumer B must have moved to a higher indifference curve—an indifference curve with a higher level of satisfaction. A combination of 6½ units of *Y* and 1 unit of *X* is obviously a better combination than 5 units of Y and 1 unit of X, if Y has any value to the consumer. We do not know how much better combination $6\frac{1}{2}Y$, $1X$ may be than combination $5Y$, $1X$ to Consumer B, but it must be better. With the new anchoring point, combination $6\frac{1}{2}Y$, $1X$ on some higher indifference curve, the investigator can set out to derive other points of indifference on that curve (i.e., combinations of Y and X that Consumer B likes equally well). Such a series of data are presented in the following table.

Y, units	*X, units*
6½	1
4	2
3	3
2	6
1½	10

Provided the patience of the consumer and the money of the investigator hold out, this process could go on indefinitely. And a very large number, theoretically an infinite number, of indifference curves for Consumer B with respect to commodities Y and X could be derived. But we shall stop with the "playlike" derivation of the fifth indifference curve; by pedagogical design, such a map enables us to illustrate all the relevant relationships. The hypothetical data for all five curves are given in Table 7-1. Those data when plotted on graph paper as in Figure 7-1 yield indifference curves I_1, I_2, I_3, I_4, and I_5, which taken together form the rudiments of the indifference map for Consumer B with respect to commodities Y and X. As in the case of a contour map describing the topography of a particular land area, as many indifference curves registering preference heights could be filled into the map in Figure 7-1 as time and money would permit. But we shall work with five indifference contours in a rather incomplete map.

Properties of the indifference map. There are several general properties —things or aspects—of indifference maps that we need to know. First, the map describes one side of a hill of satisfactions. The indifference contours, similar to altitude contours on a topographic map, describe the surface of a hill—a hill of satisfactions. But the indifference map differs from the topographic map in one important respect. We have no idea how high this hill of satisfactions may be. The height of any particular indifference contour measured in utiles (or units of satisfaction) is unknown to us. The hill of satisfactions produced out of the consumption of various combinations of Y and X by Consumer B sort of floats in space—cut loose from any bench mark of measurement.

Table 7-1. *Hypothetical Data for Constructing the Indifference Map of Consumer B with Respect to Commodities Y and X*

Curve I_1, combinations of—		Curve I_2, combinations of—		Curve I_3, combinations of—		Curve I_4, combinations of—		Curve I_5, combinations of—	
Y	*X*	*Y*	*X*	*Y*	*X*	*Y*	*X*	*Y*	*X*
5	1	6½	1	9½	1	14	1		
3	2	4	2	6	2	8	2½	15	3½
2	3	3	3	5	3	6½	3½	10	5
1	6	2	6	4	5	5	6	8	7
½	10	1½	10	3	10	4	10	7	10

Second, the indifference contours are negatively inclined–slope downward and to the right. This must always be the case because, to stay on the same indifference contour, the consumer in question must give up some *Y* every time a unit of *X* is added. And the substitution of *X* for *Y* in the commodity combinations produces a downward-sloping contour line.

Third, indifference curves cannot cross. We do not, for example, know the height of curve I_2 in Figure 7-1, but let us suppose that it is 20 utons high (to coin a unit of measure). And we do not know how high curve I_3 may be, but we do know that it *must be higher than curve* I_2; so we assume it to be 30 utons high. Now curve I_3 cannot cut downward through curve I_2 and remain 30 utons in height. If curve I_3 cuts below curve I_2, then I_3 must be less than 20 utons since this is the height of curve I_2. But it is impossible for curve I_3 to be 30 utons high and less than 20 utons high at one and the same time. Two contours, whether measured in feet or utons, which are 30 and 20, respectively, can never cross.[2]

Fourth, indifference contours are convex to the origin. This follows from the workings of the principle of diminishing marginal utility (there is no escaping this old law, no matter how hard sophisticated analysts may try). In giving up units of *Y* when he has lots of *Y*, Consumer B does not

[2] A geometric proof of the impossibility of indifference curves crossing is offered by George J. Stigler in his *Theory of Price,* rev. ed., The Macmillan Company, New York, 1952, p. 71.

require the addition of much X to hold him on the same indifference curve. Referring to curve I_4 in Figure 7-1, Consumer B trades 6 units of Y for 1½ units of X when he has lots of Y: Y is cheap in terms of X; the marginal utility of Y is low when Y is plentiful. But as Consumer B gives up more and more Y and has only a little Y left, he must have increasingly larger amounts of X to offset any further decrease in Y. In terms of curve I_4 (Figure 7-1), Consumer B trades 1 unit of Y for 4 units of X when he has only a little Y left. Y is now expensive in terms of X: the marginal utility of Y has become high. Given these utility relationships, changes in the combinations of Y and X will always be such as to yield indifference curves which are convex to the origin. And it is fortunate that the principle of marginal utility works as it does, for indifference curves must be convex to the origin, as we shall see, if a solution to the problem of the best division of expenditure between commodities Y and X is to be effected via the indifference approach.

OUTLAY CURVES

Given the indifference map for any Consumer B, we can indicate which combination of Y and X is best for Consumer B (i.e., maximizes his total utility) where we know (1) the prices of Y and X and (2) the total expenditure allotted to the purchase of these two commodities. Out of this price and total-expenditure information, it is possible to construct what are generally known as outlay curves (sometimes called consumption-possibility lines). And out of the relation of the outlay curve for commodities Y and X to the indifference map for these same commodities emerges the solution to the consumer choice problem; the best combination of Y and X is indicated by this relationship.

The question thus arises: "How is the outlay curve constructed?" To return to the illustration involving Consumer B, let us assume that he has made the decision to spend \$10 on Y and X. We assume further that the price of Y is \$1 and the price of X is \$2. With this information, we can describe all the *possible* combinations of Y and X that Consumer B can purchase. And this is what we mean by an outlay curve; it is a line connecting all possible combinations of Y and X that can be purchased with a fixed total expenditure where the prices of the commodities are given.

Where Consumer B spends the full \$10 on each combination, the possible whole-number combinations are as follows:

$$10Y, 0X = (10 \times \$1) = \$10$$
$$8Y, 1X = (8 \times \$1 + 1 \times \$2) = \$10$$
$$6Y, 2X = (6 \times \$1 + 2 \times \$2) = \$10$$
$$4Y, 3X = (4 \times \$1 + 3 \times \$2) = \$10$$
$$2Y, 4X = (2 \times \$1 + 4 \times \$2) = \$10$$
$$0Y, 5X = (5 \times \$2) = \$10$$

And we can and do plot these combinations of Y and X on the indifference map of Consumer B to derive the outlay curve (line AA in Figure 7-2). The outlay curve is simply superimposed upon the indifference map. In all cases, the outlay curve will be a straight line; the fixed total expenditure guarantees this result.

Since the outlay curve is in all cases a straight line, we do not in practice calculate all points along it. Only the extreme points lying on the Y and X

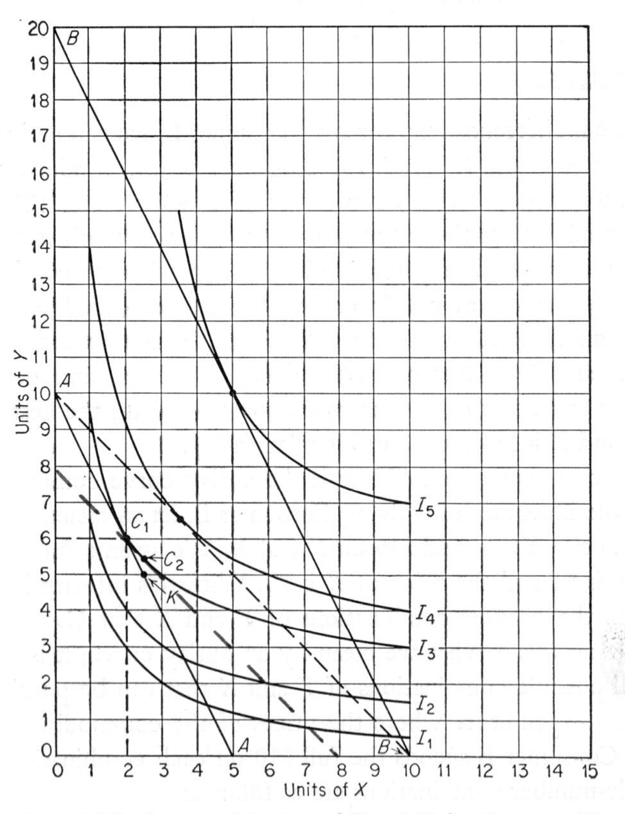

FIG. 7-2. The best combination of Y and X for Consumer B.

axes need be calculated. If all \$10 is spent on *X*, 5 units of *X* can be obtained (\$10 ÷ \$2 = 5 units); if all \$10 is spent on *Y*, 10 units of *Y* can be obtained (\$10 ÷ \$1 = 10 units). The extreme points on the *X* and *Y* axes are thus determined (5 units on the *X* axis, 10 units on the *Y* axis), and the line *AA* connecting these points is the outlay curve of Consumer B where \$10 is allocated to the purchase of *Y* and *X* and price *X* = \$2, price *Y* = \$1.

What if the total expenditure increases to \$20—what then? Assuming the prices of *Y* and *X* to remain unchanged, Consumer B could purchase 20 units of *Y* if he spent the full amount on *Y* or 10 units of *X* if he spent the full amount on *X*. With this information, we can lay off outlay curve *BB* on Figure 7-2. The position of the outlay curve is thus determined by the size of the total expenditure.

A moment's reflection makes it clear that the prices of the commodities involved determine the slope of the outlay curve. In the Consumer B illustration, *X* is twice as expensive as *Y*; hence only half as much *X* (5 units) can be purchased with the full \$10 as may be purchased of *Y* (10 units). This relationship determines the slope of the outlay curve *AA* in Figure 7-2; the slope of the line *AA* = 10/5 = 2, which means that the slope of *AA* is such that for every 1-unit change in *X* there is a 2-unit change in *Y*. But suppose the price of *X* falls to \$1—what happens in this case? In the first place, nothing has happened to the price of *Y*, which means that the extreme point on the *Y* axis remains unchanged at 10 units. But now 10 units of *X* can be purchased if the full \$10 is spent on *X*. A new point is plotted on the *X* axis at the tenth unit, and the outlay curve *AB* is ruled off. The position of the outlay curve is determined by the total expenditures allotted to the commodities in question; the slope of the curve is determined by the prices of the commodities in question.

CONSUMER EQUILIBRIUM

The equilibrium position of the consumer, the best combination of *Y* and *X*, may now be determined by relating the outlay curve to the consumer's indifference map. The best combination of *Y* and *X* for Consumer B is given by the point where the outlay curve touches the highest indifference curve. Assuming that Consumer B allocates \$10 to the purchase of *Y* and *X* and that their prices are \$1 and \$2, respectively, the outlay curve becomes *AA* in Figure 7-2; the point of tangency (C_1) with indifference curve I_3 defines the best combination of *Y* and *X*. Consumer B will choose 6 units of Y and 2 units of X if he is an economical man, for with that combination and only with that combination does he achieve the highest level of satisfaction from the expenditure of $10 on commodities Y and X.

The logic of this combination becomes apparent upon a consideration of the consequences of a movement away from point C_1. Given the condition that Consumer B spends $10 on commodities Y and X, the only possibilities of movement are along the outlay curve AA (i.e., his consumption-possibilities curve). But any movement along outlay curve AA leads Consumer B to a lower indifference curve, hence to a lower level of satisfaction. In terms of Figure 7-2, a movement away from point C_1 along curve AA leads to the lower indifference curve I_2. But we remember that the indifference map for Consumer B presented in Figure 7-2 is incomplete; we should visualize many, many indifference contours falling between indifference curves I_3 and I_2. Where this is the case, any movement away from point C_1 along the outlay curve would quickly run into some lower indifference curve. It follows, then, that the only combination of Y and X that maximizes Consumer B's satisfactions is that at the point where the given outlay curve becomes tangent to the highest possible indifference curve.

In formal terms, we say that the marginal rate of substitution of Y for X is equal to the ratio of their market prices at point C_1. The slope of the indifference curve describes the marginal rate of substitution of Y for X, since it indicates the amount of Y that must be added to a specific combination to offset the loss of one small unit of X (i.e., the rate of substitution of Y for X at the margin). The ratio of prices is given by the slope of the outlay curve. The slopes of the outlay curve AA and indifference curve I_3 are equal at the point of tangency, point C_1 (the slope of the outlay curve $AA = 10/5 = 2$ at all points; the M.R.S. $= 10/5 = 2$ at point C_1). And the equality of these slopes defines the optimum combination of Y and X for Consumer B.

Let us consider further the implications of the foregoing statement. How does the equality of the slopes of the indifference curve I_3 and the outlay curve AA at point C_1 define the optimum combination of Y and X? Consider, first, point C_2 on curve I_3. The marginal rate of substitution at that point is equal to the slope of the curve at that point, which is estimated to be $7.8Y/7.8X = 1$. Point C_2 is on the same indifference curve (curve I_3) as point C_1, and hence the combinations involved provide Consumer B with the same amount of satisfaction, but M.R.S. is equal to 1 at

C_2 and 2 at C_1. Consider further that Consumer B cannot realize point C_2 with an outlay of $10; if he has 2½ units of *X*, the consumption-possibility line will permit only 5 units of *Y* (i.e., the combination at point *K* on outlay curve *AA*). But Consumer B can reach point C_1 on indifference curve I_3 from point *K* by selling units of *X* in the market and buying *Y*. He can do this because he gains more *Y* in the market, from the sale of *X* and the purchase of *Y*, *than* the number of units of *Y* required by him to offset the loss of a unit of *X* moving along indifference curve I_3 from point C_2 to C_1. In other words, so long as the rate of exchange in the market, 2*Y* for each unit of *X*, exceeds the rate of substitution at the margin along the indifference curve I_3, 1*Y* for 1*X* at point C_2, for example, Consumer B gains, moves in the direction of indifference curve I_3, by trading *X* for *Y* in the market. Thus, the incentive of satisfaction maximization drives Consumer B to point C_1, where his marginal rate of substitution of *X* for *Y* is equal to the rate of exchange in the market (that is, 2*Y* for 1*X*).

This is equivalent to the statement in the previous chapter that the weighted marginal utilities are equal for *X* and *Y* at the optimum combination. If all conditions of the problem were the same—the consumer, the commodities, and prices and total expenditure—the solution to the combination selected would be the same by either approach.

CONSUMER EQUILIBRIUM UNDER VARYING SITUATIONS

Consequences of a change in expenditure. The indifference technique may be used to advantage to show changes in consumer behavior under varying situations of price and expenditure. And we shall use it here to demonstrate how combinations of commodities selected by a consumer vary with changes in total expenditure. Let us assume that Consumer B decides to double his expenditure on commodities *Y* and *X* (we assume the increase in expenditure grows out of an increase in income). In this event, the outlay curve for Consumer *B* becomes *BB* in Figure 7-3. Prices of *Y* and *X* have not changed; hence, the slope of the outlay curve does not change. But, with total expenditure equal to $20, Consumer B can now acquire 10 units of *X* if he spends it all for *X* or 20 units of *Y* if he spends it all for *Y*. And, with this information, we lay off on Consumer B's indifference map the new outlay curve *BB* (this is the identical case discussed in the section Outlay Curves).

A new equilibrium point, C_3, is obtained for Consumer B at the point of tangency of the outlay curve *BB* with indifference curve I_5. This equilibrium position involves a combination of $10Y$ and $5X$; this is the combination that Consumer B would choose in order to maximize his satisfaction. It should be noted that a doubling of expenditure does not result in Consumer B taking twice as much of both Y and X. His particular

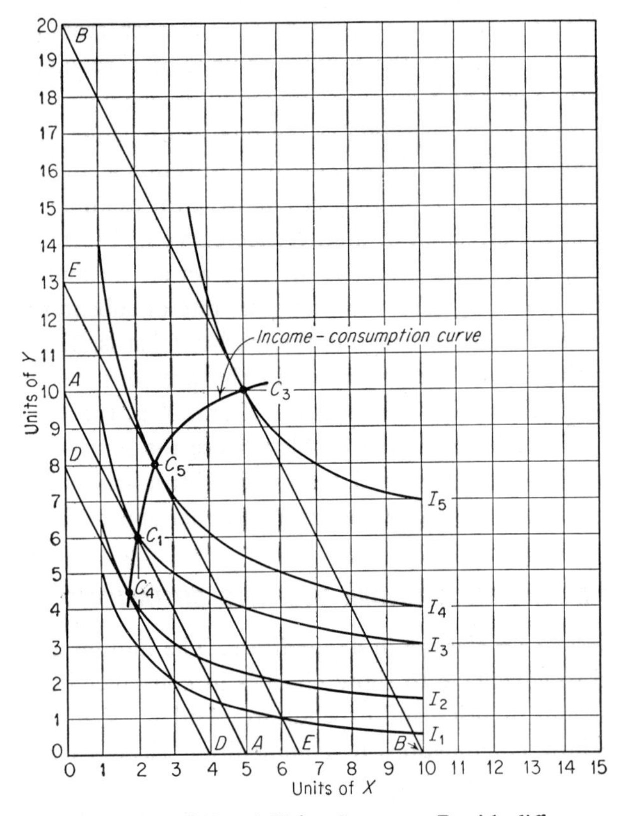

FIG. 7-3. Best combinations of Y and X for Consumer B with different total expenditures.

indifference map is such that the proportions of the combination changes slightly—he takes relatively more of X and less of Y. But some other consumer with a different indifference map would maximize his satisfaction with a combination involving different proportions.

If we continue to let Consumer B's total expenditure vary, next to \$8 and finally to \$13, outlay curves DD and EE may be superimposed on B's indifference map. Following these constructions, equilibrium points C_4 and C_5 are obtained. The line connecting points C_4, C_1, C_5, and C_3 may be defined as the *income-consumption curve.* It describes how quantities of Y and X vary with changes in total expenditure. In this case, it will be observed that increases in expenditure are first used almost exclusively to acquire more of Y, but the last increase (from $13 to $20) is used to acquire more of both Y and X. Generally, the quantities taken of both commodities involved will increase with rising total expenditures; our case is a typical case. But, on occasions, the amount of a commodity taken by a consumer will decline as his income rises. Such a commodity is known as an *inferior* good. An example of such a commodity in the United States might be beans.

Consequences of a change in price. Let us assume that we are back to outlay curve AA with a total expenditure of $10 and that then the price of X falls to $1. What happens in this situation? First, a new outlay curve which takes account of this price decline must be constructed. And this curve AB is superimposed on Consumer B's indifference map in Figure 7-4. In this case, the slope of the outlay curve changes since Consumer B can purchase 10 units of X at the new price of $1 with a total expenditure of $10. A new equilibrium point C_6 now obtains at the point of tangency of the outlay curve AB with indifference curve I_4. At this maximizing position, Consumer B selects 6½ units of Y and 3½ units of X. This is the best combination of Y and X that Consumer B can obtain, given (1) his indifference map; (2) a total expenditure of $10; and (3) price Y = $1, price X = $1.

The line drawn through the equilibrium points C_1 and C_6 is called the *price-consumption curve.* It shows how the quantity of X taken varies with a change in the price of X. Since only two commodities are involved, it also shows how the quantity of Y taken varies with changes in the price of X. In this case, the quantity of Y taken increases modestly with the fall in the price of X, but as would be expected, the quantity of X taken increases relatively more. With a fall in the price of X, Consumer B substitutes X for Y, relatively at least.

Income and substitution effects. Two interesting effects of the foregoing price decline, or any price change for that matter, may be conceptualized and isolated by means of the indifference approach. The first of these is called the *income effect;* it refers to changes in the amount of X taken resulting from the real-income consequences of the price change. In terms of our example, the increase in the quantity of X taken resulting from the rise in real income, which in turn resulted from the fall in the price of X from $2 to $1, is known as the income effect. The change in

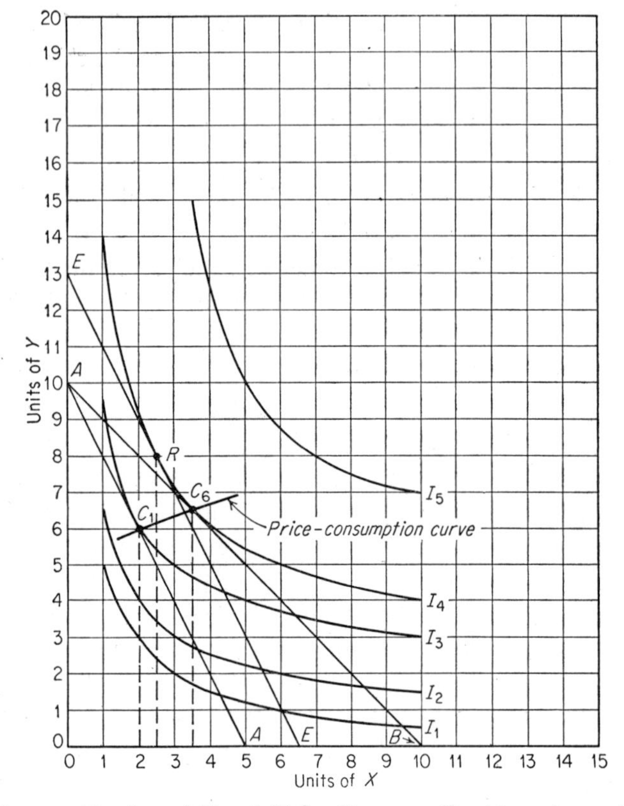

FIG. 7-4. Best combination of Y and X for Consumer B with a change in the price of X.

the quantity of X taken attributable to the change in its relative price, after subtracting out the income effect, is called the *substitution effect*. In terms of our example, the increase in the quantity of X taken resulting from the fall in its price relative to Y's price, after subtracting out the income effect, may be termed the substitution effect.

These two aspects of a price change may be viewed graphically in Figure 7-4. Consumer B maximized his satisfaction at point C_1 prior to the price change in X; after the fall in the price of X, his best combination is given at point C_6. In this change of combinations growing out of the fall in the price of X, Consumer B increased his takings of X from 2 to 3½ units. The question thereby arises: "How much of this increase is attributable to a rise in real income (i.e., the income effect), and how much is due to a change in relative prices (i.e., the substitution effect)?"

The first thing we know is that the fall in the price of X moves Consumer B from indifference curve I_3 to curve I_4. In this sense, the fall in the price of X is similar to an increase in the total expenditure by Consumer B for commodities Y and X. Hence, we ask: "How much X would Consumer B have taken if he had reached indifference curve I_4 by an increase in expenditure (income) rather than by the route of a price change?" The answer to this question is obtained by letting the outlay curve AA drift to the right in a parallel fashion until it becomes tangent to indifference curve I_4 at point R. The point of tangency, R, effected by I_4 and the new outlay curve EE, provides a measure of the income effect. The quantity of X taken increases by ½ unit by reason of a rise in real income (2½ units less 2 units = ½ unit; this may be observed on the X axis of Figure 7-4). But point R does not provide the actual combination of Y and X on curve I_4 realized by Consumer B resulting from the fall in the price of X. The actual combination is found at point C_6. The substitution effect (i.e., the increase in the quantity of X taken due to the fall in the price of X *relative* to Y) is equal to 1 unit. The full increase in the amount of X taken (1½ units) less the influence attributable to a rise in real income (½ unit) leaves a 1-unit increase in X as a measure of the substitution effect. In other words, Consumer B does not settle on that combination of Y and X that he would have if he had moved to indifference level I_4 through an increase in expenditure (that combination is given at R); he substitutes X for Y and moves along indifference curve I_4 to point C_6, where the marginal rate of substitution is equal to the ratio of prices.

The income effect may be positive or negative (i.e., the consumer may increase or decrease his takings of X when his real income increases). Generally, the income effect is positive, as we have already noted. But sometimes the quantity taken of a commodity increases very little or even declines with rising total expenditures. And when the amount of a commodity taken decreases with increasing total expenditures, we have the case of an inferior good. But the substitution effect is always in favor of X; a fall in the price of X always leads to a substitution of X for Y, and a rise in the price of X leads to a substitution of Y for X. The substitution effect of a price change generally dominates; hence, whether the income effect be positive or negative, a fall in the price of X generally leads to an increase in its consumption.

Questions and Points for Discussion

1. What is an indifference curve? What is an indifference map? How would you go about collecting the data to construct an indifference map?
2. List the properties of an indifference map.
3. What is an outlay curve? What data are required to lay off an outlay curve?
4. *a.* Given the indifference map of a particular consumer (i.e., draw in an indifference map of your own choosing) for commodities X and Y, total outlay = \$40, the price of Y = \$1, the price of X = \$2, determine the equilibrium combination of X and Y of this consumer.

   b. Demonstrate that the equilibrium combination determined above is *the* equilibrium position of this consumer.

   c. Indicate the new solution where the price of X increases to \$5.
5. What is an income-consumption curve? What is a price-consumption curve?
6. What is the income effect of a price change? What is the substitution effect of a price change?
7. How does the income effect influence the quantity of a commodity taken? How does the substitution effect influence the quantity of a commodity taken?

References

Hicks, J. R.: *Value and Capital*, Oxford University Press, New York, 1939, part I.

Norris, Ruby Turner: *The Theory of Consumer's Demand*, Yale University Press, New Haven, Conn., 1941, chap. II.

Samuelson, Paul A.: *Economics: An Economic Analysis*, 2d ed., McGraw-Hill Book Company, Inc., New York, 1951, pp. 487–493.

Stigler, George J.: *The Theory of Price*, rev. ed., The Macmillan Company, New York, 1952, chap. 5.

8. An Appraisal of the Theory of Consumer Behavior

The mechanics of a theory of consumer behavior has been presented first in direct utility terms and second in preference terms in Chapters 6 and 7. No appraisal, specific or general, of the received theory has, however, been offered to this point; we have been grubbing round the base of individual trees rather than looking at the forest. In fact, our attention may have been directed so intensely at pieces and mechanics of the theory that its meaning and significance have escaped us. Therefore, it would seem wise to pull up for a while and appraise the area which we have traversed. First, the basic meaning, or the nature, of the theory needs to be made clear. Second, the uses of the theory need to be set forth. Third, the difficulties and limitations of the theory need to be understood and appreciated. So let us turn to this task of appraisal.

THE MEANING OF THE THEORY

To some, it may seem that a new theory of consumer behavior has been presented in the previous chapters. But this is not the case. In the first place, the theory is not new; its main outlines are to be found in any good elementary or intermediate textbook,[1] and a full statement of it is to be found in any advanced textbook.[2] In the second place, it is not concerned with any unusual or peculiar behavior of consumers. On the contrary, it attempts to provide an "explanation" of consumer behavior in

[1] See Paul A. Samuelson, *Economics: An Introductory Analysis*, 2d ed., McGraw-Hill Book Company, Inc., New York, 1951, chap. 23; or Kenneth E. Boulding, *Economic Analysis*, rev. ed., Harper & Brothers, New York, 1948, chap. 29.

[2] See George J. Stigler, *The Theory of Price*, rev. ed., The Macmillan Company, New York, 1952, chap. 5; or Tibor Scitovsky, *Welfare and Competition: The Economics of a Fully Employed Economy*, Richard D. Irwin, Inc., Homewood, Ill., 1951, chaps. III–V.

the typical or normal situation. But the question remains: "In what sense has the theory provided an explanation? In short, what has it explained?"

It has not told us what is good or what is bad. It has not told us what we ought to consume or what we ought not to consume. Certainly, it has not been concerned with the establishment of goals or priorities or standards. It has rather been concerned with providing *a general description of consumer behavior*. Making use of the fundamental maximizing assumption, the theory attempts to provide a general description of the process that each consuming unit must go through in selecting the combination of goods and services that it does. The explanation provided by the theory of the household, which we have been studying, thus turns out to be a description of what the rational consumer unit *does*, acting alone, in selecting some particular combination of goods and services for living.

If the theory of consumer behavior is so pedestrian in nature, if it describes only what we do, why then must it be so complicated? The answer to this question would seem to turn on two considerations. In the first place, the blueprint describing a particular structure (e.g., a house, a gasoline motor) always appears complicated at first sight. The complete specifications of a house as shown in blueprint form must indicate accurately all elevations, pipes and wiring within the walls, type and nature of materials, etc.; and the specifications for something like a motor appear exceedingly complicated to the layman. The description on paper of a particular structure, simple as it may be, always requires more words, more drawings, and more mathematics than one might at first guess. This is because complete and accurate descriptions are difficult to achieve. Try, for example, to set forth a description of some room in a house which you know, so that a total stranger could furnish and arrange it exactly as it stands at the time of the description. Considering the magnitude of the problem (i.e., describing consumer behavior), the descriptive materials of the theory do not seem out of proportion.

But the expositor of a theory of consumer behavior, or any general theory, is confronted by a second and more formidable problem. The exposition must be of such an order as to describe not just one particular case but all typical cases. The problem is analogous to that of developing a blueprint to describe the typical house people live in, not a particular house. If the theory is to have wide and general application, it must do more than describe the behavior of any one of us. It must be of such a form that it describes in a useful way the behavior of all consumers in some group, class, or category.

But as the theory becomes more general, it becomes more abstract. This must be the case, for a general theory can be concerned only with broad, general tendencies in human behavior. It cannot be concerned with the exquisite details of shopping for my lady's hat—such experiences are more properly the subject matter of a short story in the *New Yorker* magazine. In other words, a general theory must derive from the sum of individual actions, each with its unique twist or particular quirk, the relevant and essential tendencies common to all. Thus, because complete and accurate description is difficult, and because the formulation of useful and relevant generalizations is even more difficult, the received theory of consumer behavior appears to be, and is, difficult.

USES OF THE THEORY

Provides insights. The most important single contribution of the theory which we have been studying is the insights which it provides into the nature of consumer behavior. And the word *insights* is used advisedly here. The theory of consumer behavior as it has been presented in conventional form in Chapters 6 and 7 does not provide a *quantitative* description of consumer behavior. And as we shall soon discover, it is not without other limitations. Thus, it does not provide a complete and measured description of consumer behavior. But it does provide formal insights into the nature of that behavior. It makes explicit the choice problem; it suggests how individual values, expressed either in terms of utility functions or indifference maps, influence choices; it suggests how changes in income influence choices; and it suggests how changes in price influence choices. All this is fundamental to an understanding of the economics of decision making in the household.

"But," the curious student may ask, "if we do what we do as consumers, why do we need a theory to describe that behavior? Why can't we just observe ourselves as consumers and know what we do?" This is an interesting point, and it bears on all theoretical formulations. Scientists formulate theories, which when tested and proved become laws, of the relations existing among the various phenomena in the universe. But these theoretical formulations do not bring a particular relationship into being: it is there in the nature of things; man simply discovers the relationship and perhaps puts it to work to his advantage. Take, for example, the famous story of Sir Isaac Newton and the law of gravitation. He is reputed to have formulated the law from observing an apple fall from a tree. Now apples fell to the ground for centuries prior to Newton's formulation of the law, and they have ever since. The discovery of a law by man did not bring the various gravitational relationships into being or alter them. But once man formulated a theory of gravitation—obtained some insights into the nature of the relationships involved—he could and did begin to take action based on the knowledge of the workings of those relationships.

We have a somewhat analogous situation with respect to the theory of consumer behavior. The formulation of the theory of consumer behavior presented in Chapters 6 and 7 brought into being, and altered, no consumption relationships. Those relationships were already in the nature of things, and the theory attempts only to describe them. The fact that the theory appears complicated, and is formal, need not fool us. It is complicated because accurate description is difficult; it is formal because it attempts to be general and representative at one and the same time. But it was deduced from observation and experience—observations of consuming units in action and personal experience. And it is our point that the insights provided by the theory into the nature of consumption relationships permit individuals and groups within society to take actions designed either to alter those relations or to build on them with some assurance of success. This is the purpose of all theory—to provide working hypotheses about relationships existing among phenomena found in the universe.

We know, for example, what to expect with respect to the *relative* value placed on candy bars by consumers under varying situations. We know that the consumer of candy bars, or any other good or service for that matter, will discover that the satisfaction received from the consumption of additional units will eventually fall. For this reason, the consumer cannot maximize his total satisfaction by continuing indefinitely to increase his consumption in any one line. On the contrary, he will maximize his total satisfaction with some *combination* of goods and services. And these maximizing combinations will vary by individuals because tastes and preferences, hence utility functions, vary by individuals. With this and similar generalized pieces of knowledge, we can appraise the probabilities of success from certain types of actions (e.g., expanding the consumption of milk, using the total production of nylon for parachutes).

Part of a more general theory. From previous discussions, it should be clear that the theory of the household presented here is not some isolated formulation. It is an integral part of a more general theory designed to "explain" how the limited resources of the economy are employed to produce the bill of goods and services wanted by consumers. In this conception of things, the theory of consumer behavior which we have presented finds its use in the formulation of a more general theory having the objective of explaining how the total economy works.

But we can be more precise with respect to the use made of the theory of household in this context. Out of the formulations of Chapters 6 and 7, we can and will derive the concept of demand. In other words, the decisions of a consuming unit may be formalized into the concept of consumer demand, and individual consumer demands may then be aggregated into market demand. Finally, market demand in interaction with supply determines the price of the commodity involved. All this we shall develop in Part IV. But it is important to recognize in this appraisal of the theory of consumer behavior that it has a major part to play in providing an explanation of the workings of the total economy.

More specifically, it should perhaps be noted that the demand relations which derive from the choice decisions of consumers have important implications for the decision making of other groups in society. The demand for a particular commodity tells the businessman how much of that commodity he can sell at different prices. The demand for a particular commodity, say wheat, determines how much the government will need to buy to support the price of wheat at 90 per cent or 75 per cent or some other per cent of parity. And the demand for a particular commodity can tell a consumer buying club how much its members will take at the market price. Thus, the implications of the theory of consumer behavior in this area of demand are important in the large and in the small.

LIMITATIONS OF THE THEORY

The maximizing assumption. The assumption that the consumer will always make that choice which maximizes total utility has been a whipping boy for a half century or more. Critics of orthodox theory are forever asserting that this is not a valid assumption; they argue that the individual is not a human calculating machine, weighing each set of alternatives, which then chooses in an automatic fashion the particular item which provides the greatest utility. In a more positive vein, they argue that man lives in part by habit and that many of his choices are irrational from the point of view of his long-run good.

But these arguments do not necessarily add up to an invalidation of the maximizing assumption. Economists who assume that each consumer seeks to maximize his total utility do not view the individual as a human calculating machine: they simply feel that a general tendency exists for the consumer to expend his limited income along those lines which provide him with the greatest satisfaction. And who is to say that a habitual pattern of consumption is not also a pattern which maximizes total utility? This would seem to be the very way for an individual to maximize his total satisfaction where the disutility of making decisions is great.

The argument that an individual sometimes makes choices which are damaging to himself, hence does not maximize his total utility, is a complex one. A parent giving up his (or her) life in an effort to save a child and a religious fanatic inflicting pain on himself are extreme examples sometimes given as evidence of the invalidity of the maximizing assumption. But such examples are far removed from the workaday world of food, furniture, and fishing poles. As economists, we do not apply the assumption to all forms of human behavior, although an argument can be made that the religious fanatic does maximize his total utility through masochism, and a comparable argument may be made in the case of the parent. All the economist assumes is the following: In the world of material things, there is a tendency for consumers to choose that line of expenditure from among alternatives that provides the greatest satisfaction. In the mundane world of candy bars, hats, beer, vacations, cars, and washing machines, this would seem to be a reasonable assumption.

In certain respects, however, the maximizing assumption may oversimplify the choice problem. It may be the case that the consumer in certain situations lacks the necessary information to select the combination of goods and services required to satisfy a particular want. A consumer, for example, may *want* to satisfy his hunger with a tasty, yet nutritious, diet, but lack the technical information to make the actual food choices involved. In other words, the incentive of utility maximization may not in fact lead to a maximization of total satisfaction where the consumer lacks technical knowledge.

The implications of this limitation will be explored further in Chapter 10 in the discussions of the use of consumption minima.

Tastes and preferences. One shortcoming of the theory exists with respect to consumer tastes and preferences. And this shortcoming has at least two facets. In the first place, the theory is not helpful in suggesting how tastes and preferences are formed or how or why they change. It is true that we classified and reviewed in Chapter 5 various forces bearing on want creation. But that discussion was not helpful in the way of showing how a particular preference or patterns of preferences come into being or disappear. It suggested, rather, the basis for the proliferation of human wants in our society. Certainly, no systematic treatment of want creation or preference manipulation is incorporated in the received theory of consumer behavior. The fundamental motivation of all economic activity—human want and its satisfaction—is simply taken as given. This failure to explore the mainspring of economic activity, and the driving force in consumption activity, certainly limits the usefulness of the theory.

But there is a second facet to this particular limitation. It is related to the measurement problem. Even if we know that the preferences of consumers for some product have been increasing (or dcreasing), there is no way to convert this information directly into a shift in the utility function (or the indifference map). A change in income, for example, can be converted directly into a specific shift in the outlay curve, but not so with a change in preferences. There exists no quantitative link between a known change in preferences and a shift in the indifference map. If the map is to be redrawn, it must be redrawn from new contour data derived from further research and experimental work. But this latter piece of information is not very cheering, since we have already learned that research and experimental work in this direction have not been successful.

Product divisibility. It would appear that the received theory of consumer behavior begins to break down as the products involved cease to be highly divisible. And the theory collapses completely where the items become very large (e.g., a college education, a trip to Europe, a $10,000 life insurance policy, a new house). The average consumer would find it impossible to make comparisons between the following types of combinations: (1) one college education and two houses and (2) two college educations and one house. Comparisons of this sort are nonsensical, as well as beyond the experience of the average consumer. On the other hand, the making of a comparison and stating a preference as between a combination involving 2 silver serving spoons and 3 rosebushes and 3 silver serving spoons and 2 rosebushes does not seem too unreasonable. And the reason why this latter comparison does not seem completely foolish is that it falls within the realm of possible human experience. This could possibly represent the circumstances of a choice problem confronting a person purchasing a wedding gift for friends. The items are small and divisible; hence, they can be fitted into meaningful combinations.

Referring to the candy-bar example in Chapter 6, it was not easy to find a suitable, divisible commodity to use in illustrating the principle of diminishing marginal utility. We could have settled on glasses of milk, bottles of beer, pieces of pie, or possibly pairs of shoes or pairs of hose. But the use of such an apparently harmless illustration as chicken dinners soon becomes somewhat strained, and trips to the same "movie" quickly reduce to nonsense. Each of these latter items is conceived as a whole unit and is consumed as a whole unit. It is unusual to eat one chicken dinner after another or to eat parts of one dinner at different times. These commodities, although not unusually large, are not readily divisible, hence become a problem when the theory is used to describe the behavior of consumers with respect to them. In its pristine form, the theory of consumer behavior assumes perfect product divisibility, and this assumption must come pretty close to being satisfied if the theory is to hold.

Collective decisions. The received theory of consumer behavior ignores completely the process of collective decision making in consumption. The theory focuses exclusively on the choice problem of the individual or of the individual consuming unit. But an increasing proportion of personal income is expended on choices resulting from group decisions. Consumers decide collectively the extent and composition of their educational systems, park systems, road systems, military systems, and so on. The single individual or single family does not decide what quantity of each of the foregoing items maximizes its total satisfaction and then purchase just that amount: decisions with respect to quantities consumed of these goods and services and how payment is to be made (i.e., the tax structure) are made in political arenas through political processes. In the United States, these processes involve regular elections, compromise and consensus in legislatures, and administrative determinations. We cannot investigate these processes here, but it seems clear that such an investigation would lead us far from the analyses of Chapters 6 and 7.[3]

The share of the Gross National Product acquired by all levels of government amounted to 38.5 per cent in 1945, 15.1 per cent in 1950, and 22.5 in 1952. Although these percentage shares probably overstate the extent of collective consumption in that all government activity does not

[3] Some consideration will be given to group decisions in consumption in Part V.

necessarily fall in the category of collective consumption, this type of consumption absorbs an important slice of the total goods and services produced in recent years. But the received theory has nothing to say with respect to this aspect of consumption. In this sense, the theory is incomplete, and the extent of this void has widened in recent years. In the twilight zone between peace and war in which we live in the 1950s, collective consumption approaches one-fifth of the total.

A nonoperational theory. Any theory will have limitations, and the above discussion of generally accepted shortcomings does not represent an attempt to damn the theory out of existence. It is intended only to point out the limitations of an otherwise plausible theory of consumer behavior. But the theory has, or has had, one ever-present difficulty which severely limits its usefulness. *It is nonoperational.* Now what do we mean by this phrase? By nonoperational we mean that the theory cannot be used directly in real world situations. Assuming always complete freedom of consumer choice, the theory cannot be applied to specific situations to direct or modify or adjust patterns of consumption. The theory cannot be applied to a particular choice problem confronting a consumer, to yield a solution which states that the consumer *should* take more of Y and less of X. The home adviser cannot use the theory, for example, to tell a family that it should spend more on housing and less on recreation. In this sense, the theory of the household differs from the theory of the firm. Production specialists through the use of various adaptations of the theory of the firm (e.g., the budget approach, linear programing) can advise the farmer with some authority to expand his hog enterprise and contract his beef-fattening enterprise, for example.

Now why is the theory of the firm operational and the theory of the household not? The answer to this question turns on the fact that the output of production activity can be *measured* in units of the product, and that which is being maximized by the firm, income, can be *measured* in dollars; but the product of consumption activity, utility, cannot be (or is not readily) measured in objective units, and that which is being maximized, utility again, of course, is not measurable. The fact that product and income are measurable, and utility is not, makes all the difference in the world.

Where production functions are known, or known approximately, the production specialist can advise the firm that its net receipts would be increased by substituting this input for that, or by the adoption of a new technique, or by the increased use of some particular input. This is the case because the relations, first, between input and output and, second, between output and income are known (or can be known) in measured units. But the home adviser is not so fortunate; she can advise only in terms of her personal experience. And who is to say that the satisfaction derived by a home adviser from some particular combination of goods and services is the same as that which would be derived by members of a consuming unit under consideration? It would be surprising, for example, if the utility schedule of a professional home manager for luncheon sets were the same as that of a low-income housewife with eight children. But if the home adviser knew the utility schedules of the housewife in question, or could derive the schedules involved, she could then with some assurance suggest to the housewife that the total utility of that consuming unit could be increased by more luncheon sets and fewer diapers *or perhaps the other way round.* Not knowing the utility schedules of the members of the consuming unit, the home adviser can advise only in terms of her personal experience, and there is always the possibility that this advice may be wrong. This is why we prize freedom of consumer choice so highly.

The hard facts are that the theory of the household cannot be used directly (i.e., in day-to-day situations) to aid consuming units to increase their total satisfactions until the utility functions of the consumers involved can be measured in some way. This does not preclude adapting the theory or taking another approach, either of which might lead to the use of quantitative data more readily available. But somehow, in some way, the results of choice decisions of the consumer must be converted into measured units if a basis is to be established for recommending adjustments in consumer behavior. The theory of consumer behavior as it stands now cannot be used to recommend adjustments in consumption patterns, *because where the results of those adjustments cannot be measured, it is impossible to say whether the recommended pattern of consumption yields more or less satisfaction than the previous pattern to the consumer involved.* The received theory of consumer behavior is nonoperational, and that is its fundamental weakness.

Questions and Points for Discussion

1. What type of information or knowledge does the received theory of consumer behavior provide? Of what use is this type of information or knowledge?

2. How does product indivisibility weaken or detract from the theory?

In what sense does the existence of collective decision making constitute a limitation to the theory?

3. What is a nonoperational theory? In what sense is the received theory of consumer behavior nonoperational?

References

Boulding, Kenneth E.: *Economic Analysis*, rev. ed., Harper & Brothers, New York, 1948, pp. 624–625.

Clark, J. M.: "Realism and Relevance in the Theory of Demand," *Journal of Political Economy*, vol. 54, August, 1946.

Norris, Ruby Turner: *The Theory of Consumer's Demand*, Yale University Press, New Haven, Conn., 1941, chap. III.

Scitovsky, Tibor: *Welfare and Competition: The Economics of a Fully Employed Economy*, Richard D. Irwin, Inc., Homewood, Ill., 1951, pp. 48–50.

Veblen, Thorstein: "The Limitations of Marginal Utility," *Journal of Political Economy*, vol. 17, November, 1909, and reprinted in *What Veblen Taught*, The Viking Press, Inc., New York, 1936.

9. Some Developments in the Theory of Consumer Behavior

Our appraisal of the received theory of consumer behavior leads to two major conclusions. First, the theory is plausible and useful in certain types of situations; hence, no serious student of consumer behavior would consider throwing it overboard. Second, the theory has some severe limitations, and ways must be found to eliminate or circumvent these limitations if the theory is to be of general and direct use. For these reasons, consumption economists have been building on old concepts and working with new concepts in an effort to formulate a more useful—more effective—explanation of consumer behavior. We shall now take a brief look at some of these efforts and thereby possibly provoke some further thinking along these and other lines.

This is not to suggest that beginning students of consumption economics should try to develop a new theory of the household. But it is to suggest that our knowledge of consumer behavior must continue to grow and develop. And it is the task of this chapter to point out some of the directions in which this development may take place. We shall (1) take note of the current work in the measurement of utility, (2) review briefly the ideas of such "behaviorists" as Norris and Katona, and (3) present the main outlines of vector analysis.

MEASURING UTILITY

One of the more exciting things that has happened in the field of consumption economics in recent years is the experimental work done by Mosteller and Nogee in the measurement of utility.[1] It is always difficult to trace the origin and growth of ideas, and we shall not try to develop

[1] These experiments are described in some detail in a technical appendix to Chap. 6.

the history of ideas leading up to the Mosteller-Nogee experiments, but the work done by Friedman and Savage concerned with consumer choices involving risk [2] would seem to have provided the catalyst for these experiments and, further, to have suggested the form that they took. Thus, the immediate conceptual background for these experiments was one concerned with risk—the aversion to risk (e.g., insurance) and the desire to assume risks (e.g., gambling)—and this conceptual background had a pronounced influence on the form and objective of the experiments. The objective was straightforward, although somewhat unusual in terms of our experience: it was to measure the utility of money. The form of the experiments was even more unusual in terms of our experience: the experiments, which led to specific measures of utility, took the form of a series of games of chance. The degree to which a man valued money—real money and his money—was ascertained from a series of experiments in which the man (the gambler) was subjected to varying chance situations wherein his play in those situations could lead to gains or losses. How the players used their money in these situations provided patterns of behavior which were converted into measures of the utility of money.[3]

The results of these first experiments were not conclusive. For some individuals, the marginal utility of money appears to be falling over the range of experimentation; for others, it appears to be rising. Perhaps these measures are correct; perhaps the marginal utility of money does rise for some individuals and fall for others over the rather narrow ranges of income changes involved. Or perhaps the marginal utility of money goes through more than one cycle—increasing phase to decreasing phase—over the full range of the individual's income. Or perhaps the results are simply contradictory. But the inconclusive aspects of these first experimental results should not dampen our enthusiasm. On the contrary, the experiments introduce hope, where all hope had been dead for decades. The theory appears reasonable, the experimental procedures have been established, and the results are not unreasonable; thus we have reason to believe that further experimentation can lead to conclusive results.

We must hope, therefore, that work along these lines will be continued, first, to perfect the method for measuring the utility of money and, second,

[2] "The Utility Analysis of Choices Involving Risk," *Journal of Political Economy*, vol. 56, 1948, pp. 279–304.

[3] For a description of these experiments refer to the original report, "An Experimental Measurement of Utility," *Journal of Political Economy*, vol. 59, October, 1951, pp. 371–404.

to adapt it for measuring the utility of individual commodities. The first task should not prove too difficult: if the research funds are forthcoming, the solution to this measurement problem should be only a matter of time. But the second line of work (i.e., measuring the marginal utility to consumers for individual commodities) would seem to be strewn with more obstacles. Whether experiments of a probabilistic nature can yield measures of utility for particular commodities appears doubtful. Most of us have had some experience in taking risks with respect to earning an income, many of us have had some experience gambling for money, but few of us have ever gambled for hamburgers, chicken dinners, pairs of shoes, or bedsprings. And most of us are not likely to want to participate in games of chance involving such items, for should we become a big winner, we would be forced into a merchandising operation to get rid of the stuff. Further, there exists the technical problem with respect to food of holding the state of hunger constant during the gambling experiments or constant from one series to the next. We do not conclude, however, that the method cannot be modified to permit the measurement of utility for individual commodities; we say only that the job appears extremely difficult. In fact, it would not be surprising if the measurement of the utility of commodities is realized by an altogether different approach, *but this different, and we assume successful, approach is suggested from insights gained from measuring the utility of money via the probabilistic approach.*

But the cynic may say, "So what? What if a few puttering scientists are able to measure experimentally the utility functions of a handful of individuals—how will that help?" Obviously, it would prove too time-consuming and too costly to measure the utility functions for each individual for each commodity, but no researcher is suggesting such a thing. If, however, it were possible to measure the utility functions for individuals, commodity by commodity, a great amount of utility data could be gathered from small, representative samples of individuals in their consumption of the more important commodity items. Modern statistical techniques can provide highly reliable estimates of population characteristics, in this case utility functions, from small samples, and this would be the technique used for gathering utility data. Individuals subjected to consumption experiments would be selected by a sampling procedure which would enable the analyst to estimate the utility functions for some group in the population for some commodity, say beef, and which further would enable the analyst to state the probability of this estimate being the true estimate of the utility function for an individual member of the population group.

If all the money spent by the U.S. Department of Agriculture and state experiment stations under the Research and Marketing Act of 1946 for measuring preferences of consumers for various food items (and in most cases by modern statistical techniques) had been spent on effective experiments for measuring the utility provided consumers by those items, we would now know a great deal about the utility functions of consumers for food. *If* this had been the case home advisers and nutritionists would now know much more about recommending adjustments in food consumption. *If*, further, an effective means existed for measuring utility by commodities, we may be sure that commercial research and advertising agencies would be gathering utility data to enhance their knowledge of what it is the consumer values—what type of good or service he wants more of, how much more at what prices, and so on. This type of information would be indispensable to selling campaigns, and we may be sure that manufacturers and distributors would spend large sums to obtain it.

If, and this is the all-important word here, a technique became available for measuring utility functions, that technique would certainly be used. Modern statistical procedures provide a means for estimating with reliability the utility function in question for the group in question from a very small sample. Thus, we would come to *know* with some degree of probability, for example, whether a greater expenditure on housing and less on recreation provided a family with more or less total satisfaction. And so with all other realistic and important combinations—we would know from objective measures what maximizes consumer satisfactions. We could advise the consuming unit with some authority as to the optimum, maximizing allocation of its expenditure. And it is because these first experiments in the measurement of utility raise some hope that sometime we may *know* the utility schedules of consumers that they are exciting.

THE NORRIS-KATONA ANALYSES

Ruby Turner Norris argues that the usual marginal utility approach, indifference curve approach, or any variant of either fails to provide an adequate explanation of consumer behavior in the short run.[4] In other

[4] *The Theory of Consumer's Demand*, Yale University Press, New Haven, Conn., 1941, chap. VI.

words, Norris holds that the type of analyses presented in Chapters 6 and 7 does not provide a plausible or meaningful explanation of ordinary, day-to-day consumer behavior. She argues that a useful theory of consumer behavior needs to be developed in terms altogether different from that of conventional theory (i.e., analyses deduced in a logical form from given propositions or assumptions). The Norris method of analysis is, as we shall see, essentially a behavioristic one. The expenditure behavior of consuming units is classified in accordance with the amount of consideration, or "weighing," given to each expenditure. The analysis then takes the form of indicating the extent to which expenditures fall in different categories and some of the reasons why.

Classification of expenditure behavior. Norris sets forth a classification with three principal categories: (1) areas in which careful weighing is absent; (2) areas in which careful weighing occurs; (3) the dynamic residual. Let us therefore seek the meaning and significance of these categories.

Three types of expenditure are made with little or no consideration or weighing, (1) those arising out of past commitments, (2) those for petty goods, and (3) those made to satisfy rigid habits. Commitments made in the past project into the present and the future legal and moral obligations with respect to the use of income; hence, those expenditures arising out of past commitments take place without free choice of any kind. *This type of expenditure is, in the short run, automatic.* With respect to petty goods, it would seem that each individual has a margin below which he does not think it worth his while to weigh expenditures; hence, expenditures for petty goods are also made in an automatic fashion. Finally, consumption arising out of habit (e.g., smoking) gives rise to expenditures where careful consideration is absent. Thus, Norris concludes that a very large part of each consuming unit's income is spent in an automatic or semiautomatic fashion.

The second category of expenditure behavior involves those goods which are regularly consumed but which are sufficiently costly (e.g., food, clothing) so that the consumer carefully considers, or weighs, each expenditure for them. The consumer is forced to watch, or weigh, his expenditures carefully for this category of goods to keep his budget in balance (i.e., hold total expenditures in line with income). Now what does this weighing process involve? It involves, first, a consideration and appraisal of the stock of goods on hand. It involves, second, a consideration and appraisal of future prices or costs of the goods required. It involves, third, a consideration and appraisal of the consuming unit's expected future income. Taking into account these considerations, the consuming unit then expands or contracts its expenditures in any given line as the situation dictates.

Left over after expenditures have been made, first, in areas of little or no weighing and, second, in areas of careful weighing is a *residual* amount of income. This residual may be positive or negative depending upon the relationship of expenditures in the above categories to income. But where the residual is positive, it represents an *experimental fund* to be used by the consumer in diverse ways. It may be used to try out some new type of good or service. Or it may be used to pay the first installment on some large item, hence start a commitment which carries over to future income periods. Or it may be used to go on a recreational spree. But whatever the use made of the experimental fund, it seems clear that overt choice decisions are involved. The consuming unit must choose one or more particular uses for it from among alternative and competing uses.

An appraisal of the Norris analysis. The Norris analysis is helpful in understanding the expenditure process of consumers. A moment's reflection, however, makes it clear that the analysis refers only to the short run: as a description, or explanation, of the expenditure process, it is most meaningful with respect to a point in time. Only in the short run do expenditures tend to be automatic as the result of past commitments; in the longer run, obligations assumed in the past become satisfied, and new obligations are assumed. In other words, "past commitments" become variable in the long run. Further, no attention is paid to the influences of changes in tastes and preferences and changes in income, which can only occur through time. At a point in time, expected price and income changes are considered as a part of the weighing process prior to purchase, but actual changes in relevant independent variables occurring through time are not considered. In short, the analysis is offered as an explanation of the expenditure process by consumers at a point, or short period, in time.

Even as a short-run theory of consumer behavior, the Norris analysis is, however, lacking in certain respects. It does not systematically or adequately deal with the choice problem confronting consumers. It suggests that choices are continuously made in the "area of careful weighing" and sporadically in the "dynamic residual." But no solution to the choice problem is elaborated (i.e., how consumers arrive at some particular combination of goods and services).

If, however, the Norris analysis is combined with the conventional equilibrium analyses presented in Chapters 6 and 7, a more general, and perhaps a more useful, theory of consumer behavior emerges. The Norris analysis suggests the extent to which, and the reasons why, some expenditures are made without consideration or weighing and others are made with careful consideration or experimentation at any point in time. Within the areas of careful weighing and experimentation, however, either the marginal utility or the indifference approach may be used to provide an explanation as to the allocation of income among alternative lines of expenditure. In other words, the consumer must choose, or select, a particular combination of goods and services from among those goods and services which fall in the areas of careful weighing and experimentation, but no solution to this choice problem is suggested in the Norris analysis. Thus, it would seem appropriate to employ the marginal utility or indifference analyses in this role (i.e., to provide a solution to the choice problem). In this event, the received theory would need to be adapted to take into account the causative influences of *expected* price and income changes. But this could be done without too much difficulty within the indifference approach.

The Katona position. The Katona analysis of consumer behavior would seem to represent an extension or further development of the Norris ideas: it moves farther along the road toward a purely behavioristic analysis.[5] Katona states his position unequivocally: [6] "Unlike pure theorists, we shall not assume at the outset that rational behavior exists or that rational behavior constitutes the topic of economic analysis. We shall study economic behavior as we find it."

Katona argues that insufficient evidence is available to answer the question whether consumers plan or act with foresight. But consumer behavior is susceptible of empirical investigation. And the relevant questions to be answered by these empirical investigations are as follows: [7] "When, under what circumstances, is one kind of consumer behavior likely to occur, and when, under what circumstances, another kind of behavior?" Let us therefore look at the answers which Katona draws from numerous empirical investigations with respect to these questions.

[5] George Katona, *Psychological Analysis of Economic Behavior*, McGraw-Hill Book Company, Inc., 1951.

[6] *Ibid.*, p. 16.

[7] *Ibid.*, p. 64.

Under certain circumstances, such as buying a house or a car, consumers make genuine decisions (i.e., they carefully consider alternative courses of action and select one). But otherwise, consumers follow habitual patterns of behavior. In other words, in *most instances* consumers act the same way as they acted before under similar circumstances, following habitual patterns without making decisions. According to Katona, research findings indicate that for purchases exceeding $1,000, planning and genuine decision making are frequent; for purchases of several hundred dollars, planning and decision making are less frequent; and, for purchases of less than $100, planning and decision making are infrequent.

A genuine decision once made, however, usually leads to routine behavior over a considerable period of time. In other words, once a consumer buys a house, he pays a monthly installment on that house over a long period of time. This we recognize as the past-commitment argument of Norris. But routine expenditures take many forms. Katona feels that most expenditures for food and clothing follow habitual patterns. And in general he argues that, the smaller the single expenditure, and the more frequent the expenditure, the more likely it is to take the form of a habitual or routine expenditure.

Finally, Katona argues that it is meaningless to *generalize* with respect to *the* motive (or motives) of consumer behavior. In his view, we can fruitfully search only for the motives of specific actions and decisions. And this can be done through empirical studies where (1) consumers are asked why they did or did not act in such a way and (2) the discovery of hidden motives occurs through relating forms of behavior to relevant characteristics of the persons involved.

To illustrate, Katona argues that it is fruitless to search for the basic and general motives of saving, but it is possible to discover through survey methods the particular motives that caused consuming units to increase their rates of saving during World War II. Perhaps Katona is right, but if he is, the science of economics is in difficult straits. This means that each economic problem must be studied independent of the next, since the findings developed out of the study of one situation may not be generalized to another similar situation where the motivations involved may be, and are likely to be, different. It means that conclusions with respect to economic behavior deduced from generalizations with respect to economic motivations will not be valid in particular situations because the generalizations with respect to economic motivations are not valid. In short, Katona goes the full distance and challenges the received body of economic doctrine. There is no reconciling the Katona position with the conventional views presented in Chapters 6 and 7.[8]

VECTOR ANALYSIS

Vector analysis represents a psychological approach to consumer behavior. As such, it does not conflict with the received theory presented in Chapters 6 and 7; it may be viewed, rather, as an alternative explanation of consumer behavior which with some effort can be made consistent with the more conventional theory. And since the writings of proponents of this approach are beginning to leave an imprint on the field of consumption economics, the main outlines of the approach are set forth here. In this, we follow the description of vector analysis by Warren J. Bilkey.[9]

Basic concepts. According to vector analysis theory, consumer choice grows out of an *internal psychic conflict* between the person's attractions toward certain attributes of an item and his repulsion against other attributes of the item (e.g., its costs). The individual's desire for the item is measured in terms of positive valences, his repulsion against it in negative valences. If his positive valences for the item exceed his negative valences, the purchase will be made, and vice versa. In an effort to move vector theory toward an operational state, the various attractions and repulsions to a particular item are summed into a *desire-resistance* relationship where *desire* equals the *net* total of all attractions (+ valences) minus all repulsions (− valences) except *those related to cost. Resistance*, then, is equal to the negative valences due to cost. The difference between desire (net positive valences) and resistance (negative valences due to cost) thus determines whether a particular purchase will be made.

In vector analysis, an active psychic conflict is assumed to be necessary

[8] Persons interested in this behavioristic approach should refer to Lincoln H. Clark (ed.), *Consumer Behavior*, New York University Press, New York, 1954. In this volume Katona and his colleague Eva Mueller report on a "Study of Purchase Decisions." The methods and findings of this study are deserving of serious consideration.

[9] The presentation of this section is adapted from the unpublished manuscript by Warren J. Bilkey, "The Vector Hypothesis: A Psychological Approach to Consumer Behavior Analysis," University of Connecticut, Storrs, Conn., 1952. The approach is described by Joseph Clawson in an essay entitled "Lewin's Vector Psychology and the Analysis of Motives in Marketing" in Reavis Cox and Wroe Alderson (eds.), *Theory in Marketing*, Richard D. Irwin, Inc., Homewood, Ill., 1950; and by Warren J. Bilkey, "A Psychological Approach to Consumer Behavior Analysis," *Journal of Marketing*, July, 1953.

to high disbursement efficiency. Disbursement efficiency is defined as the percentage relationship between (1) the amount of funds actually spent by a consumer for an item (this is the denominator) and (2) the smallest amount of funds which, if spent in the most satisfying of all ways, would give the consumer satisfaction equal to that obtained from expenditures indicated under (1) above (this is the numerator). If the percentage relation is low, the consumer is purchasing an item that provides little satisfaction relative to the most satisfying item that he could buy. The closer this percentage is to 100, the higher the disbursement efficiency. In indifference terms, maximum disbursement efficiency (ratio = 100) is achieved when funds are allocated in a way such that the outlay curve is tangent to the highest indifference curve. Now, in a world of constant change, the maintenance of a high disbursement efficiency requires that the consumer continuously adapt to changing conditions—requires that the consumer make new purchasing or saving decisions each time that changes occur in prices, income, expectations, or products. And continuous adaptation means continuous conscious appraisal of desirable and repulsive attributes, hence continuous psychic conflict.

But an active desire-resistance conflict involves psychic effort, which many people seek to avoid. To avoid constant psychic effort (tensions), some people adopt arbitrary buying guides or purchase by habit. Whenever consumers purchase by habit or follow an arbitrary guide, they can and do avoid active *decision making*. By such methods, they are able to reduce the psychic effort involved in choice, but the achievement of reduced psychic effort comes at the expense of efficient disbursement. In other words, decision making is work; it involves psychic tensions growing out of continuous conscious appraisal of desires and resistances; hence, many consumers try to avoid this psychic labor by purchasing by rule, habit, or impulse.

Purchasing by habit or arbitrary guides constitutes one form of disbursement rigidity. But there are other forces, too, which impose rigid expenditure patterns on the consumer. Externally imposed requirements such as taxes and dues restrict the consumer in his allocation of funds; past commitments like installment payments and insurance payments have a similar effect; finally, product indivisibility, where all-or-none expenditures are involved, create rigidities. Thus, where patterns of expenditure are tied to habit and arbitrary buying guides on one hand and are held rigid by such conditioning elements as past commitments and product indivisibility on the other hand, the consumer does not, or cannot, readily adjust his expenditure pattern as prices, incomes, and products vary.

Where expenditure rigidities predominate, active decision making is at a minimum, psychic tensions are low, and we would reason that disbursement efficiency is also low. Certainly, the latter will be the case where economic change is rapid and widespread.

The intensity of a consumer's desire for a particular good is denoted by the sum of positive valences. Without a thorough investigation of the relationships involved, it would seem that positive valences are effected by (1) psychosomatic influences such as hormone secretions and body requirements and (2) the disparity between the consumer's plane of living and his standard of living. Psychosomatic influences will vary according to age, sex, activity, and so on. The consumer's standard of living is influenced by friends and associates, socioeconomic status, and generally accepted values and activities of the society in which he lives. The consumer's plane of living is composed of the goods and services actually used up in living. Now, where a consumer's bodily needs for an item are great, or the standard of consumption for the item is greatly in excess of actual consumption, the intensity of desire for the item will be strong and the sum of positive valences relatively large. But where bodily needs are less, or the gap between the standard and level of consumption is reduced, the intensity of desire will be less strong and the sum of positive valences smaller.

Negative valences represent the intensity of the consumer's self-imposed resistance to spending money for the good or service in question. A priori, it would seem that the negative valences of the consumer would be influenced by (1) the level of the consuming unit's free, uncommitted cash balance (cash plus checking account minus committed funds) and (2) the psychological reaction to a price or income change. It is difficult to generalize with respect to the effect of the psychological reaction to a price or income change on negative valences. But it might be suggested that in most cases the psychological reaction to a price increase would be that of increasing the negative valences and to an income increase that of decreasing the negative valences. In the case of free cash balances, it may be generalized that an increase in the cash balance of the consuming unit has the effect of decreasing negative valences, and vice versa.

A vector model of consumer behavior. The basic concepts outlined above can be worked into a graphic model of consumer behavior. The disbursement pattern of a consuming unit with an income falling in the class $2,770–$3,270 as of 1944 is presented in Figure 9-1; the amounts expended on each category are measured along each axis from the zero circumference. Also shown are lines describing hypothetical minimum standards and aspired standards of living for the consuming unit. In vector theory, it is assumed that a consuming unit tends to have both a minimum and an aspired standard of living, and if there were no frictions or rigidities, the consuming unit would allocate its funds in a way such that the plane of living (disbursement pattern, Figure 9-1) would lie an equally proportionate distance between the minimum and aspired standards for each category. In practice, however, rigidities in expenditure do occur (e.g., habit patterns, past commitments); hence, the plane of living for a consuming unit may fall relatively close to the aspired standard for some categories (e.g., food in Figure 9-1) and relatively close to the minimum standard for other categories (e.g., clothing in Figure 9-1). In sum, then, we have a new approach for describing, or conceptualizing, the behavior of consumers in choosing, or selecting, a combination of goods and services for use in living.

Next, we shall use the model presented in Figure 9-1 (or rather a simplified version of it) to provide an explanation of consumer behavior in response to a particular change in the economy (e.g., a price change, an income change, a product innovation). And since time and space are limited, we shall trace through the consequence of only one type of change, namely, a decrease in income to some consuming unit C. First, however, some new features added to Figure 9-2 need to be explained. The arrows pointing outward, with positive valences, represent vectors pressing for increases in each respective disbursement—*desires*. The arrows pointing inward, with negative valences, represent vectors pressing for decreases in each category of expenditure—*resistances*. And to take into account resistance to change, or budgetary frictions, it is assumed that there must be a preponderance of 5 valences of a given sign to induce an adjustment in the consumer's disbursement pattern. If, for example, there were 50 positive valences and 44 negative valences for some category, an increase in expenditure would occur; but if there were 50 positive valences and 46 negative valences, the increase would not occur.

The effects of an income decrease are illustrated in Figure 9-2; chart *A* portrays the initial (equilibrium) situation, chart *B* the intermediary situation, and chart *C* the final (and again equilibrium) situation. The assumptions underlying this illustrative case are as follows: (1) the consumer makes purchases in monetary units; (2) *the income of consuming unit* C *declines* X *dollars per year;* (3) all prices remain unchanged; (4) taxes are fixed; (5) savings are treated as a residual claimant to a point, and thereafter as an active claimant as with any other category; (6) the standard of living remains constant; (7) there is no product innovation; (8)

valence and expenditure relationships are in equilibrium when the income decline takes place.

Since saving is a residual claimant, the first effect of the income decrease

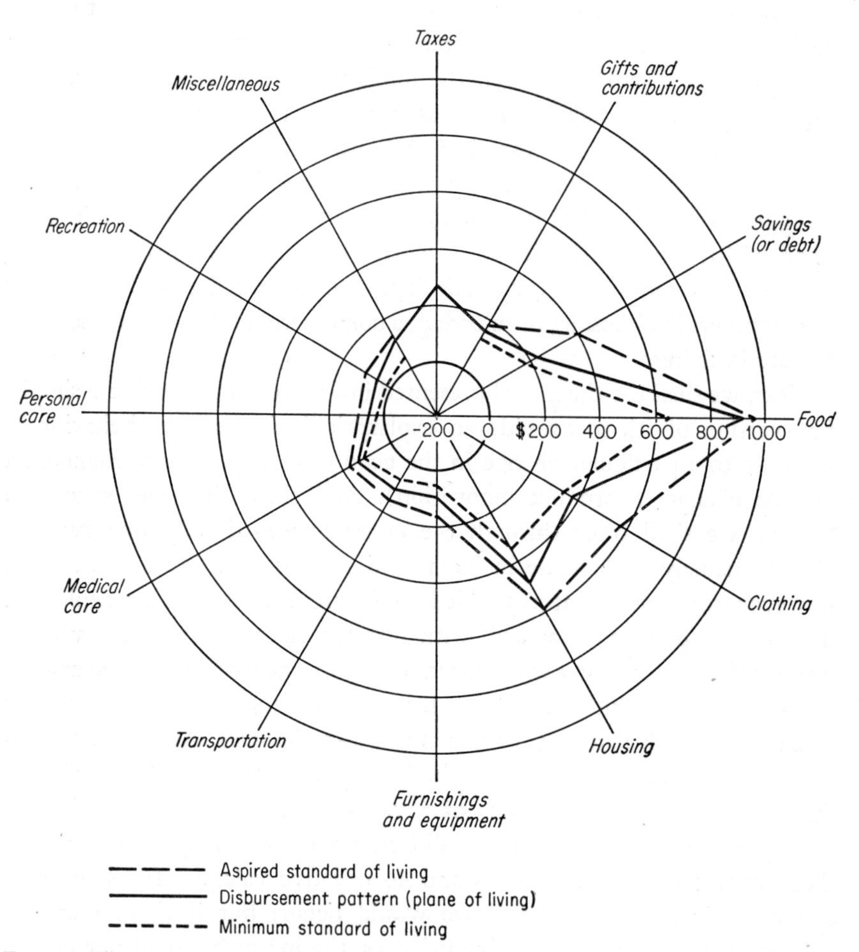

FIG. 9-1. The disbursement pattern for a middle-income consuming unit as of 1944, with hypothetical relationships to aspired standards and minimum standards of living.

is for all of Consumer C's expenditures to remain unchanged and for the rate of saving to decline by the full amount of the income decline (X amount). For purposes of illustration it is assumed that (1) the psychological effect of the income decline is to add *temporarily* 1 negative valence to each category of expenditure and (2) the cash-balance effect is to add 4 negative valences in most categories of expenditure, savings and transportation being the exceptions (see chart *B*, Figure 9-2). This moves Consumer C over the reaction threshold for the categories food

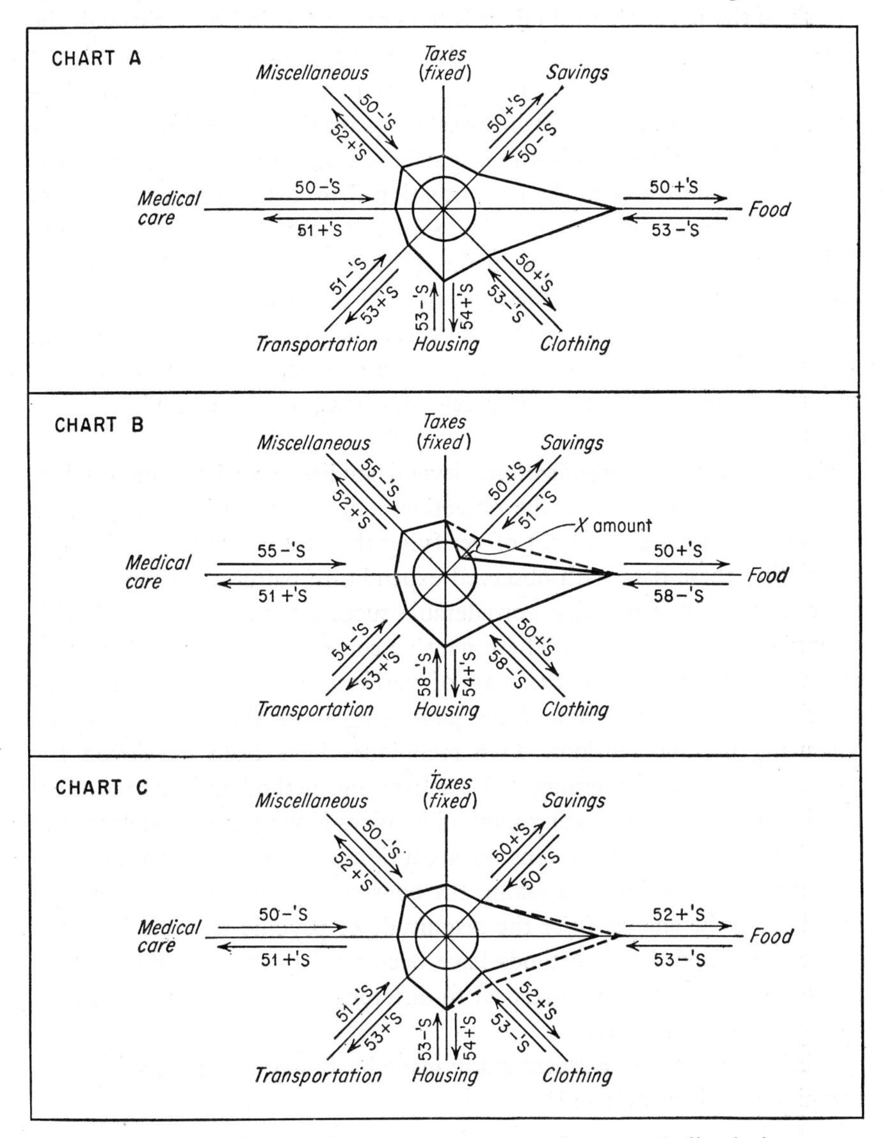

FIG. 9-2. Vector diagrams showing consumer reactions to a decline in income.

and clothing; the negative valences exceed the positive valences by more than 5 for each of these items.

In the final situation, Consumer C reduces his expenditure for food and clothing by the amount of the income decrease (X amount), and the rate of savings returns to that of the initial situation (see chart C, Figure 9-2). But since the psychological effect is temporary (lasting only through the intermediary situation) and since the free cash balance is restored, the negative valences for each category revert to their original values. Consumer C is, however, purchasing smaller quantities of food and clothing in the final situation than in the original; hence, the positive valences for these items are greater in the final situation than in the original. Increases in the positive valences for these items are not, however, sufficiently large to induce any further changes in the disbursement pattern. Thus, a new equilibrium with respect to the allocations of funds is given for Consumer C in chart C (Figure 9-2). And the vector analysis has been employed in a hypothetical situation to describe, hence explain, the nature of a consumer response to an economic stimulus (i.e., a decline in consumer income).

Measurement and verification. Several studies have been undertaken over the past decade with the objectives (1) of measuring the psychic tensions of consumers and (2) of verifying the vector hypothesis through correlating these data with observed expenditure patterns. Proponents of the vector analysis feel that considerable success has been achieved with respect to both objectives. There may be some question with respect to the successes achieved in the way of verification, but there can be no question of the importance of the pioneering work done in the way of measuring psychic tensions. Two techniques have been developed for measuring consumer tensions, (1) a self-rating method and (2) an inferential method. The self-rating method involves having the person rate the magnitude of his own tensions on a centigrade thermometer scale. The inferential method involves asking the consumer particular questions and then having the analyst *infer* the magnitude of psychic tensions from the answers received. Both methods have been used to measure the psychic tensions of consumers with respect to different food items, and both have strong and weak points.

A brief summary of a recent study made by Bilkey using the self-rating technique is given below: [10]

The research project herein described was conceived as a pilot study having the following basic objectives: (1) to ascertain the general validity of the

[10] "The Vector Hypothesis: A Psychological Approach to Consumer Behavior Analysis."

(psychological) vector hypothesis of consumer behavior, and (2) to determine whether the relationships postulated by it are amenable to objective measurement. For it 63 families were selected who had indicated a willingness to keep expenditure records for one year and to be interviewed once every month during that time.[11] Most of them were connected with the University of Connecticut and lived around the Storrs area, however, 12 of the families (mostly business) were from New London, Connecticut. Each interview involved having the family purchasing head evaluate his or her psychic feelings regarding each of their major disbursement categories (though major attention was given to food) on a modified Allport-Vernon Value Scale. The month's expenditures for these different categories then were obtained during the next interview. Since the interviews were taken as close to the middle of each month as circumstances permitted, the psychological testing preceded the month's aggregate expenditures. Once the interview and expenditure data were obtained, the analysis simply involved making correlations of the families' psychic feelings during successive months with their actual expenditures during those months, and correlations of these psychic feelings with various relevant events such as income changes, price changes, etc.

This bulletin presents data only for food as a whole, and for meat, milk and eggs each separately. For each, a relationship was found between the psychic tension ratings obtained by interview and actual purchases made. As postulated by the vector hypothesis, the reaction threshold did manifest itself–only slightly for food as a whole but strongly for milk. Evidence indicates that these families tended to think of both meat and of food as a whole in monetary terms (i.e., dollars worth purchased) and of eggs in physical terms (i.e., dozens purchased). The price of milk did not change sufficiently during the period of this study to indicate how the families tended to purchase that. The above mentioned findings imply that the concept of psychic tensions (the heart of the vector hypothesis) is meaningful with respect to consumer purchasing activities, and that these tensions are objectively measurable. Thus an affirmative answer tentatively is provided to the two questions with which this project was basically concerned.

Questions and Points for Discussion

1. Why is the measurement of utility so important to consumption economics? Is the risk approach followed by Mosteller and Nogee in the measurement of the utility of money likely to yield useful results for particular commodities?

[11] Of these households, 45 were interviewed once a month for 12 months, 8 for 6–11 months, and 10 for 1–5 months. All of these interviews did not run concurrently.

2. Describe the key ideas in the Norris approach.

3. Describe the key ideas in the Katona approach.

4. In what ways do these approaches supplement the received theory presented in Chapters 6 and 7, and in what ways are they in conflict?

5. What is vector analysis? What roles does the desire-resistance conflict play in the choice of goods? What is disbursement efficiency? How do disbursement rigidities influence disbursement efficiency?

6. Can the vector analysis approach be made operational?

References

Bilkey, Warren J.: "A Psychological Approach to Consumer Demand Analysis," *The Journal of Marketing*, July, 1953.

Boulding, Kenneth E.: *A Reconstruction of Economics*, John Wiley & Sons, Inc., New York, 1950, chap. 8.

Clawson, Joseph: "Lewin's Vector Psychology and the Analysis of Motives in Marketing," in Reavis Cox and Wroe Alderson (eds.), *Theory in Marketing*, Richard D. Irwin, Inc., Homewood, Ill., 1950.

Katona, George: *Psychological Analysis of Economic Behavior*, McGraw-Hill Book Company, Inc., 1951, chaps. 4–6.

Norris, Ruby Turner: *The Theory of Consumer's Demand*, Yale University Press, New Haven, Conn., 1941, chap. VI.

10. The Use of Consumption Minima

The appraisal of the received theory of consumer behavior presented in Chapter 8 made it clear that consumption economists were in need of a theory that is more general and that is operational. By more general, we mean a theory which does not reduce to nonsense as consumption items become large and lumpy and which takes account of group decision making. By operational, we mean a theory that admits of measurement and testing, hence that may be used in problematic situations to guide decision making at both the group and individual consuming-unit levels. Implicit in the above thought is the idea of utility maximization: it is assumed that a recommendation, or guide, to decision making will be furnished only when it contributes to an increase in the total satisfaction of the consuming unit (or units) involved. But the authors know of no theory of consumer behavior which is both general and operational, and although some interesting and important developments are occurring in the field of consumption economics, they see no such theory on the near or distant horizon.

It seems appropriate, therefore, to suggest a direct-action approach which makes use of the insights gained from the theoretical formulations presented in Chapters 6 and 7, as well as the newer developments sketched in Chapter 9, but which does not grow directly out of any of those approaches. The objective of this approach becomes the *minimization of consumer disutility*, rather than the maximization of consumer utility. The validity of the approach rests on the following lines of reasoning: Since we cannot at present measure consumer utility functions, hence are unable to recommend combinations of goods and services that maximize total satisfaction, but since minimum standards of consumption (i.e., consumption minima) can be established in certain consumption lines, let us use these standards to evaluate and appraise actual consumption patterns. The operational pieces—the mechanics—to be established under this approach are, then, the *minimum standards of consumption* (e.g., for food, housing, education, medicine).

CONSUMPTION MINIMA—THEIR LOGICAL BASES

Consumption deficiencies. The presentation of reliable measures of the extent and intensity of consumption deficiencies in the United States is not an easy task, for numerous reasons. First and foremost, a consumption deficiency is ascertainable only in terms of some standard; thus, a review of the extent and intensity of consumption deficiencies to provide a measure of the underconsumption problem leads directly into the construction and use of consumption standards, the latter of which is the subject of this entire chapter. Second, the empirical problem of measuring actual consumption in all lines for any group of consumers, and relating that data to given standards, however obtained, is a vast one. In this preliminary section, we shall deal with the first problem by accepting whatever consumption standard the original researcher employed. And the second problem is reduced to size by limiting the discussion to food, housing, and health. By this admittedly rough procedure, it is possible to gain a picture of the problematic aspects of consumption deficiencies in certain key lines.

Let us look first at the nature and extent of dietary deficiencies among American consumers. Such a descriptive picture is presented in Tables 10-1 and 10-2, where the actual food consumed per day by households in 1948 is converted to nutritive values (e.g., protein, calcium) and compared with the recommended dietary allowances of the National Research Council. The influence of income on the adequacy of diets, hence by implication on deficiencies, is made clear in Table 10-1. It will be observed that a large percentage of urban families in all income classes were deficient in the consumption of calcium in 1948. In most other lines (e.g., protein, riboflavin, and ascorbic acid), the percentage of families deficient in consumption is greatest in the lower-income classes and declines with rising incomes. A comparable story emerges from Table 10-2. Calcium is underconsumed by a large percentage of families at each family size. But, in general, the percentage of families deficient in the consumption of calories and nutrients increases with the size of family.

A careful study of Tables 10-1 and 10-2 thus leads to the following general conclusions: (1) lack of knowledge or interest, rather than limited incomes, leads to consumption deficiencies in some dietary lines (e.g., calcium); (2) in general, dietary deficiencies are inversely correlated with income—increasing with declining incomes; (3) given average incomes, dietary deficiencies increase with size of family, suggesting once again the limiting influence of income.

Table 10-1. *Adequacy of Diets and Size of Income: Percentage of Urban Families Having Diets Meeting National Research Council's Recommended Allowances for Calories and Eight Nutrients, Housekeeping Families of Two or More Persons in the United States, Spring, 1948*

Annual-income class (1947 income after Federal income tax)	Food energy, 3000 cal or more	Protein, 70 g or more	Calcium, 1 g or more	Iron, 12 mg or more	Vitamin A value, 5000 I.U. or more	Thiamin,* 1.5 mg or more	Riboflavin,* 1.8 mg or more	Niacin,* 15 mg or more	Ascorbic acid,* 75 mg or more
All classes..........	79	89	58	87	86	78	84	80	79
Under $1,000.......	70	66	40	76	72	72	65	68	56
$1,000–$1,999.......	77	83	50	86	78	72	79	78	69
2,000– 2,999.......	75	87	56	87	86	78	83	78	76
3,000– 3,999.......	83	93	62	90	87	82	88	81	82
4,000– 4,999.......	83	95	59	88	94	79	88	86	83
5,000– 7,499.......	79	93	64	88	90	81	89	88	88
$7,500 and over.....	76	92	61	88	99	76	87	85	92

* Estimated average cooking losses were deducted from the aggregate value of foods consumed.

SOURCE: *Nutritive Content of City Diets*, U.S. Department of Agriculture, Bureau of Human Nutrition and Home Economics, Special Report 2, October, 1950, p. 2. The nutritive value per nutrition unit (physically active man) per day of food consumed at home by each household was computed and then compared with the National Research Council's recommended dietary allowances for a physically active man (revised 1948).

Table 10-2. *Adequacy of Diets and Size of Family: Percentage of Urban Families Having Diets Meeting National Research Council's Recommended Allowances for Calories and Eight Nutrients, Housekeeping Families of Two or More Persons in the United States, Spring, 1948*

Family size	Food energy, 3000 cal or more	Protein, 70 g or more	Calcium, 1 g or more	Iron, 12 mg or more	Vitamin A value, 5000 I.U. or more	Thiamin,* 1.5 mg or more	Riboflavin,* 1.8 mg or more	Niacin,* 15 mg or more	Ascorbic acid,* 75 mg or more
2..........	85	91	63	89	85	81	87	85	83
3..........	79	92	64	88	91	77	87	81	82
4..........	79	88	57	87	88	78	85	78	83
5 or more..	70	83	42	84	82	73	76	76	66

* Estimated average cooking losses were deducted from the aggregate value of foods consumed.

SOURCE: *Nutritive Content of City Diets*, U.S. Department of Agriculture, Bureau of Human Nutrition and Home Economics, Special Report 2, October, 1950, p. 15. The nutritive value per nutrition unit (physically active man) per day of the food consumed at home by each household was computed and compared with the National Research Council's recommended dietary allowances for the physically active man (revised 1948).

Turning to expenditures for health, two types of consumption data will be presented: (1) community expenditures for public health programs and (2) number of hospital beds. In Table 10-3, estimates developed by the

Table 10-3. *Per Capita Health-department Expenditures Adjusted for Cost of Living in Eleven Large Cities, 1948*

City	Per capita health-department expenditure	
	Minimum need adjusted for cost of living *	Actual expenditure, 1948
Baltimore	$1.62	$1.53
Boston	1.64	1.60
Buffalo	1.54	1.74
Cleveland	1.59	1.26 †
Detroit	1.63	1.13
Milwaukee	1.64	1.66
New Orleans	1.50	1.04
Philadelphia	1.57	0.98
Pittsburgh	1.63	1.54 †
St. Louis	1.61	1.64 †
Washington	1.71	2.40

* Based on need of $1.50 for city having lowest cost-of-living index (New Orleans).
† Expenditures for 1949.
SOURCE: "Expenditures of Health Departments in Large Cities," *Public Health Reports*, vol. 67, no. 3, p. 281, March, 1952.

American Public Health Association of the minimum per capita expenditure for public health services are compared with actual expenditures in 11 cities. In this comparison, only 4 of the 11 cities (Buffalo, Milwaukee, St. Louis, Washington) make expenditures for public health services which ensure the provision of the minimum level of such services. And none of the cities reaches a level of expenditure for public health services —$3 to $3.75 per capita—which the American Public Health Association defines as an adequate expenditure.

The disparity between available supply (consumption) and need with respect to hospital beds is more dramatic than that for public health services. And since the number of hospital beds per 1,000 population serves as the principal indicator of hospital service, the important disparity between available supply and need is perhaps more disquieting. The Hill-Burton standard, as set by the Public Health Service Act, is 4.5 to 5.5 beds per 1,000 population for general hospitals, 5 beds per 1,000 population for mental diseases, 2 beds per 1,000 population for chronic diseases, and 2.5 beds per average annual deaths from tuberculosis over a five-year base period.

No state by 1952 had met the Hill-Burton standard in all four bed categories, and only three states in sparsely settled areas (Montana, North Dakota, and Nevada) had met that minimum standard for the general category. These data—the standard per 1,000 and existing beds per 1,000—for the United States as a whole are shown in the accompanying table.[1] The extreme need for hospital beds for patients having mental and chronic diseases is reflected in the low ratios for these categories.

	General	Mental	Tuberculosis	Chronic
Hill-Burton standard.....	4.5	5.0	2.5	2.0
Existing beds per 1,000 population...........	3.2	2.8	1.6	0.3

It is more difficult to define and establish standards with respect to housing than with respect to nutrition or health, but the Housing and Home Finance Agency of the Federal government defines *housing need* as follows: [2] it ". . . is nothing more than an indication of how much safe, sanitary, acceptable housing we will need by some future *date* if all the families who will want housing are to have decent homes." Applying this working definition to the housing inventory conducted by the Bureau of the Census in 1950, the following measure of deficient or substandard housing is derived:

Total nonfarm housing units reported.................		37,611,000
Standard units.....................................		31,312,000
Substandard units................................		6,299,000
Dilapidated..........................	2,756,000	
Lack bath or toilet....................	3,543,000	

[1] "Hospital Beds in the United States," *Public Health Reports*, Federal Security Agency, March, 1952.

[2] *How Big Is the Housing Job*, Housing and Home Finance Agency, 1951.

In other words, the Housing and Home Finance Agency found some 6 million housing units in the United States in 1950 which failed to meet the standard of adequacy set forth by that agency.

The analysis of future housing needs by the Housing and Home Finance Agency is perhaps of greater interest (see Table 10-4). Construction

Table 10-4. *Nonfarm Housing Units Needed in the United States in 1960*

Number of nonfarm families which will require housing in 1960		41,625,000
Add:	Allowance for 4 per cent vacancy rate for rent and sale	1,675,000
	Total supply needed in 1960	43,300,000
Subtract:	Estimated effective supply as of 1950	37,314,000
	Net additional units needed by 1960 to keep up with the rate of family formation	5,986,000
Add:	Total replacement and rehabilitation needed	8,400,000
	Total nonfarm new construction, conversion and rehabilitation needed by 1960	14,386,000

SOURCE: *How Big Is the Housing Job*, Housing and Home Finance Agency, 1951.

activity of all types—new, conversion, and rehabilitation—will be required on some 14.5 million dwelling units by 1960 if the estimated need for housing is to be satisfied adequately. Such a volume of construction activity far exceeds the amount anticipated by the Housing and Home Finance Agency. The prospects for 1960 thus are for a volume of unsatisfied housing needs equal to or greater than that in 1950. In other words, consumption deficiencies in housing have been, are, and are expected to continue to be widespread.

In retrospect, consumption deficiencies in food and nutrition, health and housing would seem to be real and widespread; this conclusion derives from a comparison of actual consumption with regularly used standards in the respective fields. In some instances, the observed deficiencies would appear to grow out of inadequate knowledge or lack of interest; this could be inferred to be a partial explanation of the widespread underconsumption of calcium and the failure to spend $2 to $3 per capita per year on public health services. But the more general and more important cause of consumption deficiencies in these fields is to be found in the limiting factor income. Certainly this is the case for diets in general and for housing.

Now, if the standards employed in the various investigations reviewed above are valid standards, the measures of consumption deficiencies cited must indicate the extent to which *the human beings involved are deteriorating or are unable to meet the numerous requirements imposed upon them by society*. In other words, if we can assume that the standards employed are valid, the measures of consumption deficiencies derived from the use of these standards become in fact measures of the extent to which individual beings are failing—failing personally in a physical or mental sense or failing organized society. Granted this interpretation, it seems reasonable and logical to recommend and facilitate consumption adjustments having the purpose of achieving in practice the accepted standards of consumption. This follows because, unless the consumption levels of the individuals involved are raised in some way to the defined standards, the individuals will be counted as failures by society. In sum, and in short, an objective measure of consumption involving kinds and quantities of goods and services has been forged which may be used in certain circumstances for recommending adjustments in consumption.

The question of freedom of consumer choice. It is reasonable to ask: "Does not the use of consumption minima to appraise and evaluate actual consumption patterns, and certainly where imposed, violate the fundamental value of freedom of choice?" The answer to this question is neither all white nor all black: it depends upon the type of social engineering employed. If the consumption deficiencies of consumers are eliminated as they are in the armed forces—through the specification of a particular bill of goods and services for all persons—then, of course, freedom of choice is dead.

But minimum standards of consumption need not be imposed with military rigor or specificity; they can in most instances be set forth in general terms wherein the choice of the particular bill of goods is left to the consumer. Nutrition standards are a case in point. Recommended quantities are specified in terms of broad food group wherein the choice of particular items is left to the consumer (see Table 10-5). Further, the use of minimum standards may in many cases make the choice process more effective—help the consumer make the actual choices that he really wants to make. This follows from the inherent nature of the problem of consumer choice. It will be remembered from the analysis of the central problem of choice in Chapter 5 that the choice problem is divided into two parts, (1) the selection of particular wants to be satisfied and (2) the selection of actual goods and services to satisfy the want pattern under

(1) above. Now it can be, and may often be, the case that a consumer makes a decision with respect to a particular want to be satisfied and then has insufficient technical knowledge to select the combination of goods and services which adequately satisfy that want. Or he may lack the income to afford the goods or services required to satisfy a legitimate want (e.g., medical service).

Take, for purposes of illustration, the consuming unit that decides that it wants a nutritionally adequate diet, but (1) it is at the bottom of the income scale and (2) it does not in fact have sufficient technical knowledge to choose a combination of foods which achieves nutritional adequacy. In this case, the establishment of a minimum standard of nutritional adequacy in terms of calories and the various nutrients (e.g., protein, calcium, vitamins, etc.) and the conversion of these nutrient requirements into food combinations at different levels of cost to serve as an informational guide to the family in question in no sense impairs free consumer choice. And an action program designed to assist the consuming unit to obtain some combination of foods of its choice which meets the test of nutritional adequacy need not impair free consumer choice. On the contrary, the establishment of and dissemination of information concerning nutritional standards would help this consuming unit realize the first and basic choice made by it, namely, to obtain a nutritionally adequate diet. And the operation of a food program which made it possible for the consuming unit to acquire a bill of goods that previously was denied to it by reason of its low income would certainly help this consuming unit to realize the first and basic choice made by it, namely, to obtain a nutritionally adequate diet.

In the field of housing, it is obvious to all concerned that there are many, many families living in dilapidated shacks across the country who want better housing, need better housing, but cannot afford decent housing. In this common case, it cannot be argued that a housing program which would make it possible for the families involved to obtain adequate housing would limit their freedom of choice. Their freedom of choice is circumscribed first and foremost by low income. It might be argued with some reason that the resources of the economy were too limited to provide all consuming units with adequate housing or that the consuming units involved would not conserve and maintain houses provided them under some sort of subsidized program. But it would be the worst kind of sophistry to argue that a program having the goal of providing each family with a minimum standard of housing would at the same time restrict its freedom of choice. On the contrary, this would widen its field of choices.

The consuming unit with an income of between $5,000 and $10,000 building its first house provides an interesting case study. The first and basic decision of the consuming unit is concerned with the selection of some particular type of shelter at some approximate cost. But anyone who has gone through the misery of building his first house will appreciate the need of this consuming unit for technical assistance, and not the type that the building contractor is likely to provide. There are the obvious technical problems concerned with the type or style of house and the quality of materials to be used, but there are other and more complex problems: the room layout needed for a family of a given age and sex composition (or a prospective family); to have or not to have a basement; the method of assessing taxes in the area involved; the type of heat to install; and so on. A long and tortuous path, liberally strewn with pitfalls, runs between the original and basic decision to build a house and the *combining* of a vast variety of materials and services into a particular structure called a house. And it is not improbable that the final combination of wood, bricks, tile, wiring, rooms, etc., which we call a house is not what the family in question *want*. They may well have a house on their hands which does not meet their basic needs, hence they do not want. If this family, and the many more like them to come, could obtain more information concerning the space needs of the family, storage needs, traffic flows, etc., there would be more families who in the purchase or construction of a house satisfied their basic want for housing.

In short, the socioeconomic goal of free consumer choice is somewhat more complex than most Fourth of July orators and newspaper editors are inclined to make it. It seems clear that two distinct steps are involved in the choice process, (1) the selection of wants to be satisfied and (2) the selection of goods and services to satisfy the wants chosen. And, in some areas of consumption, it is a long and difficult route from step 1 to step 2. In some instances, lack of knowledge creates a barrier between steps 1 and 2. But, in more instances, lack of income working in conjunction with lack of knowledge creates the barrier between steps 1 and 2. The freedom of choice in step 1 is often imprisoned and sometimes perverted by restricted income and inadequate knowledge before manifesting itself in step 2.

SOURCE OF THE STANDARDS

The question arises: "Who should formulate these standards?" Certainly, it would not be, and in fact has not been, the task of economists concerned with consumer problems to formulate minimum standards of consumption. We would expect those standards to be developed within each science the discipline of which relates to human wants (e.g., nutrition, medicine and physiology, education). And, without too much conscious direction, minimum standards of consumption have been developing within several scientific areas from the research and education going on in those areas.

Perhaps more has been accomplished in the field of food and nutrition than in any other in the way of setting forth consumption requirements. We use the general term *consumption requirements* advisedly here because, in the field of food and nutrition, requirements are sometimes set forth in absolute minimal terms and sometimes in terms of allowances suitable for the maintenance of good nutrition, depending upon the situation and the social objectives. Dietary requirements exist both in terms of specific nutrient requirements and in terms of food combinations which satisfy these requirements. The responsibility for establishing, and periodically revising, the set of specific nutrients required per person in good nutrition has been assumed in the United States by the National Research Council; these requirements the NRC calls Recommended Daily Dietary Allowances.[3] And numerous agencies, such as the Bureau of Human Nutrition and Home Economics of the U.S. Department of Agriculture, spin these allowances into diet plans under varying conditions of costs, physical activity, age, sex, and so on.[4] In some cases, diet plans are spelled out in detail, but, in the usual case, the recommended quantities are indicated only for the principal food groups (see Table 10-5). The choice of particular food items is left to the consuming unit concerned. Thus, a wide area of freedom of choice is reserved to the consuming unit under step 2 of the choice problem even where the consuming unit follows the recommendations set forth in the consumption standard.

But knowledge is accumulating in other areas of consumption which can be or is being developed into minimum standards. The Public Health

[3] Revised in 1953 by the Food and Nutrition Board of the National Research Council. See their *Recommended Dietary Allowances, Revised 1953,* Publication 302.

[4] See *Nutrition up-to-date up-to-you,* U.S. Department of Agriculture, Home and Garden Bulletin 1, 1950.

Table 10-5. A Nutritionally Adequate Food Plan with Quantities for One Week

Food group	For children 1–6 years	For children 7–12 years	For girls 13–20 years	For boys 13–20 years	For women		For men, all activities
					All activities	Pregnant and nursing	
Leafy, green, and yellow vegetables, pounds	2–2½	2½–3	3½	3½–4	3½–4	4	3½–4
Citrus fruits, tomatoes, pounds	2–2½	2½–3	3	3–3½	2½–3	3½–4½	2½–3½
Potatoes, sweet potatoes, pounds	½–1	1½–2	2½	3½–4½	2–3	2–3	3–5
Other vegetables and fruits, pounds	2	2½	3½	3½	3–4	3–3½	3–4
Milk, cheese, ice cream, quarts	6	7	6–7 *	7	5	7½–10½	5
Meat, poultry, fish,† pounds	1–1¼	2	2½–3	3	2½–3	3	3–3½
Eggs	6–7	7	7	7	6–7	7	6–7
Dry beans and peas, nuts, ounces	1	2	2	4–6	2–4	2	4
Baked goods, flour, cereals, whole grain, enriched or restored, pounds	1–1½	2–3	2½–3 *	4–5	2–4	2–2½	3–7
Fats, oils, pounds	¼	½–1	¾	1–1½	¾–1	¾	1–2
Sugar, sirups, preserves, pounds	¼–½	¾	1	1–1½	¾–1	¾	1–1½

* Larger quantities are for the younger girls.

† To meet the iron allowance needed by children 1 to 6 years, girls 13 to 20, and pregnant and nursing women, include weekly one large or two small servings of liver or other organ meats.

SOURCE: *Nutrition up-to-date up-to-you*, U.S. Department of Agriculture, Home and Garden Bulletin 1, February, 1950, pp. 14–15.

Service and other organizations concerned with medicine and health know what we need in the way of hospital facilities, beds, nurses, and doctors per thousand population to maintain the health of the population at a minimum standard. Educators know how much room space and how many teachers are required per hundred or thousand children to maintain a minimum standard. Admittedly, the degree of objectivity may be at a lower level in setting minimum standards for education than for diets and nutrition, since it is more difficult to establish objective units of measure for education than for such things as calories, protein, and the various vitamins. But this is not to say that a minimum standard for education is less important than for food or that such a standard cannot be established. There must be a level of education below which the individual is seriously handicapped in the interdependent, commercial world of the 1950s, and it would seem to be the responsibility of people working in education to determine this level, which indeed they have tried to do on many occasions. Further, considerable work has been done in such consumption categories as clothing and housing in the way of specifying consumption minima.

In addition to the work taking place in specific categories of consumption, several important efforts have been made to set forth minimum standards of living or, in some cases, yardstick budgets for workingwomen [5] and working families.[6] In all cases, the complete family budgets which have been formulated have not been *minimum* budgets; in some cases, they are more nearly representative of accepted standards at different income levels. But the experience gained in these attempts to formulate complete standards of living could be used to establish a minimum standard of living.

Consumption standards can never be precise and objective in the sense that 2 times 2 equals 4. This follows for the significant reason that "man does not live by bread alone." He is a social animal, and as a social animal he has developed forms of activity (e.g., writing) which he considers indispensable to group living. Hence, proficiency in writing becomes a part of the minimum standard for education. The level of proficiency in writing may be subject to debate, but not the judgment that a man should

[5] *Minimum-wage Budgets for Women,* U.S. Department of Agriculture, Miscellaneous Publication 549, 1944.

[6] "The City Worker's Family Budget," *Monthly Labor Review,* February, 1948; and *Quantity and Cost Budgets for Three Income Levels,* University of California, Heller Committee for Research in the Social Sciences, Berkeley, Calif., 1950.

be able to write. And so with most forms of consumption. A minimum standard, to find use and acceptance in society, must take into account factors other than purely physical ones. It must recognize and be developed in terms of accepted standards of consumption, physical productivity, economic costs, social mores, and so on. Hence, we can never expect to obtain complete agreement on any particular minimum standard. But sufficient work has already been done and sufficient experience has already been gained to indicate that reasonable standards can be established in the more important categories of consumption.

One interesting experiment in the derivation of a minimum standard of consumption should perhaps be recounted at this point. In 1945, George J. Stigler set out to determine the cost and quantities involved in a "truly minimum cost diet." In other words, where only physical requirements and costs (product prices) are considered—no attention is paid to social and environmental considerations—what are the specifications of a minimum-cost diet? The results of his inquiry for the years 1939 and 1944 are set forth in Table 10-6. The diets for both years are clearly antisocial. Except under the threat of starvation, consumers in the United States could not be made to follow these diet plans even though each is, technically speaking, nutritionally adequate. And this, of course, is what Stigler wanted to show (he may also have had larger hopes; he may have

Table 10-6. *Minimum-cost Annual Diets for a Moderately Active Man*

Commodity	August, 1939		August, 1944	
	Quantity	Cost	Quantity	Cost
Wheat flour	370 lb	$13.33	535 lb	$34.53
Evaporated milk	57 cans	3.84		
Cabbage	111 lb	4.11	107 lb	5.23
Spinach	23 lb	1.85	13 lb	1.56
Dried navy beans	285 lb	16.80		
Pancake flour	.....	.....	134 lb	13.08
Pork liver	.....	.....	25 lb	5.48
Total cost	.....	$39.93	.....	$59.88

SOURCE: George J. Stigler, "The Cost of Subsistence," *Journal of Farm Economics*, vol. 27, no. 2, May, 1945.

hoped to show the lack of objectivity, hence lack of value, in any sort of consumption standard). But the significant conclusion to be drawn from his work is the following: A consumption standard to have meaning for society must be developed in terms of all of those things which society values—cultural and environmental factors as well as physical factors.

USE OF THE STANDARDS

Once the consumption minima are established, their use is obvious. The consumption levels defined as minimum standards become the norms against which actual patterns of consumption are compared. Where actual consumption in any line is greater than the defined minimum, this approach contributes knowledge with respect to that fact, *but nothing further in the way of implications for adjustments.* But where actual consumption in any line falls below the defined minimum, we can suggest (1) the direction in which consumption adjustments need to occur and (2) the magnitude of these adjustments. Here, then, is an operational concept—an approach which can be used directly to modify or direct or adjust patterns of consumption.

The operational steps under this approach are clear:

1. The development and establishment of consumption minima
2. The use of the defined minima as measuring rods against which actual consumption is compared
3. The effecting of consumption adjustments where actual consumption falls below the defined minima

The key analytical idea under this approach is the establishment of minimum standards of consumption *in measured units.* Once the standards are specified in measured units, a measuring rod is established for appraising and evaluating actual consumption. This is the piece of the "jigsaw puzzle" that was missing in the theory of consumer behavior presented in Chapters 6 and 7. Once measurement is introduced, consumption norms enter the picture. The norms in this case take the form of minimum standards of consumption: where the defined minima are not realized, some form of human failure results. *Thus the analysis ceases to be purely descriptive; it becomes normative.* Out of this type of analysis grow recommendations for action with reference to what consumers *ought* to consume.

It needs, however, to be recognized that the nature of this approach entails certain limitations. It does not represent perfection; it is operational, but it falls in the class of halfway measures. This is true because the approach cannot be *used* to effect consumption adjustments which maximize total satisfaction. The value of the approach resides in its potential for eradicating weak or sore spots in current patterns of living. Such a potential is not to be taken lightly, but it also is true that the potential falls short of assuring maximum satisfaction for any particular consumer or all of society.

Individual responsibility. The approach that we have been considering has important implications for individual consuming units. The responsibility for effecting consumption adjustments within individual consumng units in a free society must ultimately reside in the consuming units involved. Where, for example, a consuming unit discovers from comparing its particular pattern of consumption with the established consumption minima that it is seriously underconsuming some item, say foods which provide body calcium, but is overconsuming some other item, say sugar, it alone must consider the consequences of alternative courses of action and decide on the type or manner of adjustment, if any.

In short, this general approach in no way absolves the individual consuming unit from decision making. One of the basic objectives of the approach is the provision of information for use or consideration in choice decisions. Thus, it would seem reasonable to expect that the dissemination of information concerning minimum standards of consumption would have the effect of increasing the proportion of consciously considered, or weighed, choice decisions among consumers; where relevant, such information should have the effect of jarring consumers out of habitual patterns of consumption and inducing them to consciously consider their choices.

Implications for group action. The implications of this approach, which may not be readily apparent but which flow directly out of the nature of the approach, are those for group action. Three lines of group action would seem to form an integral part of the approach. The first is concerned with the development and establishment of the consumption minima. Individual consuming units will generally lack the resources and the prestige necessary to establish minimum standards which have general acceptance. The advances in knowledge and techniques out of which minimum standards are formulated occur most generally in research and educational institutions. The biochemist studying the properties of flour or the bacteriologist studying the properties of milk will not be some fellow huddled over a Rube Goldberg contraption in his basement; he will be a member of a research team in a government research bureau, a large corporation, or a university department. And the proclamation of a minimum standard by a Mrs. John Smith does not in fact establish a minimum. Consumption minima become established, first, through the efforts of recognized scientific or educational bodies and, later, through the force of convention or law. But first must come the pioneering efforts —group efforts—of highly respected organizations. So we see that consumption minima are not likely to leap full-blown into the world of ideas from the brain of a single individual. They are more likely to emerge through long and continuous group efforts.

The second type of action is that concerned with bringing the information concerning minimum standards to individual consumers for their consideration and action. There are many means, or techniques, for carrying information to the consumer (e.g., newspapers, group meetings, home demonstration), but who is to foot the bill? It is possible that private firms in certain cases would find it to their advantage to disseminate information concerning these minima. But such information is always open to suspicion; are these consumption minima objectively derived, or are they a part of some slick advertising scheme? These are the kinds of questions that would arise out of reliance on private advertising.

It seems clear that, if the minimum standards of consumption under consideration were to become (1) widely known and (2) generally accepted, they would have to be carried to the people through public agencies. These public agencies might take the form of the existing school and university systems, or extension services attached to universities, or specially established governmental agencies. But one thing seems certain: some collective decision making would be involved. Collective decisions would have to be made with respect to (1) how much information work should be done, (2) what agencies should do this work, and (3) how should it be financed. These are some of the kinds of group decisions that consumers would be forced to make, given the acceptance of the general policy of establishing consumption minima.

The third type of group action is concerned with action programs where the provision of information cannot or does not effect desired consumption adjustments. Action programs with the purpose of effecting consumption adjustments in accordance with the dictates of the defined minima could arise out of two types of situations, (1) where incomes are so low that the consuming units cannot purchase all the goods and services defined in the minima and (2) where a national emergency exists (e.g., war) and the use of resources for emergency purposes dictates rapid consumption adjustments.

If a family has insufficient income to purchase the goods and services defined in the minima for food, shelter, clothing, education, and medical care, no amount of information is going to solve the problem. If this family is to achieve the defined minimum standard of living, its income must be increased in some way—perhaps by a cash payment, perhaps by free goods and services, perhaps by a better-paying job, but in some way its income must be increased. And, without entering into a thorough analysis of the number of consumers that might be involved—particularly where a minimum standard of living has not been spelled out—it might be guessed that every family unit with one or more children in 1950 whose income was less than $1,000 could not have achieved a minimum level of living, and probably families with incomes up to $2,000 could not have achieved such a level. The number of families falling into these very low income classes in 1950 is given as follows: 1.5 million families with incomes less than $1,000 and 6.2 million families with incomes less than $2,000.[7]

Except in relatively few cases, we would not expect these families to improve their income situation by individual action in the short or medium run; they are families who either cannot (e.g., because they are sick, aged, or ignorant) or will not (e.g., because they are shiftless) earn an income which provides a minimum standard of living. *If, then, the bulk of these low-income consuming units are to achieve some minimum standard of living, this will have to occur through group action—through society taking action to provide these unfortunates with the goods and services that society says every individual should have.* Here, then, is another group decision which would have to be made. Should the group—society—develop programs (e.g., old-age pensions, food subsidies, medical subsidies, low-cost housing) to raise the level of living of low-income people to the defined minimum?

It should be recognized that a group decision having the aim of raising the level of living of disadvantaged consuming units imposes restrictions on other consuming units. The freedom of choice of more prosperous consuming units is restricted as their incomes are taxed away to aid the disadvantaged. Hence, this policy question is a controversial one; it is one where the interests of one group are hurt in some unknown degree

[7] U.S. Department of Commerce, *Survey of Current Business*, March, 1955, p. 25.

to enhance the well-being of another group in accordance with relatively objective standards. This is a question that cannot be resolved on logical grounds alone; it can be resolved only through those governmental and institutional processes created for such purposes.

In wartime, it is usually relatively easy to take group action if it is generally felt that such action is necessary to the war effort. It is not too difficult to visualize a situation where a group decision was made to reduce the level of consumption for all individuals to a defined minimum in certain categories of consumption. This is a choice that each consumer might be willing to make if he knew that everyone was sharing in the reduction, but not otherwise. So here is another case where the realization of the minimum—a reduction to the minimum—could be effected only through group action.

The key ideas with respect to the use of consumption minima may be summarized as follows: the group—society—can develop and establish minimum standards of consumption where those standards can be set forth with some degree of objectivity. The development and establishment of consumption minima in measured units lead logically to the use of those minima in normative comparisons with actual consumption. This in turn leads to the question to be resolved by the society: "Should the minimum standards be formalized into goals to be achieved?" If the decision is in the affirmative, as is usually the case in democratic societies, then the means, or measures, taken to achieve the goals will generally be group measures—government-action programs.

Questions and Points for Discussion

1. What is the purpose of the direct-action approach developed in this chapter? How does the purpose of this approach differ from that of the received theory of consumer behavior?
2. What bases exist, or what arguments may be advanced, for the use of consumption minima? Does the use of consumption minima violate the principle of free consumer choice?
3. What constitute the logical steps in the use of consumption minima?
4. Under this approach, what responsibilities are reserved to the individual consuming unit? What responsibilities must be assumed by the community or society?

References

Cochrane, Willard W.: *High-level Food Consumption in the United States*, U.S. Department of Agriculture Miscellaneous Publication 581, December, 1945.

Hansen, Alvin H., and Harvey S. Perloff: *State and Local Finance in the National Economy*, W. W. Norton & Company, Inc., New York, 1944, chap. 8.

How Big Is the Housing Job, Housing and Home Finance Agency, 1951.

Kellogg, Lester S., and Dorothy S. Brady: "The City Worker's Family Budget," *Monthly Labor Review*, vol. 66, no. 2, February, 1948.

Nutritive Content of City Diets, U.S. Department of Agriculture, Bureau of Human Nutrition and Home Economics, Special Report 2, October, 1950.

Recommended Dietary Allowances, Revised 1953, National Research Council Publication 302, 1953, pp. 1–22.

PART THREE

The Expenditure Approach to Consumer Behavior

During the nineteenth century, classical economists developed a theory of consumer behavior as part of their general theoretical structure. This theory in its modern form was presented in Part II. It was believed that, when quantitative data on consumer behavior became available, it could be inserted directly into the theoretical relationships and hence be used to predict consumer behavior. But the quantitative data on consumer behavior which were gathered did not reveal marginal utility functions or consumer preference.

The empirical approach implies something which is measurable—a quantity like output or price rather than a quality like newness or utility. Empirical investigations of consumption, therefore, dealt with real consumers and their actual choices, in terms of pounds of food, numbers of rooms, and the money costs of clothing or rent or heat. The development of statistical techniques during the latter part of the nineteenth century led to an accumulation of large numbers of data and to generalizations from the relationships observed in those data. In this part, we concentrate on the evidence from such investigations of consumer behavior.

The generalizations, or "laws," of consumption derived from statistical studies do not contradict the theory of consumer behavior. That consumers will seek to maximize utility, or to attain the highest preference level, remains true in the same sense that water seeks its own level. The actual behavior of water in a drainage ditch, a household plumbing system, a reservoir, or a river depends on many other variables. So does the actual behavior of consumers. The great contribution of empirical studies has been to distinguish these variables. In the following chapters, we describe the empirical approach and its findings, and the implications of consumer behavior for the economy as a whole.

11. The Development of Empirical Investigations

In this chapter, we recount briefly the origins and accomplishments of the empirical approach and describe some of the more important statistical investigations of consumption. All consumption studies have dealt with problems in methodology, and we shall look at some of the solutions.

One prefatory warning may be given: The statistical approach defines consumption, for the most part, in terms of money expenditures out of income, a definition which we recognize as narrowing (and in some ways complicating) the concepts with which this volume began. In order to collect expenditure data, a distinction has been made between consumption (as spending) and saving (as not spending). The theory of consumer behavior requires no such distinction, since saving has utility just as any product or service does. But we find in the division of income between spending and saving important implications for the economy as a whole, and an approach—sometimes called Keynesian or macroeconomic—that stresses heavily the role of consumer. We find, therefore, new reasons for investigating consumer behavior in terms of actual households and their actual decisions.

PIONEERING STUDIES

The early thinkers who were later to be called economists were first concerned with wealth and how to increase the wealth of an economy. Their interest in facts and figures developed the first approach to studying actual consumption patterns. Gregory King, an Englishman living in the seventeenth century, prepared the first detailed computation of a nation's wealth, which incidentally described levels of consumption. This study classified families and households in occupational categories, with the number of households in each grouping and the number of people in each household, and listed money figures of income and wealth, including homes, land, and household possessions. King's study still provides, together with other material from the same date, a description of consumption levels in England at that time. Today's statistical methods developed, however, not from similar censuses of entire economies at one time, but from more intensive studies of particular problems.[1]

Frédéric Le Play. Every student of consumption learns the name of Frédéric Le Play, mining engineer, social philosopher, and French patriot, who lived from 1806 to 1882. In studying the living conditions of European workers, he made the first detailed investigations of family income and expenditure and grappled with problems of definition and analysis which are familiar today. Le Play called himself a social scientist, rather than an economist or a student of consumption, and was chiefly interested in the problem of human happiness. His life spanned years of great social unrest following the French Revolution, when the development of industry, changes in laws and traditions, the rise of different social classes, and a new political balance of power shook the Continent. Le Play characterized developments in Europe as catastrophic and deplored the disappearance of all harmony. He searched, therefore, for a solution to a large problem. His profession as a mining engineer had given him great respect for the scientific method, and particularly for observation. In 1829, partly to fulfill the requirements of his technical education, he made a field trip through northern Germany, with the avowed intention of observing happy peoples and discovering the secret of their happiness. Other journeys followed, during which his techniques of recording data were improved and his case studies added to. For Le Play, the greatest outcome of his search was to find that "in order to heal social suffering, there is nothing to invent"; the factors of happiness have been known for centuries: [2]

> I call "prosperous" the societies where peace reigns without any recourse to armed force; where the stability of homes, of workshops, and of communities is assured by the free mutual agreement of the fathers of families; where, finally, the preservation of tradition, founded upon the mores, is the common wish of the population.

[1] Sir William Petty and later Frederick Eden in England investigated consumption among specific groups but lacked the precision or accuracy of later workers.

[2] These and subsequent quotations are taken from the only translation of Le Play's writings, a condensation of *Les Ouvriers européens*, vol. I, in Carle C. Zimmerman, and Merle E. Frampton, *Family and Society*, D. Van Nostrand Company, Inc., New York, 1935.

After his first book, *Les Ouvriers européens,* was published in 1855, he worked and wrote to further a program of social reform in France, based chiefly on the revival of tradition and customs which he believed had been wrongly abandoned. *La Réforme sociale,* published in 1864 at the request of Napoleon III, who wished to revive paternal authority, led finally to *L'Organisation du travail,* published in 1870. We cannot but feel that Le Play, the social reformer, must have died unhappy, with none of his ideas accepted, but Le Play, the social scientist, is remembered for his contribution to empirical sociological and economic studies.

His grandiose generalizations about happiness were, in fact, founded upon thorough observation. Reasoning from society as a whole to the family in particular, he argued that detailed investigations of individual workingmen were necessary.

> Everywhere happiness consists in the satisfaction of two principal needs imposed absolutely by the nature of man (daily bread and the essential mores). Among prosperous races these needs are assured by the social structure. When the social structure is weak, happiness is no longer present.
>
> The mores are fundamentally the same for all human races . . . the conditions of living afford to observers the most characteristic distinctions between societies.
>
> Since the family is the image of a society, observing the conditions of the workman enables us to understand the social constitutions. The workman is thus the main object of study. In simple societies workmen still form the majority of producers and consumers. . . . All of the acts which constitute the existence of a working family sooner or later tend to influence its income and its expenses.

Some 360 studies of individual families, therefore, disclosed to Le Play the differences between happiness and unhappiness, and each study began with a budget of income and expenditures. These budgets, besides providing factual information on living standards and their achievement in different communities and a description of general classes of society, forced Le Play to some methodological decisions still valid today. He recognized, for example, the importance of income in kind, the food or shelter received without money payment, or the food or clothing or furniture produced at home. He described the disposition of income by broad categories—expenditures on food, housing, clothing, household operation (heating, lighting, furniture, etc.), education, recreation, and health, and he was concerned with that part of income which was not spent, going to taxes, insurance, or savings. As a pioneer in methodology, then, Le Play influenced many of the research workers who followed.

Ernst Engel. One of the first to use Le Play's data was Christian Lorenz Ernst Engel, who lived from 1821 to 1896 in Germany. Born in Dresden, Engel also became a mining engineer, and Le Play's work must have appealed to him, not only because of his own interest in the field, but because of the similarity of their vocations. Engel's chief concern was with statistics: appointment to an official commission of inquiry on industry and labor in Saxony led to his becoming director of the Saxon statistical bureau and later to the same post in the Prussian statistical bureau. In these offices, he organized official statistics covering many facets of the economy. He originated and edited source books and yearbooks, improved procedures for the German census, and founded, in 1862, the German seminar of statistics and social science at Berlin, a group adding much to the practice and theory of statistics.

Methodology in consumption studies has benefited from Engel's work, particularly his analysis of the consumption unit. He recognized that total food expenditure could not be compared between families unless the ages of family members were taken into consideration. Consequently, he invented the quet (after Quételet, a Belgian social philosopher greatly respected by Engel) to represent the value of food consumed by a child less than one year old. A two-year-old child was then taken to represent 1.1 quets, a three-year-old 1.3, and so on, a figure of 3.5 being derived for an adult male and 3.1 for an adult female. This concept, with many refinements, plays an important role in consumption studies today.

Unlike Le Play, Engel was concerned not with metaphysical but with empirical generalization. He calculated, from Le Play's data and those of other workers, the percentages of total income spent on different categories of consumption and developed two famous "laws" which are associated with his name. The first states that, the poorer a family, the greater the proportion of total spending which goes for food purchases. From this fact, he concluded that, other things being equal, the percentage of total expenditure devoted to food gives the best indication of the material well-being of a people.

The second law developed the idea that incomes are first devoted to the necessities of staying alive and that luxury spending or saving occurs only at higher income levels. Concerned with improvements in living conditions during the industrial revolutions of his time, Engel suggested that a "normal" level of welfare might exist when "the rational physical upkeep costs consume no more than eighty per cent of the income, and when twenty per cent of the income can be considered as free-income." [3] This idea, too, has its modern counterparts: the term *discretionary spending* is closely related to the idea of "free income." Market research analysts compute the amount of income needed to satisfy a given standard of basic living and plan ways of guiding discretionary spending out of the remaining sum.

Later developments in the field of minimum consumption standards can also be traced to this law of Engel's, although social-welfare considerations loom large in today's determination of basic living costs. Engel, on the other hand, planned to work out the economic value of man in terms of his cost (basic consumption) and his productivity. The first publication on this subject, *Der Werth des Menschen,* appearing in 1833, was also the last, for the data were never published in complete form.

These two pioneers, Le Play and Engel, represent two approaches to family consumption and living: the detailed case study with a psychological and sociological view of Le Play and the compilation and analysis of mass data produced by Engel. Both have their modern followers, and both methods have their uses.

LATER DEVELOPMENTS—POVERTY AND BUDGETS

The nineteenth century was a period of great humanitarian reform movements, particularly in England, and those who wished to improve education, housing, nutrition, child care, and the conditions of labor were quick to use statistical arguments for their cause. Several monumental studies of poverty appear next in our story of consumption studies. Charles Booth was the author of *Life and Labour of the People in London,* describing data collected between 1886 and 1892, and this work prompted research in other areas. B. S. Rowntree investigated the town of York, publishing *Poverty: A Study of Town Life* in 1901, and A. L. Bowley made surveys in other English cities which were analyzed in *Poverty and Livelihood,* 1915.

Like previous research, these studies provided a mass of detailed description, much of which contributed to the growing social awareness of the times. But they also contained some hard thinking in the realm of

[3] Quoted from Engel's *Die Lebenstoken* (1895) by Carle C. Zimmerman, "Ernst Engel's Law of Expenditures for Food," *Quarterly Journal of Economics,* vol. 47, p. 83.

concepts and methodology. Booth's startling conclusion that 30 per cent of London's population lived "below the line of poverty" led to the analysis of poverty and ways to measure poverty. The student at this point may ask himself what the word *poverty* means—a common term, familiar to us all, and widely used if only to emphasize the difference between living conditions in the United States and those in other nations. It is likely that our readers will decide that true poverty implies insufficient income for the necessities of life. The concept of *need* is bound to creep into a definition of poverty at a very early stage. But then the question arises: What are needs, and what is an absolute necessity? [4] According to our ideas of decent sanitation, for example, probably 90 rather than 30 per cent of London's population in 1890 would have fallen below the line of poverty. It is evident that needs change and that poverty can be measured only with respect to the standards prevailing within the time and place of study.

Rowntree's efforts to distinguish between "primary" and "secondary" poverty led to these conclusions, as did the method used in these studies. The data collected on actual family income and expenditures were compared with the costs of a predetermined pattern of living. Rowntree then concluded that families in primary poverty lacked sufficient income for the minimum necessities included in a general standard applying to that family. Families in secondary poverty used their incomes in such a way as to omit some of the minimum necessities of this standard in favor of other types of expenditures, some of which he termed useful, such as extraordinary expenses for illness, and some of which, like drinking and gambling, he termed wasteful. In a later survey, Rowntree abandoned the attempt to measure secondary poverty, recognizing that the amount of individual judgment involved was more than could be justified.

Such research into the meaning of poverty led to other definitions. In the *Encyclopaedia of the Social Sciences*, poverty is defined in terms of five separate levels: insufficiency, minimum subsistence, health and decency, comfort, and luxury. Such a classification merely multiplies the evaluations involved, necessitating five standards, five independent judgments, to illustrate these terms. Another analysis of poverty is offered by Ferdinand Zweig, whose two investigations of British workingmen after

[4] The discussion in Chap. 10 pointed out the difficulties in defining minimum consumption needs and the slow development of objective standards. All of these standards, however, are of recent date.

World War II [5] are in some ways reminiscent of Le Play's intensive approach. Zweig suggests that our ideas of poverty are indeed value judgments but that these judgments arise from three different sources. "Felt poverty"—"an acute sensation of ill-being"—depends upon the individual's or family's judgment of its poverty, with respect to past history, social grouping, occupation, environment, and personal relations. Second, the impersonal judgment of science should provide a standard of poverty, in terms of minimum nutritional requirements, for example. Third, there is the judgment of society on poverty, the standard which impels social action when families fall below it.

All this reasoning requires us to accept the idea of change in our standards, a change reflected in today's mode of living contrasted with that of our grandfathers, so that the symbols of poverty are different, but poverty itself still exists. The words of the New Testament, "For the poor always ye have with you," find objective support in economic data:

> Critics have charged that the apparent stability in the volume of inadequate incomes results from shifting standards that change with the level of the average wage or the average income and they point out that even the poorest families today have comforts, unknown two or three generations ago. . . . The inevitable conclusion from this argument is that inadequate incomes can never be eliminated in any final sense because we as human beings always tend to judge incomes below the average as inadequate.[6]

> Our interest in consumption no longer focuses only on notions of adequacy; . . . necessities we have learned to define as expenditures for goods people will not do without.[7]

With the idea of relative standards, the attack on general poverty gave way to specific problems. Surveys of particular groups provided data for particular purposes. In the early years of the twentieth century appeared a succession of "budgets," or surveys, of the cost of living, for specific groups of wage earners, often limited to one or two cities or a relatively small area.

[5] F. Zweig, *Labour, Life and Poverty*, London, 1948, and *Men in the Pits*, London, 1948.

[6] Dorothy S. Brady, *Low Income Families*, Hearings before the Subcommittee on Low Income Families of the Joint Committee on the Economic Report, 81st Cong., 1st Sess., 1950, p. 475.

[7] National Bureau of Economic Research, *Studies in Income and Wealth*, vol. 15, Introduction.

The pioneer study of this kind, made by Carroll D. Wright in 1875, listed the goods and services required by wage-earning families in Massachusetts, with a statement of the money expenditures involved. R. C. Chapin, collecting workingmen's budgets in New York City, published an account of the standard of living in 1909. Interest in such studies was fanned by the adoption of minimum-wage laws, by the growing profession of social, or welfare, work, by the attempt among labor unions to base wage increases upon increases in the cost of living, and, particularly, by the sharp inflationary pressures during and following World War I. A price index was needed to measure changes in the cost of living, and consumption studies were needed to construct the index.

In Chapter 2, the nature of a price index was explained briefly. Here, we may review the problem of determining the content of a price index, which provides a measure of price change without tabulating all the prices charged in every market. Commodities are selected and prices measured for only the most significant transactions. An index of prices paid by consumers, therefore, depends upon studies of actual expenditures, which reveal the commodities most important in household consumption. And as tastes or incomes change, new studies are made to determine whether rayon or nylon hose are part of the "cost of living" and whether price changes in canned peas are more important than price changes in frozen orange juice.

The National Industrial Conference Board, in August, 1918, published the first report on changes in the cost of living for the country as a whole. This estimate, based on a complete household budget with retail prices weighted according to actual consumption, followed an exhaustive collection of previous researches and the statistical material available and led to a periodic series of index numbers. The National War Labor Board used the index but requested further information from the U. S. Bureau of Labor Statistics, which began publishing its Cost of Living Index regularly in 1920.

Although these indices purported to measure the cost of living on a nationwide basis, they were compiled, of course, from specific reports for particular localities, chiefly urban areas where the adequacy of money wage payments was an important factor. The studies were, however, fragmentary, and much interpolation, projection, and modification entered into the final figures. As the data accumulated and statistical method developed, a nationwide survey of consumption became possible, to provide for the first time a consistent analysis of income and expenditures.

The Study of Money Disbursements of Wage Earners and Clerical Workers [8] was undertaken chiefly to provide data for the revision of the Bureau of Labor Statistics Price Index, known then as the Cost of Living Index. Forty-two separate cities with populations of over 50,000 were studied, and data collected for 14,469 families. As a result, the price index was revised by including new items, dropping others, and revising weights. But the study also provided the largest body of data on incomes, expenditures, family size and composition, racial and regional differences, and occupation which had so far been collected. The very selection of the families which were studied showed important changes in the nature of the consumption problem. The Commissioner of Labor in 1890 dealt with wage earners who were almost evenly divided between agricultural and industrial occupations, but by 1930 the number of wage earners in agriculture was less than half the number of workers in industry.

This study was followed by an even broader investigation, the Study of Consumer Purchases, conducted in 1936. The Bureau of Labor Statistics, the Bureau of Home Economics in the Department of Agriculture, the National Resources Committee, and the Central Statistical Board cooperated in this project. It was designed to give comparable information on incomes, spending, and saving for many different types of families. It showed the distribution of families by income, occupation, and family composition, and the consumption activities of these families in different regions and in urban and rural areas.

The study covered New York, Chicago, and 6 other large cities, 14 middle-sized cities with populations of 30,000 to 75,000, 29 smaller cities of 10,000 to 20,000, 140 villages, and 64 farm counties. Families were sorted into 18 income groups, ranging from those receiving less than $250 per year to those receiving more than $10,000 per year. Occupational groups included wage earner, clerical, farm worker, professional, and business groups and families with income from sources other than wages or salaries. A wealth of data provided comparisons among families classified and cross-classified by these many characteristics.

Although we may think that consumption patterns in 1934 and 1936 are far outdated now, these two studies still provide useful material for analyzing consumption and the many variables which influence it. The empirical findings of these two studies are, however, representative of the economy in depression. The Consumer Purchases Study itself was

[8] U.S. Bureau of Labor Statistics Bulletins 636–641, 1940–1941.

financed by the Works Progress Administration, and WPA workers interviewed families and tabulated data. Hence, as the economy pulled out of the depression decade, the data of the studies became less useful in providing a basis for price indices, market information for businessmen, a guide to social-welfare policies, or arguments for wage bargaining.

World War II required a new approach to consumption problems. An economy which mobilizes for war cannot provide a sufficient output of consumer goods to satisfy the growing consumer demand, and the words *shortages, rationing, inflation,* and *controls* summarize the nature of the consumption problem. Two agencies were particularly concerned with gathering new types of data: the Office of Price Administration, which controlled rationing, and the Bureau of Labor Statistics, whose Cost of Living Index was sharply challenged. Wage controls allowed wage increases only as the Cost of Living Index rose. By 1943, union officials were complaining that the index did not take account of absolute shortages, of quality deterioration, and of upgrading. The argument that these omissions underestimated the rise in the cost of living was investigated by a special committee appointed by the President. The committee found that retail prices had risen, between January, 1941, and September, 1944, some three or four points more than indicated by the index. The continual shifts in consumption patterns during the war, however, as goods increased and decreased in supply, made it impractical to revise the weights of the index. The controversy promoted, nevertheless, a better appreciation of the limitations of the index. It had never measured *the* cost of living in the United States, and after the war its revision included a more realistic title. It is now known as the Consumer Price Index, and its use should be restricted to measuring the effect of price changes on the purchasing power of urban families of wage earners and clerical workers.

Consumption patterns affected the rationing program more directly. In order to determine point values and ration allowances for foods, the Office of Price Administration needed data on the number of ration stamps outstanding, the consumer stocks of rationed goods, and the demand for various foods which could be purchased with the stamps. These data could be tabulated only from a continuous record kept by a number of families, and some 2,000 families participated in the OPA Wartime Food Diary. This experiment was particularly important because it was the first large-scale attempt to record, continuously, consumption by the same family or household over a period of time. Such an approach is of great interest to manufacturers analyzing their markets and the effect of their selling efforts, and since the war several commercial firms have furnished similar information based on continuous records kept by a sample of families.

The most recent large-scale investigation of consumption patterns was that made in 1949–1950 by the Bureau of Labor Statistics to derive a new list of items and new weights for its Consumer Price Index. The resulting data were used in the revised index beginning in January, 1953. In this study, again, extensive data on incomes and expenditures were gathered from a carefully selected sample of families, some of whom kept a continuous record of certain purchases.

An extremely important postwar development in the field of consumption studies has been the yearly Surveys of Consumer Finances, sponsored by the Division of Research and Statistics of the Board of Governors of the Federal Reserve System, and published in the summer issues of the *Federal Reserve Bulletin.* The Survey Research Center of the University of Michigan's Institute for Social Research has carried out the investigations for the Board of Governors.

These surveys cover not only the economic position but also the attitudes of consumers. The financial status of consumers is described by data on incomes, liquid assets, investments, and debts. Major consumption expenditures—houses, automobiles, household appliances, and furniture—are recorded. Beyond this, the survey explores the consumer's own appraisal of his economic well-being, his expectations, his preferences, and his plans for future consumption. With information about family composition, age, occupation, source of income, and regional location, many different analyses can be made. Data are collected from over 3,000 spending units, selected so as to represent the consumers living in private households in the continental United States, an estimated 97 per cent of the total population. The results are used by businessmen, economists, and government officials. If techniques can be perfected, the predictions of consumers themselves as to spending and saving may provide valuable insights into the future course of business fluctuations. The data have also been used by at least one writer to develop a theory of consumer behavior, discussed in Chapter 9.

An early investigator like Engel would be overwhelmed by the abundance of statistical data on consumption now in existence. These data are the raw material for a continuing series of analyses, and they provide support for a number of useful generalizations. Perhaps the single important conclusion to be drawn is that the consumption behavior of a single household or an economy cannot be predicted from objective fact —that the number of variables are too great and their relationships too unstable to permit the accurate forecasting possible in the physical sciences.

BASIC TENDENCIES AND RELATIONSHIPS

The expenditure studies, in summary, show that consumers' choices depend on income, prices, tastes, and habits. The details of consumption expenditures furnish useful data on these variables. We can compare expenditures on specific goods and services among households with different incomes. We can analyze the influence of the consumer's savings and expectations on his responsiveness to price changes. We can list many factors influencing habits and taste, including location, ethnic background, occupation, age, sex, and education. And we recognize that many of these same factors influence income and hence consumption.

The utility and indifference theories of consumer behavior assume that consumer preference can be known, that a given scale of utility or a given set of indifference curves exists. Consumption studies have pointed out the influences on consumer preference and allow us to state what factors will shape the consumption pattern.

Income effects. The voluminous Study of Consumer Purchases, like so many others, concluded that income was the predominant influence on family spending and saving patterns. The basic importance of the income factor can be seen clearly from Table 11-1. Such a table verifies Engel's law in its narrow statement with respect to food. The dollar amounts spent on food are larger in each higher-income class: thus, the $461 spent by the families receiving less than $1,000 yearly income contrasts with $836 spent on food by families receiving between $2,000 and $3,000 yearly and with $1,788 spent by families receiving over $5,000. But food expenditures are far more important to low-income families than to high-income groups. The $461 food expenditure of the poorest class represents over twice the proportion of total income that the $1,788 expenditure of the highest-income group represents. The three basic necessities—food, shelter, and clothing—required expenditures in excess of total income by the lowest-income class, and well over two-thirds of total income went on these items for all except the highest-income families, where incomes were sufficient to allow a considerable percentage for taxes, contributions, and savings.

But the influence of higher incomes on all categories of spending is

Table 11-1. *Distribution of Adjusted Family Income, White Families, New York City, 1935–1936*

Income class	Total adjusted income	Total money value of current family living	Food	Home maintenance	Clothing and personal care	Transportation	Medical care	Contributions and personal taxes	Other
				Average amount					
$ 500–$ 999	$ 850	$1,111	$ 461	$ 442	$ 81	$ 27	$ 19	$ 13	$ 68
1,000– 1,999	1,562	1,634	614	584	150	73	70	35	108
2,000– 2,999	2,450	2,435	836	811	271	157	110	77	175
3,000– 4,999	3,588	3,510	1,044	1,122	452	259	164	187	282
$5,000 and over	9,456	8,333	1,788	2,796	922	652	385	989	801
				Percentage of income					
$ 500–$ 999	100	130.7	54.3	52.0	9.5	3.2	2.2	1.5	8.0
1,000– 1,999	100	104.6	39.3	37.4	9.6	4.7	4.5	2.2	6.9
2,000– 2,999	100	99.4	34.1	33.1	11.1	6.4	4.5	3.1	7.1
3,000– 4,999	100	97.8	29.1	31.3	12.6	7.2	4.6	5.2	7.8
$5,000 and over	100	88.1	18.9	29.5	9.8	6.9	4.1	10.4	8.5

SOURCE: *Family Income and Expenditure in New York City, 1935–36*, Study of Consumer Purchases, Urban Series, U.S. Bureau of Labor Statistics Bulletin 643, vol. II, 1941, Table 44, p. 98.

not so clear as it appears on food. Expenses for housing, which includes rent, utility bills, furniture, and furnishings, are a smaller proportion of total income in successively higher-income classes, but the decline is not so precipitate as that for food. Expenditures for clothing, on the other hand, increase as a proportion of total income, but only up to the $5,000 yearly income figure. While the dollar amounts going to medical care are greater at each higher-income class, there is a striking change in this category as a proportion of total income from the lowest-income group to the next higher. Thereafter, the percentage remains remarkably constant, so that the effect of income seems minimal in this category.

It is by looking at such comparisons—and the student may well find others for his enlightenment—that influences other than income are suspected.

Family size and composition. Family income and expenditure obviously depend on the number of persons in a family, their age, and sex. The number and sex of wage earners affect total family income. Where the wife supports the household, income is usually lower than where a man is chief earner. Finally, the average size of the family is larger at higher income levels, as shown in Table 11-2. Family members are also older at higher levels of income.

Table 11-2. *Average Number of Persons, Native White Families, New York City, 1935–1936*

Income class	*Number of persons*
All families	3.62
Under $500	2.98
$ 500–$ 999	3.11
1,000– 1,499	3.29
1,500– 1,999	3.49
2,000– 2,999	3.62
3,000– 4,999	3.84
$5,000 and over	3.73

SOURCE: *Family Income and Expenditure in New York City, 1935–36,* Study of Consumer Purchases, Urban Series, U.S. Bureau of Labor Statistics Bulletin 643, vol. I, 1941, Table 16, p. 31.

The size of a family also affects its spending pattern, although some categories of expenditure are influenced more than others. Thus, the Consumer Purchases Study showed that, in New York City, families with children (regardless of income) spent less upon transportation and recreation and more upon housing and home maintenance than did childless couples. Average expenditures for food are directly related to family size, and, in most areas, clothing expenditures are higher in larger families.

Occupation and education. Both income and consumption patterns are obviously affected by occupation and education. In the New York City survey, the median income of wage-earner families was $1,500, that of clerical workers $2,060, and that of business and professional people $2,690. These income differences lead to differences in spending. Aside from this, there are other details, such as expenditures on liquor, automobiles, work clothing, and so on, where occupation has an influence, but in the broad categories described by most surveys these factors are vague in detail. Food expenditures, for example, include the cost of meals at work—a kind of occupational expense—and also the cost of meals purchased as recreation or entertainment. The low-income wage-earner families spent more for the first item, and the high-income families, particularly the professional and managerial groups, spent more for the second. Spending and occupation are closely correlated in the field of housing, where independent business and professional families spent more in every income group than did the wage earners. On the other hand, transportation and recreation expenditures were highest for the wage earners at nearly every level of income. Expenditures for clothing and personal care were found to vary little among different occupations.

Ethnic background. The New York City portion of the Consumer Purchases Study, from which we have drawn these examples of variables influencing consumption patterns, provides clear-cut data on the influence of race on income and expenditure. Table 11-1 may be contrasted with Table 11-3.

To begin with, Negroes generally were more numerous in the lower economic groups. During 1935–1936, almost half the Negro families in native areas of New York City received relief, while only 14 per cent of the white families received such aid. Among nonrelief families, only 4 per cent of the Negroes enjoyed incomes of $3,000 and over, while 24 per cent of the white families fell in this class. These differences in income account for much of the "racial" difference in consumption patterns. They do not, however, explain it all.

At the lower income levels, the Negro families' expenditures were greater for housing and less for food than among white families. The proportion of income spent for clothing and personal care was larger at higher incomes, and the increase in spending on clothing was greater

Table 11-3. *Distribution of Adjusted Family Income, Negro Families, New York City, 1935–1936*

Income class	Total adjusted income	Total money value of current family living	Food	Home maintenance	Clothing and personal care	Transportation	Medical care	Contributions and personal taxes	Other
Average amount									
$ 500–$ 999	$ 920	$ 985	$384	$ 412	$ 78	$ 29	$ 25	$ 8	$ 49
1,000– 1,999	1,432	1,450	501	559	162	58	41	38	91
2,000– 2,999	2,375	2,226	669	783	294	153	75	98	153
$3,000 and over	4,020	3,560	678	1,481	395	212	109	421	265
Percentage of Income									
$ 500–$ 999	100	107.1	41.7	44.8	8.5	3.2	2.7	0.9	5.3
1,000– 1,999	100	101.3	35.0	39.0	11.3	4.0	2.9	2.7	6.4
2,000– 2,999	100	93.7	28.2	33.9	12.4	6.4	3.2	4.1	6.4
$3,000 and over	100	88.6	16.9	36.8	9.8	5.3	2.7	10.5	6.6

SOURCE: *Family Income and Expenditure in New York City, 1935–36*, Study of Consumer Purchases, Urban Series, U.S. Bureau of Labor Statistics Bulletin 643, vol. II, 1941, Table 44, p. 98.

for Negro than for white families. The most striking difference appears in the figures for total spending compared with total income. For families with incomes of less than $1,000, spending exceeded income by an average of 31 per cent among the whites and by an average of only 7 per cent among the Negroes. At higher income levels, the surplus available for saving was a much greater percentage of Negro family income than of white family income. Less than one-half of 1 per cent of income remained after total spending to white families receiving between $2,000 and $3,000 yearly, while 6 per cent remained for Negro families in the same income class.

To see these differences as solely a product of racial custom, tastes, or habits would, however, be unrealistic. Negroes were not comparable with white families in terms of economic conditions or social status. For example, food expenditure data were complicated by the fact that many Negroes were employed as servants or as kitchen help in restaurants, where meals are provided as part of the wage. Housing expenditures reflected in part the limited choice available to Negroes, because of restricted areas and discrimination. And the smaller deficits and larger savings among Negro families do not mean a greater desire for thrift but more difficulty in obtaining credit. We may consider also a difference in standards of living among the two groups, and all the restrictions upon Negro living which affect these standards.

Region and location. As a final example of the important variables affecting consumption, the Consumer Purchases Study data for village and farm families may be briefly mentioned.

Farming as a business and as a way of life appeared as a definite influence —it led to irregular and varied income and to a pattern of consumption which appeared at all income levels. Farm families, looking to reinvestment in their enterprise, retained a surplus of income over expenses more frequently than did urban families. Housing and house maintenance took a higher proportion of urban family expenditure, as did clothing and personal care. Transportation, on the other hand, cost farm families much more than urban households, and automobile outlays were particularly high.

Interregional differences can be found in both farm and village families. Some of these reflect climate, and others seem more akin to custom or local preference. Thus we find climate forcing home-maintenance expenses of heating in the North and custom or labor supply producing home-maintenance expenditures for servants in the South. Homeownership as a tradition was more prevalent in New England than elsewhere. Transportation expenses were larger, at given levels of income, for families living in the Pacific towns and villages.

While different consumption patterns can be identified, in the Consumer Purchases Study, with different regions or areas, they frequently reflect underlying economic conditions, as was true of some characteristics of the Negro consumption pattern. In the following two chapters we shall explore further the three important variables of income, prices, and habits and taste.

Questions and Points for Discussion

1. How may the standards for minimum consumption discussed in Chapter 10 be used to define poverty?

2. Suppose you are working for a welfare committee in your home town and receive a large bequest to be used for relief of the poor. How could you use the consumption standards discussed in Chapter 10 to select poor-relief recipients? How could you use consumption studies?

3. In a 1948 study of meat consumption, two families lived in a small city and reported incomes and food expenditures of about equal amounts. Both families consisted of one small child, wife, and husband, who carried his lunch from home. One family reported consumption of about 2 pounds per person during the week; the other, about 4 pounds per person during the week. What factors might have influenced this difference? When such differences exist, is it true to say that income is the dominant influence in consumption?

4. Suppose you were asked to construct a price index for the cost of living of students at your college or university. Why would you need a consumption study, and what kind of investigation would you make to establish your index?

5. In comparing Tables 11-1 and 11-3, why do you think the proportion of income spent on medical care was so much larger for white families than for Negro families?

6. Under the heading "home maintenance," list all the detailed expenditures in this category you can think of. Compare your findings with the data given in *Family Income, Expenditures, and Savings in* 10 *Cities,* U.S. Bureau of Labor Statistics Bulletin 1065, 1952. Did you omit any subcategories because they are unimportant in your area?

7. Distinguish between the research methods of Le Play and Engel.
8. What are Engel's famous laws of consumption?

References

The Consumer Price Index, U.S. Bureau of Labor Statistics, 1953.

King, Gregory: "Natural and Political Observations and Conclusions upon the State and Condition of England, 1698," in G. Chalmers, *An Estimate of the Comparative Strength of Great Britain,* London, 1802.

"Methods of the Survey of Consumer Finances," *Federal Reserve Bulletin,* July, 1950.

Williams, Faith M., and Carle C. Zimmerman: *Studies of Family Living in the United States and other Countries,* U.S. Department of Agriculture Miscellaneous Publication 223, December, 1935, especially pp. 2–68.

12. Household Expenditure Relationships

Now that we are acquainted with the major influences on incomes and consumption expenditures within the household, we may bring our factual knowledge up to date and observe consumption patterns in the United States in the 1950s. This chapter is of a kind which needs frequent revision, and the student is urged to compare the findings here with more recent data, whether general or fragmentary. To be valid, however, comparisons of different studies require that definitions and methodology be similar. In fact, many variations exist, which the following summary may illustrate.

PROBLEMS IN EMPIRICAL STUDIES

Any student of the behavior of actual consumers must decide three questions: "*Whose* consumption?" "*What* consumption?" "*How* is consumption to be investigated?" Not all surveys have answered these questions in the same way.

Whose consumption? In Chapter 2 we distinguished among the individual consumer, the family, and the consuming unit as decision-making units, and each of these has been used in various consumption studies. Two important definitions are those used by the Survey Research Center, collecting data for the Federal Reserve System, and by the Bureau of Labor Statistics. The first defines the data-collection unit as a spending unit composed of all persons living in the same dwelling, related by blood, marriage, or adoption, who pool their incomes for their major items of expense. *Pooling* exists where people contribute more than half their income to the spending unit. The wife of a family head, or a family member under eighteen years of age or earning less than $10 a week, is always included in the spending unit. In the most recent BLS survey, the term *consumer unit* or *economic family* is used, to mean either a family of two or more persons, usually living in the same household, dependent on a pooled income for their major items of expense, *or* a single consumer, financially independent and living separately from a family group. Some decision-making units may, therefore, be classified differently by the two definitions. An adult unmarried son, living with his family and paying board of less than 50 per cent of his income, would be part of the BLS *consumer unit* but would, in the FRS data, constitute a separate *spending unit*. More importantly, the most recent BLS survey in 1950 covered only cities and excluded newly formed families. The FRS survey probably has a better analysis of consumers in high-level income brackets.

These definitions use income to define the consuming unit, and the studies include data on consuming units classified by income level. Hence, every effort is made to record income completely, to get the sum of *all* receipts, including interest on savings accounts, occasional gifts, earnings from odd jobs, and so on. The FRS data disclose income received from wages and salaries, pensions, benefits, allotments, alimony and other contributions, rents from property and those received from roomers and boarders, net farming income, unincorporated business profits, professional or other self-employment income, interest, dividends, royalties, and trust-fund income. The same sources are recorded by the BLS surveys, but the problem of computing the income received in a particular case is very great. In computing rental income, for example, costs must be subtracted from the gross amount. Some business withdrawals actually represent capital rather than income.

But for many purposes the entire year's income is not the relevant concept. Real estate operators, farmers, and other self-employed businessmen frequently have fluctuating or irregular incomes and spend according to a "normal" income which may or may not correspond to an average of several years' receipts. Most people think of spending out of their disposable income, or take-home pay, which is less than total income by the amount of withholding taxes and other payroll deductions. Defining spending units by income, therefore, involves many questions of income concepts.

The question: "Whose consumption?" also involves the area of the study—does it include all consumers in the United States, urban wage earners' families in cities of over 80,000 population, or shoppers in downtown Boston? Usually, consumption studies use "stratified random samples" because some of the variables which affect consumption are known. For example, data should include consuming units at various income levels, and so a number of units are selected at random within each of a predetermined number of income classes. Or it may be useful to have childless families specifically included, as well as those having children.

What consumption? Consumption is measured differently for different purposes, and measuring with money involves several problems. In Chapter 1, we defined consumption as the combination and use of goods and services to produce satisfaction for the consumer, and we recognize that consumer income is spent to obtain the goods and services. But income is received, and consumption takes place, over time, and hence data are collected for a specific time period, usually a year.

In measuring current consumption, we have to allow for spending out of past or future income. The family which cashes in a savings bond to buy clothing draws upon previous income which has been accumulated, or saved, by not spending, or consuming, it previously. The family which borrows money to pay a hospital bill expects to pay for its current expenditures with future income. Current consumption, in money terms, may exceed current income by the amount of dis-saving, or debt. But current consumption may also represent using up a consumer good which was paid for in previous periods. The family which owns a radio obtains satisfaction from it by using it long after it has been purchased, and current consumption occurs out of past income. The automobile purchased on time payment provides services and satisfaction, current consumption, which are paid for with future income. So current consumption may exceed current income by the amount of real goods which are being used up in the period.

In a given time period, households also spend income for past or future consumption. The family depositing regularly in a savings account is not spending this money on current consumption but accumulating future income for future consumption. The family paying an overdue doctor's bill is devoting current income to paying for consumption in a previous period. Current consumption, in money terms, may be less than current income by the amount of saving or payment of debt. But the family buying a home, a typewriter, or a washing machine is also providing for future consumption, with the gradual use of goods and services in later time periods. And current consumption, in real terms, may be less than current income by the amount of durable goods acquired.

We have already defined saving as the difference between income and consumption; so we can see that, when a consumer spends current income on an asset, whether a share of stock or a sewing machine, he is saving. And when the asset is being used up or consumed, he is dis-saving. We can now think of the net worth of a consuming unit as the sum of all the assets minus the liabilities, that is, consumer debts which are owed. Saving, whether by increasing assets or reducing debt, tends to increase net worth, and dis-saving, whether by using up assets or incurring debt, tends to decrease it.

Strictly speaking, therefore, we might measure total consumption during a given time period by income plus or minus the change in the assets and debts, or net worth, of the consuming unit over the period. But our money measure is ineffective for putting accurate dollar figures to this net worth concept.

A complete enumeration of consumers' net worth would include all assets, both financial and tangible. Houses, automobiles, washing machines, fur coats, furniture, and even the contents of home freezers may all be included in the assets of consuming units. They all represent the accumulation of saving, or income which is not spent. They all provide potential consumption in the future. But the value of these assets consists of the potential consumption which they represent, and a ten-year-old house, a five-year-old automobile, or house furnishings which have been used provide less future consumption than when they were new. There is no way to estimate the future consumption potential of most of the tangible assets, or consumers' capital goods, which belong to consuming units. Hence, for most purposes, both consumption and net worth are defined in financial terms: consumption as money expenditures during a given time period, and net worth as the algebraic sum of those assets and liabilities which have a readily ascertainable money value.

Thus the Federal Reserve Board data present selected items on consumers' balance sheets, including liquid assets (United States government bonds, checking- and savings-account balances, postal savings, and shares in credit and savings associations, but not currency), corporate stock, business investment, real estate, and short-term consumer debt. Figures are also available, however, on the ownership of homes, automobiles, and certain durable goods. One study by the Federal Reserve Board estimates that the amount of consumers' capital (defined as homes and automobiles) is almost equal to the amount of consumer investment in business, and we shall find later some interesting relationships between the purchase of consumer durable goods and saving. The Bureau of Labor Statistics survey records the net change in consumers' savings and debts over the year, with less detail than the Federal Reserve Board. The BLS classifies life insurance payments as a separate outlay, since they contain elements of both consumption expenditure and saving. The BLS analyses present the change in net worth as an addition to income or a disposition of income.

For other purposes, consumption is measured in physical terms. Surveys of dietary adequacy are concerned less with the money value than with the nutritional value of food, and data are needed, therefore, on the pounds of beef, carrots, butter, and so on, used. Here, the measurement of consumer food stocks at the beginning and end of a period is vital. Other problems involved are the measurement of waste, food loss, and nutrition loss, which frequently depend on housekeeping arrangements and cooking ability. Those market surveys which report consumer preference to manufacturers also require data in physical terms, and ingenious devices for computing accurately the cans of tomato juice of brands *X*, *Y*, and *Z* used in a home have been developed.

How to investigate? This problem involves all the others, since the extent and accuracy of data depend chiefly on the survey method used. Replies collected by interviews are far more complete than those obtained from questionnaires; yet the interview technique produces difficulties. Fieldworkers require intensive training so that questions are always posed in the same terms and interpretations made in the same manner. Many questions have a psychological effect—the respondent may wish to impress or please the interviewer or may consciously or unconsciously answer in order to gain sympathy. People differ in their willingness to answer questions—generally speaking, the percentage of "no answer" is highest for income questions and among people in the upper income brackets.

Aside from this, people frequently have honest difficulties in reporting incomes and expenditure. More accurate data can be derived by summing the answers to detailed questions covering a short time period than by asking for annual income or expenditure figures. To supply income data, the respondent answers questions about receipts from many different sources. Information given on food purchases for the previous week or two is much more reliable than an estimate of yearly butter purchases. Frequently the questions: "When did you last buy stockings?" "What kind?" "At what store?" "How much did they cost?" produce, by refreshing the respondent's memory, more accurate expenditure data than the vaguer form: "How much did you spend on stockings last year?"

Particularly for food-consumption data, a record kept by the housewife may be used to supplement the questionnaire. But such accounts also furnish problems. When people consciously keep track of their spending, they frequently change their "normal" consumption pattern, being shocked or pleased by what they discover. The record, to be useful, often involves great detail, such as the number and kinds of meals served, the food bought but not used, and the amount, type, and price of various food items purchased. The chore of keeping such accounts means that fewer people are willing to give information, while those who do may differ from a representative sample by having more education, more leisure, or more interest in household accounting. Again, such characteristics may distort the normal consumption pattern.

Some studies, particularly in the field of market research, pose hypothetical questions. A survey to elicit marginal utility or a preference map would probably ask the consumer, "How many oranges would you buy at 10 cents a pound? 20 cents a pound? 30 cents a pound?" and so on. When the item is familiar, the answers may come readily enough, but manufacturers of new products find it difficult to obtain estimates of prospective consumption when the consumer is confronted with an unfamiliar item.

Finally, wherever short-term data are collected, they must, of course, be expanded, or "blown up," to give yearly figures for comparison with income. They may be adjusted for seasonal variations, they must be checked for internal consistency, they must be edited for unusual circumstances, and all traces of bias must be eliminated as far as possible. Hence, any market or consumption survey involves a myriad of complex decisions which are not always apparent in the comparative simplicity of columns of numbers in tables.

INCOME AND CONSUMPTION

Income has a twofold effect on consumption: it provides purchasing power, and it is one indicator of economic or social status which may influence the standard of living which people seek to attain. But credit and past savings also supply purchasing power, and past or expected income may dominate a standard of living, so that classifications of consumption patterns by income levels are not always what they seem. The difficulties in obtaining income data have already been mentioned: it is possible that what a family *considers* its income is a more valid indication of both purchasing power and status than the accurate total of all receipts.

Consumption by income class. Income in dollars, whether accurate or not, does not distinguish economic status except by comparison with higher and lower incomes, and the theory has been advanced that it is the consumer's rank in the income distribution, rather than the dollars in his possession, which chiefly influences his mode of living. In this respect, the income-distribution data of Chapter 4 may be reviewed, and the point emphasized again that in 1954 most of the spending units were found in the middle income brackets—from $3,000 to $7,500 yearly—with very few inordinately wealthy or poor consumers. This middle-income class, however, covers a fairly wide range in dollars and an equal range in consumption expenditures. But the differences in consumption patterns at different levels of income are not so striking as, say, those of fifty years ago.

We find, first, that most consuming units own assets in excess of their debts and that nearly half of them had a net worth in excess of $5,000.[1] For almost two-thirds of the consuming units, net worth equals or exceeds their annual income. These figures vary, of course, with income levels. The median net worth for consuming units receiving less than $3,000 yearly income in 1952 was $1,300, that for consuming units receiving between $3,000 and $5,000 yearly was $3,500, while that for other consuming units was $10,300. There were more consuming units with negative net worth in the lower-income classes. Liquid assets (United States government securities and savings and checking accounts) were reported by almost three-quarters of all consuming units and by over half of those with incomes of less than $3,000 yearly. Over three-fourths of those in the middle-income class owned both liquid assets and automobiles, and about half of them owned their own homes. This income class also contained the greatest number of debtors, although the amount of debt in relation to income was smaller than for consuming units in the lower income brackets. The other types of consumer assets, investments in farms, businesses, or corporate stock, were much less widely owned. The number of owners and the size of holdings in real estate, unincorporated business, and corporate stock were least at low income levels and greatest among consuming units with yearly incomes of $7,500 and over.

[1] These figures based on Federal Reserve Board data exclude from net worth consumers' equities in life insurance policies and holdings of currency.

Purchases of durable goods, which combine both consumption expenditure and saving, also vary with income. Four per cent of consuming units receiving yearly incomes of less than $3,000 purchased new automobiles in 1952, while 24 per cent of those with incomes between $3,000 and $7,500 made such purchases, as did 25 per cent of those in the highest-income class. But used cars were bought by 30 per cent of the lower-income group in 1952, as compared with 58 per cent of those with incomes from $3,000 to $7,500 and only 8 per cent of those with higher incomes. Similar variation is shown for purchases of furniture and major household appliances, with more purchasers in each of the successively higher-income classes.

The effects of income on other types of consumption expenditure cannot be shown on a nationwide basis for recent years, but Tables 12-1 and 12-2, prepared by the Bureau of Labor Statistics for Detroit, in 1948, are illustrative of the changing patterns of consumption at different income levels.

Income concepts. When expenditure data are presented for different income levels, two problems are involved. First, are families within the same income group comparable with respect to the other characteristics, particularly family size, which influence consumption? Second, to what extent do the dollar receipts reported actually determine family spending?

The first point can best be illustrated by means of food-consumption analysis, a field where much work has been done on the problem. Two families in the $3,000 income bracket do not receive the same income if there are two people in one and six in the other. Two four-person families are not comparable, with respect to food income-expenditure relationships, if one consists of adults and the other includes two small children. Food income-expenditure relations have been calculated on a per capita or consumption-unit basis, where the two-person family is classified at a higher income level than the four. But this overlooks two facts: that per capita income is no determinant at all of the baby's expenditure since someone else receives and spends the money, and that family food expenditures do not add up to the sum of food expenditures for the number of individuals concerned. There are, in short, economies of scale in housekeeping, and while two cannot live as cheaply as one, living costs are not doubled, either.

The second problem—the concept of income which actually influences purchases—has received much more attention in recent years.

Table 12-1. *Average Annual Money Income and Expenditures, Families of Two or More Persons, by Net Income Class, Detroit, 1948*

Item	Under $1,000	$1,000–$2,000	$2,000–$3,000	$3,000–$4,000	$4,000–$5,000	$5,000–$6,000	$6,000–$7,500	$7,500–$10,000	$10,000 and over
Average family size	2.6	2.9	3.1	3.1	3.4	3.7	4.5	4.9	4.1
Expenditures for current consumption	$1,768	$2,119	$2,859	$3,473	$4,157	$5,348	$6,382	$8,147	$12,536
Food purchased to be served at home	609	687	889	1,002	1,199	1,309	1,489	1,710	2,349
Food purchased and eaten away from home	28	27	98	122	136	220	333	329	658
Alcoholic beverages	4	10	57	57	85	59	119	157	185
Housing	324	339	410	417	477	524	480	459	1,380
Fuel, light, refrigeration, water	113	137	169	149	184	157	240	254	215
Household operation	62	109	97	134	162	205	206	265	895
Furnishings and equipment	30	34	154	201	250	396	581	564	1,040
Clothing, materials, and service	138	173	330	408	561	713	1,017	1,470	2,210
Automobile purchase and operation	161	266	212	309	430	728	757	1,562	1,351
Other transportation	9	28	61	85	64	83	101	173	102
Medical care	62	145	135	218	208	302	242	329	656
Personal care	25	44	63	73	93	104	127	146	219
Recreation	28	30	81	137	164	349	436	462	735
Reading	18	22	29	39	44	51	51	55	104
Tobacco	5	44	52	70	69	86	92	100	110
Education	...	1	6	15	7	35	39	57	132
Other	152	24	17	36	23	27	72	56	195
Gifts and contributions	47	74	121	150	237	360	382	463	1,509
Insurance	19	38	86	123	152	207	165	278	610
Net surplus	0	0	0	0	53	0	11	0	9,188
Money income	661	1,428	2,602	3,482	4,441	5,471	6,666	8,595	23,415
Other money receipts	0	0	0	19	12	6	0	0	0
Net deficit	1,065	778	279	149	0	310	0	71	0
Balancing difference	−108	−25	−185	−96	−146	−128	−274	−222	−428
Surplus:									
Percentage reporting	0	25	26	43	58	38	61	43	71
Average amount for those reporting	0	$148	$289	$397	$466	$690	$617	$1,741	$11,705
Deficit:									
Percentage reporting	80	60	61	47	37	56	39	57	29
Average amount for those reporting	$1,331	$1,359	$577	$681	$912	$1,027	$948	$1,430	$1,168

SOURCE: Compiled from *Family Income, Expenditures, and Savings in* 10 *Cities*, U.S. Bureau of Labor Statistics Bulletin 1065, 1952, Tables 2*a*, 3, 4, 5.

Table 12-2. *Average Annual Net Money Income and Expenditures, Families of Two or More Persons, by Percentage Distribution, Detroit, 1948*

Item	Under $1,000	$1,000–$2,000	$2,000–$3,000	$3,000–$4,000	$4,000–$5,000	$5,000–$6,000	$6,000–$7,500	$7,500–$10,000	$10,000 and over
Average family size	2.6	2.9	3.1	3.1	3.4	3.7	4.5	4.9	4.1
Expenditures for current consumption	100%	100%	100%	100%	100%	100%	100%	100%	100%
Food purchased to be served at home	34	32	31	29	29	24	23	21	19
Food purchased and eaten away from home	2	1	3	4	3	4	5	4	5
Alcoholic beverages	...	...	2	2	2	1	2	2	1
Housing	18	16	14	12	11	10	8	6	11
Fuel, light, refrigeration, water	6	6	6	4	4	3	4	3	2
Household operation	4	5	3	4	4	4	3	3	7
Furnishings and equipment	2	2	5	6	6	7	9	7	8
Clothing, materials, and service	8	8	12	12	14	13	16	18	18
Automobile purchase and operation	9	13	7	9	10	14	12	20	11
Other transportation	1	1	2	2	2	2	2	2	1
Medical care	4	7	5	6	5	6	4	4	5
Personal care	1	2	2	2	2	2	2	2	2
Recreation	2	1	3	4	4	7	7	6	6
Reading	1	1	1	1	1	1	1	1	1
Tobacco	...	2	2	2	2	2	1	1	1
Education	...	...	...	...	...	1	1	1	1
Other	9	1	1	1	1	1	1	1	2

SOURCE: Compiled from *Family Income, Expenditures, and Savings in* 10 *Cities*, U.S. Bureau of Labor Statistics Bulletin 1065, 1952, Tables 2*a*, 3, 4, 5.

The tendency to underreport income has already been noted. After its most recent survey, the Bureau of Labor Statistics reported that: [2]

> There is a general tendency for . . . families either [to] understate their incomes or [to] overstate their expenditures or saving; or the understatement in income is larger than the understatement in expenditures or savings. . . . Discrepancies of this kind have been noted with almost an historical regularity. . . . *It is, therefore, quite incorrect to interpret the entire difference between reported income and expenditure as saving or dis-saving.*

Accordingly, the Bureau presents the reported data for income and expenditures with the discrepancies stated separately. We may use as an example figures in Table 12-1 for families in the $4,000 to $5,000 income class. Here the average money income, as calculated from the statements of families, amounted to $4,441. Other money receipts averaged $12, and there was no dis-saving, or net deficit, on the average. The sum of these figures, $4,453, should therefore equal the average expenditure plus saving. But the reported data show an average figure of $4,157 for current consumption, $237 for gifts and contributions, $152 for insurance, and a net surplus of $53. These figures add up to $4,599, or more than the reported money available. The discrepancy amounts to −$146.

Such a negative balancing difference appears for every income group, and obviously if more accurate data were available, either income or consumption figures would be different. Most important, the classification by incomes would be altered, and different income-expenditure relations would appear in the various income groups.

Aside from this point, there is also the question of what income actually determines what consumption. Here we may review the theory of consumer choice and give some thought to household buying practices. The underlying tendency to equalize the marginal utility of all purchases cannot literally be fulfilled by reconsidering the allocation of the entire income with every purchase. Once a family is established in a house, for example, part of the income is already committed to rent and household expense. It is, therefore, something less than total dollar receipts which the family considers in deciding whether Junior should have a baseball glove or Mother a new dish drainer in the kitchen.

[2] *Family Income, Expenditures, and Savings in 1950*, U.S. Bureau of Labor Statistics Bulletin 1097 (revised), June, 1953, pp. 5–6.

The purchasing power available for some categories is frequently much less than the total income, and hence spending within those categories varies with this subtotal of income. The housewife who receives a set sum to pay household bills and buy food for the family and clothing for the children may juggle purchases within these three categories according to the amount of her weekly or monthly household expense money. The two-person family which operates a joint checking account is much more likely to consider each of the categories in terms of total purchasing power.

Very little is known about the way in which income is actually spent in different households and the extent to which income subtotals vary with total income. Some attempts have been made to classify households by expenditure levels, but all the difficulties of comparing different families at various income levels are present in this method also.

Table 12-1 supports the conclusions which we have already drawn about wealth and debt by income classes. The proportion of those reporting a surplus and the average amount saved is generally higher at the higher income levels, while the reverse is true for reported deficits.

MEASURING INCOME ELASTICITY

The relative importance of the expenditure data in Table 12-1 by income classes and by changes in income classes may be described by a measure called *income elasticity*. This measure compares the relative change, or percentage change, in quantity (or expenditure) associated with the corresponding relative change, or percentage change, in income. The conceptual formula is thus

$$\text{Coefficient of income elasticity} = \frac{\text{relative change in quantity (or expenditure)}}{\text{corresponding relative change in income}}$$

A coefficient of income elasticity that is negative (i.e., the sign is minus) means that the quantity taken decreases as income increases; a coefficient of zero means that the quantity taken is not influenced by changes in income; a coefficient greater than zero and less than 1 means that the proportional increase in quantity taken is less than the corresponding proportional increase in income; a coefficient greater than 1 (or unity) means that the proportional increase in quantity taken is greater than the corresponding proportional increase in income. In sum, the coefficient of income elasticity describes, in one brief number, how the rate of change in quantity (or expenditures) compares with the corresponding rate of change in income.

Data from Table 12-1 are plotted in Figure 12-1 to show how expenditures for clothing and housing vary with income. Because of the discrepancies in the reported data, however, we cannot plot the expenditure data against reliable estimates of income. Hence, the horizontal axis of Figure 12-1 employs *total expenditure* as an indicator of

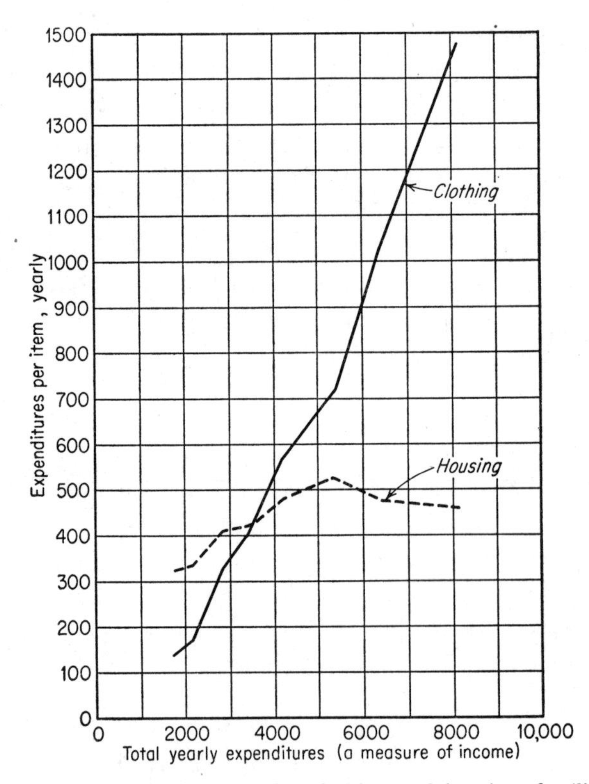

Fig. 12-1. Income-consumption curves for clothing and housing, families of two or more persons, Detroit, 1948.

income. The inescapable conclusion that one must draw from Figure 12-1 is that expenditures for clothing vary more dramatically with income than do expenditures for housing.

We can make a rigorous comparison of these income-expenditure relationships by stating each relationship in terms of a coefficient of income elasticity. In this little problem, we shall derive a measure of income elasticity between the third and fourth income class, or of a change in average total expenditure from \$3,473 to \$4,157 (reported in Table 12-1). The actual computations can be accomplished in one of several ways, but we shall use the following computational formula: [3]

$$\text{Income elasticity} = \frac{(E_1 - E_0)/(E_1 + E_0)}{(Y_1 - Y_0)/(Y_1 + Y_0)}$$

where E_1 = expenditure after change in income
E_0 = expenditure before change in income
Y_1 = changed income
Y_0 = base income

Now, substituting the income-expenditure data from Table 12-1 in this formula, we get in the case of housing

$$\text{Income elasticity} = \frac{(\$477 - \$417)/(\$477 + \$417)}{(\$4{,}157 - \$3{,}473)/(\$4{,}157 + \$3{,}473)}$$
$$= +0.07$$

And we get in the case of clothing

$$\text{Income elasticity} = \frac{(\$561 - \$408)/(\$561 + \$408)}{(\$4{,}157 - \$3{,}473)/(\$4{,}157 + \$3{,}473)}$$
$$= +1.76$$

We can now say all that we could say from looking at the graph, namely, an increase in income is associated with a much greater increase in expenditure for clothing than for housing. But we can also say considerably more; we can say, for example, that a 10 per cent increase in income is associated with less than a 1 per cent increase in housing expenditure *but with a nearly* 18 *per cent increase in clothing expenditure.* This measure thus provides us with some *precise* and useful information.

Information on the relative importance of expenditures by items can also be gained by expressing the expenditure data of each income class as a percentage of the income (or total expenditure) of that class and then by comparing the percentage of income allocated to an item, income class by income class. Where the percentage of income allocated

[3] See Chap. 17 for a more complete treatment of elasticity, although in that context the independent variable is price rather than income.

to an item (e.g., food) declines across the income scale, moving from low to higher incomes, it follows that the proportion of income allocated to the item is declining with rising incomes and the coefficient of income elasticity is less than 1. On the other hand, where the percentage of income allocated to an item (e.g., clothing) rises across the income scale, it follows that the proportion of income allocated to the item is rising with rising incomes and the coefficient of income elasticity is greater than 1. We can interpret Table 12-2, therefore, to mean that clothing in general has a high income elasticity, while food has a much lower one. This conclusion affords a new terminology to Engel's law of demand and allows us to substitute the concept of low income elasticity for the highly charged phrase "necessities of life."

Just this reasoning is implicit in the use of expenditure data on families classified by income by the Bureau of Labor Statistics to prepare an objective standard for describing an American standard of living. The consumption minima discussed in Chapter 10 have no counterparts for many categories of consumption, nor is there any scientific basis for standards. The Bureau of Labor Statistics developed, therefore, from a study of how consumers actually used their incomes, a list of goods and services to represent accepted standards of living for a city worker's family of four persons, and techniques to develop other budgets of a similar kind:

> This budget . . . can best be described as a single point on a scale of living patterns that ranges continuously from a mere existence level to levels of luxurious living where the consumer is almost surfeited with goods. The point selected for measurement is in general the point where the struggle for "more and more" things gives way to the desire for "better and better" quality. Above this level, for example, the average family is likely to be more interested in escaping from an endless round of the cheaper cuts of meat than in increasing the number of pounds of meat that it buys. Below this level, on the other hand, people find it harder and harder to economize, being unable to shift extensively to cheaper commodities and therefore forced to "do without." [4]

The budget is unique in that it represents, not an "ideal" budget, or a "judgment" budget devised by a few people, but rather the actual choices of American families.[5]

[4] A. Ford Hinrichs, "The Budget in Perspective," *Monthly Labor Review*, vol. 66, no. 2, February, 1948, p. 131.

[5] Lester S. Kellogg and Dorothy S. Brady, "The City Worker's Family Budget," *Monthly Labor Review*, vol. 66, no. 2, February, 1948, p. 134.

While scientific standards were used as a starting point for some of the items, the translation of nutritive values, for example, into actual foodstuffs was accomplished by looking at the actual purchases of representative consumers. The budget level for most items was established in the same way—by observing actual purchases.

The analysis used studies of city-family expenditures made between 1929 and 1941, including those described in an earlier chapter. By charting the relation between the amounts bought and the changes in income, a point was found where the increase in buying showed a tendency to decline relatively. Such a point would exist on Table 12-1, for example, for fuel, light, refrigeration, and water at the $2,000 to $3,000 income level, after which these items take a smaller proportion of the total. The BLS study, of course, used much more detailed analysis than this, and measured physical quantities as well as expenditures. The general relationship between consumption and incomes used to establish the budget level is shown in Figure 12-2. When such a chart was plotted for each of many items in the consumption pattern, the point where larger incomes led to decreasing proportions of purchases could be determined.

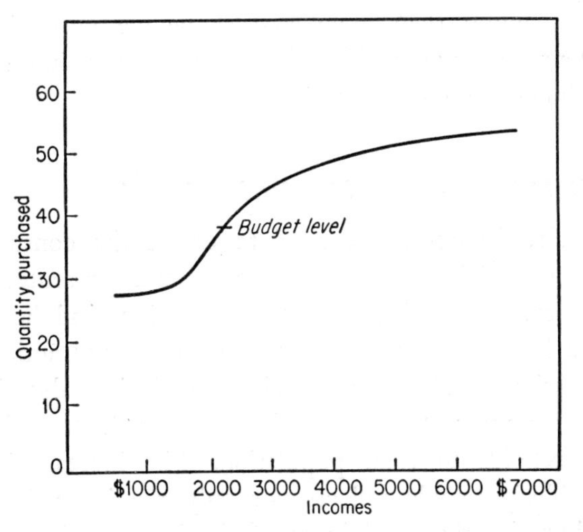

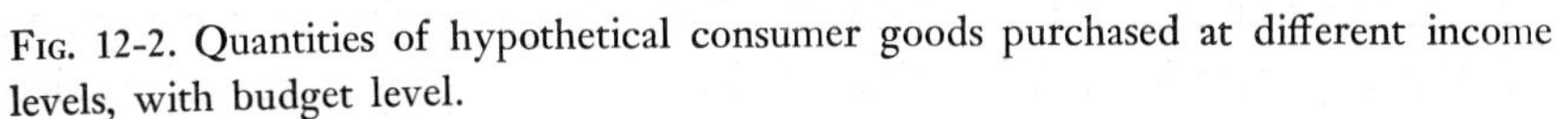
FIG. 12-2. Quantities of hypothetical consumer goods purchased at different income levels, with budget level.

It should be emphasized that this curve, and the data of Table 12-1, represent different spending patterns among consuming units with different incomes at the same point in time. It tells us nothing about the spending patterns of the same consuming unit receiving different incomes over time. The fact that consumers today are not content with the level of consumption they would have enjoyed fifty years ago at the same income levels implies that the budget derived by BLS may soon need revision and poses some interesting problems on the useful life of expenditure data for predicting future markets or consumption. We are still generally ignorant of the effect of income changes on individual consuming units, although Tables 12-1 and 12-2 show a considerable variance among different income levels. The question for businessman and economist remains: "If income changes, how will the consuming unit spend its income? Will those in the $5,500 income bracket now spending $60 yearly on liquor double their purchases with a $1,000 raise and take on the present spending pattern of those in the next higher income class shown in Table 12-1? If the junior civil servant earning $2,600 yearly is out of work for six months and receives only $1,300, will the share of his total spending going to recreation be cut in half and his household expense rise slightly as a proportion of the total, as is typical of the next lower income class?" The short answer to this question suggests that consumption patterns change more slowly than incomes—that people need time to adjust to a new level of income. We find in this reasoning the influences other than income on consumption spending.

HOUSEHOLD FORMATION AND CONSUMPTION

We have already noted the need to define the consuming unit or household for which data are collected and presented. There are important factors which influence the formation, and hence the number, of these households, with some effect on consumption.

Our population of about 160 million people includes about 53 million consuming units. Cultural and economic factors determine the ratio of households to total population. The increase in households headed by elderly people reflects not only the increasing age of our population but also the breakdown of the large family unit composed of three generations. The rise of industrial employment, of social-security provisions, and even of incomes which enable more people to provide for their retirement have all played a part. In the relatively self-sufficient families of eighty years ago, most of whom were employed in agriculture, there was more opportunity for older family members to contribute to family income and support than today, when most incomes are earned in industrial jobs, with their stricter limits on age of employment. The increase in pension and retirement plans, together with government provision for the aged, ensures some independent income to older people. And the rise in real incomes has allowed more households to be supported by the same number of people.

At the other end of the age scale, social and economic factors have also enlarged the formation of households. It is normal for young people to set up independent homes upon marriage, and over the past half century the average age at marriage has become lower. Again, we acknowledge the rise in real incomes which enables the young man to support a family sooner than his grandfather. A change in employment opportunities and in social attitudes has brought a continual increase in households headed by workingwomen—widows and divorcees who in former years would have returned to parents or close relatives. Some of the increase in family incomes can also be attributed to working wives, another fairly recent phenomenon.

Such long-term trends break down temporarily in the face of depression or war. The marriage rate fell sharply during the thirties, but household formation was even more severely cut. On the other hand, the wartime boom in marriages did not produce many households until housing became available and more normal family life became possible.

Such changes in the rate of household formation influence aggregate consumption as the decisions involved in housekeeping arrangements influence the individual consumer's disposition of his income. The purchase of housing and the consumer durables needed to furnish a home stem from the rate of household formation rather than income, once a certain level of income has been reached. The savings and debt position of consumers reflects this also.

Thus we find that the number of homeowners and house purchasers has increased most, since the war, among those where the head of the family is between twenty-five and thirty-four, and particularly among veterans' families. Both the age and the provisions for veterans' home financing are influences here. The same applies to purchasers of automobiles, many household appliances, and furniture, for these items are most frequently bought by married people with no children. Washing machines, on the other hand, are bought mostly by couples with young children.

In order to finance these purchases, young married couples find it quite normal to go into debt. The highest percentage of consuming units with some consumer debt and the highest amount of debt lie again within the age group of twenty-five to thirtv-four and the family-status group of married couples with children.

The youth and the expectations of these households diminish the effect of current income on their current consumption. Mortgages for homes, installment credit, and personal loans enable them to purchase goods and services in excess of their income. And the expectation that incomes will increase means that some future rather than current income determines their status and their consumption pattern. It also means, of course, that they are willing to go into debt with the assurance of future income to meet payments.

When consuming units are classified by incomes, age, and family status these expectations appear to be valid. Tables 12-3 and 12-4 give figures for 1952. Most of the young people up to twenty-five years of age were receiving less than $3,000 yearly. But they could expect their incomes to increase—most of the families in the next age bracket were receiving incomes over $3,000, and the numbers of those in higher-income groups were even greater at ages forty-five to fifty-five. If we recall again the fact that most of the consuming units in the country receive $3,000 to $7,500, it is not surprising that this income is attained by the middle-aged group, making up most of the families in the country.

An orderly change in income and consumption accompanies the development of the family, therefore. Newly formed households, at relatively low income levels, make major expenditures on houses and housekeeping arrangements. Sometimes credit is the chief means of finance; sometimes the working wife provides supplementary income to enable these purchases. By the time children are born, the increasing experience and usefulness of the family head have usually led to higher income, although frequently income declines temporarily if a working wife becomes fully employed at home. Some new major expenditures are required—a shift to homeownership with its accompanying requirements—and the details of other consumption expenditures shift, with more being spent on food and medical care and less on entertainment and transportation. Consumer indebtedness may well rise in this period of a family's fortunes, but income increases are still expected in the future, while the children are growing up. Some of the added income goes, of course, to paying off debt, while some of it, particularly in the

Table 12-3. *Age of Head of Consuming Units by Income Groups,* 1951, Percentage Distribution*

Age of head of spending unit	All income groups	Under $1,000	$1,000–$1,999	$2,000–$2,999	$3,000–$3,999	$4,000–$4,999	$5,000–$7,499	$7,500 and over
18–24	9	15	15	14	6	3	2	1
25–34	23	9	14	28	30	28	26	16
35–44	22	12	16	18	26	27	30	26
45–54	19	14	17	15	17	22	23	32
55–64	12	13	14	13	10	13	13	17
65 or over	13	36	22	10	8	4	5	6
Not ascertained	2	1	2	2	3	3	1	2
All cases	100	100	100	100	100	100	100	100

* Money income before taxes.
SOURCE: "1952 Survey of Consumer Finances," part III, *Federal Reserve Bulletin*, September, 1953, supplementary Table 7.

Table 12-4. *Family Status of Consuming Units by Income Groups,* 1951, Percentage Distribution*

Family status of spending unit	All income groups	Under $1,000	$1,000–$1,999	$2,000–$2,999	$3,000–$3,999	$4,000–$4,999	$5,000–$7,499	$7,500 and over
Single:								
18–44	12	18	19	20	12	3	3	2
45 or over	11	33	19	10	5	4	4	4
Married:								
18–44, no children under 18	7	3	3	7	7	10	13	8
18–44, children under 18	30	8	16	28	40	43	40	31
45 or over, no children under 18	20	19	20	18	17	21	22	30
45 or over, children under 18	11	6	10	9	10	12	15	22
Other †	5	9	11	6	4	3	1	1
Not ascertained	4	4	2	2	5	4	2	2
All cases	100	100	100	100	100	100	100	100

* Money income before taxes.
† Cases in which the husband or wife absent.
SOURCE: "1952 Survey of Consumer Finances," part III, *Federal Reserve Bulletin*, September, 1953, supplementary Table 7.

upper income brackets, is absorbed in more child-rearing expense, notably education and clothing. When the children become independent, the peak of income may already have occurred, but the family consumption pattern, achieved by indebtedness, tends to persist, as the debt has generally been lessened or wiped out. The family home is substantially paid for, as are major appliances and furnishings. When the family head approaches retirement and finally stops working, income declines but by that time the consuming unit is smaller and the type of expenditure has changed.

The pattern of saving in this family life history is particularly relevant to expenditures. Over one-third of the single-person spending units reported no liquid assets in 1952, while less than one-fourth of the childless married couples did so. The percentage of those holding liquid assets amounting to at least 20 per cent of income was greater among families than among single persons, and for consumers as a whole there has been a notable shift of liquid assets to income-bearing investments. Owning liquid assets or investments does not, however, preclude short-term consumer debt of the type we have been discussing, and almost three-fourths of all debtors (concentrated in the middle-income family groups) owned liquid assets which exceeded their indebtedness. The family attempts, then, to secure a backlog of savings despite its current debt, which is properly regarded as short-term.

Another form of spending vitally affected by the family life history is the purchase of insurance. Life insurance policies are associated with beginning a family, and insurance payments contain elements of consumption expenditure and of saving. Except for term policies, any form of life insurance requires saving on the part of the policyholder, for the premiums exceed the actual cost of death benefits, represented roughly by premiums on term policies. The larger payments in other types of insurance provide sometimes a pension or lump-sum payment to the insured at a given age, a limited number of payments, or some other features. These benefits are paid for by accumulating present income in order to derive future income, in other words, by saving. But the total amount paid by consumers for insurance is not saving, for part of it represents the premium for current insurance protection. Because company policies vary so widely, no general analysis of insurance payments can be made to divide them into spending and saving.

To the consuming unit, payments on insurance policies are a kind of commitment of income comparable to mortgage payments or payment of the utility bills which accompany housekeeping. Some three-quarters of all consuming units own some kind of life insurance policy, although the amount of insurance per family is relatively small, only about $5,500. Postwar developments in the insurance field have tended to increase the number of insured people by means of group insurance plans. Group life insurance purchases quadrupled between 1941 and 1951. Payments to retirement or pension plans are another type of saving which is somewhat difficult to include in figures for income and net worth of the consuming unit. Payroll taxes for the government social-security programs of course dispose of part of the consuming unit's income before it is received. Many of the private pension plans require payroll deductions as well as contributions by the employer, and these, too, constitute both income and saving, although, since the funds are never received, they cannot have much bearing on the calculation, by the consuming unit, of income available for consumption expenditures. The number of pension plans in force with life insurance companies rose from 1,500 to 12,000 between 1941 and 1951, while many other pension funds, independently administered, also exist.

Other types of insurance payments include those made by the consuming unit for sickness, accident, or hospital benefits and those made by employee and employer for such benefits and for unemployment compensation. Again, where payroll deductions are used to make payments, these cannot be regarded as part of disposable income by the consuming unit; yet they do provide current protection and are payments designed to bring future income. For the most part, all these developments in the insurance field mean that more middle- and low-income consuming units have become purchasers of insurance, and the net effect has been to secure to more consuming units an extension of their income when their earning power is diminished by death, ill-health, or old age. Insurance payments usually figure as an expense during the early years of family life and as income in the later years.

The consumption pattern associated with old age, therefore, is best interpreted as the final chapter in the family life history. Incomes are generally low—less than $2,000 for 62 per cent of all consuming units headed by a sixty-five-year-old, more than $4,000 for only 13 per cent of these older consumers. The older group shows the most unequal income distribution of any age bracket. Expenditures, both in dollars and percentage terms, are lowest for the highest age group, and average savings have been calculated at roughly the same percentage of income for the oldest consumers as for all consuming units. To some extent, such an arithmetic mean reflects very large incomes and savings by a few people, for, although the average liquid-asset holding is high among older people, the percentage of those having no liquid assets is higher than for any other age group. Reflecting partly the low-income, weak-asset position and partly the fulfillment of major expenditures, the proportion of consuming units with no short-term consumer debt is highest in the oldest age group. We find, therefore, that this group provides the fewest purchasers of automobiles, household appliances, and furniture. Because 65 per cent of them own their own homes (the highest proportion of any age group except that immediately preceding—the fifty-five- to sixty-four-year age), very few either plan to buy or actually purchase a house. For the most part, then, the relatively stable consumption pattern with a high proportion of savings reflects the end of expected income increases, a sufficient supply of durable goods, and probably the fixed habits which go with age.

CONSUMER PLANS AND EXPECTATIONS

Our previous discussion emphasized that household formation and the subsequent history of a family tend to modify sharply the dominant influence of income on consumption. This is particularly true for the younger age groups when the income level of the family is expected to rise. It follows that income changes of all kinds are relevant to consumption, and the Federal Reserve Board has for several years investigated this aspect of consumer behavior.

There is, first, the consumer's own attitude toward his financial status—an approach which is reminiscent of Zweig's definition of "felt poverty." Depending on past and expected income, family status, and the incomes prevailing in a family or social circle, a $4,000 annual income makes one person feel well off and another person poor. Furthermore, consumers are well aware of the difference between their money income and their real income, and their own appraisal enables them to include the effects of price changes on their financial status. While measuring real income changes by the Consumer Price Index appears more objective, it must be remembered that the index is a relatively crude average of limited applicability and that, furthermore, consumers' preferences and decisions are subjective valuations anyway.

Thus, we find that in the postwar years more people reported income increases than decreases or no change, but the people who reported that they were worse off financially, from year to year, were also more numerous than those who felt financial improvement or no change. In 1950, only three-fourths of the consuming units whose incomes had actually increased felt better off, and two years later the proportion had dropped to about half. The increases in income do not come as a surprise to many people—one-quarter to one-third of the consuming units have anticipated yearly income increases.

Along with consumers' attitudes toward their finances may be considered their opinions on the right time to buy certain major-expense items, like houses, automobiles, and consumer durables. Because most of these expenditures can be postponed, consumption in these lines is much more subject to fluctuation. From the decision-making point of view, such purchases are obviously more carefully considered than the habitual purchases of cigarettes or milk. Hence, the consumer's plans to buy can be recorded, with some interesting data on the difference between planned and unplanned purchases.

The number of consuming units planning to buy is closest to the number of actual purchasers for houses rather than for automobiles or consumer durables. There is, however, an opposite tendency with respect to the planned and actual sums involved, with actual home purchasers paying less, generally, than the planned expenditures and actual automobile purchasers paying more.

Entering into the consuming unit's plans are, of course, expectations of price changes; yet for the most part these are far less important than might be thought—perhaps because no economic predictions are trusted. Thus, for most postwar years far more people who expected their incomes to rise planned major purchases than did those who expected no income increase. Neither group was influenced by their expectation of price rises, and less than 20 per cent of those who expected price rises concluded from that fact that the present was a good time to buy.

It appears, therefore, that price changes affect consumers more after they have taken place, by their effects on real income, while income changes cast their shadows before as well as affecting status and purchasing power once they have taken effect. The whole area investigated by the Survey Research Center for the Federal Reserve Board is a developing field, in which both methodology and data are constantly being improved.

SOCIAL AND ECONOMIC FACTORS

We have already emphasized the dominance of the middle-income group in American consumption. Starting with this fact, a provocative analysis in *Fortune Magazine* [6] suggests that there is a remarkable homogeneity in this group, including social and cultural factors.

One such factor is the suburban development. The changing relationship between urban and rural communities appears in all kinds of problems—the increasing deficits of metropolitan cities, the school and road problems of mushrooming villages or towns, the migration of the shopping center to parkways and intersections, and the continuing transportation sufferings of commuters. The suburbia described by *Fortune* is probably typified by the postwar housing "development"—and the postwar rate of household formation, the building boom, and relatively high incomes all played a part in expanding the number of families who live in the open spaces and work in the city.

By *Fortune*'s definition, suburbia includes some 30 million people in metropolitan areas or near cities of 50,000 in population. These suburbs have been growing some three times as fast as the country as a whole, and even faster in the Southern and Plains regions, where they are not so prevalent.

Stressing the uniformity of consumption patterns in this area, *Fortune*'s discussion of the suburban way of life emphasizes many group characteristics. Suburbanites tend to own their own homes, to have families of two and three children, and to be concentrated in the age groups under forty. These characteristics of course influence the consumption pattern—the toys and children's clothing, the household appliances needed to cope with home and small children, and the housing expenses ranging from furniture to garden hose. Beyond this, the proximity of families at roughly the same age and income levels with broadly similar occupations and background makes, it is claimed, group customs overriding. Other characteristics of this homogeneous culture include a taste for informal and outdoor living, affecting clothing and recreational purchases, and a burgeoning market for suburban shopping centers.

The social climate of any group, not only suburbia, of course affects the consumption pattern. Thus the 1950 BLS survey shows some interest-

[6] "The Lush New Suburban Market," *Fortune Magazine*, November, 1953; and "The Wonderful, Ordinary Luxury Market," *Fortune Magazine*, December, 1953.

ing differences between the expenditures of wage earners' and clerical workers' families and those of all families, to support the idea that there are different standards between the two groups. Such differences may be found, but they tend to disappear in the smaller cities, and they are not so pronounced as the variations in the depression decades, mentioned in the previous chapter.

Housing and clothing expenditures were generally a smaller share of the total for wage-earner and clerical families than for all families, but this difference was far more noticeable in the large cities. Almost half of the cities with less than 30,000 population showed clothing expenditures among workers equal to or greater than the share for all families, while only one-fifth of the other cities, and these mostly in the South or West, showed such a relationship. Again, in housing, the proportional expenditures of wage-earner and clerical families were equal to or exceeded those of all families in one-third of the small cities, and in only 5 of the other 58 cities studied. A similar pattern can be traced for expenditures on food and liquor and tobacco. With the exception of Youngstown, Ohio, all the cities above 30,000 population revealed wage-earner and clerical family expenditure on these items well in excess of the proportion spent by all families. But in the 33 smaller cities, the difference in spending on these items was much smaller, and in about 6 cities it did not exist. One can reason that the smaller locations provide not only a more homogeneous cultural pattern but also less extremes of price variation in different shopping and housing centers.

Many of the differences in household consumption patterns among regions must be traced to similar regional differences. Thus, when the Bureau of Labor Statistics priced its budget in 34 cities, to find the "cost of living" for its objective standard, the differences in total costs were traceable chiefly to housing and food. The survey reinforces, however, the idea of a homogeneous consumption pattern by suggesting that prices and costs do not vary greatly between regions and that what differences exist are little larger than the variations among cities in the same region.

AMERICAN CONSUMPTION, CIRCA 1954

Much stress has been laid on the Industrial Revolution and more recent changes in technology which have made continually increasing production a commonplace phenomenon. Total production in this country doubled between 1900 and 1920 and by the 1950s had almost doubled again. A similar rise took place in total consumption, and since population has only doubled since the turn of the century, consumption levels per capita or per consuming unit are roughly twice what they were in 1900. In terms of household expenditures, this means that today's consuming unit is receiving and spending much more income than those at the end of the nineteenth century. These changes have for the most part been gradual, and we find, therefore, a partial answer to the question posed earlier in the chapter as to the dynamic effects of income change on the same consuming unit. We have experienced the dynamic effects of increased income, and we find that consumption too has increased.

This important increase in consumption could only take place insofar as consuming units changed their patterns of expenditure—made new choice decisions with respect to types and quantities of goods and services consumed. We should look, therefore, at changes in household expenditure patterns for the characteristics of the revolution in consumption which has accompanied the revolution in production.

One such characteristic is the expectation of change and of progress, however the latter term is defined. We have noted the importance of income expectations to the spending habits of a family in its economic cycle, and we have remarked that most income changes are foreseen by the consuming unit. We may generalize further on the familiarity of change in the American scene, on the readiness with which pioneers left their static surroundings to explore dynamic possibilities in other regions, on the upheavals of population produced by two wars and a depression, on the overwhelming change in this economy from agriculture to industry and from an isolated country to a world power. Not all these changes have been accepted readily or efficiently throughout the nation, but such events justify the American expectation of change, which may be credited with much of the increase in consumption from increased income.

Along with the attitude that expects dynamic rather than static surroundings must be mentioned a willingness, on the part of households, to experiment with new consumption patterns and with new goods and services. When increased income provides increased consumption, it also results in different patterns of consumption. The family must learn how to spend more money on food and clothing, to enjoy more travel and recreation, and to provide better education and medical care with its larger funds. Many of today's consumer goods and even forms of saving did not exist fifty years ago, and would not exist today were not consuming units ready to experiment with their increased incomes. In the following chapters, we shall examine some of these recent developments in the commodities which consumers buy. Here we must note, as an intangible but nonetheless essential characteristic of household expenditure patterns, the willingness to experiment which carries income changes through to changes in consumption.

In this connection, one further point must be made. We have already noted the fact that spending at higher income levels consists in buying better-quality items rather than more in quantity. This means, also, that consumption patterns differ in degree rather than in kind between the several income classes. There are no categories of household expenditure which are confined to the very rich and totally absent from the middle-income groups. And a similar resemblance exists between purchases of the middle-income and low-income groups. There are few commodities which do not have their low-priced counterparts, and these cheaper models make the American consumption pattern available in all price ranges to all income classes. When we say that most of the consuming units in the country receive yearly incomes between $3,000 and $7,500, we speak of a fairly wide range in dollars. But the wide range in consumption expenditures does not produce striking differences in consumption patterns. The process of change, experimenting with new purchasing habits and new commodities, can take place at almost every income level.

Because consumption patterns differ in degree rather than in kind, it becomes easier for the household to increase its purchases with increased incomes. Those goods and services which represent better quality to an individual consuming unit are already familiar. Many of them are sold where the consumer normally buys. Others are apparent in the lives of those in the community who are slightly better off. And the media of mass communication provide abundant information about all the better-quality items which exist. Our social mobility means that there are no caste or class restrictions on consumption patterns and that those who experience income increases can take naturally to their increased consumption expenditures.

We may conclude, then, that the typical characteristic of household spending is its dynamic nature; that increased incomes lead to increased consumption because consumers are ready and willing to experiment; and that the differences which we have noted in consumption patterns may be expressed as differences in quality and degree.

Questions and Points for Discussion

1. Distinguish between comparing expenditures by income classes and comparing expenditures with changes in income.
2. What is the general relationship between income and age, income and family status, and how does this affect consumption?
3. Discuss the concept of consumer's net worth.
4. Why do consuming units with liquid assets also have debts?
5. What do we mean by income elasticity? Give the conventional computational formula. What does an income elasticity of 1 mean, of 2 mean, of .5 mean?

References

Editors of *Fortune Magazine: The Changing American Market,* Hanover House, New York, 1953, chaps. 1–4, 11.

———: "The Lush New Suburban Market," *Fortune Magazine,* November, 1953.

———: "The Wonderful, Ordinary Luxury Market," *Fortune Magazine,* December, 1953.

Gilboy, Elizabeth W.: "Income-expenditure Relations," *Review of Economic Statistics,* vol. 22, pp. 115–121, August, 1940.

Kyrk, Hazel: *The Family in the American Economy,* University of Chicago Press, Chicago, 1953, chaps. 1–4, 14.

McConnell, Joseph L., and Janet M. Hooks: "The Changing Family and Its Dependents," in Hoyte, Reid, McConnell, and Hooks, *American Income and Its Use,* Harper & Brothers, New York, 1954, part III.

Stone, Richard: *The Measurement of Consumers' Expenditure and Behaviour in the United Kingdom, 1920–1938,* Cambridge University Press, New York, 1954, vol. I.

U.S. Bureau of Labor Statistics: *Family Income, Expenditures, and Savings in 1950,* Bulletin 1097 (revised), June, 1953.

———: *Family Income, Expenditures, and Savings in* 10 *Cities,* Bulletin 1065, 1952.

———: *Monthly Labor Review,* vol. 66, no. 2, February, 1948.

13. *Commodity Expenditure Relationships*

In this chapter, we shift our emphasis from the consumption pattern of the household to the effect, on particular goods and services, of the consumption patterns of many households. Our data include the findings of expenditure studies and also aggregate figures covering a span of years. We have figures on the total disposable income received by households and on total consumption expenditures out of this income. We also have figures on sales of various goods and services and sales by different types of business firms. All these are important in describing the choices of consumers.

Obviously, what is consumed depends to some extent on what is produced within an economy. The natural resources of a country make coal or oil or gas the common heating fuel. Bicycles are essential to Dutch travel and a hobby for Americans in part at least because of geography—the great spaces in the United States, the lack of land space in Holland. A country with a large unskilled labor force or considerable unemployment uses many household servants, while in the United States the high cost of labor has induced the development of many household appliances. The climate and soil conditions of one country make rice or wheat the staple food crop and in another lead to the export of sugar or rubber or tin in exchange for foods. Consumption patterns in the United States vary because of our diverse production, our abundant natural resources, and the productivity which makes us wealthy in the output of real goods and services. This chapter is devoted to further exploration of the American scene. It is a historical exploration in part, for expenditure patterns often become clearer in contrast with those of earlier years.

INCOME, TOTAL CONSUMPTION EXPENDITURES, AND TOTAL SAVINGS

We may begin with figures on total consumption expenditures, calculated not from actual spending by consuming units but from the current sales and production of firms which make consumer goods. These figures were quoted in Tables 4-8 and 4-9, Chapter 4, where it was pointed out that the total level of spending varied with prosperous or depressed times, as well as with changes in the value of the dollar. Our figures for total spending can, however, be deflated for price increases, and when this is done, they show a very real increase in the volume of goods and services consumed. Our consumption levels, in real terms, are almost double those of the 1920s.

Total consumption expenditures are related to total disposable income—the money available to consuming units after income taxes have been paid. Reflecting the vast increase in production, total disposable income in the United States in 1953 was $250 billion, or over three times that of 1929. Beginning in 1930, the depression years decreased this income, and not until 1941 were the dollar amounts of 1929 reached again. Since then, however, total disposable income has increased in every year, although not at a steady rate.

Spending and saving. How much of this income is spent on goods and services for current consumption, and how much is saved? Table 13-1 gives the totals for personal income, disposable income, consumption expenditures, and personal savings for 1929 to 1953.

Two phenomena—the depression and the war—show up immediately. During 1932 and 1933, consuming units spent more than their current incomes by using up past savings at the rate of $600 million each year. From 1941 to 1945, consuming units saved at extraordinarily high rates, partly because of the large rise in incomes, partly because of scarcities, particularly of houses and durable goods, and partly because of the new incentives to save offered by patriotic motives and small-denomination United States bonds. Aside from these two abnormal periods, what does Table 13-1 tell us about total income and its disposition?

First, that both spending and saving are high at high levels of income and low at low levels of income. This confirms the findings of consumption studies which show greater wealth and more savers among consuming units at high levels of income than at low levels. The figures do not show, however, a steady rise in the *proportions* saved at higher levels of income, as is true when the savings of consuming units in different income classes are compared.

In 1935, for example, personal saving amounted to 3.4 per cent of total disposable income of $58.3 billion and in 1936 to 5.4 per cent of a $66.2 billion income. In 1937, income increased to $71 billion, but saving dropped slightly to 5.2 per cent, and in 1938, when income declined to

Table 13-1. *Personal Disposable Income, Total Consumption Expenditures, and Personal Saving, 1929–1953, Current Dollars and Percentage Distribution*

(Dollar figures in billions)

Year	Personal disposable income		Personal consumption expenditures		Personal saving	
	Amount	Per cent	Amount	Per cent	Amount	Per cent
1929	$ 83.1	100	$ 79.0	94.9	$ 4.2	5.1
1930	74.4	100	71.9	95.4	3.4	4.6
1931	63.8	100	61.3	96.1	2.5	3.9
1932	48.7	100	49.3	101.2	−0.6	−1.2
1933	45.8	100	46.4	101.3	−0.6	−1.3
1934	52.0	100	51.9	99.8	0.1	0.2
1935	58.3	100	56.3	96.6	2.0	3.4
1936	66.2	100	62.6	94.6	3.6	5.4
1937	71.0	100	67.3	94.8	3.7	5.2
1938	65.7	100	64.6	98.3	1.1	1.7
1939	70.4	100	67.6	95.9	2.9	4.1
1940	76.1	100	71.9	94.5	4.2	5.5
1941	93.0	100	81.9	88.1	11.1	11.9
1942	117.5	100	89.7	76.3	27.8	23.7
1943	133.5	100	100.5	75.3	33.0	24.7
1944	146.8	100	109.8	74.9	36.9	25.1
1945	150.4	100	121.7	80.9	28.7	19.1
1946	159.2	100	146.6	92.1	12.6	7.9
1947	169.0	100	165.0	97.6	4.0	2.4
1948	187.6	100	177.6	94.7	10.0	5.3
1949	188.2	100	180.6	96.0	7.6	4.0
1950	206.1	100	194.0	94.1	12.1	5.9
1951	226.1	100	208.3	92.2	17.7	7.8
1952	238.9	100	218.4	92.3	18.4	7.7
1953	250.1	100	230.1	92.0	20.0	8.0

SOURCE: U.S. Department of Commerce, *Survey of Current Business*, July, 1954.

$65 billion (still higher than 1935 levels), saving dropped to 1.7 per cent. Figures for recent years are also inconclusive. In 1949, personal saving accounted for 4 per cent of a $188.2 billion income; in 1950, when income rose to $206.1 billion, saving increased to 5.9 per cent; and, in 1951, an even larger income of $226.1 billion produced even larger savings of 7.8 per cent. In 1952, however, income rose to $238.9 billion, and the proportion saved scarcely changed. Figures for 1953 show only 8 per cent saved out of still greater income. Finally, our current total income is over four times that of the 1930s, but saving has not increased by the same proportion.

There are, therefore, complicating factors which prevent a simple relationship between the amount of income and the amount of saving or spending. One such factor is the source of data, for personal saving is computed by subtracting the sum of total expenditures from total disposable income. Since saving is the smallest sum, any error in calculating the other two will affect the figure for saving disproportionately. Such errors, however, cannot wholly account for the change in the proportions of income spent and saved.

We may find part of the explanation in the changed distribution of income. The increased total income, from 1936 to 1944, especially after taxes, represented far more money for low- and middle-income consuming units than additional money for high-income consuming units. The rate of household formation began to recover in the late thirties and boomed after the war. We should expect, therefore, more spending out of a quadrupled total disposable income when it is divided up among more newly formed families at moderate income levels.

Finally, we may refer to our changing standards of living. The BLS standard of minimum decency described in the preceding chapter includes some goods and services unknown in 1900 and a level of consumption which is not at all minimum by earlier standards. What this implies, of course, is that the extra income has been spent on reaching higher levels of living, as new commodities became available. Savings increase as well, but not in proportion to the increases in income. And consuming units change their spending patterns, to make total consumption rise as income becomes higher and higher.

How have these changes in spending patterns and total consumption and saving taken place? A brief examination of some major categories of consumption spending will tell us.

FOOD

The importance of food in the consumption pattern is obvious. Purchases of food to be served at home are the largest item in total personal consumption expenditures. In 1929, such purchases represented 18 per cent of all consumption expenditures; in 1953, 23 per cent. When expenditures on meals away from home and the value of food produced and consumed on the farm are added, the food expenditures of American consumers have shown a steady growth, absolutely and as a proportion of total spending, since the depression. The aggregate figure of $71 billion spent on food in 1953, about 31 per cent of all consumption expenditure, contains many fascinating details of change and stability in food consumption.

Consumption and production. The relationship between food consumption and production is particularly interesting in the United States, and perhaps more so in these days of a perpetual farm problem. Over 90 per cent of the food consumed in this country is produced here also. The volume of imports compares or exceeds domestic production only for canned and cured fish, some kinds of fruits including bananas, figs, and pineapples, and sugar, coffee, tea, cocoa beans, and nuts (excluding peanuts), but all the imports have never provided more than 8 per cent of our total food supplies. Some changes in domestic production have decreased the proportion of imported foods since the beginning of the century, which is true for peanuts, all kinds of tree nuts, sugar, rice, dried peas and beans, dried fruits, citrus fruits, and cheese.

The total volume of food production in the United States has increased importantly over the past fifty years: total output increased from an index value of 56 in 1910 to 110 in 1954 (1947 to 1949 = 100). And output on a per capita basis has been sustained and bountiful, never falling below an index value of 87 since 1910 (again 1947 to 1949 = 100). We should recognize at this point the tremendous role that technological advance has played in increasing food production. The number of workers in agriculture has declined from 13.5 million in 1910 to 6.5 million in 1954; yet this greatly reduced labor force feeds a total population that has increased from 92 million in 1910 to 162 million in 1954. Farm technological advance has made this possible. Besides the mechanization of tractors and farm implements, great gains have been made in crop yields through the improvement of seeds, fertilizers, and pest-control methods, the breeding and feeding of livestock has progressed, and farm-management techniques in general have developed. The productivity of American agriculture has led today to the specter of surpluses rather than scarcity.

Consumption measures. The outstanding fact in food consumption is the limitations of the human stomach, which preclude much change in the *volume* of food consumed by a people. The Department of Agriculture estimates that in 1909 about 1,612 pounds of food per capita was consumed in the United States; in 1952, about 1,530 pounds. The difference between the lowest and highest figures for the other years was only 118 pounds, or 7 per cent of the average. And some of this variance can be attributed to errors of measurement.

The index of per capita food consumption, which takes into account shifts in the composition of diets (i.e., shifts from low-resource-using foods like cereals to high-resource-using foods like meats), computed on a 1947 to 1949 base, indicates that the per capita food consumption held almost constant from 1909 to 1937, rose sharply from 1938 to 1946, and has leveled off since 1946. The index value for the long period 1909 to 1939 approximates 90; the index values during the period 1938 to 1946 rise from 90 to 104 and in the latter period fluctuate between 104 and 100. Total food consumption as measured by the index of per capita food consumption has been relatively constant since 1909 with the exception of the brief upward thrust during and immediately following World War II.

How, then, shall we look at food consumption? Food consumption can be evaluated by nutrition experts in terms of the dietary needs of the population. Another approach analyzes consumers' choices among many types of food. And a third looks at the services provided with the food and the ways in which food consumption relates to other items in the consumption pattern.

Nutritional values. In measuring food supplies in terms of the nutrients available for consumption, it appears that food supplies in the United States have increased in nutritional value. The amount of calcium per capita per day, for example, has increased from about 0.8 to 1.1 grams over the past fifty years, owing chiefly to an increase in dairy products. Iron and all the vitamins have become more plentiful because of gains in fruit and vegetable production and the enrichment of staples like bread, milk, and margarine. Table 13-2 compares the National Research Council's recommended dietary allowances for a physically active man with the nutrients available for consumption in three time periods, 1909 to 1914, 1933 to 1938, and 1947 to 1951.

On their face, these figures show a healthy surplus, today, of most

Table 13-2. *Average Nutrients Available for Consumption per Capita per Day and Recommended Dietary Allowances for a Physically Active Man*

Item	1909–1913	1933–1937	1947–1951	Recommended dietary allowances
Food energy, calories	3486	3254	3228	3000
Protein, grams	100.8	89.4	94.6	70
Calcium, grams	0.85	0.91	1.03	1
Iron, milligrams	15.2	14.3	17.1	12
Vitamin A, international units	6880	8060	9760	5000
Thiamine, milligrams	1.64	1.45	1.90	1.5
Riboflavin, milligrams	1.88	1.86	2.32	1.8
Niacin, milligrams	17.6	15.8	19.4	15.0
Ascorbic acid, milligrams	104	114	118	75

SOURCE: *Recommended Dietary Allowances*, National Research Council. Nutrients available compiled from *Consumption of Food in the United States, 1909–52*, U.S. Bureau of Agricultural Economics, Agriculture Handbook 62, September, 1953, Table 44.

nutrients and a historical lack only in calcium. To be wholly accurate, the dietary needs of the entire population should be computed for reference, since babies and nursing mothers require far more calcium and iron than the adult male, and adolescent boys require more calories. Even apart from this defect, the table does not, of course, show the per capita intake of food, but only what is available. The nutrients are not all equally present in all foods, and the food loss through waste and faulty preparation methods cannot be estimated. Dietary inadequacies are prevalent in low- and high-income families. *Our food supplies are sufficient, however, to allow a proper diet for all, if distribution methods and education could equate consumption with what is available.*

Dietary changes. Consumers buy food, of course, by choosing particular food products rather than packaged nutrients, and the composition of the diet discloses consumer preference. Table 13-3 shows, for twelve major food groups, the per capita consumption in pounds during the three time periods used above. These figures explain some of the changes in nutrients—the vast increase in citrus fruits and leafy vegetables and the impressive rise in dairy products. The most notable change in the quantitative data is the steady decline in potatoes and grain products.

These changes in food consumption appear more striking in Figure 13-1, which shows the basic trend of dietary composition since 1910. The values in this diagram refer to an index of food consumption which measures both quantity and some changes in quality. The index weights the quantities of foodstuffs consumed in each year by the average retail prices of these foods during 1947 to 1949. Various foods are thus combined

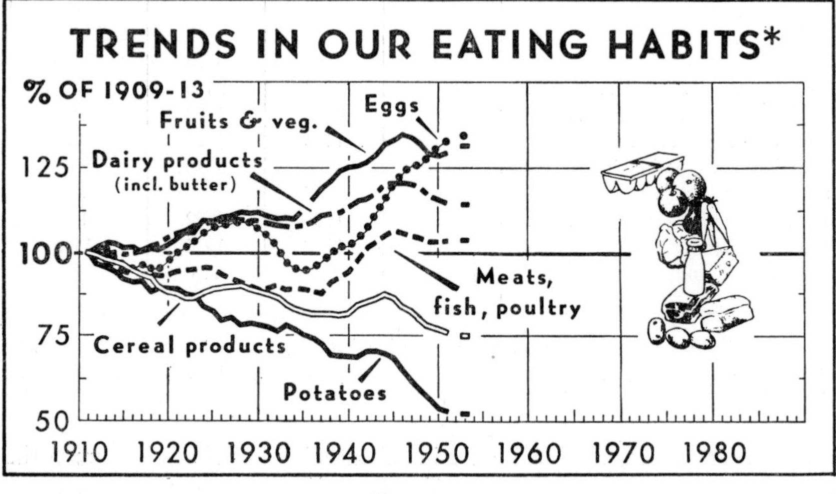

FIG. 13-1.

* Per capita civilian consumption, United States, using 1947 to 1949 retail prices as weights. Five-year moving average centered. Data for year 1953 shown by symbol. From Negative 47745-XX, *U.S. Bureau of Agricultural Economics.*

in terms of their relative economic importance, which reflects both consumer preference and the costs of producing and marketing the foods. Table 13-4 presents for a year in each of the time periods used in Tables 13-2 and 13-3 the index for seventeen groups of food products. It provides greater detail, but it tells the same story: rising per capita consumption in fruits and vegetables, eggs, and dairy products; declining consumption in cereal products and potatoes.

This changing dietary pattern reflects technological change in production and marketing as well as shifts in consumer preference. Refrigeration equipment enables more fresh fruits and vegetables to be grown for shipment to distant markets; food processing has increased sugar consumption. Certainly nutritional education has influenced the shift to vegetables and

Table 13-3. *Approximate Consumption of Food per Capita, Retail-weight Equivalent in Pounds, by Major Food Groups, Annual Averages*

Food groups	1909–1913	1933–1937	1947–1951
Total food	1,591	1,509	1,532
Dairy products, excluding butter	376	375	415
Eggs	37	35	46
Meats, poultry, and fish, excluding bacon	151	133	153
Fats and oils, including fat cuts and butter	59	64	65
Dry beans and peas, nuts, and soya products	16	17	17
Potatoes and sweet potatoes	196	146	114
Citrus fruit and tomatoes	60	87	111
Leafy, green, and yellow vegetables	62	103	106
Other vegetables and fruit	251	222	224
Flour and cereal products	287	203	168
Sugars and sirups	88	109	108
Coffee, tea, and cocoa	10	14	18

SOURCE: Compiled from *Consumption of Food in the United States, 1909–52,* U.S. Bureau of Agricultural Economics, Agriculture Handbook 62, September, 1953, Table 38.

fruit, and the dieting fad of the twenties helped discourage potatoes and grain products.

But the diet also reflects the high income of our economy. In terms of economic resources, our current food consumption represents a high-quality, high-cost diet. Producing calories and proteins from animal sources—eggs, meat, dairy products—requires far more resources than growing the same amount of nutrients in potatoes, beans, and grain products. The steady growth in real consumer income since the turn of the century, therefore, is responsible for the long-term trend to a diet of high-quality foods.

Food and other goods and services. We may now examine the food-consumption pattern in terms of what the purchaser buys at the market, aside from the changes in major raw food groups we have noted. The striking trend in food production and consumption is the increase in processing and marketing services, which provide consumers with quite a different sort of meats, vegetables, dairy products, and so on, from what existed at the beginning of this century.

Part of this increase may be seen in the figures of Table 13-4 for proc-

Table 13-4. *Per Capita Consumption of Foods, by Major Food Groups, Price-weighted Basis*

(Index numbers, 1947–1949 = 100)

Food groups	1911	1935	1949
Total food	88	87	99
Meats, poultry, fish	99	80	99
Eggs	84	72	100
Dairy products, including butter	82	92	98
Dairy products, excluding butter	67	80	98
Fats and oils, including butter	104	118	101
Fats and oils, excluding butter	59	88	102
All fruits	88	93	98
Fresh	119	110	95
Canned	20	73	102
Canned juices	2	13	98
Frozen	...	15	116
Dried	102	137	110
All vegetables	72	84	98
Fresh	91	99	96
Canned	40	66	99
Other processed products *	4	20	104
Potatoes and sweet potatoes	151	138	97
Beans, peas, nuts	79	101	100
Cereal products	128	105	99
Sugar and sirups	61	91	100
Coffee, tea, cocoa	56	79	103

* Includes frozen vegetables, canned soups, and canned baby foods.

SOURCE: *Consumption of Food in the United States, 1909–52,* U.S. Bureau of Agricultural Economics, Agriculture Handbook 62, September, 1953, Table 39.

essed fruits, juices, and vegetables. The development of quality control in the canning industry, both by arrangements with growers and by improvements in processing methods, had led, by the thirties, to universal acceptance of commercially canned fruits and vegetables. Canned fruit juices began a spectacular rise in the late thirties, as did canned baby foods.

Frozen foods made their appearance in the late thirties, but because wartime material shortages held down the supply of freezer units for retail stores, consumption of frozen foods began to rise only after the war, and then increased rapidly. Since 1947, the per capita consumption of canned fruit has risen by only 11 per cent, but the per capita consumption of frozen fruit has more than doubled. The substantial use of frozen orange juice has led to an absolute decrease in the per capita consumption of fresh oranges. Similar gains in frozen-vegetable consumption have caused a similar decline for canned vegetables. Frozen fruits and vegetables were added to the Consumer Price Index in its postwar revision, although these items are still more frequently purchased by families with incomes above those whose typical consumption is priced by that index.

More processing has been added to almost every major food group. Grains and grain products are sold not merely as flour and bread, but as waffle mix, piecrust and cake mixes, and heat-and-serve rolls. Complete dinners of spaghetti and meat or beef stew are canned and frozen. Pudding and dessert mixes, ice-cream and candy preparations allow the consumer to buy eggs and milk already processed. The consumer is buying, in short, laborsaving foods. Prepackaged meat and sorted, washed, and packaged fruits and vegetables provide further convenience and timesaving to the customer. In many cases, quality has been standardized by such preparation of foods; in any case, some part of the kitchen work has been taken over by the food seller.

These changes reflect, of course, other changes in the consumption pattern. We have already mentioned the workingwoman, who can run a home and job more efficiently with such foods and whose job is part of the reason why family incomes can pay for such items. Purchases of kitchen equipment have obviously been affected with the disappearance of the soup kettle and the introduction of the freezer. Important developments in marketing to be discussed in a later chapter have meant that all food items are available in one store and that shopping tends to be done on fewer, but more expensive, expeditions.

In an economic sense, most of these changes in consumption reflect a substitution of the consumer's capital for the consumer's labor. The outlay for an electric mixer or a deep freeze enables the housewife to save time and energy. The higher prices paid for more fully processed foods require more liquid capital or current income and less current labor. Hence, we have another manifestation of the higher incomes more generally available in 1954 than in 1909.

We may now return to food purchases as a percentage of total consumption expenditures and find the explanation for the increased spending for food since World War II. Americans are not eating more food in terms of pounds, and for the most part they have not increased the quality or richness of their diet since 1946, *but they have been purchasing more and more services with their food.* Consumers are buying new products with their food—all kinds of conveniences—saving both time and work. One change in consumption patterns which has led to increased spending out of increased income results from the consumer preference for laborsaving items and for the services supplied by the processors, distributors, and retailers of food.

HOUSING AND HOUSEHOLD OPERATION

Food, shelter, and clothing have been so often quoted as basic human needs that it is logical to consider housing and home maintenance next in our categories of consumption. These two subdivisions take, from the total of personal consumption expenditure, sums which have in recent years declined as a share of total expenditures. In 1929, housing amounted to $11.4 billion and household operation to $10.7 billion out of a total of $78.7 billion, or about 28 per cent. In 1933 occurred the lowest expenditures, $7.9 and $6.5 billion, respectively, which accounted for 30 per cent of all expenditures. Beginning in 1935, the expenditures on household operation began to exceed those on housing, but the total declined to about 23 per cent of all consumption spending. The most recent data show expenditures, in 1953, of $28 billion on housing and $30 billion on household operation, which account for 25 per cent of total consumer spending. We need to analyze, therefore, what these relative shifts in consumption expenditure mean in terms of the kind of "shelter" attained in our consumption patterns.

Housing expenditure data. The amount of housing "consumed" each year is essentially a service, provided by the stock of houses in existence at that time. Consumption figures are therefore derived from a census of the dwellings in the country, for the amount of housing services purchased is taken to be the space-rental value of these dwelling units. The Census of Population and Housing provides data on the number of dwelling units, the average monthly rent of rented dwellings, and the fair market value of owner-occupied units. Many rents include payments for utilities or furnishings supplied by the landlord, and these are deducted in order to give a figure for payments for "space rent," which were the housing expenditures quoted previously. Over half the families in this country own their homes, and the value of the shelter they receive must be computed by allowing a rental value for these homes, based on the actual rents paid for similar houses in the same neighborhood.

It follows that expenditure data are far from precise, subject to much estimate, and above all dependent on rents, which normally lag behind the movements of other prices and which, since 1940, have been affected by rent controls of varying stringency and duration. Nevertheless, the data show some striking changes since 1929. In that year, less than $6 billion of the $11 billion spent on housing represented the value of owner-occupied homes, and $4.5 billion was rents paid. During the depression and late thirties, housing expenditure was almost evenly divided between rentals and homeownership values, as in 1933, when $3.8 billion represented owner-occupied homes and $3.3 billion rents paid. But the postwar housing boom brought a noticeable change. In 1953, out of a total of $28 billion housing expenditure, some $16 billion represented the imputed value of owner-occupied homes, while only $9 billion represented rents. We find, then, a growing tendency for consumers to own their homes and for such homes to provide a larger share of the total consumption of shelter in this country.

Housing construction data. Purchases of new houses, of course, represent an addition to consumers' capital rather than consumption expenditures, and the new houses built, beyond those needed to replace old houses, add to the economy's wealth, or stock of income-producing goods. New residential building accounts for a little more than one-third of all new construction and in recent years for over one-half of new private construction activity. It represents, therefore, an important productive activity, but one which is subject to spectacular fluctuations.

Housing in recent decades was restricted first by the depression and then by the war. In 1929, the value of new residential construction amounted to about one-third of the current expenditures on housing, but it dropped to less than 10 per cent during the thirties and regained its former levels only in 1940 and 1941. But from then on the building industry was subjected to severe shortages and restrictions, so that new housing again dropped to depression rates. Because the demand for housing could be postponed, there occurred in 1946 the beginning of a housing boom, and the value of new construction in 1948 to 1950 was over half the amount currently paid for housing shelter. The depression years left their mark, however, in the large number of old houses and the persistence of substandard units.

Over half the dwelling units are over thirty years old today, as opposed to only one-third of the stock which were that old during the late twenties. There is some evidence, also, that the houses added since the war are considerably less in value than earlier houses. The greatest increase has occurred in houses valued at less than $12,000, and the number of houses valued at over $22,500 has decreased. Much of this trend reflects the government aids given to low-cost housing; much more of it probably reflects the gains in homeownership.

Despite the widespread interest in mass-construction and low-cost housing, the chief technological change responsible for these housing figures is probably the revolution in mortgage agreements. Prior to the depression, mortgage rates were 2 to 4 per cent above the 4 to 4½ per cent prevailing in recent years. Long-term agreements were not at all the standard contract which is signed today. The short-term mortgage required regular interest payments, but no reduction of principal by consumers in the 1920s. Hence, the risk was substantially greater and fewer consumers were able to borrow mortgage money with which to buy a house. Today's long-term agreements provide for the steady reduction of principal, which increases the owner's equity in his home. Such developments, plus the Federal Housing Administration guarantee of mortgages, enabled an entirely new group of consumers to become homeowners, as did the housing provisions for veterans enacted after the war. Thus, in 1950, we find 55 per cent of the dwelling units occupied by their owners, as opposed to 46 per cent in 1900, a change whose social implications have been mentioned earlier.

Housing characteristics. What types of shelter do the expenditures noted above provide? How can the housing sector of our consumption pattern be described? The Census collects data on structure, facilities, and other characteristics of our housing stock.

Most of the dwelling units are single detached homes. These accounted for almost two-thirds of all dwelling units in 1950, while houses with two to four dwelling units amounted to 25 per cent. The 1950 Census gives the first record of trailers, which in prior decades had been negligible but amounted at that time to 290,000 units. The type of dwelling reflects, first, the shift to an urban population; since 1900, nonfarm dwelling units have trebled in number. Second, it represents the trend to independent families we have been discussing; although the cities have required apartment buildings, there has been a marked increase since World War II in the proportion of single-family homes erected. Half the homes in the country contain 4½ rooms or more, but half are smaller. The proportion of homes with private inside toilet facilities has gone up from 60 to 71 per cent in the past decade, while 64 per cent of the dwellings had private bathing facilities with hot running water.

Figures on substandard homes have been quoted elsewhere. We may end this section by quoting from the BLS budget described in the previous chapter, which designates minimum accepted American standards of housing: [1]

> The city family almost universally lives in an individual home—either an apartment or a house. Family privacy is believed to be so important that any other living arrangement is considered only as a last resort. In general, two or more families share one dwelling only under extreme pressure of circumstances. . . . It is a fact that the four-person city family in the United States considers five rooms, including a kitchen and bath, with modern plumbing, heating and lighting, as basic to satisfactory housing. . . . Privacy requires a separate house or apartment containing a common living room, a kitchen and bathroom, and the necessary number of sleeping rooms. . . . Sanitation necessitates a pure water supply, adequate in quantity for personal and household cleanliness, to be piped under pressure to kitchen sink, wash bowl, toilet, bathtub, or shower. Other requirements are that doors and windows are screened where necessary; that structure is protected against contamination from sewage; and that neighborhood is free from accumulations of refuse that harbor disease-carrying vermin. . . . One or more windows in each room is a minimum requirement for ventilation. . . . Safety precautions are that the dwelling must be of sound construction, with foundation, roof, walls, porches and stairs repaired as necessary to prevent any danger of collapse; it must have adequate provision for escape in case of fire; and safety precautions in electric, plumbing, and heating installations as required by municipal authorities. The neighborhood must have space for outdoor exercise and children's play, and must be free from worst hazards of traffic, such as railroad or elevated tracks or unregulated thoroughfares of automobile traffic. . . .

Household operation. This is something of a catchall category, in which the changing details of spending reflect many facets of our consumption pattern. The increasing totals, representing in 1929 less than the value of housing and in 1950 almost one-third more, have taken about the same share of total consumption expenditures. But the $30 billion spent in 1953 on household operation includes furniture, furnishings, household appliances and repairs or cleaning of these, utilities like fuel, water, telephone,

[1] Lester S. Kellogg and Dorothy S. Brady, "The City Worker's Family Budget," *Monthly Labor Review*, February, 1948, pp. 140–141.

and telegraph, domestic service, and minor payments such as fire and theft insurance and moving expense. Table 13-5 shows these items in detail, so

Table 13-5. *Expenditures on Household Operation, 1953*

(In millions of dollars)

Item	Amount
Total	$30,070
Durable goods:	
Furniture	3,294
Kitchen and other appliances *	3,488
China, glassware, tableware, utensils	1,398
Other durable house furnishings †	2,420
Nondurable goods:	
Semidurable house furnishings ‡	2,461
Lighting, cleaning, and paper supplies	1,613
Stationery and writing supplies	538
Fuel (except gas) and ice	2,873
Services:	
Household utilities	7,830
Electricity	2,692
Gas	1,550
Water	715
Telephone, telegraph, cable, and wireless	2,640
Domestic service	3,051
Other §	1,337

* Refrigerators, ranges, washing and sewing machines, cooking and portable heating equipment, and miscellaneous electrical appliances except radios.

† Floor coverings, bedding, art products, clocks, lamps, writing equipment, tools.

‡ Chiefly textile house furnishings; also brooms and brushes.

§ Includes maintenance services for household furnishings, moving and warehouse expenses, postage and express charges, and premiums on fire and theft insurance.

SOURCE: U.S. Department of Commerce, *National Income Supplement to the Survey of Current Business*, 1954, Table 30.

that their relative importance may be gauged. The durable goods on this list amount to about 35 per cent of the total, the services to 40 per cent, and the nondurable commodities to 25 per cent. This classification has not changed much over the years; in 1929, durable goods accounted for 35 per cent, services for 37 per cent, and nondurable goods for 28 per cent of the total expenditures on household operation.

The consumption pattern must be sketched in greater detail than this. Thus, while purchases of durable goods today are three times the level of 1929, spending on household appliances is five times the 1929 amount, and within this category other significant changes have taken place. The demand for durable goods, like housing, depends on new buyers and those who are replacing older equipment. The spending of the thirties concentrated chiefly on refrigerators and washing machines; that of the fifties, a host of new appliances including deep freezes, room air conditioners, and television sets. Some of the spending, therefore, is for replacement of the older appliances, which necessarily means a smaller demand once most consumers possess such equipment. But such a decline may be offset as the use of dishwashers, garbage disposals, and automatic ironers becomes more widespread. Production of consumers' durables, therefore, seems to necessitate constant innovation to maintain a high level of spending, which may give us wholly new products like the rotisserie or a completely revolutionized familiar product like the washing machine.

The widespread introduction of many such products is reflected in an enormous increase in electricity consumption, and this service, like many of the other utilities, cannot be gauged merely in terms of spending. Thus, while expenditures on electricity trebled between 1929 and 1950, the number of kilowatt-hours used by residential consumers has increased almost six times. Perhaps more important is the fact that 12 million households were added, between 1947 and 1953, to the number of users of electricity then in existence. Many of these are farms benefiting from the program of rural electrification. In 1930, about 10 per cent of all farms had electricity; in 1949, the proportion was almost 90 per cent. Similar changes may be noted for telephone expenses. Some 12 million new subscribers were added between 1947 and 1953.

The details of household operation expenditure deserve more study than can be given here. We may summarize by quoting from the most recent statistics and the BLS budget. In 1952, 99 per cent of all households owned a radio, 32 per cent a television set, 91 per cent an electric iron, and 80 per cent a mechanical refrigerator. Half the homes possessed electric vacuum cleaners, and more than half electric toasters, washing machines, and clocks. Almost half owned electric coffee makers, food mixers, sandwich grills, or waffle irons. The description of accepted American standards includes the following: [2]

> The family dwelling . . . contains . . . a kitchen and a bathroom, and is supplied with hot and cold running water. . . . The home is equipped with the usual house-furnishings and the mechanical electric cook stove, a mechanical refrigerator, and a washing machine. . . . The family owns a small radio . . . the husband has a haircut about once every 3 weeks, the son every 5 weeks,

[2] *Ibid.*, p. 136.

and the wife and daughter every 3 months. . . . A telephone in the dwelling is not considered essential, but an average of three local calls are made each week. Stationery and stamps are included to provide for about one letter a week.

CLOTHING

Clothing and personal care accounted, in 1950, for about 13 per cent of total expenditure, a fraction which does not seem to alter much with changes in total spending. The kinds of clothing purchased with these sums are influenced by climate, occupation, the number of children and older people in a family or population, and above all by production and marketing techniques. When we speak of fashion, we think of women's clothing, and yet the changes in consumption are more basic than varying hem lines, waistlines, or hats.

Clothing fabrics and styles have provided, along with the prepackaged foods and the household appliances, increasing amounts of comfort and less work. The "miracle fibers" make their appeal in terms of easy laundering, but new finishes have been developed for cottons so that they remain competitive. The garment trade has disclosed an increasing preference for casual wear, with "coordinated separates" replacing women's suits, and slacks with sport shirts or jackets lessening the sales of men's suits. And the hat industry deplores the trend among both sexes to do away with headgear of all kinds.

Since World War II, these trends in clothing have led to a consistent increase in clothing sales with a decline in prices. In other words, consumers are getting more clothes for their money, which may be one reason why they have not expanded the share of total spending which goes for clothing. For the most part, the increase in clothing sales is made up of casual, informal clothes—the children's uniform of dungarees and cotton jerseys, which can be found in older age groups as well; women's adoption of blouses or sweaters and skirts; and the enormous increase in separate jackets and slacks for men and boys.

The kinds of clothing worn today go with American homes, American recreation, and American living. They reflect the homogeneous culture referred to earlier. Thanks to national magazines, movies, and television, consumers all over the country can be acquainted with prevailing clothing choices. And, thanks to a garment industry which turns out low-priced copies, there is little noticeable difference in the styles available to low- and high-income families.

AUTOMOBILES

The automobile is perhaps the most distinctive feature of American consumption. It has developed from a rich man's novelty to a necessity at low income levels, except for city families. Automobiles are responsible for the vast increase in suburban homes and in travel and tourist expenditure and for such consumption items as drive-in theaters and toll fares. Aside from such related expenditures, payments for cars and their upkeep required, in 1953, 10 per cent of total consumption expenditures. This is considerably higher than the 6 to 7 per cent spent twenty-five years ago.

The increased spending had to come from somewhere, and it is interesting to speculate, in this connection, on the relative decline in expenditures on housing. The extent to which our cars have become our homes cannot be spelled out merely in terms of money expenditures. Again we must look at what is bought with the money.

In 1929, there were about 23 million passenger cars registered; in 1954, over 43 million cars were on the roads. About 6 out of every 10 spending units own an automobile, and the number of two-car families has risen sharply since the end of the war. Estimates of the miles traveled by passenger cars show a rise from 211 billion miles in 1936 to 324 billion in 1948, which can easily be projected to a much higher figure today. There are almost 3 million miles of roads, outside of municipalities, and, since 1930, most of them have been improved and surfaced.

The demand for automobiles, like that for other durable goods, depends on new purchasers and those who are buying replacements. The total number of cars depends, also, on the rate of scrappage, and since the twenties the cars have been scrapped at increasingly older ages. But the amount spent on cars depends not only on the number of cars but also on the amount of car in each sale. Again we must note the effect of technological change in the fact that today's Chevrolet is more car than its 1929 counterpart. Not only do automatic transmissions, power steering, radios, and heaters figure here, but also the increased durability which makes cars last longer these days. Technological change is also relied upon to speed up or maintain the rate of replacement.

FORMS OF SAVING

Total personal saving has increased, accompanying the rise in income since the 1930s, and the forms in which savings are made have changed. Personal saving in our economy includes time deposits ("savings accounts") in banks, shares in savings and loan associations, postal savings deposits, demand deposits, United States savings bonds and other government and industrial securities, ownership of real estate and business, equities in life insurance and pension plans, accumulation of currency, and the repayment of debt. All these are paid for with income which is not spent on goods and services for immediate consumption. Table 13-6 shows the

Table 13-6. *Personal Saving, 1953*

(In billions of dollars)

Currency and bank deposits	$ 4.72
Savings and loan associations	3.68
Private insurance and pension reserves	5.08
Securities	6.21
United States government	1.36
State and local governments	1.82
Corporate and other	3.03
Increase in equity in nonfarm dwellings and nonprofit institutions	2.15
Liquidation of other debt	2.83
Increase in equity in nonfarm unincorporated business	3.79
Increase in equity in farm enterprises	−1.61

SOURCE: U.S. Department of Commerce, *National Income Supplement to the Survey of Current Business*, 1954, Table 6, pp. 166–167.

relative importance of major categories of private saving for 1952. These figures are estimates of the changes in total personal assets and liabilities during the year, and statistical errors and omissions make the total sum vary from personal saving as shown in Table 13-1, which is computed by subtracting consumption expenditures from income.

The figures on mortgages and the liquidation of debt are of course closely tied to the pattern of consumption expenditures. Since over half the consuming units in the country own their homes, the equity obtained by the reduction in mortgages is now an important form of saving. About half the homes are mortgage-free, but the average owner's equity in mortgaged homes in 1954 was about $8,200. Over half the consuming units who owned their homes had an equity of at least $5,000 in their mortgage. Housing expenditures are less, as a proportion of income, than in earlier years, chiefly because the postwar housing boom has taken place in low-cost construction. But such homes can be owned by consuming units with relatively low incomes, and this form of saving has therefore become more widespread. The accumulated equity of all consuming units owning their homes was about $250 billion in 1954.

The figure in Table 13-6 for the liquidation of other debt is net: that is, it represents the total amount of consumer credit extended less repayments during the year. When it is negative, it means that consumers as a whole are increasing their purchases faster than they are paying off their debts. The positive figure for 1953 represented a rate of repayment which was higher than the rate at which new debt was incurred.

Consumers also save by investing in farms and business, including real estate. About 1 out of every 7 consuming units owns real estate, other than their homes, most frequently a one- or two-family house or a lot of land. Fewer consuming units, about 7 per cent, own an interest in unincorporated business or shares in corporations, but the amount of personal saving in corporate securities has increased yearly since World War II. Approximately $236 billion has been accumulated by consuming units in business investment.

The rise in saving by means of insurance has already been discussed. These savings now amount to over $60 billion and represent the purchase of future income for the consuming unit. United States savings bonds held by consuming units increased from $2,800 billion in 1940 to $42,900 billion in 1945, but after that their popularity as a form of saving diminished. Deposits in postal savings, savings banks, and savings and loan associations are equally liquid forms of saving, readily available for spending, and these plus currency show the greatest fluctuation from year to year. During the recession of 1948–1949, the total of currency and bank deposits was drawn down by some $3 billion, as consuming units attempted to maintain their accustomed spending patterns with a decline in income.

Very few consuming units hold all these forms of saving, and little is known about the decisions to save in one form or another. The Federal Reserve Board surveys the investment preferences of consumers with yearly incomes of $3,000 or more, who actually save most of the money recorded in Table 13-6. Such surveys show in general that consuming units first prefer forms of saving which will provide security, and after that their preferences are for assets with higher income return at the risk of fluctuating value. Forms of saving may then be classified as to the type of consumption expenditure they allow: currency and bank deposits may be transferred at any time into consumption expenditures, although the value of such holdings, in real goods and services, may change with time. The ownership of homes and consumer durables provides future consumption of homes and consumer durables; if such assets are converted to income, there is generally a loss in value. Reserves in insurance companies provide future money income, which again is subject to changes in value. Business investment also provides future income, but with less security.

Finally, it should be noted that most of the forms of consumer savings which produce money income are subject to business or government control. When the consuming unit takes out a mortgage which is reduced by saving, the house produces real services to the consumer. The decision to buy, to invest, and to save is taken by the consuming unit, presumably in terms of the income (shelter) to be received from the house. But when the consuming unit buys insurance, the money which is paid is invested by the insurance company. The same is true for business investment and for government bonds. The process of making decisions, which produce the income expected by consuming units when they save, lies outside the competence of the consuming unit.

Questions and Points for Discussion

1. Does the fact that food expenditures have increased as a proportion of total spending disprove Engel's law? Why or why not?
2. What is the relationship between housing expenditures and home-ownership?
3. Explain the difficulties in using dollar values to measure consumption patterns or consumption changes.
4. What have been the important innovations in consumption since 1900?
5. The amount of saving is calculated by subtracting total expenditures from disposable income. Does this mean that saving is in fact what is left over from the consuming unit's income after expenditures are made? Argue for and against the point that savings are a residual.

References

Editors of *Fortune Magazine: The Changing American Market,* Hanover House, New York, 1955, chaps. 5–10.

———: "The Big, Baffling Food Market," *Fortune Magazine,* October, 1953.

———: "The Sunny Outlook for Clothes," *Fortune Magazine,* April, 1954.

———: "$30 Billion for Fun," *Fortune Magazine,* June, 1954.

———: "Upheaval in Home Goods," *Fortune Magazine,* March, 1954.

U.S. Bureau of Agricultural Economics: *Food Consumption in the United States, 1909–1952,* Agriculture Handbook 62, 1953.

U.S. Department of Commerce: *National Income Supplement to the Survey of Current Business,* 1954.

14. Consumption, Production, and Income

In the last three chapters, we have explored the ways in which people spend their incomes and the kinds of goods and services they buy. If we add up all the consumption expenditures, we can picture a flow of payments from consuming units or households to business firms. There is a flow of consumer goods and services in the opposite direction, from firms to consuming units. The major part of the entire economy is employed in turning out and distributing these goods and services—or, to quote Adam Smith, "Consumption is the sole end and object of all production." We have now to examine this flow of payments, in one direction, against the flow of goods and services, in the other direction, in order to analyze the role of consumption in the economy.

THE CIRCULAR FLOW

The money which households spend on consumption goes, for the most part, to business firms. Some services are supplied to consumers by gardeners, cooks, maids, and other servants, who are not really businessmen. Some money is spent abroad and does not go to American business. But, out of total consumption expenditures of $194 billion in 1950, $185 billion represented purchases from business firms. What happens to the money firms receive? Nearly all of it is paid out to consuming units as wages and salaries, as rents, as profits of proprietors and partners, as dividends, and as interest. So we may visualize a circular flow of payments, from consuming units to business firms and from firms back to consuming units. Consumers spend their money for goods and services supplied by business, and business in turn spends money to pay for the services supplied by households. These two streams may be pictured in a diagram.

In Figure 14-1, the solid lines represent goods and services and the broken lines spending or income payments. On the right, the solid line denotes consumer goods and services—all the categories of consumption discussed in previous chapters. On the left, the solid line denotes services supplied by consuming units to firms—mostly labor, but also the use of land and capital—which are used to produce goods and services. Household employees provide services shown by a solid line going from consuming units to consuming units, while the line circling around the sector of firms denotes capital goods, or investment goods, sold only to business. These

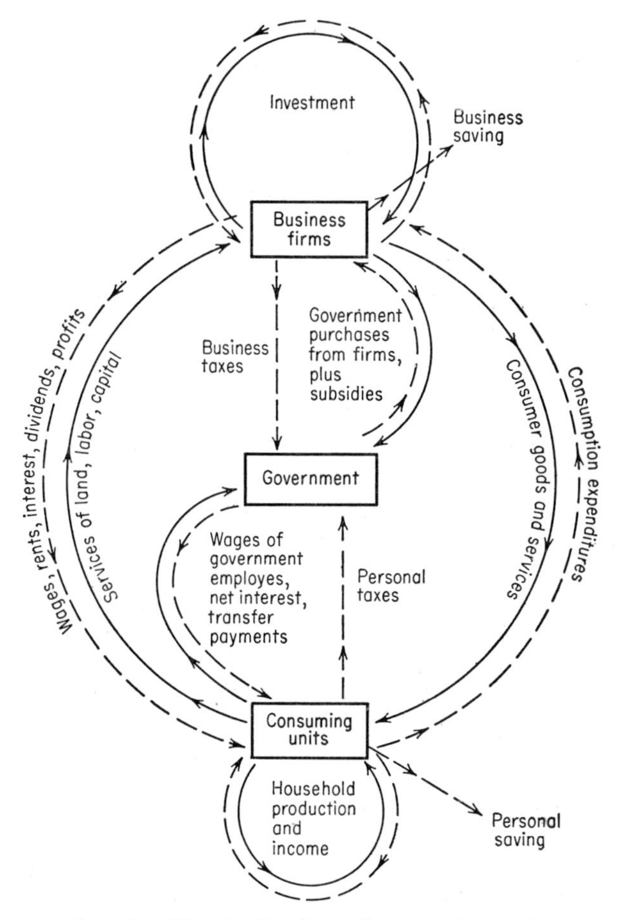

FIG. 14-1. The circular flow of economic activity.

are the machinery, buildings, and inventories of materials or finished goods which are used in production. Business supplies goods and services for government use—the solid line to the government sector—and consuming units provide land and labor to government—the solid line connecting these two sectors. All these lines, then, sum up the total output—the goods and services produced in the economy.

The broken lines show payments which provide income to all parts of the economy. On the right of the big circle, consumers pay firms for the goods and services they buy. Government also pays for its purchases from business, sometimes at artificial prices called *subsidies*. And firms, of course, pay other firms for the capital goods bought. Business and consuming units pay taxes to government, shown by the broken lines leading into the government sector. On the left, firms and government pay consuming units for their productive services. Government also subsidizes some consumers by means of transfer payments. And consuming units pay wages to their household employees. All these lines represent the income in the economy, derived from payments by consuming units, business, and government.

Neither consuming units nor business firms pay out all the money they receive for goods and services for immediate use. Total income after taxes is divided by consuming units into spending and saving. Business also saves part of its receipts, and so the income streams show two pools of saving, one for business and one for consuming units.

There are two omissions from this circle: a solid line for the goods and services produced by government, and lines for the transactions with the rest of the world. The first is omitted for the sake of reality; the second, for simplicity.

Government supplies real goods and services—output—just as business and households do—but, in our economic system, the output of government cannot be valued by the prices paid. Government supplies some services to business and consuming units which are paid for like any other commodity—stamps, water from municipally owned utilities, and toll highways are examples—but other services are supplied to all without charge. The payments received by government differ from payments to firms or consuming units because taxes are not levied according to the government services used. It is more realistic, therefore, to set government apart from the wheel of economic activity directed by the price system.

Income and output relations with foreign economies require two sets of lines for each sector—government, firms, and consuming units. Business exports goods and services, some Americans supply land, labor, and capital to foreign economies, and government exports goods and services. Foreigners pay for all this output, and the money enters each of the income streams. At the same time, consuming units pay for goods and services received abroad, firms pay for imported goods and services, and government pays for land, labor, and capital supplied by other economies.

Rather than show all these transactions with twelve additional lines, it is easier to balance all the payments to and from this country and record the differences as a net addition to or subtraction from production and income.

THE QUANTITATIVE DATA

The reader should already realize that Figure 14-1 is more than a schematic picture of the economy, for money values for personal disposable income (after taxes), consumption expenditures, and personal savings were discussed in the previous chapter. These figures obviously apply to the income streams going to consuming units, their payments for the goods and services shown on the right of the big circle, and their savings in various forms. Dollar values may also be applied to the rest of the diagram from data prepared by the Department of Commerce, which were mentioned in Chapter 2. The figures for 1953 appear in Table 14-1. Before we insert these figures into the diagram, however, we must understand some of the adjustments which are made in moving from a schematic model to the real economy. Basically, the money values for the circular flow come from business and government accounting records, which show payments to productive factors and sales of goods and services. Values for the output of the economy are computed from the sales figures, broken down to show purchases by households, business, government, and the rest of the world. Values for income are derived from the payments made by business, government, consuming units, and the rest of the world to each of these sectors.

Production. The entire circle of solid lines, representing the output of the whole economy, is called *Gross National Product* and in 1953 amounted to $365 billion of goods and services. Most of this output, some $230 billion in 1953, was sold to households, whose payments are called *personal consumption expenditures*, and who used the goods and services for current consumption.

Goods which are not used up in a year are capital goods sold to business, whose purchases are called *gross private domestic investment*, amounting in 1953 to $51 billion. On the diagram, this sum is represented by the lines circling the sector called "firms." This meaning for investment refers to the purchase of productive equipment, and not, as the word sometimes means, the purchase of financial assets or securities, which produce money income. Our highly industrialized economy requires many investment

Table 14-1. *Gross National Product, National Income, and Disposable Personal Income, 1953*

(In billions of dollars)

The sum of:	Personal consumption expenditures		$230.1
	Gross private domestic investment		51.4
	Net foreign investment		−1.9
	Government purchases of goods and services		85.2
Equals:	Gross National Product		364.9
Less:	Capital consumption allowances		27.2
Equals:	Net National Product		337.6
Less:	Indirect business taxes		30.0
	Business transfer payments		1.0
	Subsidies and statistical discrepancy		0.5
Equals:	National income		305.0
Less:	Undistributed corporate profits		8.9
	Corporate profits tax liability		21.1
	Corporate inventory valuation adjustment		−0.9
	Contributions for social insurance		8.8
	Excess of wage accruals over disbursements		−0.1
Plus:	Net interest paid by government		5.0
	Government transfer payments		12.8
	Business transfer payments		1.0
Equals:	Personal income, the sum of		286.1
	Wage and salary receipts	$198.1	
	Other labor income	6.3	
	Proprietors' and rental income	49.0	
	Dividends	9.4	
	Personal interest income	13.5	
	Transfer payments	13.8	
Less:	Personal tax and nontax payments		36.0
	Federal	32.5	
	State and local	3.5	
Equals:	Disposable personal income		250.1

SOURCE: U.S. Department of Commerce, *Survey of Current Business*, July, 1954.

goods–locomotives, power plants, machine tools, factories, and warehouses–in order to turn out billions of dollars' worth of goods and services. All these capital goods are continually wearing out and must be replaced to maintain production. And our expanding economy, producing more goods and services each year, requires new capital goods, added to the existing supply. When firms produce and sell more, they need larger inventories with which to work, and some investment buys raw materials and finished goods, part of the total output of the economy, which are not used up during a year. Gross private domestic investment also includes consumer spending on new houses, which provide shelter for many years.

The homeowner is a businessman supplying shelter to his family, just as a landlord is a businessman renting space to another family. All these purchases, therefore, are for investment rather than current consumption.

The value of total production includes transactions with the rest of the world, and a net figure is used, representing either a surplus or a deficit in the total balance of international payments for the year. If, on balance, we send fewer goods and services to other countries than they send to us, we have a debt to pay abroad, which reduces the Gross National Product and decreases international investment. So we find a minus figure for *net foreign investment* in 1953 of $2 billion. This value, of course, need not always be negative. If, on balance, we send abroad more goods and services than we receive, we have a surplus which adds to Gross National Product. The net figure is always, however, a very small part of total production, for domestic investment and consumption take most of the output of this country.

Finally, part of total output goes to government. Government buys some services directly—the postman, schoolteacher, judge, soldier, and game warden are examples—and government spends about as much for goods and services supplied by business. In 1953, this part of our Gross National Product—*government purchases of goods and services*—amounted to $85 billion and corresponds to the solid lines from firms and consuming units to government.

Income. In general terms, national income is equal to national output. Since the productive factors in the economy turn out all the output, the payments for these factors must equal the value of their output. For consumption analysis, however, the income data are more useful than data on output. Income payments, derived from government and business accounting records, can be related to the Gross National Product by computing the current income derived from current production. *National income* and *disposable personal income* consist of Gross National Product minus some values which represent current output but not current income and plus some values for current income which does not result from current production.

In the first place, part of our national output, included in gross private domestic investment, serves to maintain our productive capacity. The households which supply productive factors to make new machines, factories, or houses receive income payments for their services. But if their output goes to replace worn-out machinery, factories, or houses, their income payments are not part of current national income. Another way of looking at this concept is to say that current production furnishes all the goods and services available for current consumption—the definition of real income. But the capital goods needed to keep our productive economy going are not available for current consumption, any more than the money received for selling a house is used for current consumption by the individual family. These sums, needed to maintain our current productive capacity, must be deducted from the total of gross private domestic investment, and from Gross National Product, to arrive at national income. The money values involved are called *capital consumption allowances* and are based on business methods of accounting for capital goods.

Firms allow for the fact that machines are used up gradually by charging depreciation. The total cost of a factory, a machine, or a house is divided into annual expense for each year of its useful life. Thus the baker's yearly sales pay the cost of all the flour he has used during the year, and also one-tenth of what his ovens cost, if ovens will serve for ten years. During any one year, then, the sum of all the depreciation charges will tell us roughly how much of our productive capacity has been used up during the year.[1] This figure is used to measure all the capital goods produced for replacement purposes during the year and is subtracted from Gross National Product. The result, *Net National Product,* is very close to national income and is also a close approximation of the goods and services actually available for use in the year.

The next adjustment necessary stems from the origin of the data in

[1] The capital consumption allowance computed by the Department of Commerce includes not only the depreciation expenses reported by firms but also some capital outlays which are treated as current expenses by the firms themselves. Depreciation allowances are estimated for farms and for unincorporated business including real estate and institutions, and a figure for the accidental damage of capital goods due to fire, flood, and so on, is added. Depreciation accounting can be complex in theory and inconsistent in practice, and one of the major controversies should be noted here. The purpose of depreciation accounting in the financial sense is to charge the original cost of a fixed asset as expense over its useful life and to recognize the decrease in the value of the asset with age. Provided that no losses exist after depreciation expense, the firm's total assets should, therefore, remain the same in value. In the economic sense, maintaining the money value of assets, or capital goods, is not the same as maintaining the productive capacity, or income-producing ability, of these assets. Particularly in times of rising prices, it is claimed, capital consumption allowances may understate the extent to which our economy's productive capacity is diminishing or overstate the rate at which national income is increasing.

business records. The total money sales of firms include taxes—such as sales and excise taxes on cigarettes and automobiles, tariffs on imported goods, and property taxes on some of the business assets. These taxes are paid by firms but they are recouped from the prices charged by firms, so that consuming units are the ultimate taxpayers. It would be wrong, therefore, to take income as the total dollar sales recorded by firms when these money values include taxes which merely transfer income from households to government. From the Net National Product figure must be subtracted, therefore, the sum of *indirect business* taxes—those which are shifted to consumers—which do not become income to the suppliers of productive services for their output.

What is left—$305 billion in 1953—represents *national income*—the values earned during a year by the owners of productive factors. But the broken lines in Figure 14-1 representing income paid to consuming units do not include some of the income which is earned, and they do include some income which is not earned. So we adjust further to find *disposable personal income*, the amount available for households to spend on current consumption or forms of saving.

National income represents the earnings of labor and land and capital, the basic productive factors. Some of these earnings are accumulated by corporations in the form of profits but belong to the consumers who own the stock of the corporation. The total of these profits is never paid as dividend income to consuming units. The *profits tax* paid by the corporation goes to government. *Undistributed corporate profits* is money which is earned but never received by consuming units because it is "plowed back into the business," or retained by the corporation, perhaps to provide for new factories or more machines to increase productive capacity. This figure is not always positive—that is, sometimes corporations pay out to consuming units more than the earnings of a single year, and then the figure represents earnings which were retained earlier and are currently distributed. Such a situation existed during the depression, when the total of undistributed corporate profits in the economy was negative, because some companies made great losses and others paid more dividends than they had earned. In recent years, the undistributed profits have been positive and large. One further adjustment of income earned by corporations for their consumer-owners occurs in valuing inventories. This is a technical problem which need not be explained here, except to say that the statistics adjust business statements to provide a currently consistent value for income. The sum of capital consumption allowances, undistributed profits, and *inventory valuation adjustments* represents income which is currently received but not spent by business firms, in other words, the business saving stream in Figure 14-1.

The major service which consuming units supply to firms and government is, of course, labor, so that wages and salaries make up most of the income stream, but what consumers earn from their labor is not exactly the same as what they receive. *Contributions for social insurance*—the payroll taxes paid partly by employers and partly by employees—are subtracted from national income because this money is earned but not received. A further adjustment to labor income results from *retroactive wage and salary payments.* If a company is ordered to give back pay, the income may be received by consuming units a year or two after it has been earned.

Money capital is another productive factor supplied by consuming units both to firms and to government. When consumers provide business capital—by purchasing bonds or making bank deposits—their money earns a return by financing current production, and this interest income is part of the stream of payments from firms to consuming units, and hence of national income. But money loaned to government does not earn a return from current production. The amounts borrowed by governments and the interest paid for this capital vary with the financial policy of the government rather than with the use of productive factors in current production. Hence, the sum of *interest paid by governments* is added to the national income, to represent income received by consuming units but not earned.

The most important form of consumer income received but not earned from current output is *transfer payments.* Government payments of direct relief, pensions, veterans' aid, and so on, provide income to consuming units on the basis of their needs rather than their productive services. In recent years, such payments have amounted to large sums, and they will increase with the extension of social legislation. Income is also paid by business to consumers who do not earn it—notably in the form of gifts to colleges, hospitals, and other nonprofit institutions, which are classified as consuming units rather than firms. Other income is received but not earned by consumers who are awarded payments for personal injury or cash prizes for contests. Finally, those households which never pay their debts or who enjoy stolen or shoplifted property are also benefiting from business transfer payments, receiving income which is not earned.

Summarizing all these data in the order which we have used to explain them, Table 14-1 gives us a figure for the total income stream to consuming units—*personal income*—shown in the circular flow of Figure 14-1. Personal income represents first, then, the income which is currently *earned* from the year's production, plus income which is currently received. Households cannot, however, dispose of this sum until they have first paid taxes. For consumption analysis, therefore, we deduct the sum of *personal tax payments* to local, state, and Federal governments, which in 1953 amounted to $36 billion. Were Table 14-1 to be continued, it, too, would illustrate circularity, for disposable personal income provides, of course, the personal consumption expenditures with which the table begins. The income of an economy, then, is derived from the production of that economy, which goes to firms, government, and consuming units, all of whom spend their income to buy the economy's output. We may now analyze further the role of consumption in this wheel of economic activity.

CONSUMPTION AND PRODUCTION

The total spending of consuming units—the $230 billion with which Table 14-1 begins—provides the largest demand for the output of business. Production is high when consumer spending is high, and retail sales, automobile sales, and housing-construction figures give important clues to the level of business activity. Most of our labor force is employed in turning out the food, clothing, shelter, and other goods and services bought and used in households.

Total production, however, depends on total demand, and business purchases of capital goods together with government purchases of goods and services must be added to consumption expenditures in determining the entire output of the economy. Consumption appears to affect business spending more directly than it does government spending.

Business purchases. We have already seen that gross private domestic investment consists of increased inventories and capital goods. Part of this total, estimated by the capital consumption allowances, is spent to replace used-up productive facilities. The rest—called *net investment*—serves to enlarge productive capacity. In terms of Figure 14-1, this investment enlarges the total circle of current output. Some new plant and equipment is built to produce more of the goods and services which are already in existence, and some investment is made to turn out new kinds of commodities and offer new services.

It is obvious, first, that maintaining the capacity of a factory is profitable only when consumers are buying and using the factory's products. The enormous rise in total consumption over the past fifty years has made productive capacity in the economy soar in some lines and dwindle in others, with the shifts in consumer demand and the introduction of new products. So current consumption dictates what part of the producing sector is to be maintained and what part to be abandoned. Such business spending, about half of gross private domestic investment in recent years, stems directly from consumption.

Second, productive capacity is usually enlarged in response to a growing consumption demand. Investment in factories and inventories to increase steel output and provide larger numbers of automobiles and more yards of textiles and cans of orange juice is called *induced investment*—induced by rising consumption. The demand of such investing firms for machine tools and capital goods is called *derived demand*—derived from consumer demand. The dependence of business investment on consumption spending deserves further analysis.

Consumer demand and inventories. Let us take, as a hypothetical example, the retailer of widgets, who finds that his normal sales are 150 units a month and that a satisfactory inventory is about twice this figure, or 300 units. He buys monthly, then, 150 widgets from his supplier to replace those he has sold. Should consumers begin to buy more widgets, the retailer would find his inventory depleted and would place a larger order with his supplier. If sales go up to 200 widgets a month and the retailer decides this new level will continue, he may want to increase his inventory so that the ratio of stock to sales is the same. He will buy 300 widgets from his supplier, then, so that he can maintain an inventory of 400 while monthly sales amount to 200. We have already seen that purchases of inventories are a kind of investment, spending for goods which are not immediately consumed, and we see now that a 33⅓ per cent rise in consumption expenditure has led to a 100 per cent growth in investment expenditure. The demand for inventories is derived from the demand for final products, and an increase in inventory purchases is induced by an increase in consumption purchases.

Spending on inventories will continue to increase if consumption purchases increase, but never at the same rate. If consumers step up their spending and buy, say, 50 per cent more, or 300 units a month, the retailer's order will again go up. But his inventory should now be maintained at 600 units, and so he buys 500 from his supplier, or 66 per cent more than his previous order. His investment spending has increased less than at first. If consumption does not continue to increase, the retailer's purchases will drop and induced investment will fall. When sales continue at 300 units a month, the retailer can keep up his inventory of 600 by ordering now only 300 widgets a month. And if consumers shift their demand from widgets to fledgers, the retailer will fill the declining demand out of inventories and make no purchases at all. A decline in sales from 300 to 200 leaves the seller with surplus stocks, and not until he has drawn down his inventory to less than 400 will he place a new order. This decline in inventories represents *disinvestment*, which is induced directly by a decline in consumption expenditure.

We may set out this example in Table 14-2 followed, for the realistic

Table 14-2. *Sales and Inventories of Widgets, Hypothetical Retail Store*

Monthly sales (consumption)	End-of-month inventory (sales × 2)	Monthly purchases (investment)
150	300	150
200	400	300
300	600	500
300	600	300
200	400	0

reader, by figures on monthly sales and stocks for 296 department stores in Table 14-3. This table shows, between 1945 and 1946, an increase in monthly average sales (consumption) of $69 million, or 25 per cent. In order to maintain the existing stock ratio of 2.3, the orders outstanding at the end of the month increased by $189 million, or 32 per cent, and $163 million additional investment had taken place in inventories. Again, the drop in consumption between 1948 and 1949 was only $20 million, or about 5 per cent. But outstanding orders declined by $121 million, or 24 per cent, and disinvestment of $54 million had occurred with a drop in inventories.

Consumer demand and capital goods. The retailer's demand, derived from consumption, is filled by wholesalers and producers, whose investment in inventories is similarly affected by changes in the rate at which consumption is increasing or decreasing. At the producing level, these

Table 14-3. *Monthly Averages of Sales, Stocks, Orders, and Stock-Sales Ratios for 296 Department Stores, 1944–1952*

(Dollar figures in millions)

Period, monthly average	Sales (total for month)	Stocks (end of month)	Outstanding orders (total for month)	Ratio of stocks to sales
1944	$246	$ 574	$596	2.4
1945	276	604	775	2.3
1946	345	767	964	2.3
1947	365	887	588	2.5
1948	381	979	494	2.7
1949	361	925	373	2.7
1950	376	1,012	495	2.8
1951	391	1,202	460	3.2
1952	395	1,093	433	2.9

NOTE: These figures are actual dollar amounts reported by a group of department stores located in various cities throughout the country. In 1952, sales by these stores accounted for about 50 per cent of estimated total department-store sales.
SOURCE: *Federal Reserve Bulletin.*

changes affect not only the rate of current output but also business decisions to purchase new productive facilities or scrap some existing equipment. This part of induced investment or disinvestment brings us back to the capital consumption allowances and the machines which are replaced each year, and we may use the hypothetical Widget Manufacturing Company, Inc., as an example.

Widgets require, of course, labor and tons of widgetine, the raw material used in their making. Basic to the process, however, are a number of specialized machines, which can be used for nothing else and which, owing to corrosion and vibration, are replaced every 5 years. The company owns 15 of these machines when it turns out widgets at the rate of 150 million a year, and it purchases 3 new machines each year. When sales all over the country increase by 33⅓ per cent, the company decides to increase its capacity so that it can turn out 200 million widgets with an increased labor force instead of working overtime. In the new wing of its factory, then, it will need 5 new machines, and its purchases that year go from 3 to 8. These purchases of capital goods are part of gross private domestic investment, and we find that a 33⅓ per cent increase in consumption spending has led to an increase in investment spending of 150 per cent. Again, however, the rate of increase in investment will not coincide with the increase in consumption, for if sales go up again by 50 per cent and the company plans to expand further, it will buy 13 new machines to produce 300 million widgets, or only 60 per cent more than the previous purchase. If sales are then maintained and the plant stops expanding, its investment spending will drop. Machinery must be bought for replacement, but with 30 machines the firm needs to buy only 6 new ones each year. When widgets are abandoned by the consumer and the company's sales drop to 200 units again, it buys no new machines, and may even decide to cut down its investment by scrapping 10 machines and renting the factory wing—all of which represents disinvestment to the corporation. Table 14-4 summarizes the changes.

Table 14-4. *Sales, Machines, and Machinery Purchases, Widget Mfg. Co., Inc.*

Sales, millions of widgets	Machines	Purchases
150	15	3
200	20	8
300	30	13
300	30	6
200	20	0

Consumption and investment in the economy. The story of the fortune and failure of widgets reflects, of course, the way in which industries expand and contract in the face of changing consumer demand. But when we look at the economy as a whole, we find that expansions and contractions of total consumption expenditures are reflected and enlarged in the fluctuation of gross private domestic investment, which includes both purchases for inventories and for added productive capacity. The realistic data in Table 14-5 are more complex than those in Table 14-4, but they illustrate the same process.

The depression years show the most dramatic results. While consumption expenditures declined between 1930 and 1931 some $9½ billion, or about 13 per cent, investment dropped almost 50 per cent, with inventories declining as business cut back production and fewer factories and homes were constructed. The beginning of recovery, in 1934, meant $5 billion, or only 11 per cent, more spent on consumption than in 1933. But it encouraged investment spending to increase over 100 per cent, and although inventories were still being reduced, some firms stepped up their purchases of durable equipment. The same sensitive response to consumer demand can be found in the investment figures for 1946 to 1952. When consumption expenditures leveled off in 1949, total investment dropped sharply as retailers and producers everywhere sold off their surplus inventories, which had been expanded after the previous year's sizable increase in spending.

Table 14-5. *National Income, Personal Consumption Expenditures, and Gross Private Domestic Investment, 1929–1937 and 1946–1952*

(In billions of dollars)

Year	National income	Personal consumption expenditures				Gross private domestic investment			
		Total	Durable goods	Non-durable goods	Services	Total	New construction	Producers durable equipment	Change in inventories
1929	$ 87.4	$ 78.8	$ 9.4	$ 37.7	$31.7	$15.8	$ 7.8	$ 6.4	$ 1.5
1930	75.0	70.8	7.3	34.1	29.5	10.2	5.6	4.9	−0.3
1931	58.9	61.2	5.6	29.0	26.6	5.4	3.6	3.2	−1.4
1932	41.7	49.2	3.7	22.7	22.8	0.9	1.7	1.8	−2.6
1933	39.6	46.3	3.5	22.3	20.6	1.3	1.1	1.8	−1.6
1934	48.6	51.9	4.3	26.7	20.9	2.8	1.4	2.5	−1.1
1935	56.8	56.2	5.2	29.4	21.7	6.2	1.9	3.4	0.9
1936	64.7	62.5	6.4	32.9	23.3	8.3	2.8	4.5	1.0
1937	73.6	67.1	7.0	35.2	24.9	11.4	3.7	5.4	2.3
1946	180.3	146.9	16.6	85.8	44.5	28.7	10.3	12.3	6.1
1947	198.7	165.6	21.4	95.1	49.1	30.2	13.9	17.1	−0.8
1948	223.5	177.9	22.9	100.9	54.1	42.7	17.7	19.9	5.0
1949	216.3	180.6	23.8	99.2	57.5	33.5	17.2	18.7	−2.5
1950	240.6	194.6	29.2	102.6	62.7	52.5	22.7	22.3	7.5
1951	278.4	208.1	27.3	113.4	67.4	58.6	23.1	24.6	10.9
1952	291.6	218.1	26.7	118.8	72.7	52.5	23.4	25.4	3.7

SOURCE: U.S. Department of Commerce, *National Income Supplement to the Survey of Current Business*, 1954, Tables 1 and 2.

Table 14-5 shows how consumption and investment spending work together to produce changes in total output, but it also shows varying degrees of sensitivity in the different kinds of output. The purchases of consumers' durable goods vary most widely in consumption spending, dropping some 63 per cent in the depression years from 1929 to 1933, when total spending declined by only 41 per cent. Our previous analysis of consumption gives us the reasons for this. Automobiles and household appliances are bought both as new purchases and as replacements, and replacements can be postponed. Food consumption, as we have seen, declined in money terms but not in quantity during this period. And, for the most part, the decline in spending on nondurable goods and services meant a shift to lower-priced goods, for food and clothing needs must be met somehow. The old car, the old icebox, the old radio set, however, could be made to do, and the decline in spending on durable goods meant that fewer quantities were bought. The decline in housing reflects, of course, the same effects.

Business investment in new construction and equipment can also be postponed. Not only production but the productive capacity of the country declined during the depression. Capital consumption allowances, which indicate the expenditures needed to replace plant and equipment, exceeded the total of gross private domestic investment from 1931 to 1935. In a very real sense, the economy was living off its capital, producing and using goods and services without maintaining the factories and machines which turned them out.

By the same reckoning, purchases of durable goods, both consumers' and producers', cannot be postponed indefinitely, unless the economy collapses entirely. Eventually, the machine wears out and has to be replaced if only to maintain a low rate of production. Eventually, the old automobile is too costly to run and the old home not large enough for the growing family. And the rise in spending on durables and housing, the growth in purchases of producers' durable equipment, from 1935 to 1937, from 1946 to 1948, and from 1949 to 1951, is just as spectacular, percentagewise, as its decline.

The especial sensitivity of inventories may be mentioned here, for if consumption changes are multiplied in changes in inventory, this relationship also carries a self-limiting factor. Consumer purchases of nondurables cannot decline too far, and once the inventory has been reduced, then consumption spending leads to investment spending to replenish stocks. So the fluctuations in inventories are more violent than in other types of investment, but they can neither increase nor decrease indefinitely.

Aside from the investment which is induced by rising consumption expenditures on established commodities, our figures for new construction and expenditures on producers' durable goods include another type of expansion. Some productive capacity turns out new goods and services, or innovations, which appear in the consumption pattern or the purchases of firms. Spending in this area cannot be separated from the figures on expansion of existing facilities, but some theories suggest that the entrepreneur who introduces an innovation does so most successfully when consumption spending is first beginning to rise from its depression depths and that new techniques or commodities are less appealing at peak levels of spending, when consumption is beginning to level off.

Government spending. We have now to consider the two remaining factors determining Gross National Product, or total output—government purchases and net foreign investment. To a considerable extent, government expenditures provide goods and services for use by consuming units, but since they are not sold at market prices, there is no way of calculating the value of consumption by expenditures in this area. Figure 14-1 would be more elegant if we could show the output of government services flowing to firms and households, but in the absence of market prices those services cannot be valued.

Since 1929, however, state and local expenditures have more than doubled, and these provide schools, hospitals, highways, police and legal systems, the preservation of natural resources and of health and sanitation—in other words, a host of services to the community, as much a part of the family's consumption as food or housing or shelter. Federal government purchases of goods and services, of course, have increased much more since 1929, and the bulk of the payments have been for war and defense. In recent years, our net foreign balance has been chiefly affected by government programs for relief and military aid. Aside from these, services are provided to consumers by housing measures, conservation and research programs, highways and the post office, and the regulation of finance, commerce, and labor in the public interest. Such measures may be called *collective consumption,* and their further analysis postponed until a later chapter.

It may be noted here that the consumer's choice in this area is effected not by his purchase but by his vote. We need not expect, therefore, consumer income to have a predominant influence on expenditures for collective consumption. And since government can borrow so that its expenditures exceed the flow of taxes from firms and households, we need not expect government income, or receipts, to circumscribe its purchases of goods and services.

INCOME AND CONSUMPTION

Since we are already aware of the general identity of national production and national income and of the way figures for disposable personal income are derived from those for the Gross National Product, the fluctuation of disposable personal income with total expenditures by households, business, and government is obvious. To explain changes in income over the years, we have only to look at the changes in total spending. Our study so far, however, has provided us with a good many explanations for these changes.

The consumption function. No matter how important family size, location, occupation, or individual taste may be to the particular spending pattern, *consumption in the entire economy operates within the framework of national income.* Aggregate consumption expenditures are a component of and vary with national income. It is true that, from 1931 to 1935, the economy used up more than the earnings from current production, by not replacing capital equipment. This was possible to the consuming units involved because some used past personal savings, some were paid corporate dividends from earnings retained in the past, and some received government transfer payments for welfare and relief. Such payments allowed personal income to exceed national income during the entire period from 1930 to 1937. But an economy cannot consume more than its current output indefinitely; hence we say that total consumption depends on, or is a function of, total income.

Table 13-1 showed that total consumption expenditures and total personal saving varied with disposable personal income. Table 14-5 shows a similar relationship between consumption expenditures and national income. The consumption function describes this relation between income and consumption, stating at each level of income the fraction, or percentage, of income that is expended on consumption; it tells what fraction of the income stream is maintained in the circular flow as consumption spending. This fraction, or percentage, is defined as the average propensity to consume. Thus, in terms of Table 14-5, total income in 1950 amounted to $241 billion and personal consumption expenditures to $195 billion, which gives an average propensity to consume of 0.81.

When income increases or decreases, we expect that consumption expenditures will change. So we can express changes in consumption spending as a fraction, or percentage, of the change in income which is called the *marginal propensity to consume.* Thus, when income rose by \$37 billion from 1950 to 1951, consumer spending increased by \$13 billion, illustrating a marginal propensity to consume of 0.35 (13 ÷ 37 = .35).

Since total income is divided, by households, into consumption and saving, we may also derive average and marginal propensities to save, by relating savings figures to income. In 1950, when income amounted to \$241 billion and consumption to \$195 billion, the average propensity to save was 0.19 (46 ÷ 241 = .19). This tells us what fraction of the income stream, in Figure 14-1, is not returned to the circular flow, but held in the two pools of saving. And when income rose \$37 from 1950 to 1951, savings increased by \$24 billion, which gives a *marginal propensity to save* of 0.65 (24 ÷ 37 = .65).

In sum, the consumption function describes a relation between income and consumption, and average and marginal values are computed from this relation. The average propensity to consume describes the percentage share of income that is spent for consumer goods and services *at any level of income.* The marginal propensity to consume describes the percentage share of income spent for consumer goods and services *out of an addition to income.* The saving function and the average and marginal propensities to save are defined similarly. And since consumption and saving exhaust income, it is the case that the average propensity to consume plus the average propensity to save equal 1, and the marginal propensity to consume plus the marginal propensity to save equal 1. Further, these relations are extremely important, for, as we shall see, they play leading roles in the determination of the level of national income—the size of the economy as a whole.

Consumption, saving, and the determination of income. We may now use our data on spending to understand how the total national product is determined. We have already seen that total output, or national product, is the sum of consumption spending, government purchases, and investment spending (both domestic and foreign). But consumption spending is determined by the level of national income and is a fraction, or percentage, of national income. Consumers put back into the income stream only part of what they receive; personal taxes are paid, and personal saving is nearly always positive. Total spending therefore depends on how much business and government put into the income stream compared with the amounts which are taken out by taxes and saving. If we assume for the moment that government spending exactly equals taxes, then total output, or national product, will be determined by the level of spending where investment exactly equals saving.

We may arrive at the same conclusion from the identity of national product and national income. Since consumption spending plus investment spending determines national product, national income must be at a level where the fraction going to saving equals investment spending.

In terms of our circular flow diagram in Figure 14-1, part of the income

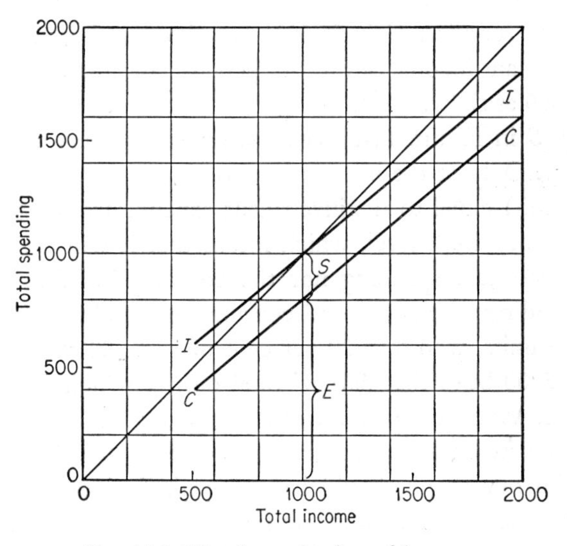

FIG. 14-2. The determination of income.

stream is returned, via consumption spending, to the circular flow, but part is drawn off into saving. If the level of total income remains the same, therefore, or is in equilibrium, investment spending must add to the circular flow exactly as much as saving withdraws. We may show this graphically, omitting the activities of government, in Figure 14-2.

Income is plotted along the horizontal axis and total spending along the vertical axis. All the points plotted lie on a 45-degree line, which merely pictures graphically the fact with which we began, that total income equals total consumption spending plus total investment spending. But we can show consumption expenditures as a function of income on this graph. Let us assume that, where income is \$2,000, consumption spending amounts to \$1,600, and where income is \$500, consumption spending amounts to \$400. Joining these two and other points on our graph gives us the line *CC*, the rate of consumption spending out of income. But if consumption is determined by the level of income, investment spending is not so strictly limited. Business can borrow to finance its spending to a much greater extent than can consuming units, and investment purchases are, as we have seen, influenced by factors other than current income. The line *II*, therefore, represents investment purchases which are assumed to be constant—$200 regardless of total income—and which are added to the total of consumption expenditures.

The level of income determined by the consumption function *CC* and the investment function *II* is $1,000, or where savings and investment are equal. At an income level of $1,000, consumption expenditures amount to $800 as shown by *E* in Figure 14-2 and savings amount to $200 as shown by *S* in Figure 14-2 (i.e., the difference between income and consumption). Only at the income level of $1,000 is this $200 of savings (*S* on the graph) equal to the investment expenditures of $200. This income is the equilibrium level, which means that it will continue as long as neither investment spending nor the consumption function changes. The total spending of business and consumers provides $1,000 of income to consuming units, who save 20 per cent of it, or $200. But business investment of $200 buys that part of total output which consuming units do not, and investment expenditures offset saving.[2]

Our previous investigation has shown, however, that both the limiting assumptions in our graph should be removed. Business investment purchases are not constant but fluctuate from year to year, and the amount of consumption spending out of income is not a constant either. When investment spending and consumption are such that saving equals investment, the total income is determined and is in equilibrium, but we know that national income does change.

In terms of our circular flow diagram in Figure 14-1, we may think of saving as continually *diminishing* the total money flow and of investment and consumption spending as continually *replenishing* the total. When investment spending puts more into the circular flow than saving withdraws, obviously the total stream increases. Conversely, when saving takes more from incomes than investment is adding, the total must decrease. We can explain these changes in national income more precisely with the aid of the consumption function, which defines the multiplier effect of changes in spending on the national income.

[2] The reader will find a clear and helpful discussion of this analysis of income determination in *Economics: An Introductory Analysis*, 3d ed., by Paul A. Samuelson, McGraw-Hill Book Company, Inc., New York, 1955, part 2, chaps. 11 and 12.

The multiplier effect follows from the increase in consumption expenditures out of additional income—the marginal propensity to consume. When consumer spending increases, it generates further increases in income.

Using the data from Figure 14-2, let us assume that income is $1,000, made up of $200 investment expenditures and $800 consumption spending, in time period one. Now, if firms decide to increase their investment to $300 (perhaps by borrowing from banks), total income expands, for the $800 of consumption spending plus $300 investment spending results in national output and income of $1,100 *in the second time period.* If consumers spend at the same rate, 80 per cent of income, consumption expenditures out of the new, higher income will be $880. If business continues to invest at the $300 level, national output and income then rise, *in the third period,* to $1,180. The amount of this spent on consumption will now be $994, and this plus investment spending of $300 will make a new total income of $1,244. Out of this higher income, consumer spending at the same rate will amount to $995, and this plus the same amount of investment spending raises output and income to $1,295, and so on. Additional consumption expenditures out of higher incomes generate additional income, or *multiply* the original income increase from investment.

But as incomes increase from one time period to the next, total savings increase, causing the additions to income, period by period, to dwindle. This condition keeps income from expanding indefinitely. These ideas can be expressed more precisely with the aid of the concept of the marginal propensity to save. The reciprocal of the marginal propensity to save expressed in fraction form describes the number of times that the original increase in spending will be multiplied, or generated, into income. The marginal propensity to save in the example under consideration is 0.2,[3] or in fraction terms ⅕, and the reciprocal of ⅕ is 5. Hence

[3] It happens in this example that the average propensity to save and the marginal propensity to save are both equal to 0.2. This is an unusual case and results from the fact that the consumption function *CC* in Figure 14-2 intersects the *X* and *Y* axes at 0, the point of origin. Where this does not occur, and in the more typical case, the values for the average and marginal propensities to save will differ, as they did in the calculations based on actual data from Table 14-5. In the more typical case, the marginal propensity to save will be higher than the average propensity to save, and the value of the former becomes greater at higher incomes. This means that the fraction becomes larger and the multiplying effects smaller at higher incomes.

the original increase in spending of $100 is multiplied five times, and total income is increased to $1,500 at the end of the income-generating process. This example of the income-generating process through successive time periods is set forth in the accompanying table.

Time period	Consumption expenditures	Investment purchases	Total output or income
1	$ 800	$200	$1,000
2	800	300	1,100
3	880	300	1,180
4	944	300	1,244
5	995	300	1,295
6	1,036	300	1,336
7	1,069	300	1,369
8	1,095	300	1,395
9	1,116	300	1,416
.	.	.	.
.	.	.	.
.	.	.	.
N	1,200	300	1,500

This analysis is reproduced graphically in Figure 14-3. Given the consumption function *CC* and investment expenditures equal to $300, so that the investment function *I′I′* parallels the consumption function *CC* at all income levels, the equilibrium level of income is determined to be $1,500 where savings of $300, or *S* on the graph, are equal to investment $300. This occurs in Figure 14-3 at the point where the function *I′I′* intersects the 45-degree line and total spending $1,500 ($I = 300$, $C = 1{,}200$) equals total income $1,500. In sum the additional investment expenditure of $100 has generated a $500 increase in total spending and income.

Since the level of income is determined by the amount where total saving equals investment spending, changes in the level of income result from a tendency for saving and investment to be unequal. In our example, when income was $1,000 and consumption $800, total saving would equal $200. But when firms increased their investment spending to $300, there was a tendency for investment to exceed saving, and this produced the expansion of income, since total product increased to the level of total spending. Again, out of the new $1,100 level of income, when consumption was $880, total saving would equal $220, or less than the investment of $300.

Such a divergence between saving and investment led to the rise in income which finally provided sufficient saving to equal investment.

The chain reaction of the multiplier enlarges any initial change in spending, whether it is an increase or a decrease. If, in our example, investment spending *decreased* by $100, total product and income would fall and this would lead to lower consumption expenditures. Total spending would decline eventually to $500, where consumption at the rate of

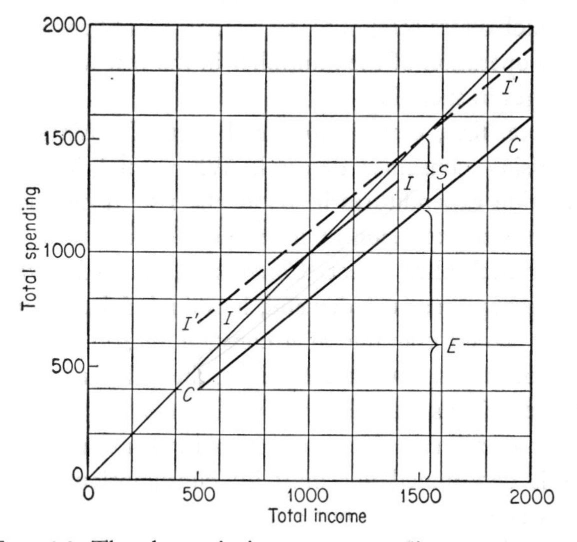

FIG. 14-3. The change in investment spending and income.

80 per cent of income would allow $100 of saving, exactly equal to the amount of investment. The reader should plot this change in investment on Figure 14-3.

In more realistic terms, it is both possible and likely for the amounts consuming units and business plan to save to differ from the amounts firms plan to invest. In the previous chapter, we analyzed the forms of savings purchased by consumers and pointed out that life insurance, bank deposits, and business investments were all means by which consumers provide money capital for investment by business. The decisions to save are taken by consuming units as well as business; the decisions to invest are taken chiefly by business. There is no reason, therefore, for the amounts involved in these decisions to be equal. But such a tendency for saving and investment to diverge brings about changes in the total income. If firms begin to invest more than the amount of planned saving, total spending goes up, as larger amounts of investment purchases are added to consumption expenditures. On the other hand, if saving tends to exceed investment, then total output (and hence income) must fall, for business spending does not use up all the output which consuming units, who are spending less, do not buy. If the investment decisions of firms are exactly matched by total saving, income remains stable or unchanged.

The multiplier has so far been explained in terms of change in business investment which alters total output or income and hence total consumer spending. The operation of the multiplier in the real world is complicated by other changes in spending.

We may note, first, that a substantial part of business investment is induced by rising consumer demand. When total income and hence total consumption expenditures increase, the rise in purchases may very well lead to further expansion of investment expenditures, which would have a further multiplier effect. Conversely, since disinvestment is induced by declining consumer demand, it is doubtful that business investment spending would continue at a constant rate in the face of falling consumer expenditures. Investment might, then, decline even more, with added multiplier effects on the shrinking income.

We may now examine the role of government in this analysis, for total output is determined not only by consumption expenditures and business investment spending, but also by government fiscal policy (i.e., the spending, taxing, and borrowing policies of the government). In fact, the fiscal policy of the government has become one of the principal policy instruments for influencing total expenditures, hence the size of the national income. When the government runs a deficit by increasing expenditures by more than taxes, economic expansion results; income is generated via the multiplier in a manner similar to an ordinary business investment expenditure. And when the government runs a budget surplus, national income must decline, unless the budget surplus is offset by an increase in business investment. In short, the size of the national income is importantly influenced by government fiscal policy.

The role of government spending and taxing may be visualized in terms of the circular flow of economic activity portrayed in Figure 14-1. Government purchases reduce the amount of productive services that can be used to make consumer goods or capital goods. But the income of consuming units and business is reduced by just this amount if taxes are used to finance the spending of government and the national income is maintained. If, however, government spends less than its tax receipts, it is paying out less than it receives and disposable incomes are reduced. Out of this smaller income, consumer spending will be less, and the multiplier will begin to work, contracting income until a level is reached where total saving equals total investment plus the government surplus. If government spending exceeds the amount of income taken from the rest of the economy, however, then total income goes up. Additional consumption expenditures, and additional saving, are generated until income provides sufficient saving to balance the amount of government deficit which initiated the change.

Finally, we must note that saving will tend to be unequal to investment plus government deficit or minus government surplus when consuming units themselves alter their rate of spending or saving. If business and government expenditures remain unchanged and consumers decide to save less, total spending increases, providing more income for consuming units. There is a tendency for saving to be lower than investment plus the government surplus or deficit, and the divergency between saving and investment generates additional income, until the level where sufficient saving is provided to balance investment.

The word *tendency* is used because our national income accounting figures show what has happened in the past. They present totals for actual saving and actual investment and cannot show a divergency between these two. This follows from our definitions. Since consumption plus investment plus government spending equals total product, total product equals total income, total income equals consumption plus total saving, then saving must equal investment. We may also understand this in terms of buying and selling at the consumer level. If consuming units do increase their purchases, say, of widgets and lower their saving, the immediate effect is to deplete the retailer's inventory by exactly the same amount saving has been cut. But inventories are part of investment, and so the two values, saving and investment, remain equivalent. The *tendency* in this example, however, is for saving to be less than investment, and hence to expand income. As our example showed formerly, the change in consumption spending leads to an increase in investment spending, and this by generating new income would also provide an increase in saving.

CONCLUSION

The role of consumption in our economy appears to be extremely significant. *Consumption expenditures make up the largest part of the demand for total output.* Changes in consumer spending influence business decisions to purchase investment goods, another large part of total output. And the increases in consumption out of increased income can generate a multiple income expansion, as decreases in consumption spending out of lower income can force a multiple contraction.

Consumers' decisions to save are equally important to the economy as a whole. The national income is determined by the relationship between the rate of total saving and the rate of total investment, and a tendency for saving and investment to diverge can occur only when these decisions are separately made. We speak of households as *consuming units* to emphasize their chief economic decisions, and we define their saving as income which is not spent on consumption goods—a negative concept. We speak of business firms, on the other hand, as *producers*, and we are interested not only in their current output but also in their decisions to buy new plant and equipment or to increase inventories—the positive concept of making investments. We can, therefore, think of business plans to invest as unrelated to consumers' plans to save. The emphasis on separate decisions was, when introduced, a highly useful analytical tool, since it stimulated research into the way business investment decisions are made and the way consumers save.

The total saving, however, consists partly of personal saving units and partly of saving by business on behalf of consuming units. In recent years, business "saving" has ranged from two-thirds to three-fourths of the annual total. Furthermore, more of the investment expenditures made by business have been financed by such saving. Business firms tap personal savings by selling new issues of stock, but these have served to pay for only about one-fifth of business investment in recent years. Retained earnings have increased, and business executives justify the retentions by their plans for future investment. Some data have been advanced to show that business spending on new plant and equipment bears a consistent relationship to business depreciation charges—that this form of saving is always invested. At any rate, owing to the growth of all kinds of business saving, many of the decisions to save and invest are, in fact, taken by the same units—the management of business firms—and we may expect less divergency between these two activities.

Much attention has been given to government's ability to expand income by deficit spending, and government's decisions are also separated from those made by consumers as a whole. But, for this reason, the consumer's role in spending and saving becomes even more important, since, somewhere in the economy, saving must compensate for the sums spent by business and government deficits if the current rate of output is to be maintained. When consuming units decide to save more or less of their income, the dynamic effects on the economy equal those of investment decisions. The multiplier can generate income changes from a change in consumption expenditures or a change in saving decisions. Some of the factors which affect such changes will be discussed in the next chapter.

Questions and Points for Discussion

1. Why is investment spending derived from consumption spending?
2. Find the average and marginal propensities to consume, using national income and total consumption expenditures, for 1932, 1933, 1952, and 1953. Explain what your results mean.
3. Find the average and marginal propensities to consume, using Table 12-2, for consuming units at the $3,000 to $4,000 income level and the $4,000 to $5,000 income level.
4. What causes the level of national income to change?
5. Why are depreciation allowances counted as part of total saving in the economy?
6. Explain the multiplier effect from an increase in net foreign investment.
7. Draw a chart similar to Figure 14-2, illustrating a consumption function with an average propensity to consumer constant at 0.75 and investment spending of $300. What determines the level of national income?

References

Clemence, Richard V.: *Income Analysis,* Addison-Wesley Publishing Company, Cambridge, Mass., 1952.

Hansen, Alvin T.: *Business Cycles and National Income,* W. W. Norton & Company, Inc., New York, 1951, chaps. 10–12.

Samuelson, Paul A.: *Economics: An Introductory Analysis,* 3d ed., McGraw-Hill Book Company, Inc., New York, 1955, part 2, chaps. 11 and 12.

U.S. Department of Commerce, Office of Business Economics: *National Income Supplement to the Survey of Current Business,* 1954.

15. Consumption and Economic Stability

In this chapter, we shall look at the total economic activity of the country with the aid of the analysis developed in Chapter 14. Earlier in the volume, we described how the price system regulates the whole economy, with relative price changes determining what is produced, how much is produced, and how the total output is divided up among all the firms and consuming units which use it. The circular flow of the national-income approach suggests how the total economy expands and contracts, and also indicates where prices operate, in the exchange of money income for goods and services of all kinds.

Thus the stream of consumer goods and services from firms meets the stream of income from consuming units, and the exchange of money income for goods determines the general level of prices for consumer goods and services, as well as the total business output of these goods and services. Again, the stream of income payments by firms meets the stream of productive services offered by consuming units, and the exchange of money payments for services determines the general levels of wages, interest, profits, and rents, as well as the total employment of these services in business. We can see now that many government transactions take place outside such streams and do not result in market prices —a point which was made in the previous chapter.

THE IMPLICATIONS OF ECONOMIC INSTABILITY

National-income changes occur in both streams—goods and services in one direction against income payments in the other—of our circular flow. The quantities of goods and services produced vary, and the amounts of income paid out vary. When both these quantities are high, we enjoy prosperity; when they are low, we suffer from depression.

Deflation and unemployment. National-income analysis was introduced during the Great Depression of the 1930s, to answer the question: "What is depression, and why does it occur?" We have already seen that, when saving tends to exceed investment plus the net effect of government spending, national income declines. Out of a lower income, consumption expenditures are less, and smaller total spending means less output. But the social and political implications of a depression are the problems of human unemployment, where no jobs exist for people who are willing and able to work.

How does a decline in total output bring about depression and unemployment? First, the decline in spending provides less payment to the services of land, labor, and capital for the finished goods and services they turn out. Beginning at the retail level, if the store selling widgets to consumers suffers a drop in sales, the retailer's earnings decline. He may have less income of his own to spend or less rent to pay his landlord. He will cut back his purchases of widgets, he may postpone paying for his last order, and he may ask his employees to take lower wages. At the producer level, similar adjustments take place, and prices are lowered to encourage sales. Unless sales increase, such price cuts may mean a loss, for the cost of the goods has already been paid. When lower sales of widgets reflect a general decline in total spending, then total earnings, and payments to all the productive factors of land, labor, and capital, must go down.

If everyone's income and spending were reduced more or less simultaneously and prices were generally lowered, the dollar value for the national income would decline but this would not be depression. If the same amount of output were available and purchased, then *real* income would be maintained and the only adjustment would be in price levels, or the value of money. But a depression involves both price deflation and a loss in total output. Price and income payments do not adjust simultaneously so that production, with a smaller money value, continues at the same rate. Instead, output and employment decline, and the fall in real income means a decline in consumption spending, which generates a multiple contraction of income.

When the retailer's sales decline, he finds that a smaller sales force can take care of his customers and that he has lost a substantial sum by having to sell his inventory at the new low prices advertised by the manufacturer. A clerk loses his job. The factory can produce all that people are willing to purchase by working thirty hours a week instead of forty, and pay envelopes contain smaller amounts, while some employees are laid off. The landlord unable to rent his house receives less income, and the vacancy means less real income—shelter—enjoyed in the economy. Fewer new firms begin doing business in the face of declining sales, while some firms' losses are great, and they go out of business. Inventories of unsold goods pile up, production shuts down entirely in some factories, and the machines stop. It is the idle resources, the unemployed men and unused machines and materials, which spell a decrease in real output and real income.

The loss in production is a vital problem to the economy, not so much because of the smaller output of goods and services as because of the effect on human lives. Technically, a severe depression means that consumers are not maximizing their satisfactions with the available resources. In reality, lower income and unemployment mean that children lack shoes to go to school and milk to gain health, that men cannot support their families and begin to despair, and that consumption levels decline.

The analysis explains why such a depression can persist. National income is determined at that level where saving equals investment plus the net effect of government spending. This level of total spending may be below the demand for output which provides employment to all the labor force. Whether or not unemployment exists, national income will not rise until the amount of investment plus government deficit or minus government surplus tends to rise above the amount of saving. Unemployment, then, may reflect a fairly stable level of income, but one which lies far below the level preferred by consumers, businessmen, and government officials.

Full employment and inflation. Economic instability has an opposite extreme which is equally subject to national-income analysis. When national income rises, consumption spending increases, leading to a rise in total output. What does this expansion mean?

It means, first, that more productive services are employed and more income is paid. The retailer hires an extra clerk, the factory begins working overtime. As the expansion of income leads to more spending, prices begin to go up in order to attract more productive services into turning out finished goods and services. The buyer making the best offer gets the empty house, and one retailer hires an extra clerk by paying him $5 per week more than another store's wages. The factory recruits employees from a labor force with many job opportunities, and people work where the pay is highest. Such increases in spending induce some firms to expand capacity, and investment spending increases. The resources of land, labor, and capital become fully employed, and prosperity means a rise in both production and income.

When full employment exists, the economy is working to capacity. If total spending continues to increase, total output cannot, because there are no productive factors available to increase the supply of goods and services. Extra spending will mean extra income, but this can be spent only on the same amount of finished goods and services, at higher prices. The situation is then no longer prosperity, and the economy has met inflation. Again, if inflation meant that all prices and incomes went up more or less simultaneously, while production continued at a high rate, the dollar value of the national income would rise but real income would be maintained, with the only change in price levels or the value of money. Such adjustments do not occur.

Some prices go up faster than others; some incomes rise, while others do not. Those goods which are bought with the amount of extra spending typically rise in price faster than other goods in the economy. Wage earners usually receive pay increases before civil servants or bondholders. A rapid advance into inflation can precipitate the economy into a decline in production when the major occupation both of firms and of consuming units is to buy real goods with their money before it becomes worthless. Money savings are not available to business for investment spending as people purchase land, or jewelry, or raw materials against future price rises. Since this kind of investment adds nothing to total output, the increase in spending leads only to further price rises.

The problem of inflation has been more familiar, in recent years, than that of depression. National-income analysis provides not only tools to explain these two situations but also devices to remedy them. Before investigating such measures, we must look further at the role of consumption and saving in these cases of economic instability.

DISPOSABLE INCOME AND INSTABILITY

We have already seen that total consumption as a function of total income is not a simple constant. National, or total, income differs from personal disposable income, and total consumption is the sum of expenditures made by many different consuming units. The distribution of income among consuming units therefore affects the propensity to consume, as do taxes and the availability of credit. Consequently, the multiplier effect on the national income is influenced by all these.

The distribution of income. Every study of consuming units' income and expenditure shows that saving takes a larger proportion of income among families with high incomes than among those with low incomes. The average propensity to consume for poorer consuming units may be 1, meaning that all their income is spent for current consumption, and it may exceed 1 where families are using up past savings or going into debt. On the other hand, the average propensity to consume is substantially less than 1 among upper-income consuming units whose saving is large. More important are the different values for the marginal propensity to consume of households at various income levels. Any extra income received by a poor family is likely to be spent entirely on consumption or on paying off past debts—the value for the marginal propensity to consume is very high. Extra income to a wealthy family which already is saving 60 per cent of its income is rarely spent. If the total income of the economy is distributed unequally, therefore (as all national incomes are), the multiplier effect will depend on which consuming units get most of the income and who is affected by changes in income. When the marginal propensity to consume is high, additional saving out of additional income is low and the multiplier, which is the value of the reciprocal of the marginal propensity to save in fraction form, is high.

In an economy where most of the income is received by a relatively few very wealthy consuming units, the marginal propensity to consume will be small, and the marginal propensity to save will be large. In this situation any expenditure injection, either by government or by business investors, will have a small income-generating effect; in this situation the value of the multiplier is low, and its income-generating effects are relatively unimportant.

If most of the income were received by low-income classes in an economy with few very wealthy consuming units, the multiplier effect would, of course, be just the opposite. Gains in income by poorer families growing out of some sort of an expenditure injection into the national-income stream would result in increased spending, and the large multiplier would affect a large part of total income, with a substantial rise as a result. Also, if such consuming units suffered a loss of income, the contracting effect of the multiplier would be very great indeed.

Since the multiplier itself is a sign of economic instability, we should expect major swings and declines in an economy where income is distributed unequally, with a large share of the income going to low-income families. On the other hand, we should expect a stable level of production and income, although at very low values, where a few extremely wealthy consuming units received a large share of the national income. Most of the people in such an economy would be poverty-stricken, and poverty would tend to persist until more of the total income was available to them.

There is a third possibility, where most of the income is received by consuming units in the middle-income brackets, with a relatively small share of total income going to either very rich or very poor consuming units. Here, the consumption function would be less than unity, and the marginal propensity to consume might be very close to the average propensity to consume (as in the case of Figures 14-2 and 14-3). Income increases received by the wealthy would have a minor effect on total income, because of their low marginal propensity to consume. Gains by the poor would also be unimportant for the economy as a whole because of their small share of total income. Additions to income received by the middle classes, as a result of increased business investment or a government deficit, would certainly produce a multiplier effect, but one which would be more moderate than in the case of extreme instability just described.

All these possibilities may be summarized in Table 15-1. Although the

Table 15-1. *Income Distribution, the Marginal Propensity to Consume, and the Multiplier Effect*

	Income classes		
	Low	Middle	High
Percentage of total income received...	5	5	90
Marginal propensity to consume....	Very high	Moderate	Very low
Multiplier effect on total income of income changes................	Slight	Slight	Slight
Percentage of total income received...	80	15	5
Marginal propensity to consume...	Very high	Moderate	Very low
Multiplier effect on total income...	Extreme	Slight	Slight
Percentage of total income received...	10	80	10
Marginal propensity to consume...	Very high	Moderate	Very low
Multiplier effect on total income...	Slight	Moderate	Slight

table is exaggerated, the reader will undoubtedly think of real economies which correspond roughly to these cases. The first represents underdeveloped countries with a wealthy ruling class, where income gains received by any class have little effect on the rest of the economy and the country enjoys economic stability, of stagnation, at a very low level. The second sheds some light on the course of depression and inflation in countries where the bulk of income is received by people who are not sufficiently well off to save a significant portion of their income. The third represents relative economic stability at a higher level than either of the preceding cases. It should be noted that total income, or income per capita, would probably be smallest in the first case and largest in the third.

Consumer taxation. Consumption expenditures out of income, and hence the multiplier effect, depend on taxation and its influence on the income distribution. We differentiate proportional, progressive, and regressive taxes according to their effect on income and spending. A proportional tax takes the same share of income from all who spend it. Progressive taxes take a larger share of income from those with higher incomes, and regressive taxes take a larger proportion of incomes from those with smaller incomes.

Examples of proportional taxation are very hard to find. Some states levy a straight 1 or 2 per cent tax on income, but because of personal and family exemptions the tax is not strictly proportional. The Federal income tax illustrates progressive taxation most clearly, since the tax rates are successively higher at higher levels of income. Regressive taxation may result from any system. Property taxes, a flat percentage of the assessed valuation of real or personal property, may take a larger share of income from the poor than from the rich, even though the upper-income classes usually hold more property.

The usual example of regressive taxation is sales taxes, and consumption analysis shows why this is so. Total spending takes a larger share of income from consuming units with low incomes than from those with higher incomes. Any tax on consumer goods or services, therefore, bears more heavily on those who spend most of their income. The taxes which are paid by business—indirect business taxes in national-income accounting—come out of consuming units' income directly or indirectly. If the taxes are not included in the prices paid by consumers, they are necessarily deducted from the earnings of business which provide income payments to consuming units.

Taxation affects the multiplier, and changes in the national income, by shaping the distribution of disposable income out of which expenditures are made. We have shown, in Chapter 4, that the Federal income tax tends to equalize income somewhat, by reducing the disposable income of wealthy consuming units more than the income of poorer consumers. But the total effect of taxation cannot be measured precisely because of the vast numbers of tariffs, excise taxes, sales taxes, and other taxes which are paid by business and alter either consumer income or expenditures. The final effect, or incidence, of each of these taxes is practically impossible to determine. Nor do our consumption studies give enough detailed or accurate information on expenditures by different income classes for such taxed goods and services.

Taxation affects consumption, therefore, by reducing personal disposable income, and by influencing consumption patterns, so that expenditures shift from Swiss to American watches, or from telegrams to letters. Income and consumption are altered by a change in taxes, and the way in which income changes are spent is influenced by the tax system.

Consumer credit. We have already noted that, for different consuming units, consumption reflects not only income but also assets and debts. The various forms of consumer credit and the ways they are used influence total consumption expenditures and the value of the multiplier.

Consuming units at low income levels may spend all their income or more by going into debt. Such credit is used to purchase the food, clothing, and shelter (the "basic necessities") which take the largest share of income among poorer consuming units. If it is widespread, this type of consumer credit indicates another symptom of stagnant, poverty-stricken economies. Credit extended in small amounts is expensive, and high prices make consumption expenditures larger than they would otherwise be. If such low-income consuming units receive extra money and use it to pay up back debts, the multiplier is stifled, for the gains in total income have been transferred to creditors, who are likely to have high incomes where the propensity to consume is low. There is little or no extra spending, therefore, which would lead to an expansion of income.

In the economy of the United States, we have found that homes, automobiles, and consumer durable goods are usually bought with credit and that such debts are frequently incurred by newly formed households as a normal part of their consumption pattern. Many of the consuming units with debts have assets, or even liquid assets, which exceed the amount of their debt. This type of consumer credit differs markedly from the previous case.

In the first place, buying a home, or automobile, or consumer durable represents investment to the consumer—he expects to enjoy future income in the services from such purchases. His payments represent savings which have already been committed to investment. Technically, the amount of future income produced by such consumer investment depends upon the course of prices after the purchase is made. Signing a mortgage note at the top of a housing boom may require future payments far greater than those needed later to buy a similar house which has declined in price. Or the cost of the credit may be too great to show any net return in buying as opposed to renting a home. Fortunately or not, relatively few consuming units make the precise calculations of income and expenditure needed to analyze such possibilities, and their behavior assumes some net return from incurring debts of this kind.

Although, by borrowing, the consuming unit can spend more than its total income currently, repayments in the future in effect reduce future incomes, so that no income increases or multiplier effect result from the availability of credit per se. But where relatively high-priced goods or services are widely purchased by using mortgages, installment sales, and personal loans, two other possibilities of income increases exist.

In the first place, consumption on a wide scale allows mass production and the economies that accompany mass production. Such economies lead to lower prices and further consumption as more people are able to buy these goods. An increase of production with the same or lower prices also represents an increase of real income within the economy. The development of the automobile industry, providing employment and income in a host of related fields, required investment with a multiplier effect on the national income. And the automobile industry, like most of the appliance industries, expanded with the aid of consumer credit.

Second, this kind of consumer credit does not nullify the multiplier effect of income increases. Most consuming units incur such debt as a form of convenient fractional payment. Current income provides the money to meet such payments, and when one debt is liquidated, another frequently takes its place. When the newly formed household which buys a home and furnishings on credit pays for the refrigerator, it will be time to buy a washing machine. The last payment on the automobile allows the purchase of a new rug or perhaps a newer-model automobile. Consuming units contract such debts because they expect future income to cover them, and most of the total consumer debt is held by younger families who may reasonably have such expectations about income. The individual consuming unit does not, of course, go on borrowing indefinitely, for older people have a small share of the total debt. But their drop in consumption expenditures when debts are paid is matched by loans made to newly formed households borrowing for the first time. If in such a situation total income increases, some consuming units will of course use income gains to wipe out debt without buying something else on credit. But, to other consuming units, extra income becomes a means of financing a bigger home, a better automobile, or a new appliance. And the availability of credit means that such purchases can be made.

When a sizable share of consumption spending depends on credit, then any change in the availability or cost of such financing of course affects spending. Some developments in home financing have already been mentioned, which altered forms of saving as well as spending for housing and household operation. The decline in purchases of consumer durable goods during the depression reflects not only income decreases, but the expectation of future cuts in income, which has the effect of forestalling purchases on credit.

THE ROLE OF GOVERNMENT

The distribution of income and the effects of taxation and consumer credit involve many ramifications which, if explored, would further modify or complicate the original analysis of the multiplier effects of income changes. Without elaborating, however, we may now look at two real situations and the government policies suggested by this analysis. In thinking of total income and consumption, as we have been for several chapters, it is easy to forget that the aggregate figures represent millions of decisions by consuming units and firms, all influenced by varying motives, surroundings, and expectations. It is easy to see, for example, that, when national income drops, an increase in business investment would, through the multiplier effect, prevent the decline or that inflation could be averted if everyone began to save more from his income, instead of spending faster than ever. The individual firms or consumers, however, act for their own welfare, and this does not always jibe with what is best for the economy as a whole. Such an interest is the concern of government, and we turn therefore to government economic policies.

Countercyclical policies. The Full Employment Act of 1946 affirmed, as a definite objective for the United States economy, a level of national income which would avoid unemployment and inflation. Under the terms of this Act, the President and his Council of Economic Advisors report to Congress on the state of the economy and make recommendations for actions. The possible countercyclical measures available for government action are derived directly from national-income analysis.

The solution to a decline in national income is, of course, an increase in total spending, which can come from consumption, investment, or a government deficit. Government policies for taxation, credit regulation, and transfer payments can affect all these.

Consumption spending need not decline in proportion to falling income if government revenues come chiefly from progressive income taxes. When income falls, personal taxes are lower also, so that the disposable personal income declines less than total income. And purchases for consumption, of course, come from *disposable* personal income. This sum can also be maintained by providing abundant credit at low cost, a government policy to encourage consumption spending and business investment. Finally, continued government spending at the same or a higher rate will produce a deficit if tax revenues shrink. Such an increase in total spending must, however, be distributed to consuming units with a fairly high propensity to spend in order to result in a large multiplier effect. Hence, government transfer payments, to provide income directly to the unemployed or to other low-income families, will increase total spending.

When the economy tends to inflation, government policies can reduce the amount of total spending. Taxes increase more than income, cutting down the amount available for spending both by consumer and by business firms. Credit regulations can reduce the amount of available credit and increase its cost to deter purchases. Less government spending, if tax revenues expand sufficiently, will produce a government surplus to contract the total income.

Some of these measures are built into the economy. Tax revenues fluctuate with income, affecting both consumption spending and the government deficit or surplus. Unemployment compensation provides transfer payments to low-income consuming units during depression and a tax on income during prosperity. The Federal Reserve System regulates credit to provide the countercyclical measures described.

The government budget, however, is not planned solely to compensate, with a deficit or surplus, for changes in total spending. In the depression years, when national income dropped from $75 billion in 1930 to $59 billion in 1931, $42 billion in 1932, and $40 billion in 1933, the government deficit of $2 billion to $3 billion a year was obviously insufficient to deter the fall in spending. Government budgets are planned in advance, and to prepare for a deficit or surplus requires prediction about consumption and investment spending. Economic data are far from sufficient to allow accurate prediction, and government policies may be ill-timed as a result. Furthermore, production and income are extremely sensitive—a *tendency* for saving to diverge from investment is enough to make income change—

and the response in the economy to changes in the government spending program may differ from what was planned.

Aside from the sums involved, the administration of compensatory policies brings other difficulties. In a depression, government cannot go into business, and compete with private production, in order to provide income by giving jobs to the unemployed. But paying income to unemployed men and women without providing work—the dole—offends both the taxpayers and the unemployed, who lose not only human dignity but valuable skills and experience. Some sectors of the economy, notably the heavy industries producing capital goods, suffer more losses than others. Agriculture brings a special problem, as falling income encourages farmers to try to produce more rather than less, and the surplus makes farm income decline farther. The attitude of firms and consuming units is overwhelmingly important. The enmity between businessmen and the New Deal, together with the unfamiliar threat of a growing government deficit, probably bred pessimism in the 1930s rather than the optimistic expectations which accompany an increase in private spending.

There are similar difficulties in budgeting for a surplus in prosperous times. The government surplus which should have accompanied the postwar years has been conspicuously absent, and the question of whether taxes should have been higher or government spending less goes beyond the realm of national-income analysis and, indeed, of economics. The chief threat of inflation, however, comes not with prosperity but with war or defense preparations.

Wartime inflation. Inflation in the economy occurs when most productive factors are fully employed and total spending increases. If such extra spending comes either from consuming units or from firms, it is not likely to persist, because total output can expand even in times of full employment. Additional investment spending shifts some of the labor force (attracted by higher incomes) to turning out capital goods, and once these are completed and productive capacity is larger, total production increases. Inflation means that such investment spending does not take place, that firms and consuming units buy real goods which are not used in further production, but hoarded. The built-in regulators in the economy also prevent a boom in private spending from progressing to inflation. Increased taxes slow down consumer spending, and rising costs of credit deter business spending.

Runaway inflation, therefore, has always been associated with *government deficits,* and government spending for war occasions the most serious deficits. Payments to a larger army and to firms for tanks, uniforms, bombs, and instruments result in income to consuming units. But when full employment exists and these sums are paid for war material, then fewer productive services are available to expand the output of consumer goods and capital goods for private investment. These payments also take labor, materials, and equipment from making automobiles, suits, telegraph wire, and kitchen gadgets, at the very time when consumer incomes are increasing to provide larger purchases of consumer goods. If government purchases were exactly equaled by taxation, total spending would be decreased as much as the total output of goods and services for private purchase. When a deficit exists, however, the payments by government provide extra income and additional spending can result only in price rises rather than an expansion of output.

Such a case of inflation goes beyond the built-in regulators for the economy, although the special measures for war or defense finance are along lines we have described. Since government spending can scarcely be cut, taxes can be raised as far as possible in order to diminish the deficit. Credit regulations can prevent extra spending by either business or consuming units. Consumer saving can be encouraged by special government securities or by forced payroll deductions. And here the distribution of income is again involved. In order to reduce total consumption spending, taxes and other regulations should bear most heavily on consuming units who spend most of their income—in other words, on the low-income classes. Consuming units at high income levels, who save much of their income, add little to the inflationary pressures through extra spending in wartime. The progressive income tax is inadequate to cut total spending, and the sales tax is admirably suited to war finance precisely because it is regressive and reduces disposable income most at low income levels.

No government has ever succeeded in imposing such financial measures, and no war or major defense program has ever been paid for without government deficit. Typically, inflation has been stemmed by direct controls on consumption, including price ceilings and rationing, rather than by reducing disposable income.

Questions and Points for Discussion

1. What factors influence the propensity to consume?
2. What is the effect of additional spending during prosperity? During inflation?

3. What are the built-in regulators for the economy? How do they work to avert depression and inflation?

4. How can national income be stabilized at a less than full employment level?

5. Why are figures on the amount of consumer credit an indicator of business activity?

6. Look up the figures (in the *Federal Reserve Bulletin* Study of Consumer Finances) for the sales of television sets by installment plans. What do you think is the effect of this credit on the economy as a whole?

References

Editors of *Fortune Magazine: The Changing American Market,* Hanover House, New York, 1953, chaps. 3, 12.

———: "The Consumer Markets: 1954–1959," *Fortune Magazine,* August, 1954.

Hansen, Alvin T.: *Business Cycles and National Income,* W. W. Norton & Company, Inc., New York, 1951, chaps. 12, 25, 26–28.

Kyrk, Hazel: *The Family in the American Economy,* University of Chicago Press, Chicago, 1953, chap. 7.

McKenna, Joseph P.: "Consumption Patterns," in Harold F. Williamson and John A. Buttrick (eds.), *Economic Development: Principles and Patterns,* Prentice-Hall, Inc., New York, 1954.

Reid, Margaret G.: "Distribution of Income and Consumption," in Hoyt, Reid, McConnell, and Hooks, *American Income and Its Use,* Harper & Brothers, New York, 1954, chaps. 6–8.

Shultz, William J.: *Social Security and the Economics of Saving,* National Industrial Conference Board, 1948.

PART FOUR

The Consumer in the Market

In Part II, we presented a theory of consumer behavior; in Part III, we observed the behavior of consuming units in the receipt and use of income—in spending and saving. And the implications of this spending and saving behavior for the operation of the economy as a whole were also developed in Part III. Now we want to observe consuming units as decision makers in markets. We want to learn how the choice decisions of consuming units are translated into demand and influence prices and to see how business practices and government actions impinge on consumer behavior in markets. We shall try to formulate a general picture of the operation of retail markets and the role of the consumer in them.

In the first three chapters of Part IV, we shall concentrate on the concept of demand: the derivation of individual consumer demand, the conceptualization of market demand, and the role of market demand in price formation. In the following chapters, we shall look at business practices which affect the consumer in the market and see how the consumer's choices are influenced by marketing institutions and services. Finally, we shall give some attention to the influence of government on consumer incomes and expenditures in the market.

16. The Derivation of Consumer Demand

The concept of demand is widely known in a vague sort of way, hence is widely used and misused. It needs defining and development to make its meaning unmistakably clear, and this we shall do in this chapter. Now, it turns out that the concept of demand grows out of the theory of consumer behavior developed in Part II. The concept of demand can be derived logically by either the utility or the indifference approach; and the precise demand relation of some Consumer A for some commodity X can be derived if either the utility function or the indifference map of Consumer A for commodity X is known.

But we know that the theory of consumer behavior involving either utility or indifference techniques is nonoperational (i.e., we are unable to obtain the relevant utility or indifference data); hence, we are unable to derive empirical demand relations. Thus, the question may be asked: "What is the use of deriving a concept where the process involved does not admit of measurement?" The first answer to this question is that the process, in terms of either the utility approach or the indifference approach, does yield the concept of consumer demand. And this concept becomes a powerful analytical tool for thinking and reasoning logically about many economic problems. Second, knowing the concept of demand inside and out—knowing how to work with it and bend it to our needs—we are able to derive measures of market demand from market data by various types of statistical analyses.

CONCEPT AND DEFINITION

As the name implies, consumer demand involves the *wanting* of some good or service by the consumer. But by demand the economist means more. He has in mind that the consumer wants and is willing (or has the ability) to buy the good or service in question. Thus, by consumer demand the economist means the quantity which the consumer stands ready to buy —or take—under certain conditions. Now, these conditions may be listed as follows:

1. As price varies
2. As all other conditions are constant, unchanging

Thus, by consumer demand we mean *the quantity of a good or a service that the consumer stands ready to buy—to take—at varying prices where all other conditions are constant.*

There are many things besides the price of a product that may influence the quantity of it taken by a consumer (the more important nonprice influencing factors will be considered in later chapters of this part), but the demand relation is concerned exclusively with the variation in the quantity of a commodity taken associated with the variation in the price of that commodity. To derive the demand relation, then, all factors other than price which influence the quantity taken must hold, or be held, constant. Where this is not the case, it is impossible to know which part of the variation in the quantity taken is attributable to a change in price and which part to a change in some other factor. In the development of statistical demand functions from market data, this problem is not easily, and never perfectly, solved. But the successes that have been realized in this direction (i.e., holding all independent variables other than price constant) result from the fact that these other factors seem to subsume under three principal headings:

1. Consumer income
2. Consumer tastes and preferences
3. Prices of substitute goods or services [1]

These are the "other" conditions that must hold constant in order that the true relation associating quantities taken with varying prices for any consumer may be measured. When we undertake to derive the demand relation of some Consumer A for some commodity X, by either the utility approach or the indifference approach, we know now what conditions bearing on Consumer A must be held constant. His income must not change, his tastes and preferences must not change, and prices of competing goods and services must not change during the period in which the utility data or the indifference map of the consumer is obtained. These factors held constant, the quantity of commodity X which Consumer A stands ready to buy—to take—at varying prices may be ascertained. And this is what we mean by consumer demand.

[1] A logical inconsistency is involved with respect to this category, but no attempt to elaborate the nature of the problem will be made until the concept of demand becomes more familiar.

DERIVATION OF DEMAND BY THE UTILITY APPROACH

We can derive the demand relation of an individual for a particular product if we know (1) the utility schedules of the individual for the product and (2) the marginal utility of money to this individual. We are familiar with the notion of utility schedules; the meaning and interrelation of total, marginal, and average utility schedules for an individual were explored in Chapter 6. Some hypothetical utility data of a hungry man for candy bars were presented in Table 6-1; we shall now use that utility data to derive the demand curve of this man for candy bars.

The concept of the marginal utility of money has been touched upon before, but we shall review its meaning here. Although it is customary to value goods and services in units of money, it is not uncommon to value money in terms of the units of goods and services that it will buy. Hence, it is not unreasonable to value money in terms of the units of satisfaction —utiles—that the goods and services acquired by means of that money provide the consumer. In this view, the value (or the worth) of the last (or marginal) dollar to a consumer measured in utiles may be defined as the marginal utility of money. Further, it seems realistic to assume that the value (or the worth) of a dollar to a consumer will eventually decline as he acquires more dollars.

Mechanics of derivation. The marginal utility schedule of a hungry man for candy bars is given in column 2 of Table 16-1. We need to find some way of expressing those units of satisfaction—utiles—in money units. For when the valuation placed on candy bars measured in utiles is converted to money units, the worth of candy bars to the hungry man can be expressed in terms of dollars and cents. And once we know what money valuation he places on candy bars, we know in fact what he is willing to pay for candy bars. This conversion from valuing candy bars in utiles to valuing candy bars in dollars and cents becomes possible once the marginal utility of money is known. And since we assume the marginal utility of money is known, the trick has been turned.

Where the marginal utility of money to the man in question is known to be $1 = 50 utiles, it follows that 1 utile = 2 cents ($1 ÷ 50 utiles = 2 cents). The value of 2 cents, which measures the money value of 1 utile to this consumer, is called the *marginal revenue of utility*. The marginal utility schedule for candy bars in column 2 of Table 16-1 may be converted from a valuation in utiles to the more conventional valuation in

Table 16-1. *The Money Value of Candy Bars to a Hungry Man Where His Marginal Utility of Money Equals 50 Utiles per Dollar*

No. of candy bars (1)	Marginal utility of candy bars, utiles per bar * (2)	Marginal utility of candy bars expressed in money values, cents per bar † (3)
0	0	
1	10	20¢
2	30	60
3	20	40
4	12	24
5	8	16
6	4	8
7	0	0
8	−12	−24
9	−18	−36

* Taken from Table 6-1.

† Sometimes defined as the marginal rate of substitution.

dollars and cents by multiplying the marginal utility values in column 2 by the marginal revenue of utility (or 2 cents in this case). It will be observed that the values in column 3 of Table 16-1, sometimes defined as the *marginal rate of substitution*, state in money terms what the marginal candy bar is worth to the hungry man.

We now have all the information, or data, needed to formulate the specific demand relation of the hungry man for candy bars. The marginal utility data converted to money terms presented in column 3 of Table 16-1 when related to the schedule of units in column 1 yield the demand relation, although this may not be self-evident at this point. And these data when plotted on graph paper yield a curve which, in fact, becomes the demand curve (see Figure 16-1).

Why a demand curve. The question that needs to be asked is the following one: "In what sense is the curve presented in Figure 16-1 a demand curve? In what sense does it show the quantities that will be taken by the consumer as price varies?" We see that the number of bars varies as the money value, hence price per bar, varies, but in what sense does the consumer stand ready to take those quantities?

The curve presented in Figure 16-1 may be conceptualized as a demand curve, if we make certain assumptions and then ask the right questions. Let us assume that the price of this type of candy bar is 16 cents (either this is a high-class candy bar, or we have had some more inflation). How many candy bars will this hungry man buy at a price of 16 cents? He will buy 5. The 4th bar provides him with 24 cents worth of satisfaction, but it costs him only 16 cents. This is a good buy; he gets 8 cents worth of

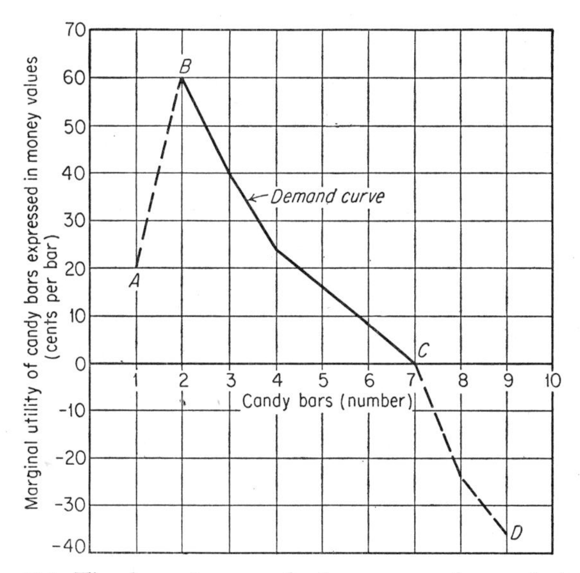

FIG. 16-1. The demand curve of a hungry man for candy bars.

satisfaction free of charge. So he will certainly buy 4 bars and consider buying the 5th. But when he buys the 5th bar, he discovers that it provides him with only 16 cents worth of satisfaction, or just what it costs. And this is where he will stop if he is a rational man. For if he buys the 6th bar, he will derive only 8 cents worth of satisfaction from it, although it still costs 16 cents. This is a poor buy, and he will not make it. Given his utility schedule, his marginal utility of money $1 = 50 utiles, this consumer maximizes his total satisfaction from the purchase of 5 candy bars at a price of 16 cents.

The same line of reasoning can be developed if the price of candy bars is assumed to be 24 cents, or 8 cents, or any other price. In every case this consumer moves out along the curve presented in Figure 16-1 to that point where the money value of the utiles provided by the last unit is equal to the price of that unit. Thus the curve *BC* in Figure 16-1 may be defined as the demand curve of this hungry man for candy bars; it indicates how many candy bars he will buy at each price.

We limit the concept of the demand curve to the phase *BC* in Figure 16-1 and eliminate phases *AB* and *CD*, because these latter phases are outside the range of rational decision making. No rational man is going to pay a price for a unit of a good which provides negative satisfaction. And, in this illustration, candy bars 8 and 9 yield negative satisfaction. Thus, we throw out this phase of the curve as being meaningless–noneconomic. The phase *AB* is eliminated for just the opposite reason. No matter what the price of candy bars may be, this consumer is better off with two candy bars than one. If for any reason he is willing to buy one, he is better off by buying two, *for the satisfaction provided by the second unit is greater than the first.* Thus, we eliminate this phase of increasing marginal utility as being noneconomic and construct the demand curve from that point where diminishing marginal utility sets in. In this case, the diminishing phase begins with the second candy bar; hence, the meaningful demand curve of this consumer for candy bars extends over the range 2 to 7.

It may be that no one will ever actually derive the demand curve of a consumer for a commodity in the way just described. Whether this will be the case depends on the successes realized in measuring utility in the years to come. But *given* the utility schedule of a consumer for a commodity, we see how these data may be used to derive the demand curve of the consumer for the commodity involved. But we see more. We see that the configuration of the demand curve conforms to the configuration of the utility schedule. The demand curve of the consumer slopes downward because it is derived from the marginal utility schedule in its diminishing phase. And where the marginal utility schedule falls rapidly, so does the demand curve, and vice versa. In other words, the demand curve of a consumer for a commodity is nothing more than his marginal utility schedule, measured in money units, and restricted in the typical case to that phase where the marginal utility schedule is declining but is still positive.

DERIVATION OF DEMAND BY THE INDIFFERENCE APPROACH

Those persons who find the utility approach distasteful, for whatever reason, may be pleased to discover that the concept of demand may be derived by an alternative approach–the indifference approach. Here again we must limit our statement to include only the derivation of the *concept* of demand, for actual indifference data, just as utility data, continue to escape us; hence, specific, empirical demand relations do not emerge out of the indifference approach. As in the previous section, we shall derive from hypothetical data the demand curve of some Consumer A for some commodity X. By this procedure, we develop the concept of consumer demand–showing its foundation in consumer behavior and the interrelations involved.

The mechanics of derivation. We can derive the demand curve of Consumer A for some commodity X by the indifference approach if we let Y represent money rather than some specific commodity. In this case, money is taken to represent all other commodities–all the other commodities which in some degree are substitutes for X. The indifference map, involving money on the Y (vertical) axis and commodity X on the X (horizontal) axis, thus presents along given contour lines combinations of commodity X and all other commodities to which Consumer A is indifferent. This procedure admits of substitutional relationships between X and all other commodities for which it is a substitute, *as is implicit in demand relationships,* but which is not the case where only two commodities are involved in the construction of the indifference map.

What we need now is the indifference map for Consumer A involving commodity X and money. But since we cannot obtain the data out of which to construct such a map from observation or experimentation, we shall use hypothetical data. The indifference map constructed from these hypothetical data is presented in Figure 16-2. We assume also that the maximum amount of funds that Consumer A will spend on commodity X is \$10.

If, now, we know the price of commodity X, the outlay curve of Consumer A for money and commodity X may be constructed and the equilibrium quantity of X determined. Where the price of X = \$2, the outlay curve may be constructed as follows: If all the \$10 is held as money, 10 dollar units of money are involved (\$10 ÷ \$1 = 10 dollar units). This provides one point on the outlay curve–the point where the outlay curve intersects the Y axis. If, however, all the \$10 is spent for commodity X, 5 units of X may be obtained (\$10 ÷ \$2 = 5 units). This provides a second point on the outlay curve–the point where the outlay curve intersects the X axis. The outlay curve is obtained by connecting these two points with a straight line; we see this curve AA in Figure 16-2. This outlay curve becomes tangent to indifference curve I_1 at point P. The equilibrium position at point P indicates that Consumer A will purchase

3 units of X at a price of \$2. These data provide one observation on the demand relation for Consumer A for commodity X: at a price of \$2, he stands ready to take 3 units of X.

A second point on A's demand curve for commodity X may be obtained, if we permit the price of X to vary. This we do; we assume the price of X falls to \$1, and all else remains constant. A new outlay curve AB is constructed at the lower price of \$1, where Consumer A may obtain 10 units of X if the full \$10 is spent on X (\$10 ÷ \$1 = 10 units). This second outlay curve becomes tangent to indifference curve I_3 at point P_1. This equilibrium position involves the purchase of 6 units of X at the price of \$1. Thus, we have a second observation on the demand relation of Consumer A for commodity X: at a price of \$1 he stands ready to purchase 6 units of X. These observations are plotted in Figure 16-3 to yield the demand curve D_xD_x of Consumer A for commodity X. And we could repeat this performance over and over again to obtain other price-quantity observations on A's demand curve; all we have to do is let the price of X vary and read from the new point of tangency the quantity of X that would be taken. But the derivation of these two price-quantity points by the indifference approach makes clear the general approach by which the demand curve is derived.

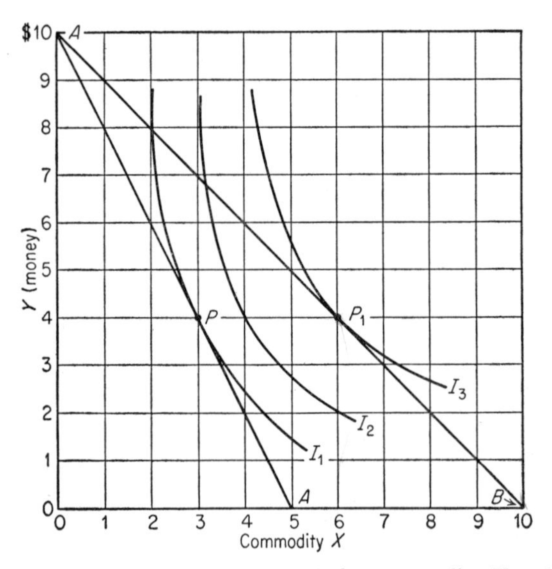

FIG. 16-2. The indifference map of Consumer A for commodity X and money, showing different equilibrium combinations.

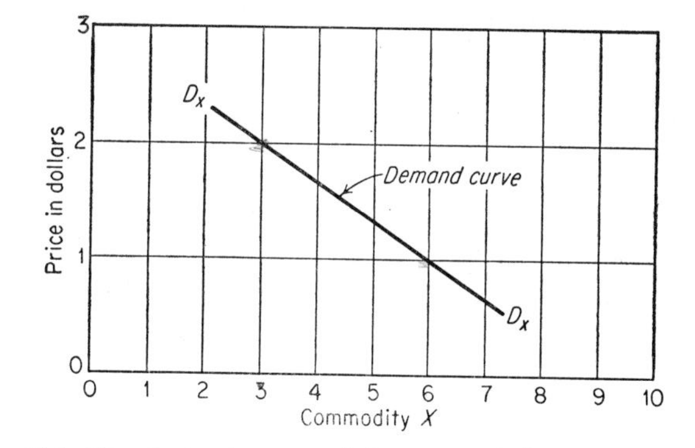

FIG. 16-3. The demand curve of Consumer A for commodity X.

The slope of the demand curve. The demand curve D_xD_x in Figure 16-3 is negatively inclined–slopes downward and to the right as all good demand curves are supposed to. But what is the rationale in this case? The negative slope cannot rest on the proposition of diminishing marginal utility, for that principle does not come into play in the determination of the quantities involved at equilibrium points P and P_1, except indirectly. We say that the curve D_xD_x in Figure 16-3 slopes downward and to the right for two reasons, (1) the *income effect* and (2) the *substitution effect.* As we remember from Chapter 7, these two effects grow out of any price change. Given a fall in price, more of a commodity is taken, hence the demand curve slopes downward and to the right, because of (1) the income effect of that price decline and (2) the substitution effect of that price decline. This is the case, because (1) the income effect of a price decline leaves the consumer with more money income out of which to buy more of all goods and services including X and (2) the substitution effect takes the form of substituting the now cheaper commodity X for the other commodities, now relatively more expensive. In other words, a price decline in X has the effect of providing the consumer with more income to spend and induces the substitution of a lower-priced commodity for higher-priced ones; a rise in price obviously has the opposite effects. Thus, a fall in price gives rise to larger quantities taken and a rise in price to smaller quantities taken, with the result that the demand curve slopes downward and to the right.

The workings of these two effects in expanding the takings of Consumer A from 3 units of X to 6 units as the price of X falls from \$2 to \$1 may be viewed graphically in Figure 16-4. In this graph, the income effect may be said to account for 2 of the 3 units increase in X, or from the 3d to the 5th unit. The substitution effect accounts for the remaining unit increase, or from the 5th to the 6th unit. The reasoning runs as follows: With the fall in the price of X from \$2 to \$1, Consumer A moved to the higher indifference curve I_3; this we know. *If* he had realized this level of satisfaction through a greater expenditure on Y and X, the new combination of Y and X would have been realized at point P_2. This point is obtained by letting the original outlay curve drift to the right until it becomes tangent to I_3 at point P_2. *If* this had been the process by which Consumer A had moved to indifference curve I_3, the equilibrium quantity of X would be 5 units. *Thus, we get a measure of the income effect of the price decline—an increase in the quantity of* X *taken by* 2 *units.* But Consumer A actually stands ready to purchase 6 units of X after the price decline. The increase from 5 units to 6 is accounted for by the substitution effect. We may visualize Consumer A moving from point P_2 to P_1 along curve I_3 through the process of substituting X for money (all other goods). The twin roles of the income effect and substitution effect in expanding the consumption of X following a fall in the price of X are thus portrayed in Figure 16-4.

We have said that demand curves typically slope downward and to the right—are negatively inclined—and we have provided an explanation for this phenomenon, first, in utility terms and, second, in indifference terms. But it has been suggested that demand curves on occasion slope upward and to the right—are positively inclined.[2] This would seem to be the case for certain important food staples in the budgets of low-income consumers (e.g., rice in the budget of a Chinese coolie, flour in the budget of an English coal miner in the nineteenth century). In other words, a fall in the price of a food item, which bulks large in the budget of a low-income consumer, may actually lead to a reduction in the quantity of that item consumed.

How could this be? And how can such behavior be made consistent with the utility and indifference explanation? It is difficult to rationalize such behavior in utilitarian terms, but the income-substitution explanation provides a way out.

What would seem to happen is this: A decline in the price of wheat flour, where bread is the principal food, gives rise to an important income effect. The real income of the consumer is expanded significantly by reason

[2] The so-called Giffen Paradox reported by Alfred Marshall, *Principles of Economics*, 8th ed., The Macmillan Company, New York, p. 132.

of the fact that the price of one of the largest items in his budget has fallen. Being, in fact, a richer man, he now buys more of the things he has been wanting (e.g., meat, clothes), but not more flour. More precisely, the consumption of bread contracts to make way for the expanded consumption of animal products; the composition of the diet shifts from

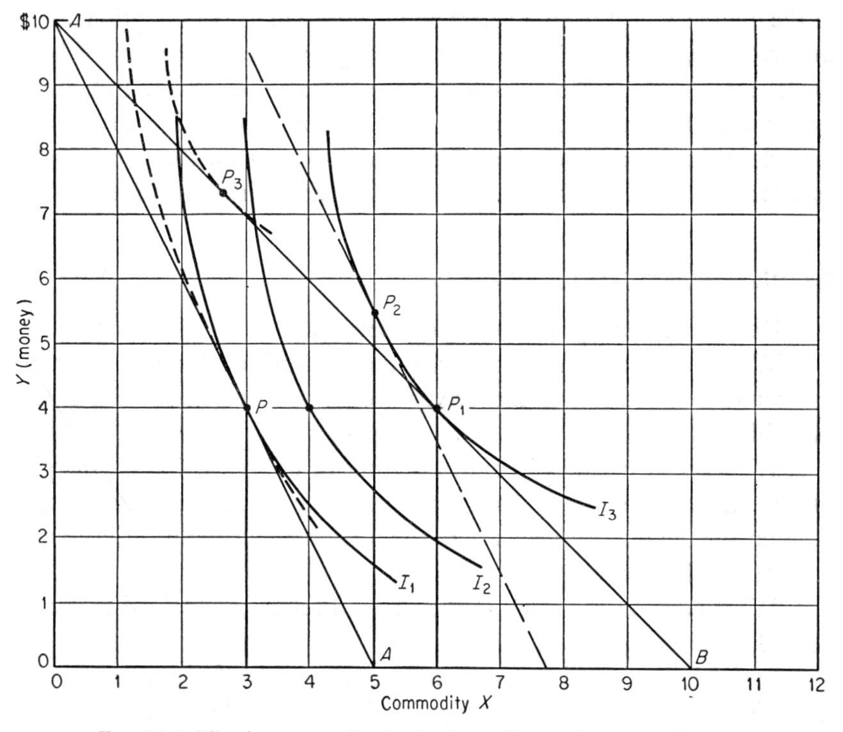

FIG. 16-4. The income and substitution effects of a price change.

one heavily weighted with bread to one less heavily weighted with bread. In the language of economists, the negative income effect on the amount of flour purchased overrides the substitution effect, with the result that the consumer buys less flour after the price decline than before. Such cases are uncommon, but they have been reported. And they can be rationalized in terms of the income-substitution explanation. Such results may be visualized graphically from Figure 16-4; if the contour map of Consumer A were such that indifference curve I_3 became tangent to the outlay curve *AB* between the second and third unit of *X*, we would have just such a case. The outlines of a contour map answering this description are shown by the dashed indifference curves in Figure 16-4; and the quantity solution leading to a positive-sloping demand curve for commodity X is given by point P_3. This is an improbable solution, but not an impossible one.

In any event, we see that the income effect of a price change may be either positive or negative (i.e., the income effect of a fall in the price of the item may lead to an increase or a decrease in its consumption). And, in rare cases, the negative income effect of a price change may be so great as to override the always positive substitution effect. But, in the typical case, both the income effect and the substitution effect are positive —work in the direction of the price change—thus cause the amount taken to increase with a fall in price and decrease with a rise in price.

Questions and Points for Discussion

1. Define the concept of consumer demand.

2. What data are required to derive the demand relation of a consumer for some commodity via the utility approach? Are these data readily available?

3. What do we mean by marginal revenue of utility? Using the marginal utility schedule for candy bars given in Table 16-1, derive the demand relation for the hungry man where the marginal revenue of utility equals 1 cent; equals 5 cents.

4. What controls the slope of the demand relations obtained under (3) above?

5. In the derivation of the demand relation via the indifference approach, why do we use money on the Y axis? And where this is the case, what does the indifference map of the consumer describe?

6. Construct an indifference map of your choosing involving money and commodity X; assume some relevant price for commodity X, and lay off the outlay curve; now, let the price of X vary, and observe how the quantity of X taken varies. With the data thus derived, construct the consumer demand curve for X, and label all parts of the graph properly.

7. Can you explain, in terms of the indifference method, how the demand relation of a consumer for some commodity could possibly slope upward and to the right—be positively inclined?

References

Boulding, Kenneth E.: *Economic Analysis,* rev. ed., Harper & Brothers, New York, 1948, pp. 617–620.

Marshall, Alfred: *Principles of Economics,* 8th ed., The Macmillan Company, New York, 1936, book III, pp. 93–137.

Stigler, George J.: *The Theory of Price,* rev. ed., The Macmillan Company, New York, 1952, pp. 74–80.

17. Market Demand: Determinants, Elasticity, and Statistical Measures

The concept of consumer demand developed in the previous chapter derives from the theory of consumer behavior presented in Part II. Thus, we understand the nature and the source of demand; it grows out of the decision making of consumers in their choice of goods and services. But the concept of consumer demand, as with much of the theory of consumer behavior, does not exist in a usable, operational form. One of the first steps in converting the concept of consumer demand into a usable tool is that of aggregating the various individual consumer demands into a concept of market demand. And this we shall do in the present chapter. We shall formulate the concept of market demand—the force that operates in the market—and consider procedures for appraising and measuring this important market force.

MARKET DEMAND

The concept. By market demand we mean the quantity of a good or a service that all buyers in the market stand ready to buy—to take—at varying prices where all other conditions are constant. In other words, the market demand for a commodity is nothing more or less than an aggregate of the individual consumer demands for that commodity. And the conditions which must be held constant in order that a true relation between price and quantity may obtain subsume again under three principal headings:

1. Consumer incomes
2. Consumer tastes and preferences
3. Prices of substitute goods and services

In a more precise manner, the market demand curve for a commodity is equal to the sum of the quantity abscissas of the individual consumer demand curves at each price ordinate. In Figure 17-1, the market demand curve D_mD_m is equal to the sum of the abscissas of the individual consumer demand curves D_aD_a and D_bD_b at each price ordinate.

Properties of demand. Three properties, or characteristics, of market demand curves need to be made explicit at this point. We have already observed (or assumed) these properties of demand in the derivation of the concept of consumer demand. But, heretofore, they have not been pointed out as distinguishing characteristics. In order, then, to be able to

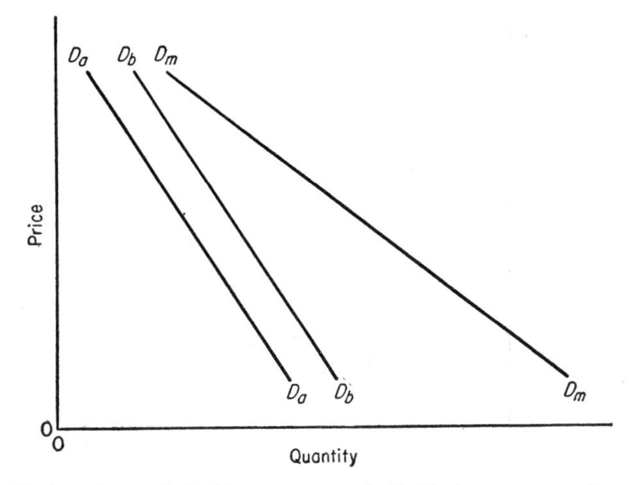

FIG. 17-1. Market demand D_mD_m summates individual consumer demands D_aD_a and D_bD_b.

identify or to recognize the demand relation readily and correctly, these properties are reviewed here. They are to the demand relation as the hop is to the jack rabbit or the red breast is to the robin: "By these properties ye shall know them."

1. A market demand curve describes a functional relation between price and quantity (i.e., the quantity value is dependent upon the price value, and vice versa). Thus, given the price of a commodity, the quantity purchased may be determined from the relationship existing between price and quantity (i.e., the demand relation).

2. Market demand curves typically are negatively inclined—slope downward and to the right. We have already worked through the explanations as to why this should be the case—first, in terms of the utility approach and, second, in terms of the indifference approach.

3. The market demand relationship is timeless. We should not visualize a movement along curve D_mD_m in Figure 17-1 as occurring through time.

The curve D_mD_m describes *without reference to time* the quantities of the commodity in question that the two Consumers A and B stand ready to buy at different prices.

A change in demand. By a change in demand, we have in mind a shift in the position of the curve. The movement of the demand curve from position D_xD_x to $D_{x1}D_{x1}$ in Figure 17-2 represents a change (an increase) in demand for commodity X. This change in demand can be defined, and

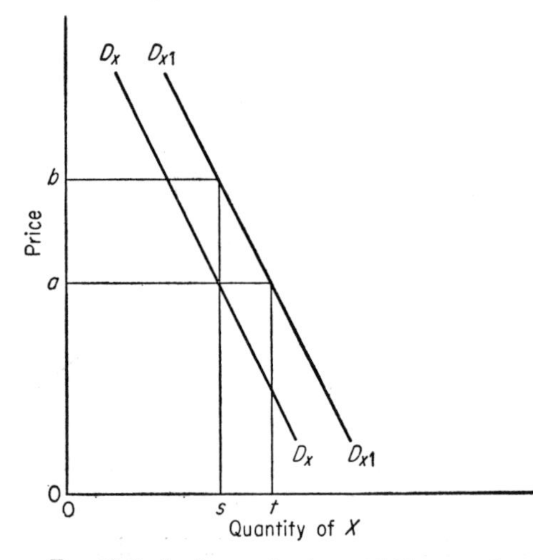

FIG. 17-2. A change in demand illustrated.

can only be defined, by observing what happens to the quantity taken *as price is held constant*, or what happens to price *as quantity is held constant.* At price *oa* in Figure 17-2, consumers stand ready to take more X—*st* more—at $D_{x1}D_{x1}$ than at D_xD_x; or, at quantity *os*, consumers stand ready to take the same quantity at a higher price—a higher price by the value *ab*. By either line of reasoning, we conclude that the demand for X has changed—increased in this case. It is customary, however, to define a change in demand in terms of a given price, and that will be our procedure. The demand for a commodity may be said to have increased when buyers stand ready to take more of it at a given price; demand has decreased when buyers stand ready to take less of it at a given price. For this to be the case, the demand curve must have shifted to the right in the first instance and to the left in the second.

Sometimes the term *change in the amount demanded* is used in economics. This term is not to be confused with the term *change in demand.*

They mean quite different things. By *change in the amount demanded*, economists have in mind a movement along the same curve; they have reference to the change in the quantity taken associated with a change in price which a particular demand curve describes. A *change in demand*, on the other hand, always has reference to a change in the position of the demand curve itself. A change in demand is concerned with changes in the quantity taken at some given price. Such changes in demand, furthermore, take place over time. The demand for a product changes with the passage of time; the individual demand curve describes different amounts demanded at varying prices at a point in time, or without reference to the passage of time.

DETERMINANTS OF DEMAND

The determinants involved. The determinants of demand are those forces which give rise to a change in demand. They shift the demand curve from one position to another—in effect, determine its position—hence, the name *determinants*. Now what are these forces which buffet the demand relation about and determine its position? They are, with one exception, those forces which had to be held constant in the derivation of the concept of consumer demand. The determinants of demand of some particular consumer for a commodity thus turn out to be:

1. Personal income
2. Tastes and preferences
3. Prices of substitute commodities

A change in personal income may be expected to influence the quantity taken by increasing or decreasing outlays for the commodity. A change in tastes or preferences for a commodity obviously means that the consumer cares more for a commodity or less for it, hence wants more of it or less of it relative to other commodities. A change in the price of commodity substitute influences the quantity taken of the commodity in question by making it a better or poorer buy relative to the substitute. These were the forces which had to be held constant in order that a net relation between price and quantity (i.e., the demand relation) might be obtained for any one consumer. But these forces do not hold constant in the world of reality: they change with the passage of time and influence the quantity taken at any particular price. In sum, changes in these forces, now defined as determinants, change—shift—the demand relation.

In the case of market demand, another, a fourth, determinant comes into play, namely, the number of persons in the market. If the number of persons in a market increases by 100 per cent *and all else remains constant,* then we would expect demand to increase by 100 per cent. In a national or world market, numbers in a market can increase only through population changes, and this is usually a slow process. Thus, this determinant is often considered to be a long-run determinant of market demand. But, in a local market, the number of buyers may expand or contract rapidly for any number of reasons: the opening or closing of an army camp, the success or failure of a real estate development, the success or failure of a sales-promotion campaign. Hence, the number of buyers in a market cannot in many cases be treated as a long-run determinant of demand.

But, in any event, numbers in the market are not a determinant in the sense of personal income, or tastes and preferences, or prices of substitutes. Numbers influence the position of the market demand curve through the addition of individual demand curves, whereas the other three determinants influence the position of the market demand curve through their influence on the demand relation of the individual consumer. Thus, it is to the workings of the determinants—income, tastes and preferences, and prices of substitutes—in fixing the position of the individual's demand curve that we now turn.

The determinants at work. The influence of changes in income, changes in tastes and preferences, and changes in the price of substitutes on the position of individual consumers' demand curves, and thence through addition on the position of the market demand curve for a commodity, may be conceptualized and illustrated by means of the indifference analysis. In the indifference analysis, a change in income is reflected in a shift in the position of the outlay curve, a change in tastes and preferences by a change in the configuration of the contour map, and a change in the price of a substitute by a change in the slope of the outlay curve resulting from the change in the price of the substitute. In the derivation of the concept of consumer demand in Chapter 16, we did not permit any of the above forces to manifest themselves: on the contrary, personal income was assumed to be constant, and hence the outlay curve did not change positions; tastes and preferences were assumed to be constant, and hence the contour map did not change configurations; and prices of substitutes were held constant, and hence the slope of the outlay curve did not change for that reason. Only the price of commodity X was permitted to vary, and this action resulted in the derivation of demand curve D_xD_x in Figure 16-3.

But now we are going to permit those forces other than the price of the commodity in question to vary and see what happens to the position

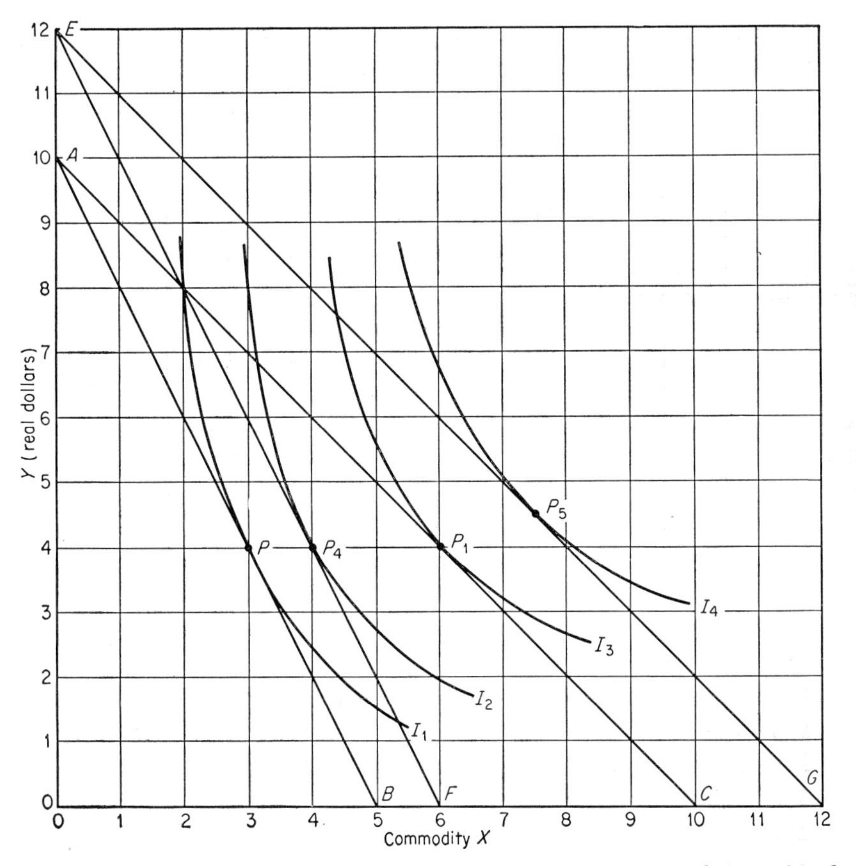

FIG. 17-3. The influence of a change in money outlay on the quantity of X purchased.

of the demand curve D_xD_x. Working through the indifference analysis, we shall observe what a change in the outlay for X means in terms of the position of D_xD_x, what a change in the indifference map means in terms of the position of D_xD_x, and what a change in the price of substitutes means in terms of the position of D_xD_x.

To facilitate this analysis, we reproduce, with one minor modification as Figure 17-3 here, Figure 16-2. The Y axis in Figure 17-3 is labeled "real dollars" to permit the number of dollar units to expand or contract with changes in the price of substitutes. The Y axis is made to measure bundles of all goods and services, called *real dollars,* that substitute for X; by this trick, we can illustrate the consequences of a change in the price of substitutes.

A change in income. Let us turn, first, to the effect of a change in income—in this case, an increase. A change in personal income will be reflected in a change in the outlays for commodities, and here we assume

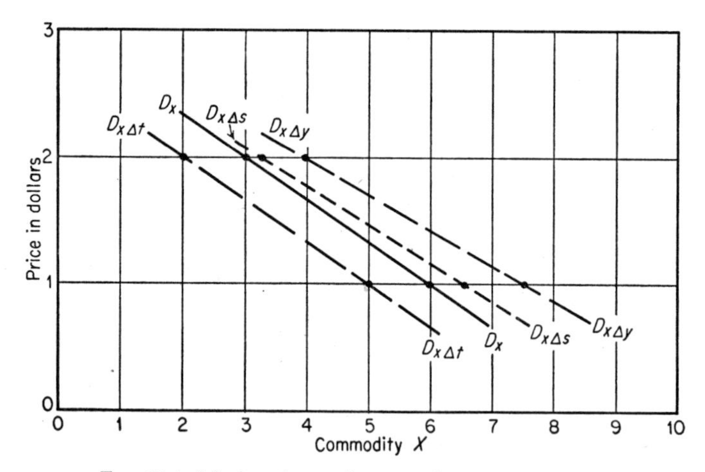

FIG. 17-4. Market demand curves for commodity X.

that the increase in personal income causes this consumer to increase his maximum outlay for commodity X from \$10 to \$12. Where the price of X is assumed to be \$2, the outlay curve EF is constructed (see Figure 17-3). Given the indifference map, the outlay curve EF becomes tangent to the indifference curve I_2 at point P_4. This point provides one price-quantity point on the new—expanded—demand curve for commodity X; at a price of \$2, this consumer stands ready to take 4 units of X. Now, let the price of X fall to \$1. Where the maximum outlay holds constant at the increased figure of \$12, we construct the new outlay curve EG. Given the indifference map, the outlay curve EG becomes tangent to indifference curve I_4 at point P_5. Thus, a second price-quantity point is obtained on the new demand curve for commodity X: at a price of \$1, this consumer stands ready to take 7½ units of X. The effect of the increase in income through an increased outlay may be seen graphically in Figure 17-4; the demand curve for this consumer has shifted to the right, taking up the new position $D_{x\,\Delta y}D_{x\,\Delta y}$. As the result of an increase in income, this consumer stands ready to take more of X at each relevant price.

A change in tastes and preferences. The effect of a change in tastes and preferences is easily shown. A change in tastes and preferences in-

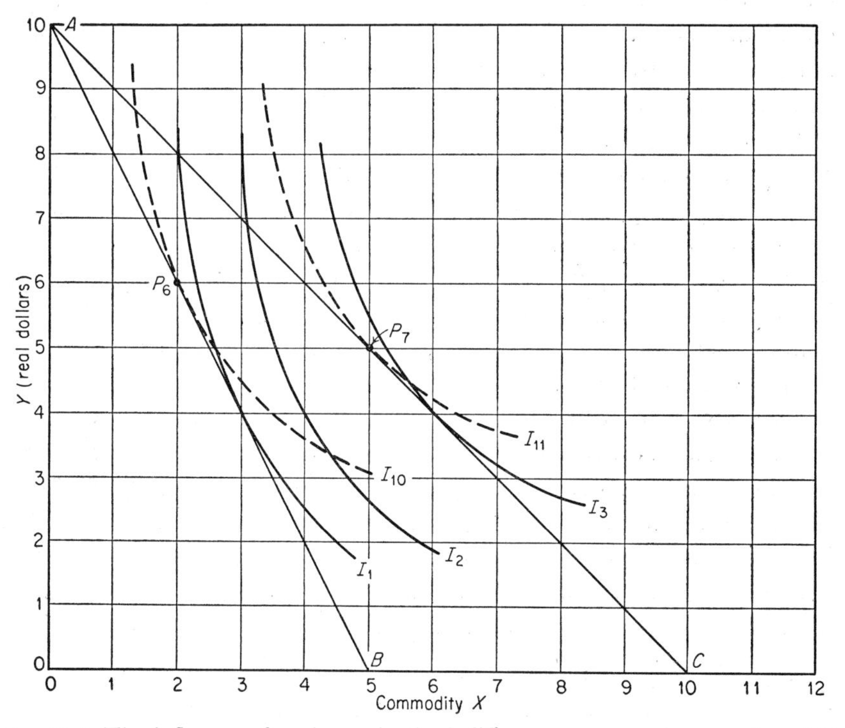

FIG. 17-5. The influence of a change in the indifference map on the quantity of X purchased.

volving commodity X will be reflected in a changed indifference map for X. This we see in the dashed indifference curves I_{10} and I_{11} in Figure 17-5. Assuming no change in income, hence outlay for X, the outlay curves AB and AC are once again the relevant curves for the prices \$2 and \$1, respectively. The points of tangency P_6 and P_7 provide the data out of which to construct the new, changed demand curve of this consumer for commodity X: at price \$2, he stands ready to take 2 units of X; at price \$1, he stands ready to take 5 units of X. These price-quantity data are plotted in Figure 17-4 to yield the demand curve $D_{x\Delta t}D_{x\Delta t}$. The change in tastes and preferences revealed in the new contour map in Figure 17-5 results in a contraction in demand by this consumer for commodity X. At each relevant price, he stands ready to take less X than was the case at demand D_xD_x.

A change in the price of substitutes. The determinant, price of substitutes, gives economists and students alike more trouble than all the others taken together.[1] It is difficult to keep the respective roles of the principal commodity and its substitutes separate and straight, and it is difficult to illustrate these roles in an indifference analysis. So first let us be clear that the force that we are investigating originates in a change in the price of the substitute commodity, and the consequences of this initiating force are registered in terms of a change in demand for the commodity in question or the principal commodity. In other words, we want to see how the demand of some consumer for a commodity such as apples is influenced by a change in the price of one or more of its substitutes—say a change in the prices of oranges and bananas.

In this analysis, we assume that the prices of substitutes for commodity X fall. As a result of this fall in the prices of substitutes, the number of *real dollars* available to the consumer increases; the number of actual dollars has not increased, but since he can now buy more units of all substitutes, we can say that the number of real dollars has increased. In Figure 17-6, the number of *real dollars* increases from 10 to 13. In other words, if the consumer spends all of his money dollars ($10) on goods other than X, he can acquire an increased number of units of other goods equal in value to $13 prior to their fall in price. Or if he spends all his $10 on

[1] The determinant, price of substitutes, gives rise to a logical difficulty with respect to the concept of demand that is not easily resolved. The demand relation describes the net relation of price on quantity only in so far as all other influencing forces hold constant. But a movement along the demand curve of the principal commodity to a changed price-quantity position must mean that some substitution between the principal commodity and its substitutes has occurred. Now, if the quantity demanded of the substitute changes by more than an infinitesimal amount by this substitution process, the demand for the substitute will have changed, and hence its price. In other words, a change in the price of the principal commodity has caused one of the determinants to change—namely, the price of a substitute. But a given demand relation holds only so long as its determinants hold constant, for a change in a determinant causes the demand relation under investigation to change. The only solution to this problem is to assume that a price change in the principal commodity is "absorbed," by infinitesimal quantity changes on the part of its many substitutes. By this not very realistic assumption, the never-ending chain of response between a given commodity and its substitute is stopped.

X, where the price of X is \$2, he can acquire 5 units of X. Thus, we construct the new outlay curve EB, which has a steeper slope than the original curve AB, because the prices of all other goods have fallen. The out-

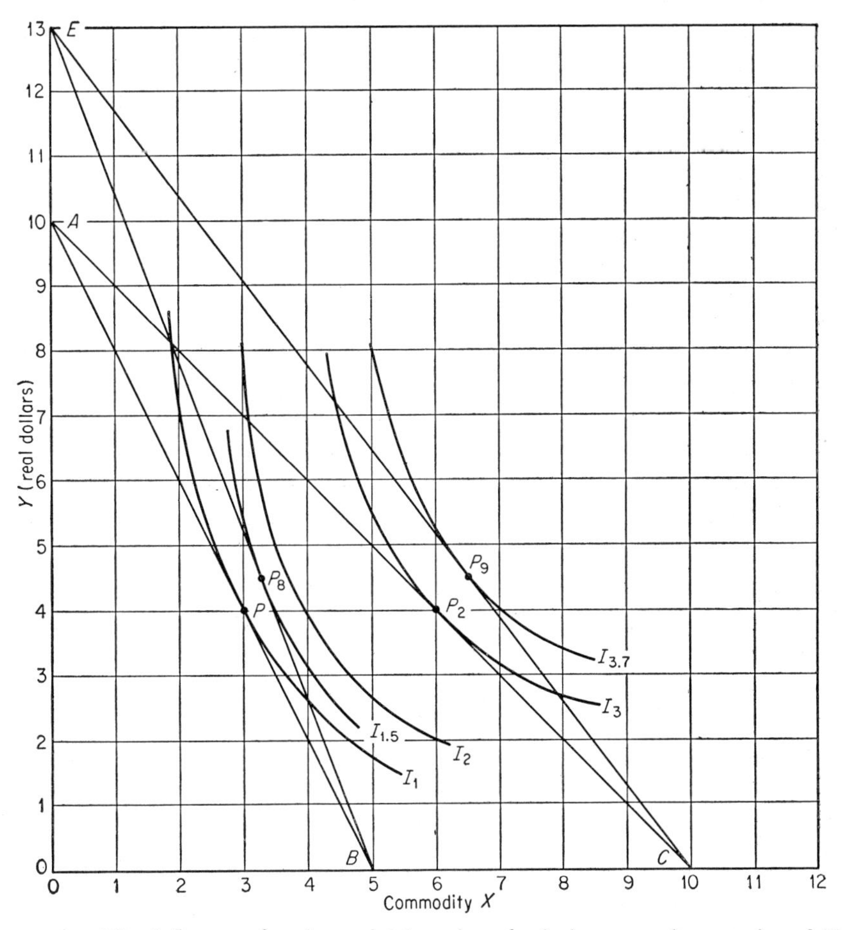

FIG. 17-6. The influence of a change in the price of substitutes on the quantity of X purchased.

lay curve EB becomes tangent to indifference curve $I_{1.5}$ at point P_8. This point yields the price-quantity data for one observation on the consumer's demand curve: at a price of \$2, he stands ready to take 3.3 units of X. Now, we let the price of X fall to \$1 to obtain a second observation on the new demand curve. The outlay curve EC emerges where the price of X is \$1, and becomes tangent to the indifference curve $I_{3.7}$ at point

P_9. A second observation is obtained on the new demand curve: at a price of $1, the consumer stands ready to take 6.5 units of X. Thus, the demand curve for this particular consumer shifts from D_xD_x to $D_{x\Delta s}D_{x\Delta s}$ with a fall in the price of substitutes. With a fall in the price of substitutes, this consumer stands ready to take more of X at each relevant price of X than previously was the case.

It would not have been unreasonable to guess that this consumer would have restricted his purchases of X in favor of its substitutes with a fall in the prices of those substitutes. This is probably the typical response for minor items in the budget and would have been the response in this illustration if the indifference map of this consumer rose vertically more rapidly than it does. For the substitution effect of a fall in the price of substitutes will always be in the direction of the price change (i.e., if the prices of substitutes fall, more of the substitutes will be purchased, and conversely). But there is the income effect of the fall in the prices of substitutes to be considered, too. The income effect is such in this illustration that the consumer takes more of X, and enough more to more than compensate for the contraction of X due to the substitution effect. In other words, the income effect overrides the substitution effect, with the result that the consumer stands ready to take more of X after the fall in the price of substitutes than previously was the case. Hence, the fall in the price of substitutes causes the demand curve to shift to the right in this case.

In more general terms, a fall in the price (or prices) of substitutes sets up two strands of consequences, (1) an income effect which can result in either an increase or a decrease in the quantity of X taken and (2) a substitution effect which always results in a decrease in the quantity of X taken. Consequently, whether the demand curve for X shifts to the right or left depends on the nature of the income effect and whether it or the substitution effect dominates.

The working of the three determinants of demand–personal income, tastes and preferences, and prices of substitutes–has now been illustrated. And many, many more illustrative cases could be presented–in fact, an infinite number–though such a presentation would quickly become tedious. But the nature of the influence of each of these determinants on consumer demand, and the limitless number of possible changes in these determinants and combinations of these determinants, needs to be understood and appreciated.

ELASTICITY OF DEMAND

The concept. We know what is meant by market demand, and we know what forces come into play, and in what ways, to shift or change the demand relation. But we have not as yet a concise and accurate means of describing a particular market demand function—say the market demand for lettuce in the United States in 1954. Such a measure is to be found in the concept of demand elasticity (or price elasticity, as it is sometimes called to distinguish it from income elasticity). This measure provides a meaningful and precise means of describing particular demand relations.

We could perhaps describe one demand curve as being gently sloped and another as being steeply sloped, but such a method of description is not precise, to say the least. What is a gentle slope to one observer may be steep to another. But this, it may be argued, could be overcome by measuring the slope of the curve, where the slope is equal to the height of the triangle divided by the base,[2] and then describing the demand curve in terms of the measure of the slope. Such a method would yield a precise measure. But such a measure is presented without a frame of reference—without telling anything about the context in which the change in price and quantity takes place. And descriptions involving dimensions, or changes in dimensions, that do not include a frame of reference tend to be meaningless or misleading. For example, the following sets of data yield identical slopes, but the situations are greatly different:

1. Price falls from $2 to $1; quantity increases from 3 units to 6 units; slope equals −0.33.

2. Price falls from $2 to $1; quantity increases from 103 units to 106 units; slope equals −0.33.

Certainly the increase in quantity taken from 3 units to 6 units repre-

[2] The slope of the demand curve in the accompanying diagram is given by

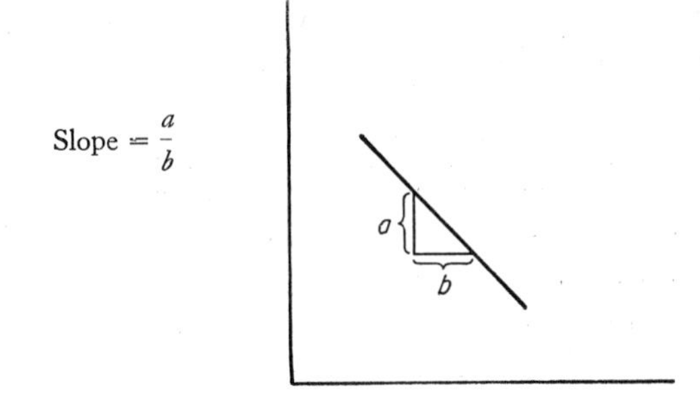

sents a more important quantity response than the increase from 103 to 106 units where the price change is the same in each case: in the first situation, the quantity response is 100 per cent; in the second situation, the quantity response approximates 3 per cent. But the slopes of the curves are the same in each case, because the absolute differences in price and in quantity are the same. Hence, it is recognized that descriptions of demand in terms of the slope of the curve are not useful in many cases and in some cases may be actually misleading. Further, it should be recognized that the precise measure of slope obtained is dependent upon the units involved on the X and Y axes. And this limitation, too, should be avoided if possible.

What we want in the way of a measure is one which compares two rates of change: the rate of change in quantity with the rate of change in price. And this is precisely what the concept of elasticity does. The fundamental definition of the elasticity of demand is

$$E = \frac{\text{relative change in quantity}}{\text{corresponding relative change in price}}$$

where we denote elasticity by E. The elasticity of demand describes how quantity changes *relative* to its base as price changes *relative* to its base. And since this measure of elasticity involves a comparison between two ratios (or rates of change), it is independent of the units in which the quantities and prices are quoted.

Measurement of elasticity. When changes in price and quantity are infinitesimally small, the elasticity of demand E may be calculated by the following formula:

$$E = \frac{\Delta q/q}{\Delta p/p} = \frac{\Delta q}{\Delta p} \times \frac{p}{q}$$

where q = quantity
p = price
Δq = infinitesimal changes in quantity
Δp = infinitesimal changes in price

But the price-quantity data, with which we typically work, are discrete in character (i.e., discontinuous rather than continuous), and the changes in prices and quantities, in which we are typically interested, occur in distinct breaks, or jumps. For example, we are likely to be concerned with the following type of problem: How do quantities of the commodity taken change as its price changes from $1 to $1.20?[3] In this type of measurement, the above formula does not yield accurate results. It will be observed that the term $\Delta q/q$ is identical with the formulation used to compute percentages if we interpret Δq as a change in quantity rather than an infinitesimal change. But percentage calculations are not symmetrical; a 2-unit change from 8 to 10 does not yield the same percentage change ($2 \div 8 = 25$ per cent) as a 2-unit change from 10 to 8 ($2 \div 10 = 20$ per cent). Thus, in the calculation of demand elasticities, where the changes involved occur in jumps, different measures of elasticity obtain from the use of the above formula for the same price change, depending upon whether the change is considered an increase or a decrease.

This difficulty is overcome by the use of the arc formula for computing elasticity. This computational formula is given by

$$E = \frac{(q_0 - q_1)/(q_0 + q_1)}{(p_0 - p_1)/(p_0 + p_1)}$$

where q_0, p_0 = one quantity and price
q_1, p_1 = second quantity and price

What this formulation does essentially is to provide a measure of the average elasticity over the range, or arc, of the demand curve involved. Or, more precisely, it provides a measure of elasticity at a point midway between the price-quantity observations involved. To illustrate, the arc elasticity of the demand curve D_xD_x in Figure 17-4 may be computed by the above formula between the observations $p_0 = 2$, $q_0 = 3$ and $p_1 = 1$, $q_1 = 6$ as follows:

$$E = \frac{(q_0 - q_1)/(q_0 + q_1)}{(p_0 - p_1)/(p_0 + p_1)} = \frac{(3 - 6)/(3 + 6)}{(2 - 1)/(2 + 1)} = \frac{-3/9}{1/3}$$

$$= -3/9 \times 3/1 = -9/9$$

$$= -1$$

The value $E = -1$ measures the elasticity of demand midway between the two points $p_0 = 2$, $q_0 = 3$ and $p_1 = 1$, $q_1 = 6$ on curve D_xD_x. The value of E will be different at every other point along the demand curve D_xD_x, increasing as we move up the curve and decreasing as we move

[3] Persons interested in measuring point elasticity by geometric means should consult George J. Stigler, *The Theory of Price*, rev. ed., The Macmillan Company, New York, 1952, pp. 33–34.

down it. Thus, it is not strictly correct to say that the elasticity of demand is -1 at all points over the arc involved, *but since the measure describes the elasticity of demand correctly at the mid-point of the arc, it is taken to represent the elasticity of demand over the entire arc.* And where the range or arc involved is relatively small, the computed elasticity for that range by the above formula will be representative and useful.[4]

By economic convention, a demand curve is called *inelastic* where elasticity is numerically less than -1, it is said to be of *unitary elasticity* where elasticity is equal to -1, and it is called *elastic* where elasticity is numerically greater than -1. Thus, in our example, the demand curve D_xD_x may be said to be of unitary elasticity for the arc involved. The other demand curves presented in Figure 17-4 are of different elasticities for the same price range. The arc elasticities of demand over the price range \$1 to \$2 are, for example,

$$D_{x\,\Delta t}D_{x\,\Delta t}\colon \quad E = -1.29$$

$$D_{x\,\Delta y}D_{x\,\Delta y}\colon \quad E = -0.91$$

In sum, the curve $D_{x\,\Delta t}D_{x\quad t}$ with a slope identical to that of demand curve D_xD_x over the price range \$1 to \$2 has greater elasticity, and the curve $D_{x\,\Delta y}D_{x\,\Delta y}$ with somewhat less slope (a greater absolute quantity response) than demand curve D_xD_x has less elasticity. In other words, the rate of change in quantity associated with a constant rate of change in price is greatest for demand curve $D_{x\,\Delta t}D_{x\,\Delta t}$ and the least for $D_{x\,\Delta y}D_{x\,\Delta y}$.

Explanation of elasticity. Why is the market demand relation for one commodity more elastic than that for another? If we think in terms of the utility approach, we recall that the *slope* and *position* of the demand curve are determined by the marginal utility schedule of the individual for the commodity involved. Thus, we might say that the elasticity of market demand for a commodity is determined by the configuration of the marginal utility schedules of the consumers in the market. When the marginal utility schedules are gently sloped (i.e., the marginal utility of the commodity falls slowly), market demand will be relatively elastic, and

[4] The discussion has been conducted here as if all demand relations are straight lines. Such, however, is not the case; the demand relation may be curved as well as straight. Measures of elasticity computed by the arc formula, where the demand curve is in fact curved, do, however, yield less reliable results. This is the case because the arc computational formula assumes a straight line between the price-quantity points involved.

when the marginal utility schedules are steeply sloped (i.e., the marginal utility of the commodity falls rapidly), market demand will be relatively inelastic. Or, stated differently, where the marginal utility of a commodity falls slowly, the consumer is placing relatively greater value on additional units than where the marginal utility falls rapidly, and he will want to purchase a relatively large number of additional units of the commodity should its price fall. And this, of course, is what we mean by an elastic demand for the commodity.

But why is the marginal utility schedule of consumers gently sloped for some commodities and steeply sloped for others? The answer to this question turns on the extent to which a commodity may be *used* in different ways, be *used* to satisfy different wants, hence is the substitute for many commodities and in turn has many substitutes. If a commodity is consumed to fulfill only one narrow and specific need, as, say, in the case of salt, then the utility of additional units of it will fall rapidly and the demand for it will be inelastic. But if a commodity has a close substitutional relationship with many other commodities, meaning that it can be combined and used in many different ways to satisfy many different needs, then the utility of additional units of it will fall slowly and the demand for it will be elastic. Money is an extreme case in point; the marginal utility of money falls slowly because it can be used in so many different ways. At the product level, the automobile is used to satisfy many different needs in many different situations; it can be used for business or pleasure, in place of walking or trains, to haul people or supplies, and so on. Thus we would expect the demand for automobiles to be relatively elastic. *Product substitution is the important idea here.* If a product or service has many and close substitutes, we would expect to find that its demand is relatively elastic. The converse would, of course, be true for a commodity which has few or no close substitutes.

If we think, now, in terms of the indifference approach, we recall that the quantity taken increases with a fall in price, hence the demand curve slopes downward and to the right, as the result of two effects: the income effect and the substitution effect. Thus, the size of the quantity response associated with any particular price change will depend upon the nature and magnitude of these two effects. In others words, the elasticity of demand will depend upon the nature and magnitude of these two effects.

The income effect being ignored for the present by assuming it to be zero, the quantity response, hence the elasticity of demand, will vary directly with the substitution effect. The greater the substitution effect, the greater the elasticity of demand, and conversely. Now, when will the substitution effect be large? It will be large when the commodity in question *has many and close substitutes.* For when a commodity has many and close substitutes (i.e., commodities that are almost the same or fill the same needs), a small increase in the price of this commodity will lead to a relatively large reduction in the quantity taken and a small decrease in price will lead to a relatively large increase in the quantity taken. And this, of course, is what we have in mind when we say that the demand for a commodity is elastic or highly elastic.

Translating these ideas into an indifference map where Y is money and X the commodity, we discover that a commodity with many and close substitutes gives rise to an indifference map where the contour lines tend to be linear (i.e., have little curvature). Where such is the configuration of the indifference map, a given price change as reflected in a change in the slope of the outlay curve gives rise to a relatively large quantity response, hence a relatively high demand elasticity, via the substitution effect (see Figure 17-7). The converse is true with respect to a commodity with few or poor substitutes. A commodity with few or poor substitutes gives rise to an indifference map where the contour lines are sharply curved and the substitution effect of a price change is relatively small.

The income effect, however, must be considered. If the income effect of a price change is positive (i.e., a price decline leads to increased purchases of the commodity, and conversely), then the income effect is added to the substitution effect to contribute to an increased quantity response, hence an increased elasticity of demand, for the commodity. If, on the other hand, the income effect is negative, the quantity response and the demand elasticity are reduced, by reason of the fact that the income effect cancels to some degree the substitution effect.

For an important class of commodities—minor items in the total budget with close substitutes—the substitution effect of a price change tends to be large and the income effect small or nonexistent. Pork chops, for example, have many and close substitutes and are relatively unimportant in the total budget; hence, we would expect a change in the price of pork chops to lead to a relatively large change in the quantity taken through a large substitution effect and a small income effect. This situation is illustrated in Figure 17-7; it will be seen that the full influence of the price change on the quantity taken of the hypothetical commodity X is felt through the substitution effect (the income effect is zero). The arc elasticity in this case over the price range \$1 to \$2 is computed to be -1.36.

The substitution effect above results in an elasticity of demand greater than 1.

The case illustrated in Figure 17-7 certainly is not representative of all types of consumer goods and services. It does not, for example, represent the case of a large item in the budget (e.g., a fur coat) or any commodity

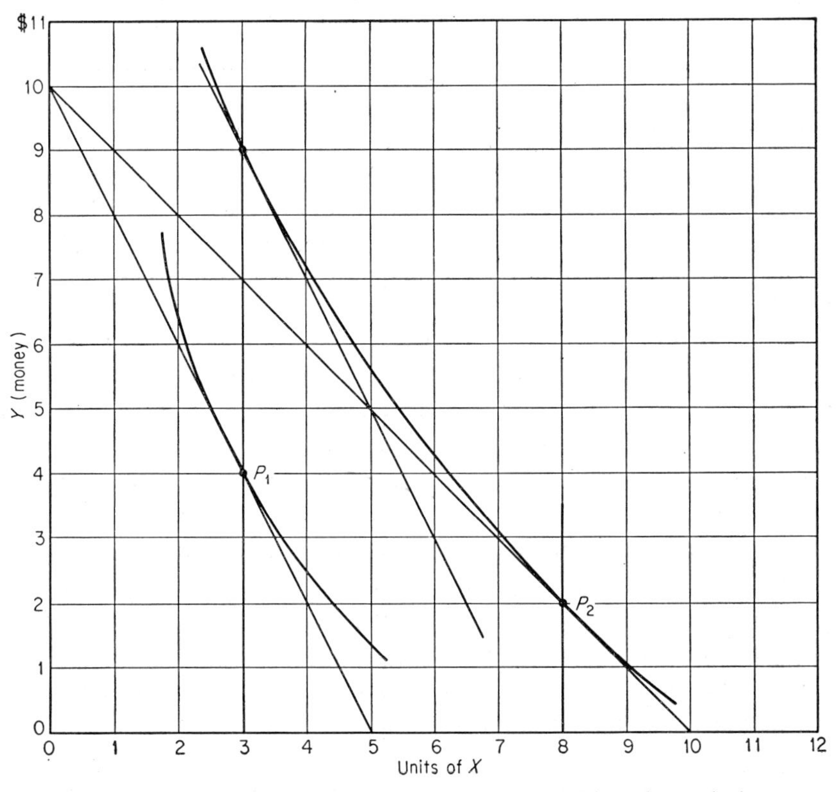

FIG. 17-7. The quantity response where commodity X has close substitutes.

with a demand elasticity of less than 1. The configuration of the indifference map for such cases would involve contours of greater curvature, with either positive or negative income effects. But the situation portrayed in Figure 17-7 would seem to be representative of many minor items in the budget (e.g., a particular brand of bread, cheese, or canned peas). The income effect of a price change in one of these commodities would hardly be noticeable to the consumer. But a small price change in one of these commodities would be very likely to lead to a relatively large quantity response for the commodity involved through the process of substitution.

STATISTICAL MEASURES OF DEMAND

Since utility functions and indifference maps for consumers for particular products are nonmeasurable, the true market demand relation for particular commodities cannot be "known" or stated in measured units. But the demand concepts are known, as we have learned. And these concepts can and have been employed to guide statistical studies having the purpose of estimating the true demand relation for particular commodities. These studies, as we shall see, have dealt almost exclusively with agricultural commodities, and the estimates are generally concerned with (1) the functional form of the demand relation (i.e., the absolute relation between price and quantity) and (2) the elasticity of the demand relation. It is impossible to *know* by statistical techniques the form and elasticity of the market demand relation for a commodity at any particular time. But it is possible to *estimate* under certain conditions the approximate form and elasticity of the market demand relation existing over a period of time. And we shall review briefly at this time what is involved in such estimating procedures, some estimates that have been made, and reasons why estimating attempts have been limited largely to agricultural commodities.

The data out of which statistical estimates of demand are made are market price-quantity quotations. It is assumed that each datum describing a particular quantity sold in a particular market at a particular price at a particular time represents one point on some unknown demand curve. Now, *if* it is known that none of those forces which influence the position of the market demand curve (i.e., personal income, tastes and preferences, prices of substitutes, and number of persons in the market) changed during the period under investigation, then each datum describing a different price and quantity must represent a particular point lying on the *same* demand curve; the market price-quantity observations, in fact, trace out the demand curve.

But since (1) the investigator can never know with certainty what has happened to each of these shifters of demand and (2) it is extremely unlikely that all these shifters would hold constant over a reasonable period of time, it becomes the task of statistical analyses to remove the effects of these influencing forces on particular price-quantity observations. After the effects of the influencing forces have been removed as completely as possible relative to the average for the period under investigation, the relationship existing between the adjusted quantities and prices is presumed to yield the average demand relationship for the period.

The elasticity computed from this average demand relationship thus provides an estimate of the elasticity of demand for the product in question and the period involved.

To illustrate what has been and can be done in the way of estimating demand elasticities, an empirically derived demand curve for food for the periods 1929 to 1942 and 1947 to 1949 is presented in Figure 17-8. This aggregate demand relation for food was constructed from average price-quantity data for each year of the period involved, where the quantity datum for each year was "adjusted" or "corrected" to take account of the effects of the determinants at work in each year. The curve *DD* thus states a relation between (1) food prices at retail and (2) the per capita consumption of food after the net effects of income and trend (tastes and preferences) have been removed. The curve *DD* does not fit the adjusted price-quantity observations perfectly, because all the influence of each determinant could not be removed by the statistical procedure followed. But the fit is sufficiently close to provide a useful measure of the elasticity of demand for food before and after World War II. The estimate of elasticity at point *A* in Figure 17-8 is -0.24.

Some empirical measures of the elasticity of demand for various food categories are presented in Table 17-1. Some of these measures are computed at the retail level (involving retail prices and consumption); the others are at the farm level (involving farm prices and production). The results of only a few of the many, many studies that have been undertaken in this food area are presented in the table, but they illustrate the nature of demand for food. It will be observed that the demand for all food is severely inelastic. Consumers do not expand or contract their consumption of food importantly as food prices rise and fall. And this result makes good sense when we consider the continuing day-to-day needs of the human stomach. Most of us try to eat three meals a day whether food prices are high or low.

With respect to individual food commodities, the demand for beef and apples is relatively elastic, whereas the demand for potatoes and wheat is severely inelastic. In other words, consumers do expand and contract their consumption of beef importantly as the price of beef changes relative to other items, but not so with potatoes.

It is no accident that measures of the elasticity of demand for various nonfood items are omitted from Table 17-1. Few empirical studies have been made of such items as washing machines, fur coats, or houses—or, for that matter, any nonfood items. And the few studies that have been under-

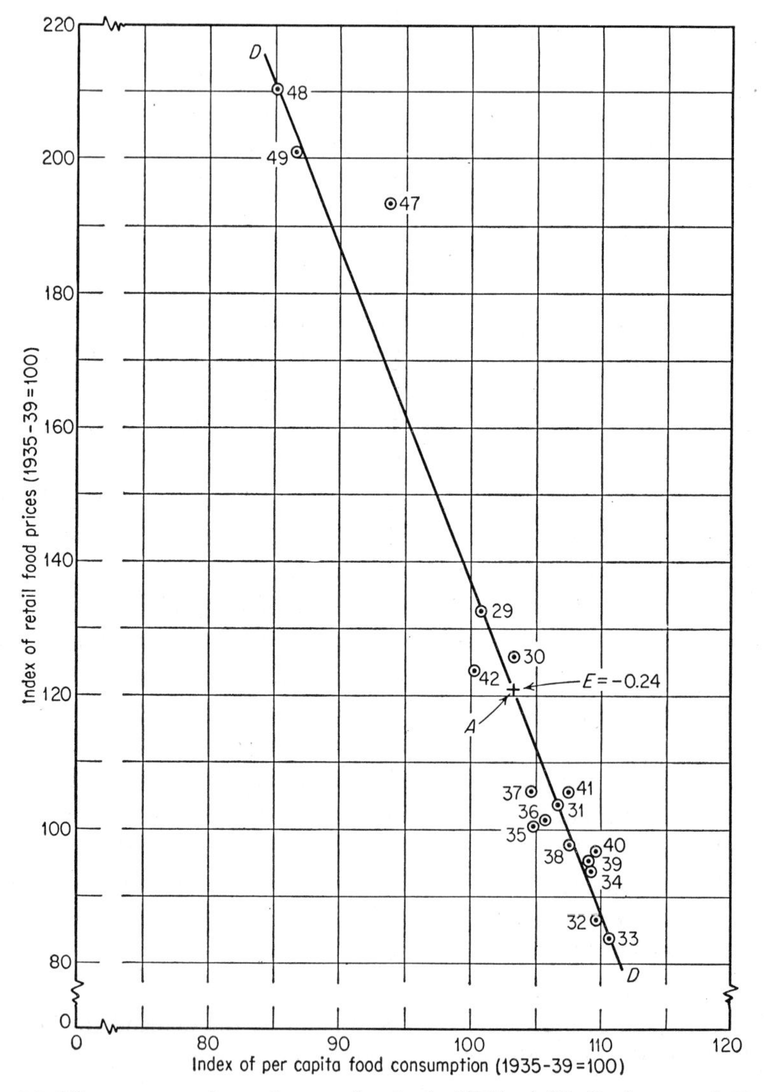

FIG. 17-8. The aggregate demand curve for food. (*Willard W. Cochrane and Harlan C. Lampe, "The Nature of the Race between Food Supplies and Demand in the United States, 1951–75," Journal of Farm Economics, May, 1953.*)

Table 17-1. *Elasticities of Demand from Selected Statistical Studies*

Commodity	Elasticity	Period
Retail level		
Food [a]	−0.25	1922–1941
Food [b]	−0.24	1929–1942, 1947–1949
All meat [c]	−0.67	1922–1941
All meat [d]	−0.66	1922–1941
Beef [c]	−0.94	1922–1941
Pork [c]	−0.86	1922–1941
Eggs [c]	−0.43	1922–1941
Eggs [e]	−0.58	1921–1941
Farm level		
Milk for fluid uses [c]	−0.30	1922–1941
All fruit [c]	−0.82	1922–1941
Apples [c]	−1.21	1922–1941
Potatoes [f]	−0.19	1923–1941
Wheat [g]	−0.21	1921–1934
Sugar [g]	−0.31	1915–1929

[a] M. A. Girshich and Trygve Haavelmo, "Statistical Analysis of the Demand for Food: Examples of Simultaneous Estimation of Structural Equations," *Econometrica*, vol. 15, pp. 79–110, April, 1947.

[b] Willard W. Cochrane and Harlan C. Lampe, "The Nature of the Race between Food Supplies and Demand in the United States, 1951–75," *Journal of Farm Economics*, vol. 35, pp. 203–222, May, 1953.

[c] Karl A. Fox, "Factors Affecting Farm Income, Farm Prices and Food Consumption," *Agricultural Economics Research*, vol. 3, pp. 65–82, July, 1951.

[d] Elmer J. Working, "Studies in the Measurement of Demand with Special Reference to the Demand for Meat," Ph.D. thesis, Harvard University, Cambridge, Mass., March, 1952.

[e] George G. Judge, "An Econometric Analysis of the Demand for Eggs," Ph.D. thesis, Iowa State College, Ames, Iowa, 1952.

[f] Roger W. Gray, Vernon L. Sorenson, and Willard W. Cochrane, *An Economic Analysis of the Impact of Government Programs on the Potato Industry of the United States*, Minnesota Technical Bulletin 211, 1954.

[g] Henry Schultz, *The Theory and Measurement of Demand*, University of Chicago Press, Chicago, 1938.

taken have not yielded conclusive results. To some degree, the explanation for the paucity of empirical demand studies outside of food and agriculture may be found in the failure of responsible public agencies to provide funds for this type of work. But this explanation cannot be pressed too far, for consider the great number of budget studies leading to measures of income elasticity that have been undertaken by public agencies.[5] A more plausible explanation would seem to be that empirical measures of demand are more difficult to come by in most nonfood commodity lines, for two reasons: (1) conceptually, the problem is more difficult where commodities are nonhomogeneous and are, in fact, purposely differentiated and (2) the kind of price-quantity observations that emerge where prices are administered do not lend themselves to the type of statistical manipulations necessary to the derivation of empirical demand relations.

Now what is the conceptual difficulty? In the case of a commodity category such as washing machines, two different concepts of demand are involved. There are, first, the concept of the demand for washing machines and, second, the concept of the demand for some brand, or "make," of washing machine. Now, which concept of demand does the analyst seek to measure, and how does he handle his observed data to measure one concept or the other—not something in between? Measures of the two concepts would certainly be greatly different if they were obtainable. For example, the demand for washing machines must be rather inelastic since most of us must have our clothes washed by someone, somewhere; the principal substitute, washing by hand, has for all practical purposes become obsolete in modern America. But the demand for some particular brand, or make, of washing machines is probably rather elastic, since there are many different makes, all of which are substitutes for one another to some degree. We might hazard the guess that the elasticity of demand for washing machines is in the neighborhood of -0.5, but the elasticity of demand for any leading make of machine is in the neighborhood of -2. Now, a statistical method that blurred these two concepts would be misleading, and one that provided measures of only one concept or the other would be telling only a part of the story. Thus, the job of deriving empirical measures of demand elasticity becomes more involved and difficult of solution where each category of commodity is differentiated into brands and makes.

The second problem is, however, more difficult. Every attempt to meas-

[5] Refer to Chaps. 11–13.

ure demand relations quantitatively must depend upon the market price-quantity observations to trace out the demand curve after the influence of such forces as changes in income or tastes and preferences has been removed from the price-quantity observations. The objective is always that of removing the influence of the various determinants of demand from the quantity data so that the adjusted quantities when associated with their corresponding prices trace out the demand curve. *But this assumes that price varies.* Now, where prices are *administered* by firms, groups, or agencies, prices do not vary readily through time. In fact, the price of a commodity may be held constant over a great number of years (e.g., Hershey candy bars). Thus, where price does not fluctuate with changes in supply and demand, statistical analysts simply cannot obtain the variable price-quantity observations out of which to derive empirical demand relations. And since the prices of most nonfood items are administered, hence are "sticky" and slow to change, the statistician labors under a serious handicap with respect to measuring demand in this broad segment of the economy.

In thinking about demand relationships and problems of elasticity, we would do well to bear in mind the different concepts of demand that are involved for most items. There is, first, the demand for the general product of the industry that fills some class of human needs (e.g., food for satisfying hunger, houses for shelter, automobiles for transportation, shoes for covering the feet). But, within each class, there are several to many different makes, or brands, or types of commodities. In each case, the demand for the general product to meet a general class of human need will be more inelastic than the demand for a particular brand, or make, or type produced within the industry. This generalization follows from the nature and role of the process of substitution. Houses in general have substitutes: people can and do live in hotels, trailers, and tents; hence, the demand for housing in general is not perfectly inelastic. But any *one* house has many more substitutes than houses in general. Any one house has all the substitutes of houses in general, plus the fact that every other house serves as a substitute for the one house under consideration. In sum, the elasticity of demand will depend upon the categories chosen for investigation, and these categories are not always easy to define or to keep conceptually straight.

Questions and Points for Discussion

1. How does the concept of market demand differ from consumer demand?

2. What do we mean by determinant of demand? List the various determinants of demand, and indicate how and in what way each influences demand.

3. What do we mean by elasticity of demand? Plot the following price-quantity schedule on graph paper, and compute the arc elasticity between each price-quantity point:

Price, cents	*Quantity*
70¢	25
60	50
50	75
40	100
30	125

Observe what happens to the measure of elasticity as you move along the curve.

4. Why is the demand for some commodities elastic and others inelastic? Make a list of commodities that tend to be elastic and a list of commodities that tend to be inelastic.

5. Why do economists have more luck estimating the elasticity of demand for farm products than for nonfarm products?

6. Can you think of some uses to which estimates of the elasticity of market demand can be put? Why do we refer here and in (5) above to *estimates* of market demand rather than the *true* market demand?

References

Dean, Joel, and Associates: *Managerial Economics*, Prentice-Hall, Inc., New York, 1951, chap. 4.

Stigler, George J.: "The Early History of Empirical Studies of Consumer Behavior," *Journal of Political Economy*, vol. 62, April, 1954.

———: *The Theory of Price*, rev. ed., The Macmillan Company, New York, 1952, chap. 4.

Waite, Warren C., and Ralph Cassady: *The Consumer and the Economic Order*, McGraw-Hill Book Company, Inc., 1949, chap. X.

Working, E. J.: "What Do Statistical Demand Curves Show," *Quarterly Journal of Economics*, vol. 41, pp. 212–235, 1927, and reprinted in *Readings in Price Theory*, Richard D. Irwin, Inc., Homewood, Ill., 1952.

18. The Role of Demand in Price Formation

The focus of this chapter is upon the operating role of demand in the market. We want to observe how the choice decisions of consumers, which have been translated into demand functions, manifest themselves in the market. How does demand act to determine price in the market? And where prices are fixed by law or administrative determination, what role does demand play? Answers to these questions, and their many ramifications, will be developed in this chapter, with the emphasis on retail markets.

We might consider the role of demand in price formation in the highly abstract situation of a perfectly competitive market or in the infinite number of real market situations that exist in the economy of the United States. But we shall do neither. In the first place, conclusions deduced from an analysis of a perfectly competitive situation have limited applications in the world of real markets, and, in the second place, we would never arrive at any conclusions if we set out to catalogue all possible market situations—the latter task would bog us down in a maze of detail.

Our method will be that of setting up three hypothetical situations—market models—that are representative of three different classes of markets important to consumers. These three market models are not representative of all classes of markets important to consumers, but an analysis of these three situations will provide a several-sided picture of the role of demand in the market and some appreciation of the part played by consumers in price determination. The hypothetical market situations that will be analyzed are (1) a freely competitive model involving many buyers and many sellers; (2) a monopolistic model involving one seller and many buyers; and (3) an oligopolistic model involving few sellers, many buyers, and resale price maintenance.[1]

[1] A review of the classification of market structures presented in Chap. 3 will provide a background for this discussion.

THE FREELY COMPETITIVE MODEL

The market situation defined. There are few retail markets to be found in America today that have both many buyers and many sellers. It is not uncommon for a retail market (i.e., a shopping center for groceries or shoes or dry goods) to have many consumer-buyers, but it is rare indeed to find many sellers in such markets (i.e., many grocery stores, many shoe stores, and many drygoods stores). For remember, by *many* we mean so many buyers and so many sellers that no single agent in the market has any perceptible influence on price. But consumers do purchase a variety of items, principally food items, whose prices are formed in freely competitive markets involving many buyers and many sellers. The prices of such commodities as potatoes, lettuce, wheat, and eggs are formed in such markets.

These price-making, competitive markets are to be found at the wholesale level and are usually located at a terminal point in the transportation system where the commodity involved is assembled from numerous production centers and in turn is distributed to many retail outlets. Hence, these markets are often called *terminal* markets. At these terminal points, supplies moving up from the farm are visually inspected and purchased by dealers and representatives of retail outlets. The existence of these terminal points acts to attract buyers in search of supplies, and supplies in search of buyers, with the result that organized markets develop in terms of physical facilities and rules governing trading and practices.

The conditions of supply are interpreted and reservation prices formed by sellers, the needs of consumers are interpreted and offers made by buyers, and, out of this higgling in the market, price is formed. A price is formed that equates the demand for and supplies of the commodity involved. This price *plus* the handling charges covering the movement of these supplies up to the retail level then becomes the price to consumers at the retail level.

The consumer buying potatoes in his local grocery store or supermarket does not, of course, see the price-making forces at work in the terminal market for potatoes, hence is generally unaware of this price-making process. What the consumer sees is a clerk sticking a card in a bin of potatoes, reading, say, "60 cents for 10 lb"; hence, he reasons that the store management is fixing the price. And to some degree the consumer may be right in this surmise, as we shall discover from a consideration of the institutional factors in retail pricing in the next chapter. But here we exclude from the discussion the part played by institutional factors and concentrate on the role of consumer demand in price formation. We want to discover how the demand for potatoes at the retail level, when converted into purchases of potatoes in the retail store, operates to help determine price in the terminal wholesale market.

The over-all market situation, and the part played in it by demand, can perhaps be best described in terms of an illustration involving the food item potatoes. We assume that consumers on the average purchase potatoes at some given rate (e.g., so many pounds per week) and that this rate of purchase when related to supplies available yields a price in the terminal market of $1 per bushel. This price plus handling charges becomes the price at retail. Now, suppose that corn- and wheat-producing areas suffer a drought, with the result that the prices of meat and cereal products rise. This means that the prices of products which are substitutes for potatoes rise and consumers begin to substitute potatoes for these now more expensive food items. Hence, the average rate of potato purchases per week increases. Confronted with this situation, store managers probably would not raise the price of potatoes immediately, *but they would observe that they were selling more potatoes at a given price* (our definition of an increase in demand). And they would increase their orders to dealers in the price-making terminal market. These dealers would then go into the market to buy more potatoes for the retail outlets that they represent. But this is a general phenomenon; hence, all dealer-representatives are trying to buy more potatoes. The result of this activity to acquire more potatoes is that of forcing up the price of potatoes in the terminal market; we assume that the wholesale price rises to $1.30 per bushel. Now potato prices at retail become $1.30 plus handling charges.

The final result of the increased consumer demand for potatoes is thus an increase in the retail price of potatoes. But the result was not immediate and direct; the increase in consumer demand had to be transmitted back through the marketing channel to the terminal market, where the force of the increased demand drove prices upward, and then the increased price was transmitted back through the market channel to the consumer. Let us, therefore, inquire into the nature of the process whereby prices were formed and changed in the terminal market.

Price determination in a terminal market. All the relevant information concerning the supply and demand situation for potatoes in this market is summarized in the supply and demand schedules presented in Figure 18-1. The quantity of potatoes that dealers in the market stand ready to offer at varying prices is described by the supply curve *SS*. An entire story lies back of this relation—in fact, an even more complex story than that which we have developed with respect to demand in Part II and Chapters 16 and 17. But this is a story that cannot be developed in a volume concerned with the economic decision making of households.[2] We take as given to the analysis the supply curve *SS*.

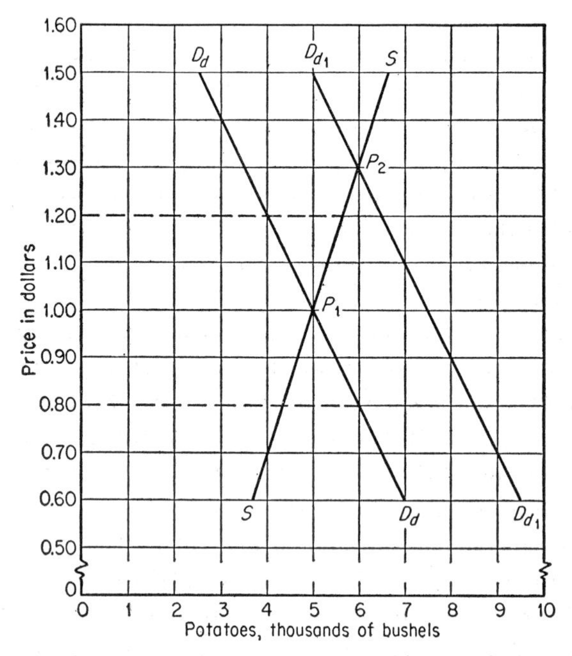

Fig. 18-1. Price determination in a competitive terminal market.

The demand curve D_dD_d is the derived demand curve for potatoes in the terminal market. It is the demand for potatoes by dealers in the market *derived* from the sum of consumer demands for potatoes at retail. It describes the quantities of potatoes that dealers in this market stand ready to purchase at varying prices. It is perhaps more elastic than the market demand of consumers for potatoes on one account: Dealers do not purchase potatoes to eat; they purchase potatoes to resell or deliver to retail

[2] Persons interested in the ramifications of the decision making of producers should turn to Kenneth E. Boulding, *Economic Analysis*, rev. ed., Harper & Brothers, New York, 1948, chaps. 21–24; or George J. Stigler, *The Theory of Price*, rev. ed., The Macmillan Company, New York, 1952, chaps. 6–8; or Earl O. Heady, *Economics of Agricultural Production and Resource Use*, Prentice-Hall, Inc., New York.

outlets. In this operation, they often purchase potatoes in large lots for storage with the intention of "feeding" the retail market at an even rate over time. And these dealers purchase large lots after a fall in price and when they think price will not fall further. In other words, dealers *try* to buy and store at low prices and get out of the market when prices are high. This type of operation tends to give the short-run demand relation at wholesale greater elasticity than the basic consumer demand for potatoes.

Now what price will be established for potatoes in this market? Most students after a glance at Figure 18-1 will say a price of $1 where 5,000 bushels of potatoes move through the market. There seems to be some fascination about point P_1 that pulls the observer to it. "It is the equilibrium price," both the newspaper editor and the economist say. And this is true, since we define an equilibrium price to be that price which makes demand and supply equal. But does the price in the market tend to be the equilibrium price?

We shall never find the answer to this problem by focusing on point P_1: such an action is comparable to trying to find out why a tree is growing in a particular spot by looking at the tree. To discover why a tree is growing in a particular spot, the interested party must inquire into the *causes* that could have put it there. And so with price P_1—what *caused* the market to establish this price, if indeed it did?

Let us begin this little inquiry by asking the question: "What would happen if a price of $1.20 were established in some way?" And let us assume that it was established in the following way: A dealer rushes into the market on a particular morning and, without taking the time to learn what new developments have taken place since the market closed on the previous day, offers to buy, and does in fact buy, 100 bushels at $1.20. This is a real transaction involving a specific quantity at a specific price. This price is quoted as *the* price of the opening sale in the market. Will there be more transactions at this price? There could be. Remember, we have postulated a situation involving many independent buyers and sellers, each trying to make a purchase or a sale advantageous to himself, and it is possible that more transactions would be consummated at this price. *But if information concerning demand and supplies in the market is good, it is unlikely that any more transactions would occur at a price of* $1.20. At a price of $1.20, it is clear that dealers stand ready to sell more potatoes than are demanded; at a price of $1.20, there exists an excess of supply. In this situation, demanders could be expected to stand firm and wait for the sellers "to come to them" (i.e., come down in price). It is true that dealers do not have a nice, neat diagram to guide their actions, such as we have in Figure 18-1. But, by reading market news reports, and in the give-and-take of conversation, dealers are able to appraise the conditions of the market rapidly and accurately. In this situation, then, a pressure in the form of excess supply exists in the market for driving down the price of potatoes.

Following this illustration a step further, let us suppose that some dealers now offer to sell at a price of $1.10. At this price, they might find some takers, hence make some sales. But a condition of excess supply continues to exist, and most buyers in the market would recognize this and hold off with their purchases. In order to make some sales, the sellers would once again have to come down in price—let us assume to a price of $1.05. At this price, a great deal of trading might take place, with the result that most sales in this market occurred at a price of $1.05 for this day. If information in this market had been perfect, there would have been no "false" trading at prices of $1.20, $1.10, and $1.05; the market would have moved directly and perfectly to the equilibrium price of $1, wherein the equilibrium price and the market price were identical. But information can never be perfect: hence, trading at prices other than the equilibrium price is common, and it may well be the case that the bulk of trading in freely competitive markets occurs at prices approaching, but not at, equilibrium prices.[3]

What precisely is the relation of market prices to equilibrium prices in freely competitive markets involving many buyers and many sellers? We might generalize as follows: There exists a *tendency* for market price to

[3] In point of fact the final position of equilibrium is dependent on the *path* by which it is reached. George J. Stigler, in the 1947 edition of *The Theory of Price* (The Macmillan Company, New York, p. 29), illustrates the possibilities thus: "Suppose, for example, that the equilibrium price of cotton is 10 cents per pound this year, in the sense that if this price were established immediately, there would be no tendency for it to change. If in fact the price begins below the equilibrium point and rises as the excess of the quantity demanded over the quantity supplied becomes apparent, it may continue to rise to perhaps 12 cents, merely because, on the basis of experience, sellers withhold a portion of the supply in anticipation of further price increases. On the other hand, the initial low price may never rise to the original equilibrium level because consumers have stocked up at low prices and divert a portion of their incomes to other clothing materials.

"There is no general theory of the effect of the path of movement of economic phenomena on their ultimate equilibrium, and the phenomena are so complicated that it is not likely that such a theory will be developed. . . ."

move toward the equilibrium price; a higher than equilibrium price will be pushed downward by the excess supply existing at the higher than equilibrium price; a lower than equilibrium price will be pushed upward by the excess demand at the lower than equilibrium price. But the forces at work in the market pushing transaction prices in the direction of the equilibrium price, namely, excess supply and excess demand, become increasingly weak as the equilibrium point is approached. This fact coupled with inadequate information makes it improbable that the bulk of trading takes place at equilibrium prices.

A change in demand. In defining the market situation involved in this model, it was reasoned that increased takings by consumers at retail would lead to larger orders at wholesale and hence be reflected in an expanded demand in the price-making terminal market. Finally, this expansion in derived demand would increase the price of potatoes at wholesale and thus mean higher prices to consumers. The effect of this increase in derived demand upon the price of potatoes in the terminal market is also portrayed in Figure 18-1. The demand curve $D_{d_1}D_{d_1}$ is the expanded derived demand relation in the terminal market. It describes the quantities of potatoes that dealers in the market stand ready to purchase at varying prices *after* consumers have stepped up their average rate of purchases and store managers have increased the size of their orders.

The expansion in demand in this case moves the equilibrium price level up from \$1 to \$1.30 (this is consistent with the earlier example). Whether the price in the market would move directly to \$1.30 is problematical and again depends upon the state of knowledge or information in the market. A price change of 30 cents on a base of \$1 represents a large price change, and dealers in the market might discover the new equilibrium level with considerable difficulty. In other words, the market might move toward the new equilibrium level of \$1.30 in a halting and awkward manner, but the excess of demand over supply at a price of \$1 would start prices moving up, and it would then be the task of dealers in the market to "feel their way" toward the new equilibrium level. A contraction in the derived demand for potatoes would, of course, have just the opposite effect on price.

THE MONOPOLY MODEL

The market situation defined. The role played by demand in the determination of price will now be considered in a market situation involving one seller, the monopolist, and many buyers. This, like the previous case, is a limiting case, in that these two represent the opposite poles of a wide range of market situations. And, like the case involving many buyers and many sellers, this case is not often found in its pure form. But we do find some real-world situations that approximate the market model (e.g., the single milk distributor in some towns, the only shoe repairman or barber or hairdresser in a particular market or shopping area, and the holder of a dealership or franchise in a given market area). The importance of this case, like the previous one, however, rests on conceptual and perhaps pedagogical grounds; once the range of possible market situations is known, together with the nature of the price solutions involved in those limiting situations, the economist and the student can begin to infer and speculate as to the nature of the price solutions in the many, many market situations in between.

To provide concreteness, we shall develop this model and price solution in terms of a specific illustration; but the conclusions hold for any market situation involving one seller and many buyers. Let us assume that a particular oil company is granted a franchise to operate the *only* gasoline station in a national-park area (anyone who has traveled by car through the national-park system of the Far West will immediately recognize the reasonableness of this assumption). The gasoline station holds a monopoly position in this particular area; it has no direct competition in selling gasoline to motorists in the area involved. It is true, of course, that experienced motorists may "fill up" before entering the park area and then wait to "fill up" again outside. And then there is always the option open to the sight-seer of walking or hiking in the place of driving. These forms of substitution on the part of consumers would keep the demand curve for gasoline in the park area from being perfectly inelastic. But it is also true that the single seller of gasoline in the park has no rivals to consider and take into account in the setting of the price at which gasoline is to sell there. And this is the crux of the matter in the case under consideration—how price is determined and what the role of demand is in this determination where the seller does not have to take into account the action of rivals.

Some new relationships. We require some new relationships to obtain a solution to this price problem. The goal of the gasoline monopolist is, we assume, similar to that of all firms—namely, to maximize net returns. In other words, the monopolist will seek to set a price on gasoline which maximizes his net revenue. To arrive at this optimum price, optimum from the viewpoint of the monopolist, that is, we need to know something of the cost situation of the firm. The cost structure of the assumed firm is presented in two relationships in Figure 18-2. The curve *ATUC* (average total unit costs) shows how the unit costs of selling gasoline vary over

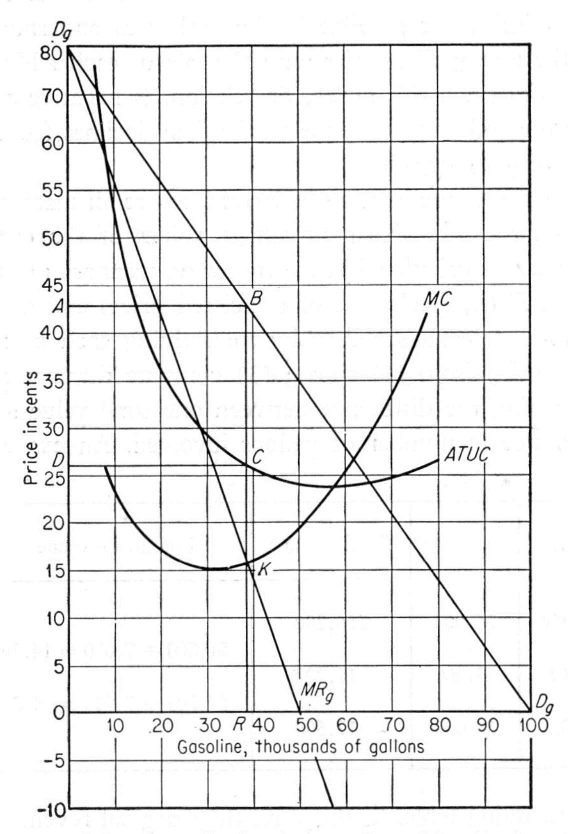

FIG. 18-2. Price determination in a market with a single seller.

the range of possible sales for this firm. Unit costs fall rapidly at first, level off, and turn up gradually at larger volume of sales. This type of cost relationship is probably typical for this class of firms. The curve *MC* (marginal costs) describes how the costs of selling an additional (or marginal) gallon of gasoline vary. It will be observed that the marginal cost curve cuts through the average cost at the lowest point of the latter and then rises rapidly as additional gallons of gasoline are sold.[4] These cost

[4] For a complete discussion of the interrelations of costs and supply see the sources cited in footnote 2 of this chapter.

relationships describe for this single seller of gasoline how the costs of selling gasoline vary with respect to the average gallon sold and the marginal gallon sold.

We have, however, a new demand relation to consider in Figure 18-2. It is the marginal revenue curve MR_g. This relationship is derived from the demand relation for gasoline in the park area and shows how the revenue to the monopolist varies with the sale of each additional gallon of gasoline. And since this curve, or relation, is negatively inclined, it follows that the additional revenue to the firm declines from each additional gallon of gasoline sold.

This marginal revenue relation is derived, as are all marginal relations, from the total relation. The approximate values of the curve MR_g in Figure 18-2 may be calculated in the following manner: (1) read off the demand curve D_gD_g, a schedule of associated prices and quantities; (2) obtain the total demand schedule by multiplying each price times the associated quantity from (1) above; (3) compute the marginal revenue values by dividing the difference between one total value and the next by the difference in number of gallons involved. An example is given

Price	Quantity	Total revenue	Marginal revenue
45¢	36,000	$16,200	
			$1,000 ÷ 7,000 = 14.3¢
40	43,000	17,200	
			$ 300 ÷ 7,000 = 4.3¢
35	50,000	17,500	

in the accompanying table. In this case, the marginal revenue of the 39,500th gallon (the mid-point between 36,000 and 43,000) sold is 14.3 cents; the marginal revenue of the 46,500th gallon sold is 4.3 cents. These marginal revenue values fall almost exactly on the curve MR_g presented in Figure 18-2.[5]

[5] Where the demand curve is a straight line, it is a property of such curves that the marginal revenue curve cut the abscissa of each price ordinate half the distance between zero and the quantity demanded (see Stigler, *The Theory of Price*, 1947 ed., p. 38). Thus in Figure 18-2, the curve RM_g cuts the X axis at 50,000 gallons, or half the distance between zero and the point where the demand curve cuts the X axis. The curve RM_g is constructed by connecting points $p = 80¢$, $q = 0$ gallons and $p=0$, $q=50{,}000$ gallons with a straight line.

A relationship exists between elasticity of demand, marginal revenue, and total revenue which should be recognized and which can be illustrated in terms of Figure 18-2. The elasticity of demand approaches infinity at the point $p = 80¢$, $q = 0$ gallons, falls to 1 at point $p = 35¢$, $q = 50{,}000$ gallons, and approaches zero at point $p = 0$, $q = 100{,}000$ gallons. In other words, the elasticity of demand falls over the entire range of curve D_gD_g. Now, we observe that marginal revenue values are positive so long as E (elasticity of demand) is greater than 1, marginal revenue is equal to zero where $E = 1$, and marginal revenue values become negative once E is less than 1. It is also the case that total revenue increases with increased sales so long as E is greater than 1, but total revenue falls once E becomes less than 1. In general terms, total revenue increases with increased sales when E is greater than 1 and falls when E is less than 1. And, of course, marginal revenue is positive when total revenue is increasing and negative when total revenue is decreasing. This latter relation may be illustrated in the accompanying table from the calculation of some additional marginal revenue values from Figure 18-2:

Price	Quantity	Total revenue	Marginal revenue
			−$ 400 ÷ 7,000 = −5.7¢
30¢	57,000	$17,100	
			−$1,100 ÷ 7,000 = −15.7¢
25	64,000	16,000	
			−$1,800 ÷ 7,000 = −25.7¢
20	71,000	14,200	

Our interpretation of demand curve D_gD_g in Figure 18-2 is somewhat different from that for the market demand curve for potatoes in the previous model. The demand for potatoes in the terminal market, emerging through the actions of dealer-buyers, *confronted* all sellers; out of this interaction, a particular transaction at a particular price occurred, and then other buyers and sellers had to decide whether to enter into transactions at that price. In a market comprised of many buyers and sellers, the question calling for a decision takes the following form: "Should I as buyer (or seller) enter into a trading transaction at the current price or hold off a while longer?"

But the situation confronting the single seller differs markedly; the entire market demand confronts the single seller. In this case, demand curve D_gD_g, which sums up the choice decisions of motorists in the park area with respect to gasoline, confronts the single gasoline station. The question posed for this single seller is then the following: "At what price shall I sell gasoline?" In this context, the demand curve D_gD_g becomes a revenue curve—an average revenue curve—describing for the monopolist the price (the average revenue) at which he can sell different volumes of gasoline. From this average revenue curve, it is a simple matter to calculate the total revenue schedule and hence the marginal revenue schedule (the mechanics of the calculation have already been described).

The key point to keep in mind is that the question of price policy posed for a single seller is very different from that posed for one seller among many. The one seller among many must decide whether to *take* a specific price when offered, whereas the single seller conceives the market demand relation confronting his firm as an average revenue curve and uses it in conjunction with his cost structure to *determine* the price which yields the greatest net revenue.

The price solution. Given the cost structure of the single firm selling gasoline in the park area and the demand relationship for gasoline in that area (see Figure 18-2), the monopoly price is easily determined. To realize maximum profits, the monopolist should set the price of gasoline at 42.75 cents per gallon and sell 38,700 gallons. And he will make profits equal to 16.75 cents per gallon, or equal to the rectangle *ABCD* in Figure 18-2.

The monopoly price and quantity are fixed by the relations of marginal costs to marginal revenue. To the left of point *K*, or at volumes less than 38,700 gallons, the sale of an additional gallon will increase the net return to the firm, as seen by the fact that marginal revenue exceeds marginal costs at these quantities. To the right of point *K*, or at volumes greater than 38,700 gallons, the sale of an additional gallon will reduce the net return, as seen by the fact that marginal cost now exceeds marginal revenue. Thus, the intersection of the marginal revenue curve with the marginal cost curve at point *K* determines the optimum volume of sales from the viewpoint of the monopolist; this quantity maximizes net returns. As indicated by the vertical line *RKCB*, this quantity sells at an average price of 42.75 cents per gallon. Given the conditions of this market, the pricing policy of the monopolist is determined, and he may be expected to hold to the price of 42.75 cents until demand and cost conditions change *or some restraint is imposed from the outside.*

There are two characteristic features of monopoly market situations that emerge from the above analysis. First, monopoly profits are involved (rectangle *ABCD* in Figure 18-2); these profits may be relatively greater or smaller, but they are generally present. Second, the firm does not operate to the point of lowest average unit costs. Average total unit costs are at a minimum at or around 57,000 gallons, but this firm limits its sales to some 39,000 gallons.

Because of these results, monopolies often are regulated or controlled by society. And, in this case, we might expect the park authorities to impose controls designed to lower prices, expand sales, and reduce profits. We should recognize, however, that the price-quantity solution obtained in this analysis is for the short run. An analysis which considered all long-run factors, particularly technological advance, might turn up with a different set of general conclusions—conclusions which were not so damning to the monopolist's position.

OLIGOPOLY AND PRICE MAINTENANCE

The market situation defined. We turn now to the role played by demand in a market situation characterized by few sellers and resale price maintenance. This is a common market situation at the retail level. Manufacturers of small appliances, drugs, and photographic supplies, for example, often pursue a general business policy somewhat as follows: (1) they manufacture the good; (2) they create the demand through advertising and sales-promotion campaigns; (3) they grant a limited number of dealerships in a given market area; and (4) they fix the price at which the good is to be sold at retail with the aid of various resale-price-maintenance laws.[6] The pursuit of this general business policy by manufacturers creates a market situation at the retail level involving relatively few sellers and a predetermined price. Individual dealers at retail are not free to establish that price which maximizes their net return. In a general way, this is what the manufacturer has already done with respect to the larger national market; he has set a price which, all things considered, appears to be an optimum price from his standpoint.

This type of market situation is portrayed in Figure 18-3. The situation depicted in the figure is one of a retail market for a particular "make" of electric toasters. The demand curve $D_{ET}D_{ET}$ shows those quantities of this make of electric toasters which can be sold at varying prices in the local market. We assume that two dealerships have been established in

[6] Resale price maintenance is discussed in more detail in Chap. 19.

this market area: one to a small-scale, relatively high-cost firm and one to a larger-scale relatively low-cost firm. The different firm cost conditions are shown graphically in Figure 18-3; firm A is the high-cost firm, firm B the low-cost firm. And perhaps it should be pointed out that the cost structures presented in the figure have reference only to the cost of retailing electric toasters, not to other product items handled by the

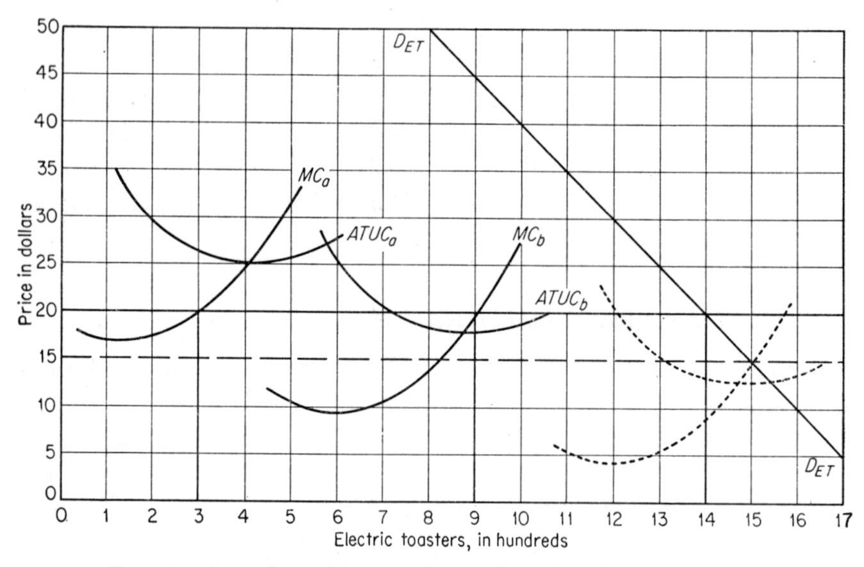

FIG. 18-3. A market with two sellers and resale price maintenance.

retail establishment; hence, these are cost structures for the electric-toaster *enterprise*.

An analysis of the situation. We have no problem of determining the price at which this make of electric toaster is to sell; the selling price is given to the problem. It was fixed by the manufacturer at $20 (see Figure 18-3). There does, however, remain the problem of determining the number of toasters that will be sold by each firm. But more important is a recognition of the fact that the price-quantity solutions that emerge in this market situation are not stable. Basic conflicts of interests are involved which make the overt price-quantity solutions unstable. Hence, we shall want to explore these conflicts of interest and consider their implications for the market.

Although the curve $D_{ET}D_{ET}$ describes the number of electric toasters of this make that will be taken at varying prices in the local market, the effective demand confronting each dealer-distributor is the price line of $20. For any quantity less than 1,400 units, the price line describes the price at which these toasters will sell, hence is the average revenue curve of these firms. Where the average revenue curve is perfectly elastic as in this case, marginal revenue is identical with average revenue, as is illustrated in the accompanying table. Thus, the price line of $20 is also the marginal revenue curve.

Price	Quantity	Total revenue	Marginal revenue
$20	100	$2,000	
			$2,000 ÷ 100 = $20
20	200	4,000	
			$2,000 ÷ 100 = $20
20	300	6,000	
			$2,000 ÷ 100 = $20
20	400	8,000	

Each firm in this market situation, as in any other, may be expected to operate to that point where its marginal revenue is equal to its marginal costs. At any volume short of this point, marginal revenue exceeds marginal costs, hence is not optimum; and, at any volume beyond this point, marginal cost exceeds marginal revenue, hence is not optimum. This being the case firm A will sell 300 toaster units and firm B 900 units. These quantities represent the "best" volume of sales for each firm, but it will be observed that the best is none too good as far as firm A is concerned. Firm A is losing about $6 on each toaster sold, whereas firm B is making a profit of $2 on each toaster sold. Thus, we say that firm A is minimizing its losses at a volume of 300 toasters and firm B is maximizing its gains at a volume of 900.

Given the market situation portrayed in Figure 18-3 and the quantity solutions derived above, three points should be noted which do or could give rise to a conflict of interests, hence lead to market instability. First, firm A is losing money. This situation firm A would probably like to see remedied by the manufacturer setting a higher retail price for this make of electric toaster. Second, firms A and B are selling only 1,200 units between them, whereas the market will take 1,400 units at a price of $20. This fact would be disturbing to the manufacturer, and he might consider establishing a third dealership in the market to fully exploit the market. Third, firm B is making a good profit and might be happy to leave things as they are. On the other hand, if firm B has reduced its costs below those of A through the development of new selling methods, modernization of his retail establishment, and other efficiency-creating techniques, it might wish to continue these aggressive methods and shift its short-run cost structure down and to the right, as suggested by the dotted cost structure in Figure 18-3. Firm B might also be considering the implications of price cutting. If it cut its selling price to $15, as indicated in Figure 18-3, it would pull all sales away from firm A and, with its new, lower cost structure, increase its total profits.

In short, this market situation involves some basic conflicts, and the market could develop in a number of ways, depending upon the strength of the contending interests. Assuming firm B to be the aggressor, it is desirous of cutting costs, breaking the resale maintenance clause, and capturing the entire market for itself. The manufacturer has already set the retail price at an optimum level from the viewpoint of his operation, but he would like to see a full 1,400 toaster units sold at a price of $20. This the manufacturer might accomplish by adding more dealerships, but such action would be likely to cut into the sales of firms A and B so that they could no longer sell 300 and 900 units, respectively. Firm A would like to see the price raised to $25 or above, but neither the manufacturer nor firm B would favor this action. Raising the price of these toasters to $25 would cut total sales in this market to 1,300 units. And at a price of $25 firms A and B together would want to sell some 1,365 units (400 + 965), or 65 more units than the market would take at a price of $25. Besides, firm B would have little interest in cooperating in a price policy designed to keep firm A in business; on the contrary, B, it has been assumed, has visions of capturing the entire market by just the opposite price policy.

The outcome of the market struggle that we have sketched above will depend on the economic strength, tenacity, and tactical skill of the contending parties. Sometimes, but not often, the aggressive firm employing price-cutting tactics in the face of legal and conventional restraints wins the day. In more cases, the manufacturer floods the market with dealerships and holds prices in line at retail with the aid of various state and Federal resale maintenance laws. And, in most cases, the manufacturer sets the retail price sufficiently high to keep most of the small and unaggressive dealers in business.

THE MEANING AND SIGNIFICANCE OF MARKET MODELS

The market models developed and presented in this chapter were in no case designed to replicate all the details of a particular market or to yield the specific price-quantity solution of a particular market. Their presentation was for a different purpose. They were developed and presented to illustrate the workings of the basic price-making forces in different classes of markets. The key forces of supply and demand were abstracted from the maze of detail surrounding actual markets and related in models representative of different classes of markets to show the influence of those key forces in the determination of price in those categories.

Such items as physical facilities in the terminal market for potatoes, restraints and regulations imposed on the gasoline station by the park authorities, and particular features of the resale-price-maintenance law involved in the market for electric toasters, along with many other particular circumstances, were not included in these models, even though each might have an important bearing on the ultimate price-quantity solution. This is because the inclusion of all the special circumstances surrounding any one market would (1) have made the model so complicated and so complex that we would have lost sight of the key forces at work—supply and demand and (2) have limited the usefulness or applicability of the conclusions reached to the *one* market under analysis. As it is, our simple, and admittedly somewhat unreal, models permit a conceptualization, hence an understanding, of the key roles played by demand and supply in the market involved. And wherever market conditions are similar to those hypothesized in the models, we know what the influence of supply and demand will be in the determination of price.

Our method of analyzing a market in terms of a simplified model is somewhat comparable to viewing the bone structure of a man or animal through an X-ray machine. From looking at the bone structure of a patient, the medical doctor cannot describe in full what the patient may look like or how he will react in a given situation. The flesh, blood, and nervous system not seen through the X-ray machine have a part to play in these determinations. But the use of the X-ray machine does permit the practitioner to see and investigate the bone structure of the patient, and this knowledge is useful in understanding many things concerning him.

To continue the analogy, the use of market models has helped us gain a conceptual picture of the basic structure of three different classes of markets. In later chapters, we can add flesh and blood to fill out the complete picture. But we must remember two things. First, there are many classes of markets at retail, but because of space limitations, we selected only three, in which to illustrate the role of demand in price formation. Second, once we begin to fill in market detail—the particular circumstances to be found in each market—we have an infinite array of market situations and our ability to generalize with respect to market behavior is lost in that maze of detail.

Questions and Points for Discussion

1. What is a freely competitive market? Are freely competitive markets common at retail? Where do we find this class of markets?
2. What role does market demand play in the determination of price in a freely competitive market? What is an equilibrium price? Are market prices always equilibrium prices?
3. What do we mean by a market monopoly? What role does demand play in the determination of price in such markets? What is the marginal revenue curve? How are the marginal revenue data obtained? How is the marginal revenue curve used in price determination?
4. What do we mean by a market oligopoly? Is this a common type of market at retail? What kinds of market problems are encountered in the oligopolistic market situation described in this chapter?
5. Specify, describe, and indicate the implications for consumers of two other *classes* of markets commonly found at retail.

References

Boulding, Kenneth E.: *Economic Analysis*, rev. ed., Harper & Brothers, New York, 1948, chaps. 4–5.

Samuelson, Paul A.: *Economics: An Introductory Analysis*, 2d ed., McGraw-Hill Book Company, Inc., New York, 1951, chap. 20.

Tarshis, Lorie: *The Elements of Economics*, Houghton Mifflin Company, Boston, 1947, chaps. 10–12.

19. *Business and Pricing Practices in the Market*

Our analysis of consumer demand in the market has led to an examination of the way in which prices are formed. It is clear that the seller sets price in the sense of writing out price tags, but it is also clear that he chooses a price in response to the market forces in his particular situation. Price, however, is not the only point at issue, for the seller must also determine the volume of output, the type of product sold, and the way in which he sells it. Furthermore, he makes all these decisions in response not only to consumer demand but also to institutional factors associated with his business and trade. These decisions of firms are important to a study of consumption because households obtain most goods and services from business firms, and household consumption depends on what firms make available in the market.

We turn, therefore, to factors which were ignored, for the sake of simplicity, in the market models of Chapter 18. Although we cannot present all the market situations which exist in reality, we can show the important differences between the hypothetical and the real and can present some alternative solutions to the problem of consumer demand in the market. In a later chapter, we shall analyze in more detail the different kinds of firms with which the consumer has most contact—chiefly retailers. But the retail market is also affected by the decisions of manufacturers, wholesalers, and even bankers and truckers; so we shall not confine our discussion here to any one type of firm.

BUSINESS MOTIVES

Businessmen, like other people, act from a number of motives. Inherent in each of the solutions of the previous chapter was the assumption that the firm chooses price and output in order to maximize profits. This singling out of the profit motive is not meant to be an accurate description of concrete business situations, but it does provide a useful method of analysis. Economic analysis resembles the diagrams and occasional three-dimensional models constructed by physicists to represent molecular structures. No claim is made by scientists that the "chain" of molecules describing a synthetic textile fiber exactly pictures reality. It does, however, serve to explain the derivation of the fiber. Likewise, no claim is made by economists that profit maximization accurately represents the motivations of businessmen, but such a tendency certainly exists, and a rational course of action can be derived from it. Other motives enter, however, which make business practice vary from the theoretical models.

The time involved. First of all, businessmen may prefer to maximize profits as a rate over time rather than as a lump sum. A profit of 10 per cent on sales for three months differs from 10 percent on sales for three years and may bring about different courses of action.

When a temporary monopoly is present, the firm which sets its price and output to equate marginal revenue and marginal cost enjoys monopoly profits. These may be high enough to attract new firms into the field or, if entry is impossible, to induce the development of substitutes. The existence of high profits may arouse public opinion or the attention of the Department of Justice, and the firm may find itself subject to an antitrust suit or some form of government regulation. Even an investigation of its pricing practices is a threat to the average firm. Precisely because all these possibilities are foreseen by the firm, it may refuse to take advantage of its monopoly position. With prices set at a less than optimum position and a larger volume of output, the firm may continue to enjoy substantial, if not maximum, profits, *over a longer period of time,* by escaping from the alternatives just set forth. The firm may seek stable profits, rather than maximum returns.

Such decisions typically face the manufacturers of new products. In most cases, they can enjoy only a temporary monopoly. Other firms will eventually begin to produce ball-point pens, automatic washing machines, synthetic textiles, and the only advantage remaining to the original innovator is his early entry into the field. The firm must, therefore, decide whether to set prices high and reap monopoly profits for a limited period or to sell immediately at competitive price levels in the hope of capturing most of the market demand and obtaining experience in production which will enable it to retain a lead over its rivals, when they appear later. The ball-point pen, first introduced by Reynolds at an extremely high price, is a good example of the first course of action. The Bendix Duomatic washer-drier, priced just under the cost of two separate machines for washing and drying, is undoubtedly keyed to later competition.

Nonprofit motives. Some choices between alternative lines of action are made with the firm's reputation or prestige in mind, rather than maximizing profits. Has the business made a name for itself in large-volume, low-priced operations? If so, then the possibility of larger profits from a smaller output sold at higher prices may appear unattractive. On the other hand, a firm known for high-priced "quality" merchandise may be uninterested in maximizing profits by changing its operations to emphasize low-priced items.

A firm's reputation means different things to different managements. For small business, such considerations are very personal, since the behavior and reputation of the firm are identified with the owner-manager. The filling-station operator in a National Park serves different customers each day, most of whom he will never see again. But his counterpart in a small town or suburban market area deals with a clientele many of whom he knows socially. Along with his desire to maximize profits goes the natural inclination to be liked and accepted socially and to enhance his own and his firm's reputation. The concept of a "fair price" is far from dead among both buyers and sellers, and the firm may prefer the reputation of always offering a fair price to the position of maximum profits.

For larger firms, the question of prestige and reputation is somewhat differently formulated. Although the corporation is a "fictitious personality," it is managed by men whose personalities are real.

> Among the more potent nonfinancial incentives which have been urged are pride of place or position in the community, love of action, "business is the greatest game there is," love of power, the desire to be a good social person, family considerations, concern for community welfare, patriotism, and religion. They range all the way from petty vanities to the most exalted forms of altruism, sometimes with an admixture of both.[1]

Company profits may, then, have a twofold purpose: they serve as scores in the game of business, and they serve to keep the company in the game as an active player. But more and more attention is being given to the corporation as a social unit as well as a business enterprise centered solely upon profit. The responsibilities of corporations to the communi-

[1] Thomas H. Sanders, *Effects of Taxation on Executives,* Harvard University, Graduate School of Business, Cambridge, Mass., 1951, p. 22.

ties where they are located, to higher education, to charity, to the children of their employees, and to the strengthening of the American economy are merely a few of the duties which have recently been accepted by or suggested to firms theoretically engaged in making price and output decisions. "The business of business is business" is no longer a complete description of our larger firm, and the single goal of maximizing profits may be less and less realistic.[2]

The corporate form itself mitigates to some extent the pursuance of any one single aim, such as maximizing profits. Price and output decisions, along with many other major business questions, fall within the realm of conference and committee work. Not only does company policy reflect the conflicting ideas and interests of the board of directors, but the execution of that policy is a joint effort. When the sales manager, the production manager, the treasurer, and the vice-president in charge of the future meet, each has a different immediate concern. The personal incentives of these men may differ, and their interpretations of company welfare are not likely to be uniform. The factory manager sees output in terms of production methods, the supply of materials, and personnel. He relates prices to costs. To the sales manager, output means quotas for the selling force and potential orders from previous and new customers. Prices, to be quoted and perhaps shaded, are related to sales. The meeting of minds which is the outcome may or may not represent an optimum position for the company. It is possible for it to reflect one dominant personality or a coalition of several against an overaggressive one.

The functions of the company treasurer, interested chiefly in the financial position of the firm, deserve a second glance, for the need to remain solvent outweighs the desire to maximize profits in many cases, particularly in the distributive trades. In the short run, firms may wish to improve their current ratio—the ratio of current assets to current liabilities. The high-cost retailer described in Chapter 18 may know that cutting prices will reduce profits, but if he is faced with bills to pay and a shortage of cash, lower prices will at least, by bringing in cash, keep him solvent for a time. This view, presumably with plans to readjust as soon as possible, may be overriding. Sellers generally make commitments re-

[2] Cf. Howard R. Bowen, *Social Responsibilities of the Businessman*, New York, 1952: "The day when profit maximization was the sole criterion of business success is rapidly fading . . . the executive is likely to be a man who is more concerned with the broader aspects of management and who is more attuned to the social implications of his job than the manager or owner of an earlier day."

quiring future outlays of cash for materials, labor, rent, and other business costs, which they hope to pay when goods are sold. If their predictions of sales are incorrect, their obligations remain and funds must be found to meet these commitments. Over the short run, in particular, the maintenance or improvement of the ratio of current assets to current liabilities may outweigh maximizing profits as a motive.

DATA FOR BUSINESS DECISIONS

The market situations described in Chapter 18 assume not only that the seller chooses that solution which will maximize his profits but also that his data are sufficient to indicate that solution. This condition of perfect knowledge rarely exists in reality, and we may examine some of the factors which prevent it.

Estimating demand. In the freely competitive model, prices change in response to changes in consumer demand as the rate of buying alters. We can recognize many situations where consumer demand does translate readily into such price movements.

Price determination or price changes do not always depend, however, on an existing demand. In markets which are not freely competitive, the seller controls the price and tries, therefore, to estimate demand in order to set an appropriate price. Such prices do not fluctuate readily but must be changed by an administrative decision which involves a new estimate of demand. The solutions in Figures 18-2 and 18-3 assume that the sellers know the shape of the demand curve. In reality, business spends large sums of money trying to find out something about such curves, and much of the information comes from attempts by competitors to change prices.

Estimating demand is one part of market research, and the functions and organization of market research are still developing among business firms. The data which are useful for estimating demand, and the technical tools for analysis, provide much more crude alternatives than the smooth, definite curves of Chapter 18. The market research analysis must consider not only price and quantity but also advertising, packaging, distribution methods, competitors' offerings, consumer incomes and tastes, and so on. There are, first, the data on past and current sales. Changes in volume may be analyzed in terms of a change in demand, and the cause sought in one of the factors listed above. Second, reports from salesmen and dealers amplify the sales figures themselves with a picture of consumer acceptance or dissatisfaction. A market survey uses all kinds of statistical data, including the results of consumption studies described earlier, to describe the income, location, and characteristics of buyers and potential buyers. A special consumer survey may be called for, to investigate not only price and quantity relationships but also preference in product, quality, design, packaging, distribution, and so forth.

In large firms, elaborate data may be collated and analyzed to predict demand; in many cases, the effort is far too expensive for the businessman to undertake. But even where there is no deliberate attempt to gather and interpret information, some estimate of demand is made, if only by default, to justify a given course of action. Because the demand schedule is vague and indefinite to the seller, he does not always select the position of maximum profit. And because consumer demand depends not only on price but also on all the other factors we have mentioned, the seller cannot verify his estimate of demand by experimenting with price changes. His inability to predict sales volume at alternative price levels makes him consider other solutions to the problem of consumer demand.

The determination of costs. The solutions in Chapter 18 depended on unit cost data, and such information is very difficult to come by in real-world situations. Furthermore, most firms sell more than one product, and price and output decisions involve many alternatives.

Any firm producing two or more commodities will have some costs that apply to all the output: rent, interest, taxes, utilities, and salaries of the managers, including that of the accountant who struggles with the problem. In order to derive unit costs for each product, these indirect or overhead costs must be divided between the products or lines sold.

For manufacturing and processing concerns, the problem may be intensified because of joint costs (i.e., those which cannot be avoided by dropping one item, like meat and hides, or gasoline and lubricating oil). The usual accounting technique is to allocate costs to such products on the basis of their market prices. But then how can prices be determined in relation to costs? A good example of this problem is a recent advertisement by the American Meat Institute, pointing out that prices paid to farmers for meat are higher than the prices charged to retailers for the same meat. The institute explains that meat-processing costs are covered by the sale of hides, medicinal products, and other by-products of the meat industry. Meat packers could equally well explain, to the tanning industry, that low prices on hides exist because processing costs are covered by the sale of meat.

Among distributors, both at wholesale and retail, the problem of costing an individual item is infinitely complex. The hardware dealer or druggist can estimate the total cost of a garden tool or toothbrush only with an unprofitable use of time and effort, and then the figure will be arbitrary. Costing by departments or lines handled is sometimes useful, but the manager or accountant must decide how much of the rent or taxes or heat or supplies shall be charged to each department, and many methods exist, each giving different results. Cost to a dealer, therefore, includes two sets of data: the cost of goods sold and his expenses of doing business. To determine individual prices, the dealer generally adds a standard markup to his purchase price or uses a manufacturer's list price less discounts. His profit then depends on the relationship between his expenses of doing business and his gross margin, which is the difference between sales and cost of goods sold. Sales volume may vary greatly with the same expenses of doing business, and this way of looking at costs and profits emphasizes the role of output rather than price.

Manufacturers also sometimes use a markup to determine prices, either to allow for a profit over total cost or to avoid allocating all the overhead costs. And in many cases this provides a new approach to the problem of costs and profits. With an existing plant capable of many different rates of output, unit costs may appear to decrease continually as volume of output increases.

Figure 19-1 shows a common graphic analysis of this approach, in terms of a "break-even" point. Variable costs are those which increase or decrease directly with the volume of production; fixed costs are those which give such trouble when we try to allocate them to a given product. Variable costs are roughly those which determined marginal costs in our previous analysis. But the break-even approach assumes that marginal costs are constant and that variable costs increase at a constant rate as output increases. Such an assumption may be relevant and valid to a given plant within a given range of productive capacity.

In Figure 19-1 the variable cost line is drawn on the assumption that, after a 40,000-unit volume of output is reached, the variable costs amount to $1 per unit. Fixed costs total $10,000. Total costs at the 40,000th unit equal $105,000: $10,000 of fixed costs and $95,000 of variable costs. With a volume of 80,000 units, the total revenue from sales exactly covers the total fixed costs plus the variable costs incurred at that volume. When total sales increase beyond this point, they increase profits. Looking at cost and output in this fashion leads to some interesting decisions when costs change or when prices change. These will be discussed at a later point in this chapter. At this point, it is sufficient to note the dramatic effect of a change in volume on total profits.

Finally, one more difficulty faces the manager who estimates demand and costs in order to determine prices and output. His data relate to cur-

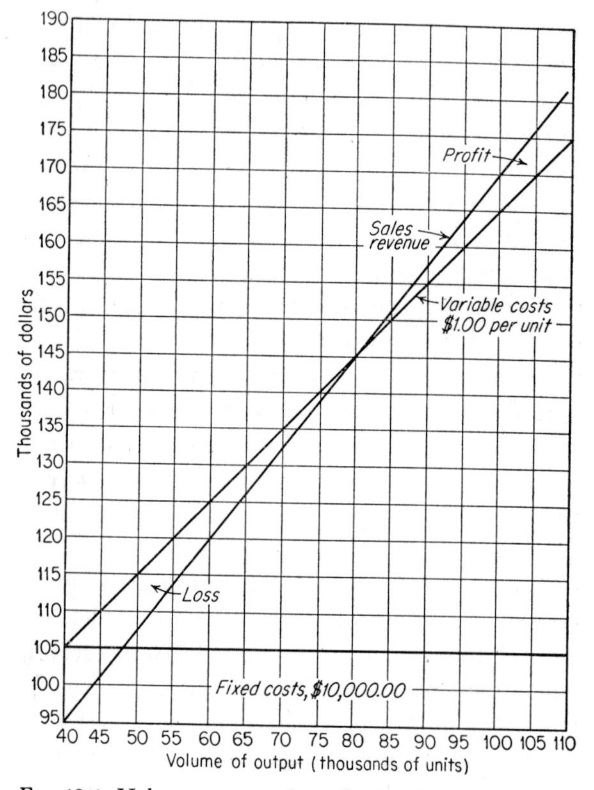

FIG. 19-1. Volume, cost, and profit: break-even analysis.

rent or past costs and demand; he needs data on future costs and demand in order to choose a course of action. The surveys of consumer plans to buy, conducted by the Federal Reserve Board, contribute vital information in this area. Many estimates of future demand and costs, however, are based upon projection of current trends, which allow large errors. Estimates of the future, therefore, are far from precise, and business decisions may be quite different from the theoretical solution based on known costs and demand.

PRICE MAINTENANCE

Aside from the difficulties of obtaining reliable data on costs and demand, the businessman in a real situation must deal with variables other than price. We can recognize a number of situations where prices change very little and sellers, accordingly, make decisions with respect to other variables (e.g., the type of product). Price stability stems sometimes from convention or inertia and sometimes from more formal action to maintain prices. These may be legal or illegal agreements between sellers or the result of government intervention. To the seller, any of these situations means that price is predetermined: it has been made stable and certain by some type of administrative action. He is therefore more concerned with varying costs, the type of product, or the volume of sales. Before we turn to such alternatives, we may examine different situations where price is predetermined to the seller.

Customary prices and price lines. The prices of many products are determined, sometimes precisely, by the existence in the market of a number of products already selling at such prices. Candy or chewing gum, at either 5 or 10 cents, is an obvious example. In other fields, with a wider range of choices and prices, the influence of *price lines* is very strong. Products which vary in quality sell for different prices, but there is a definite pattern of prices corresponding to the different qualities. Such a pattern may contain many exact prices or several price ranges. Thus, women's dresses sell, at retail, for $10.95, $14.95, $17.95, $22.95, $35, and so on. Similar price lines are found in the apparel field generally, furniture, books, periodicals, and stationery, many service industries including hairdressing, hotels and restaurants, and so on. In the automobile industry, prices fall within three ranges. Thus, although prices are not exactly the same among competing firms or from year to year, the low-priced, middle-priced, and high-priced automobiles are well known. Similar price ranges in other areas are recognized by consumers and sellers alike. A department store offers "better" dresses and "economy" styles; a prospective buyer may ask for a "low-priced" radio and have a fairly definite range of prices in mind.

Customary prices or price lines have never been adequately analyzed, and we cannot completely explain why they exist. Our decimal system of money obviously produces 5- and 10-cent prices and others ending in multiples of 5 and 10. By the same token, some common prices exist at a few pennies below the next dollar—$0.98, $4.95, $199.95—presumably to sound like an attractive economy and to permit offering values at "less than $1" or "less than $200."

This explanation is obviously not sufficient. Prices of fruit and meat vary by the cent, and no consumer expects peas to be 15 cents a pound forever. And price lines are much more apparent in automobiles than in household appliances. For the lack of a more reasoned explanation, we must fall back on the strength of convention and the inertia operating to maintain such conventions in the absence of any strong reason to change. Price lining is a customary trade practice in certain fields, and "customary trade practices" is a catchword used to explain many things: the discounts given to certain classes of customers, the weights or sizes of packages or containers, the channels of distribution used, and so forth.

An example of the strength of such convention is furnished by a minor incident during the days of price control. Individual producers could petition the Office of Price Administration for price increases when costs had increased to the point where their continued output was threatened. A manufacturer of work gloves was told, on the basis of his increased costs, that he might add $0.58 per dozen to his price, but he turned down the opportunity, saying that he would prefer to discontinue the style in question rather than to sell at "a price in odd cents, nobody in the trade ever heard of such a price. They wouldn't know what I was selling." There were many attempts to modify price lines during price control, as, for example, the increase to 6 cents a bar for candy, but resistance was very great. Price control furnished, therefore, excellent opportunities for varying the product, discussed later in the chapter.

The phenomenon of customary prices and price lines is far from permanent in some fields, however, and the reader can think of many examples where definite prices have become blurred. The optional equipment and "extras" available for automobiles remove the distinction between some models in the low and middle price ranges and between others in the middle and high price ranges. New producers have blurred the customary prices in various appliance fields by pricing their appliances midway between the prices of existing goods. Frequently, however, the change from a customary price also involves a change in the customary markup.

Since price lines at retail require predetermined prices at the manufacturer's level, they are closely tied in with customary trade margins. The manufacturer who plans to have his face powder retail at $1 rather than $0.79 or $2.50 does so with the knowledge that the retail druggist gets a 40 per cent discount, or a 66.6 per cent markup on cost, and that the wholesale distributor must therefore charge $0.60 a box to the retailer. And the 40 per cent discount is just as conventional as the phenomenon of price lines. The manufacturer must take these margins into account in planning his final price, and the retailer thinks in terms of his "historical" or "conventional" margin rather than his prices when contemplating a change. Most cut-price stores, cut-rate outlets, or discount houses operate on a lower margin than is customary and emphasize this fact by quoting list prices, together with their discount of 10, 20, or 30 per cent off. While the legal definition of price cutting as an unfair trade practice restricts it to selling below cost, many dealers believe that selling below the customary margin is equally unfair.

Administered prices. In many markets, prices can be determined by the sellers because they control some aspects of supply or demand. The monopolist, or single seller, by definition controls the entire supply. Where there are a few sellers, they are likely to set prices which are quite similar and to compete by various forms of nonprice competition. The antitrust laws outlaw agreements on prices among sellers, but the existence of such agreements, whether overt or implicit, should not be overlooked because of the difficulties in proving conspiracy. Similar prices also result from the use of a common pricing formula by all the firms or from price leadership by one dominant firm.

Aside from these institutional factors tending to limit sellers' price decisions or actions, consumer demand plays a strong role. The markets for most consumer goods take the form of monopolistic competition, where each seller controls the price and output of his own product but other suppliers offer close substitutes. In such a case, there is a strong tendency to price similarity and price stability.

In the first place, a price drop by one seller may lead to retaliation in the form of even lower prices by another, until a disastrous "price war" ensues where the prices received do not cover costs. Since each seller realizes this possibility, he is reluctant to compete by price changes when other means are available to increase sales. Second, while the downward slope of a demand curve means that larger quantities can be sold at lower prices, a drop in price sometimes leads to a decrease in sales. Consumers may expect the price reduction to be the first step in a general decline and postpone their purchases. Or, well aware of price wars, buyers may anticipate future price cuts by other sellers. Finally, strong associations tend to develop between a given product and a particular price. Since the seller does control the price, any rise will need explanation to overcome consumer resistance. A price reduction may need explanation as well, because of consumers' twofold interpretation of the term "cheap" and the suspicion that a lower price represents less quality.

Predetermined prices represent to the seller, therefore, considerable advantages in reducing the number of decisions to be made and in accepting the institutional factors present in the market.

Resale price maintenance. Many of the advantages of stable prices and of predetermined prices are secured to manufacturers and distributors through the use of resale-price-maintenance agreements, commonly known as *fair trading*. Contracts between the manufacturer and the distributor provide that the distributor agrees to charge the prices set by the manufacturer, subject to certain qualifications in the case of changes in the product, distributors' surplus, and so on. The legal status of such agreements has had a long and tumultuous history.

In 1911, a court decision held that resale-price-maintenance agreements violated the terms of the Sherman Act, which forbids conspiracy in restraint of trade. The Sherman Act applies, of course, only to interstate commerce, and similar statutes covering intrastate business exist in the separate states. Developments in retailing, plus the business losses of depression years, renewed interest in fair-trade contracts and, in 1931, led by California, a number of individual states enacted permissive legislation. These laws exempt resale-price-maintenance agreements from the state's antimonopoly legislation. In 1937, the Miller-Tydings Act amended the Sherman Act to permit contracts in states with fair-trade laws. A later Supreme Court decision upheld the constitutionality of the Act, and many more states passed permissive legislation, until, in 1953, only three states and the District of Columbia lacked such laws.

Perhaps the most controversial detail of the state legislation is the so-called "nonsigner" clause. The terms of an agreement are of course binding on the manufacturer and any dealer who signs the contract, but a separate clause provides that the contract, once signed by a single dealer, is binding on all dealers who are properly informed. Any sale below the fair-trade price not only violates a contract but is construed as illegal unfair competition.

In 1951, the Supreme Court decision in *Schwegmann v. Calvert Distillers Corporation, Ltd.* [341 U.S. 384 (1951)] declared the nonsigner clause illegal in interstate commerce. Justice Douglas's opinion pointed out that the whole basis of fair trade is the contractual one between manufacturers and distributors. "Contracts or agreement convey the idea of a cooperative agreement, not a program whereby recalcitrants are dragged in by the heels and compelled to submit to price fixing." Following this decision, retailers all over the country cut prices, and spirited but short-lived price wars occurred in New York City and elsewhere. By 1952, a new law, the McGuire Act, provided that sales below the manufacturers' established price violated the Federal Trade Commission Act, which spells out certain forms of unfair competition. Lower courts have upheld the constitutionality of this law, and, in 1953, the Supreme Court refused to hear an appeal.[3]

The extent of fair trading and its effect on consumption will be discussed in a later chapter; here it suffices to point out its implications for sellers' decisions. State laws permit resale price maintenance only on commodities which bear the trade-mark, brand, or name of the producer, on the theory that the manufacturer needs to determine price in order to protect his proprietary interest. But fair-trade agreements are difficult to enforce and hence are seldom used in several distinct areas. Branded food products, for example, are rarely fair-traded because fresh produce, which is not branded, competes so closely. Processed food prices also fluctuate sharply with the prices of raw materials. Although the brand name is extremely important in appliance sales, fair-trade contracts do not exist for automobiles, most television or radio sets, or other major purchases where the price paid by the consumer depends upon a trade-in.

Resale price maintenance covers the majority of items in drug retailing, however, including cosmetics and surgical supplies. Agreements exist for many hardware items, some clothing and household products, small appliances, cigars, and liquor. Much of the pressure to legalize fair trade and to secure contracts from particular manufacturers has come from dealers' trade associations. The contracts obviously reduce the threat of price competition. In some cases, this lack of competition, and the artificially high margin provided by the contract, keeps dealers in business who would otherwise be forced out by more efficient firms.

[3] As this book went to press, the status of fair trade was again uncertain. The Department of Justice recommended in 1955 that resale price maintenance legislation be abolished, and several prominent manufacturers abandoned their fair-trading policy on many appliances.

COST DECISIONS

Price maintenance and predetermined prices mean that sellers frequently emphasize costs and output in their decisions. Rather than accepting marginal cost as given in order to determine output and prices, the firm attempts to determine output and costs to fit a given price, or to lower costs in order to increase profit.[4]

Costs at the producing level. Earlier in the chapter, we distinguished direct and overhead costs, noting that an increase in volume tended to reduce the overhead costs per unit of output. The firm using a break-even analysis will be sharply aware of the effect on profit of a change in costs, as can be seen in Figure 19-2, where a cost increase of approximately $0.10 per unit wiped out the former profit and a cost decrease of approximately $0.15 per unit reduced the volume necessary to break even. The obverse of a decrease in costs is an increase in efficiency, or in the productivity of the labor or materials or capital used.

The firm may, therefore, seek to change the shape of its marginal cost curve or lower its break-even point by increasing productivity. The use of substitutes, recapture of wastes, an increase of the yield of final product from raw materials, or even a change in suppliers may lead to a lower materials cost. A change in productive process, the substitution of machine for handwork, a reorganization of layout or rescheduling of work may reduce the costs of turning out the same product. Many cost changes, however, involve a change in the product, as where simpler lines or a different finish are used, the styling or packaging is altered, or more basic changes are made in the functions or performance of the product.

Selling costs. Of particular interest to the study of consumption are selling costs—the economist's term for costs incurred in distribution, or marketing, or merchandising. The physical process of getting finished goods from producers to consumers is worth considerable analysis by any seller. The manufacturer has a variety of choices. Should he maintain his own selling organization to supply retailers, should he sell to a few wholesale distributors, or should he employ the services of a manufacturer's agent? Should the firm sell its products to all dealers or restrict it to a

[4] Cost control or reduction may be particularly important in a period of rising prices or wages. Although prices depend upon costs, not all costs rise at the same rate. Higher prices paid by the seller for raw materials, or component parts, or labor may provide the impetus to programs for reducing costs rather than raising the price of the finished goods.

few selected outlets? The retailer must decide whether to provide order and delivery service or pay for transportation. Any seller has a problem in defining his market—should he attempt to enlarge the number of his customers, searching for buyers in other localities? Detailed plans for dis-

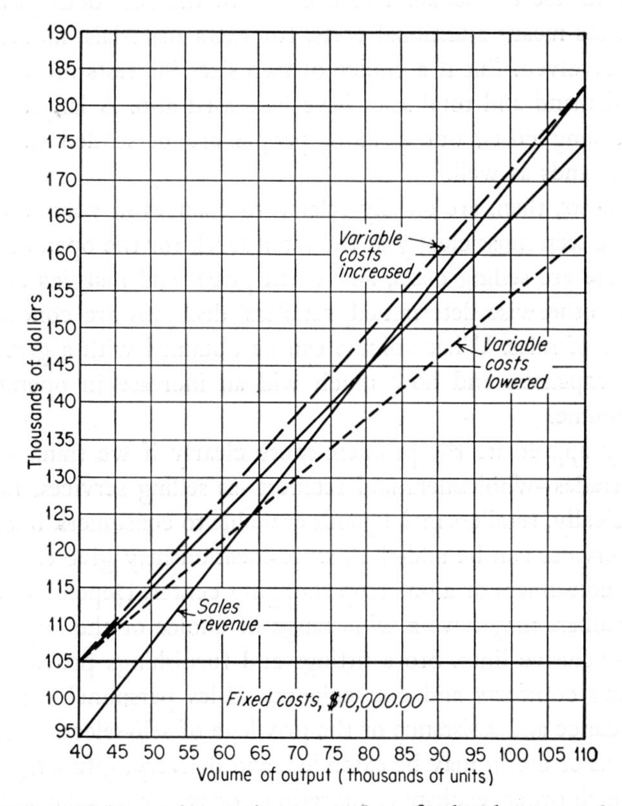

FIG. 19-2. Volume, changes in cost, and profit: break-even analysis.

tribution affect consumption, not only by making goods physically available, but also by the various costs involved in different methods.

But marketing includes not only physical handling but selling or merchandising functions. At a minimum, marketing requires that orders be taken and filled, that goods be shipped or otherwise transferred to buyers, and that purchasers are billed or charged and payment is received. More inclusively, marketing or merchandising may involve planning the product (including quantities, style, and packaging), providing information (including market research, consumer surveys, and advertising), and providing a selling effort (to assist or persuade potential customers). These marketing functions are performed differently by different firms and hence result in widely varying costs.

Selling costs reflect, however, not only the operations of the firm but also an influence on demand. A decision to market tooth paste in two package sizes means additional costs, for extra materials, machinery, and labor are involved. But if a choice of two sizes interests more customers, then the demand and total sales have increased also. A larger sales force enlarges selling costs, but if more people are persuaded to buy, total demand expands as well.

Selling costs, then, are closely related to changes in volume or output. This can be seen most clearly at the retail level, for the operating costs of a retail store are selling costs, and when prices and margins are conventionally or otherwise determined, retailers' decisions are concerned with the volume of sales. What volume can be obtained with a given level of operating expenses, and how much will an increase in operating costs expand volume?

We may appreciate the problem more clearly if we think of the distributive trades—wholesalers and retailers—as selling services, rather than goods. Basically, retailers make goods available to consumers, but a number of other services can be added. A store location may give easy transportation for consumers or a one-stop shopping center. Depending on inventory, consumers may have a wide range of choice or the opportunity to purchase exclusive lines. Store fittings and furnishings provide a variety of shopping comforts and conveniences. Sales personnel may give the buyer guidance and assistance or the privilege of self-selection. Many different forms of credit may be extended, and delivery, gift wrapping, telephone or mail order, exchange, alterations, or repair may be added to the list of services offered. It is these services which give rise to the retailer's costs of doing business, his expenses to be covered by the gross margin. These are the costs of selling. At the same time, these services influence his volume of sales directly. Shall he offer a more convenient location—and incur a higher rent? Shall he increase his inventory—and find more working capital? Shall he carpet his store, put in indirect lighting with background music to attract customers—or minimize his maintenance costs? Shall he pay higher wages for expert sales clerks—or shall he cut labor costs by using self-selection? Shall he offer charge accounts—and pay for investigating credit references or for collecting overdue accounts? Each of these decisions is a problem in volume of sales and costs. How many customers spending how much will be attracted by these services, and how much will the services cost? [5]

Because the factors leading to predetermined prices loom large at the retail level, *retail competition consists chiefly in varying services rather than varying prices.* In a later chapter, we shall investigate the principal type of distributive services available to consumers and the division of markets among different types of retail outlets. It should be pointed out here, however, that the individual retailer is less concerned with expanding total consumption than with obtaining the largest possible share of consumer purchases in his market. The facts of local geography limit a retailer's market (with the exception of mail-order houses, which form a special case). Total consumption, furthermore, depends upon population and income characteristics which cannot be influenced by a single retailer. The established retail outlet, therefore, seeks to increase its volume of sales at the expense of other competitive outlets: if two stores survive profitably where only one existed before, this is usually the result of forces other than the selling efforts of the second store—an increase in population or income, a change in shopping habits, and so forth.

Selling costs are also important at the manufacturer's level, but, for the producer, many changes in merchandising involve changes in the finished good.

Influencing demand. In a previous chapter, changes in demand, where the demand curve as a whole shifts to right or left, were distinguished from changes in the quantity demanded, or a movement along the same demand curve. Instead of increasing the quantity sold by lowering prices, many sellers attempt to increase the demand at the same price, and various methods exist of influencing demand.

To the individual seller, an increase in total sales may result from two

[5] Cf. Margaret Hall, *Distributive Trading*, London, 1949, p. 49: "The trader has fundamentally two types of problem in deciding what is his best trading policy: first, to get the most profit from servicing his existing customers at any time (by equating marginal cost with marginal revenue) and secondly to increase expenditure on expanding his circle of customers (increasing goodwill) up to the profitable limit until he finds himself confronting potential buyers who are so far distant from him (either because they live so far away or are resistant to his particular selling appeals) that it would require more expenditure on salesmanship than the net receipts (total receipts minus prime costs) from their purchases."

kinds of increased demand. If the total sales of radios increase, each manufacturing firm may expect to increase production. But each firm may also try to increase sales at the expense of the other sellers, to expand not the total demand for radios but the demand for Crosley radios, or Zenith radios, or Admiral radios.

Efforts aimed at expanding the sales of the product of one firm require, as an initial prerequisite, that the product of that firm be *differentiated* in some way from those of the rest of the industry. Consumers will not demand Zenith radios rather than Admirals unless the Zenith is distinguishable and, for some reason, preferable. We find, therefore, the use of brand names and trade-marks, and also the deliberate differentiation of product, among sellers. The objective is to create or increase a demand for Zenith radios, not for radios in general; the objective of each firm is to make its product unique so that consumers will not substitute the product of other sellers for it. In technical terms, each manufacturer seeks a demand for his product which is expanding and becoming more inelastic. Real differences in the product serve this purpose, but if real differences do not exist between the products of competitors they may be "created" through persuasive advertising, attractive packaging, the adoption of brand names, and model change-overs.

This type of market situation is characterized, we will recall, as one of *monopolistic competition.* Each firm holds a monopoly position in the market with respect to its own product, but since each product has close substitutes the firms involved must compete with one another. The competition in this situation generally does not take the form of price competition; it takes the form of *product competition* where each seller tries to put on the market a more eye-catching item. Thus, product competition becomes one of the more important forms of *nonprice competition.*

The effects of technological change. The changes in American industry and consumption over the past century have been mentioned in earlier chapters. Our homes and living conditions today are dependent on products that did not exist fifty or even twenty years ago. A majority of the sales of many firms are of products which were nonexistent ten or twenty years previously. The automobile, the classic example of an industry new to the twentieth century, tends to overshadow the myriad of other new products. But modern living reflects other innovations—synthetic textiles, household appliances, radio and television, drugs and insecticides, frozen foods and pressure cookers, aluminum storm windows and electronic calculating machines. For the most part, the new products have originated from the research and development efforts of business. The day of the lone inventor in his attic is over.

Consumptionwise, the effect of technological change has been complex. A constantly widening range of new products presents the consumer with more choices than ever. Beyond this, the consumer has come to expect change. Newness, difference, up-to-dateness are a part of what he buys. The store in which he shops differs markedly from that patronized by his grandfather, and he does not expect to find within it goods that were available fifty years ago. Finally, the consumer who sees something new does not distinguish between superficial change, technological change, and improvement.

Producers, recognizing the consumer's taste for innovation, have encouraged its growth while seeking to satisfy it. Innovation occurs both in product change and in completely new items. If a product is described in terms of its functions and its performance of these functions, technical change may be defined as an additional function or characteristic. Thus, textile fibers may be toughened, may be made shrink-resistant, or may develop colorfastness. An automobile engine may use gasoline more efficiently or require less oil, thereby improving its performance. Cigarettes appear with filter tips or a new length—a change in both function and performance. Aside from such technical changes, many innovations do not affect either function or performance. Altering the finish, color, shape, size, design, or packaging changes the product in the consumer's eyes, perhaps more so than a hidden structural change discernible only to engineers. To some extent, the package is changed to whet and satisfy the consumer's desire for novelty when no functional change can be made. As a result, change, of and by itself, has become a part of what the consumer buys and the producer sells. In the struggle to influence demand, then, firms rely on product variation and on constant innovation to keep their product unique and to satisfy the demand for change.

Advertising. Nonprice competition which seeks to influence demand is not confined to variation of the product. We have already seen that retailers compete by offering various combinations of services, and manufacturers can also seek to increase demand in this way. Factory warranties, repair service, and information or instructions accompany the sales of many consumer goods. *The most important weapon used by producers, however, is advertising, aimed directly at shaping consumer demand.* Industry-wide advertising, promoted usually by trade associations, attempts to increase the total demand for a product. The individual firm advertises in order to make the demand for its product more inelastic and to expand that demand. As such, advertising is a selling cost and clearly related to volume.

Advertising is a special form of communication. At a minimum, the seller uses it to describe to the buyer what can be bought. Since consumers need information about all the possible choices, such a use of advertising obviously assists consumption in the market. In a society replete with technological change, such advertising is probably essential, for when new or changed products are developed, consumers must be told about them. A full description of the item—what it is, how to use and enjoy it—encourages new consumer tastes and habits and helps to modify the existing consumption pattern. Such information about new or changed products, or new uses for old products, may result in an increased total demand.

Advertising is also used by sellers to inform consumers about product differentiation. Making an individual product unique is only the first step in shaping demand: the second is to make consumers want the unique product. At this point, the informational function of advertising is often subordinated to the persuasive. The consumer must be told about the individual seller and his product, why it differs from competing substitutes, and why it should be preferred. Successful advertising leads first to consumer *recognition* of the particular product, then to consumer *preference*, and finally to consumer *insistence*. The reader will recognize that each of these steps represents a successively more inelastic demand curve to the individual firm.

Recognition of the product involves a name, trade-mark, brand, or other identifying device. Advertising must then make this identification familiar; hence the simple repetition of a name on billboards, posters, or radio. Preference and insistence require that consumers have a stronger motive for buying product A than product B, and various motives may be instilled or encouraged by advertising.

Finally, sellers influence demand, not only by advertising product variations, but in some cases by creating product differences through advertising. The well-known examples of the same drugs sold at high prices under an advertised brand name and at low prices without benefit of the trade-mark need not be repeated here. Instead, a surely authoritative source may be quoted—a major advertising concern advertising its advertising services to business.

Though on the surface your product and competing ones may be "as like as two peas," yet there *is* a way *to make your product stand out from all the rest.*

In your product or in its use, just as in you yourself, there is *genuine individuality*. This lies, not in any superficial differences that others may match next season, not in any trick presentation, but in the creation of a unique and distinctive personality that belongs to you, alone. Determined, consistent association can fix this individuality more and more firmly, until it *is* your product.

In our economy of technological change, the best product variation to advertise is, of course, a technical change or improvement. And even where such technical differences do not exist, advertising copy can always create them or enhance the value of a minor alteration.

CONCLUSIONS

In this chapter, we have seen some of the many courses of action open to sellers confronting the market demand of consumers. Depending on their analysis and forecasts, sellers in monopolistic competition may plan to vary prices, output, costs, or the product itself. Nonprice competition is characteristic of most consumer markets today and has deeply affected consumption patterns. On the one hand, competition by innovation has undoubtedly produced many of the consumer goods which make us well off today. On the other hand, competition by advertising and other merchandising efforts has undoubtedly added to the costs of many products. In the next chapter, we shall investigate further the effects of nonprice competition on consumption.

Questions and Points for Discussion

1. Explain how the marginal analysis—weighing additional costs against additional revenues—applies to the businessman's decisions on a change in product, an advertising campaign, or "free services" offered.
2. Both the theory of consumer behavior and the theory of business behavior are based on marginal analysis. What corresponds, for consumers, to profit maximization by firms? What corresponds, in firms, to the consumer's limited income? What other parallels can you draw?
3. What is the current status of resale-price-maintenance laws in your state?
4. Of the consumer goods and services discussed in Chapters 12 and 13, which do you think are sold chiefly by price competition? By nonprice competition?
5. How do consumers' wants affect the nature of nonprice competition?

References

Bowen, Howard R.: *Social Responsibilities of the Businessman*, Harper & Brothers, New York, 1952.

Dean, Joel: "Cost Forecasting and Price Policy," in Malcolm P. McNair and Harry L. Hansen, *Readings in Marketing*, McGraw-Hill Book Company, Inc., New York, 1949.

———: "Pricing a New Product," *Harvard Business Review*, November, 1950.

Editors of *Fortune Magazine:* "New Gasolines: Boon or Ballyhoo?" *Fortune Magazine*, September, 1954.

Grether, E. T.: *Price Control under Fair Trade Legislation*, Oxford University Press, New York, 1939.

Hall, Margaret: *Distributive Trading; An Economic Analysis*, Hutchinson's University Library, London, 1949.

20. Nonprice Factors in Choice Decisions

The many different courses of action open to businessmen provide many choices for consumers and much of the yearly variation in consumption patterns. In this chapter, we shall look at some customary trade practices from the point of view of the consumer.

FORMS OF NONPRICE COMPETITION

Consumer choice in the real world is far more complex than that envisaged by the price-analysis models of previous chapters. The prospective buyer faces a bewildering array of objects to satisfy his wants, and a constant pressure to develop new wants. Once having decided that he will buy an automobile or a winter coat, a children's record or a box of peaches, he finds a number of different automobiles, coats, records, and boxes of peaches, some at different prices and some at the same price. He can make his purchase in a number of ways—by going to a store and asking for and receiving the item, telephoning an order and taking delivery within a day or two, or writing an order. He can choose whether to pay cash for his purchase, to charge and be billed monthly, or in some cases to receive extended credit. These and more choices surround the consumer as firms intensify their use of nonprice competition, varying the product and the services accompanying it.

For consumers to make a purchase, they need information on what is available, a means of making their choice known, a means of payment, and the transfer of their purchase to their person or home. Shopping, to perform all these functions, requires time and effort on the part of consumers, and business firms offer a number of different services to minimize the effort of purchasing. Marketing personnel have divided consumer purchases into *convenience goods* and *shopping goods* on the basis of the consumer's willingness to devote his energy to making purchases. Thus cigarettes, newspapers, soap, and many drugs or grocery products are purchased in the most convenient manner, as opposed to automobiles, household appliances, and most clothing items, for which consumers generally prefer to "shop around." But since one buyer finds one type of service convenient and another finds it awkward, many combinations of various services exist.

The information on what is available comes partly from advertising, partly from seeing goods displayed, and partly from having observed the consumption activities of other people. Business performs the first two functions in a variety of ways. As we have seen, advertising frequently mixes information with persuasion, but in some fields there has been a notable trend to informative labeling and advertising. Manufacturers tag their products with detailed descriptions and instructions for use and maintenance, while some advertising programs explain and demonstrate ways to use the product. The retailer also gives information and, more important, displays products for the consumer's inspection. This function also depends on the manufacturer, who decides whether goods are packaged in "see-through" materials and often provides special display materials for use on retail-store counters or in shop windows. Demonstrators or samples give the consumer a chance to try the product, and for some commodities such sampling is essential. A new car gets a road test, a home appliance a demonstration, clothing must be tried on and swatches of drapery materials must be matched to paint or wallpaper. Other items, like processed foods or hotel rooms, are rarely sampled in advance, although one attraction of motels is the privilege of viewing the room before registering, and morsels of cheese or meat or candy frequently appear in food store promotional campaigns.

Once having decided on a purchase, the consumer must inform the seller of his choice. Despite the mail-order business, most consumers go to stores to buy, and the latest development in purchasing convenience is the shopping centers which have burgeoned since World War II. But other kinds of convenience also exist—the corner grocery for last-minute purchases, telephone service for ordering flowers, laundry service, bakery or dairy products, the exclusive shop with a specialized knowledge of its customers, and the urban store open late in the evenings. Once in the store, the consumer may need a clerk to take his order, or the store may offer self-selection. For goods like groceries, variety store items, books, and some lines of apparel the consumer gains convenience by self-selection.

In other lines it is a burden to the buyer seeking information or guidance, or a burden to the retailer whose pilferage losses increase.

The physical transfer of goods to the consumer depends partly on the product and partly on the kind of services offered. Delivery by mail or by the seller's trucks may be convenient to some consumption purchases and inconvenient (or unprofitable to the seller) for others. Carpets, major appliances, oil burners, or household fittings which require installation have long been sold on the basis of service as well as the product itself. And although cash-and-carry stores were first introduced to offer lower prices, they now offer convenience, as the consumer's own automobile solves the problem of transportation. Closely related to the transfer of purchases to consumers is the privilege of returning merchandise or obtaining repair service in case of dissatisfaction. For some goods, only the manufacturer can make adjustments, while others reflect varying retail policies. To some extent, this depends on the guarantee or warranty offered with the product, together with the seller's wish to compete pricewise or by varying his services. The seller incurs additional costs by offering repair or return privileges, and these may be reflected in his prices.

CONSUMER'S CHOICE

For the consumer to exercise a wise choice among all these alternative services, two conditions must be met. First, the consumer in a local market must actually have access to different firms offering different services—a number of outlets must exist. Second, the consumer must recognize and evaluate those differences which do exist.

The number of competing sellers and the ways in which they compete vary widely in different locations. Only the mail-order houses provide the same services throughout the nation, and because of freight charges the prices to consumers vary by areas. With automobiles, intrinsic to our consumption pattern, however, any local market for consumer goods has widened appreciably. Sellers find more potential customers and also potential competition from more distant sellers. Store location, a complex problem, depends partly on whether transportation for consumers is convenient or inconvenient.

Although the typical consumer has, by using a car or public transportation, many alternative shopping services, his choice with some consumer goods is limited by a trade practice known as *selected distribution.* In many fields, including shoes, automobiles, some cosmetics and jewelry, some appliances and high-grade clothing, the manufacturer sells his output only to retailers whom he selects within a given market area. The exclusive agency allows only one dealer to sell the manufacturer's product within a given geographical district, and joint agency distribution limits the number of retail outlets selling the product in a given area.

Selected distribution limits competition, of course, and may or may not provide compensating services to the consumer. From the manufacturer's point of view, he can expect more energetic selling, and hence larger sales, especially where the agency contract prohibits the dealer from selling other brands. At the same time, the potential consumer demand depends entirely on the chosen dealer's effectiveness and may not be fully explored. The dealer's prices and margins are protected to cover certain costs—for example, a substantial inventory investment in shoes or china or silverware, or a complete servicing organization for automobiles or appliances. In some cases, therefore, the consumer benefits from a wide selection of styles within a given brand and from the servicing or guarantees of the chosen dealer. Against this must be weighed the inconvenience of seeking out the agency and of being forced to visit many outlets in order to compare different brands. Furthermore, if selected distribution limits rather than expands the potential market, higher costs, particularly selling costs, may be passed on to the consumer. The shopping methods actually available to consumers, therefore, may be limited not only by the number of different outlets within reach but also by the manufacturer's distribution policy.

Theoretically, the consumer's preferences enable him to gain maximum satisfaction from his consumption purchases. But there are utilities and disutilities in the purchasing process itself, and the consumer may choose not only to buy more oranges and fewer apples but also to buy more services instead of less. In order to maximize satisfaction, therefore, the consumer must recognize and understand not only the differences between products and their accompanying services but also, where prices differ, the extent to which price variations represent real differences in product or services. He must compare not only the utility from Libby's and Del Monte's foods but also the utility from driving to a supermarket, collecting a week's food, and paying cash and from telephoning to another store, having the order delivered, and paying a monthly bill.

Two factors hamper the consumer's ability to analyze these differences rationally. One is the staggering amount of time and effort involved, that is, the costs of analyzing differences in costs. An individual evaluation of all the available choices to satisfy any want would require a major touring expedition, comparing prices, product differences, and variations in shopping services. Very few consumer purchases are worth this approach, so that consumers tend to form shopping habits—presumably those which on the whole maximize their utility—which govern their purchases. It should be pointed out that price competition as well as nonprice competition depends, for its effectiveness, on consumers' awareness of and interest in differences among different sellers. If consumers neither know nor care that a penny a pound can be saved on *X* brand butter at *Y* store, the increased sales associated with lower prices will not be forthcoming. It is possible, therefore, for consumers themselves to change their consumption patterns rather markedly by changing their shopping habits.

The second factor inhibiting the consumer's ability to evaluate his alternative choices is his lack of knowledge—a subject to be treated more extensively in a later chapter. At the moment, we should note that an exhaustive and accurate comparison of utilities is well-nigh impossible even for those consumers who might devote time and energy to the problem.

A major effect of nonprice competition on consumer's choice, therefore, is to narrow the area of rational conscious decision and increase the effect of habit, impulse, or ignorance. And many types of nonprice competition themselves intensify these factors, as when advertising substitutes emotional appeals for facts, when the location or display of merchandise leads to spur-of-the-moment buying, or when a sound reputation for quality and service keeps satisfied customers returning to the same store.

THE COSTS OF NONPRICE COMPETITION

Although we can offer no general rule to the consumer wishing to compare the utilities of various trade practices, a word on costs to consumers seems in order. In the last chapter, we pointed out that various means of increasing demand are open to sellers. When such means as advertising, product variation, special packaging, or servicing *increase the volume of sales at a given price*, they do so because consumer demand has expanded—the demand curve has shifted to the right. Sellers must weigh the costs of their efforts to expand demand against the revenues from the sales resulting.

Variations in the product. Technical differences and innovations among competing substitutes have increased consumption efficiency and provided a wide range of choice. Excessive product differentiation can, however, increase the costs to the consumer. Such cost increases may occur in one of three different ways, and all stem from the fact that the total demand for a product such as cornflakes consists in a number of demand schedules for individual brands—Kellogg's, Post's, and so forth—and that the demand curve for the individual brand is more elastic than for all brands. To the breakfast cereal industry as a whole, consumer demand takes the familiar shape of a curve sloping downward to the right. But because the consumer can substitute products, the demand for cornflakes is more elastic than for all cereals, and the demand for Kellogg's cornflakes is more elastic than the demand for all cornflakes.

Assume first that firm A's established price on A's Kornflakes allows a considerable profit over production and selling costs. The prospect of like profits induces other firms to make and sell B's Flakes-o-corn, C's Corn Toasties, and D's Corn Flecks. If the total quantity of cornflakes sold does not expand, each new firm's sales will cut into that of firm A. All are producing at a smaller volume, and hence higher costs, than before new firms entered the field. The total profit is divided among the firms, who may increase in number to the point where no profits exist or actual losses ensue. But no savings in price need accrue to consumers, because the volume of production of each seller is low and hence cost is higher.

Second, the competition among sellers of differentiated products creates other costs. Firm A and its new rivals need brands or trade-marks to maintain their identity. They must introduce variations in the product or offer additional services. The uniqueness of each brand must be thoroughly explained in advertising. These selling costs must be passed on to the consumer in the form of higher prices, unless the total demand for the product is enlarged.

Third, consumer choice is actually limited by the process of product variation and constant innovation. Sellers of most consumer durable goods rely heavily on replacement demand, maintained or expanded by progressive obsolescence. Many items today have a shorter useful life than formerly, and repair parts for older models are difficult to obtain, simply because most consumers buy newer models. The emphasis on newness requires yearly model changes in the automobile industry, and the practice has spread to other lines. (Style goods, of course, including cosmetics and accessories as well as clothing, are the outstanding example of rapid obsolescence.) If structural changes require retooling or a temporary loss of output, production costs may be increased by the innovation, and not all new models embody structural or technical changes. Whether constant change or innovation is producer- or consumer-bred, it leaves no choice to anyone who prefers less novelty or a stripped-down model at a lower price.

Advertising. The effects of advertising on consumer demand and the cost of advertising to the consumer have been hotly debated. One argument maintains that advertising increases demand by informing or convincing potential buyers of the product, that larger sales result in expanded output, which creates additional employment and lower costs through economies of scale, so that consumers can buy at lower prices. This line of reasoning confuses the demand for Chesterfields with the demand for cigarettes and contains other fallacies as well. If firm A's special advertising campaign results in higher sales, production and employment presumably expand for firm A. But if the increased sales means that fewer people are buying firm B's product, production and employment there decrease. Firm A's production costs may very well decline, but the consumer is not likely to benefit from a lower price. Some of the revenues from increased sales will pay for continued advertising to maintain the firm's advantage over firm B, and price competition continues to be studiously avoided. The fluctuations of sales of different firms in industries which compete chiefly by advertising—gasoline, cigarettes, cereals, tooth paste—show how temporary the gain or loss from a shift in demand can be.

In some cases, of course, sales expand for all firms, as consumer demand for cigarettes in general increases. But the demand for some other consumer goods may well decline, so that production and employment contract in one industry to provide the productive factors needed in another. An increase in demand which expands total production and employment means that consumers are spending more and saving less. In previous chapters, we looked at changes in consumption patterns over the years and noted many influences on consumer tastes and habits—household formation and family size, housing, population location, and the distribution of income. How much has advertising shaped consumers' tastes and habits?

There can be no accurate evaluation of the results of advertising—even, to the executive's dismay, of the results of one campaign—because these other factors enter in and can neither be isolated nor properly weighed. By the same token, it cannot be proved that advertising is worthless. One analysis suggests that, if the underlying conditions favor an increase in demand, advertising may speed up the trend. Cigarette sales boomed during the 1920s as men abandoned cigars and women began smoking.

Both these reflect changed social customs. Advertising cannot, however, counteract a decline in demand, as evidenced by the sales of cigars, silk stockings, and the movies during the first years of television. *The nature of most advertising, moreover, shows that it is designed to get the firm a larger share of total sales rather than to expand total demand and sales.* Hence, most advertising emphasizes product differences and reinforces nonprice competition.[1] The notable exception is cooperative advertising by trade associations, where an attempt is made to increase the total demand for walnuts, oranges, or dry cleaning, because the individual firms supply nearly identical products and each is too small to incur large advertising costs.

Aside from its debatable effects on the demand for existing products, advertising poses other problems to the consumers who pay its costs. While aesthetic and even ethical condemnations of advertising can be made, its function in spreading information—particularly in a society of innovation—plus its financial support of the press and radio make a complete condemnation difficult. Presumably, the consumer information problem could be solved more efficiently, and other schemes exist for paying for the radio and the press. Inefficiency, however, exists in many other spheres less fraught with emotional appeal to the consumer. It has been observed that the waste and inefficiency involved in advertising are indications of the wealth of our economy—that, where people lack sufficient food, there is no need to advertise cornflakes and there are no resources to devote to advertising.[2] If advertising in our economy were to be abolished, would the men and materials be used elsewhere any less wastefully?

Resale price maintenance. All the means of nonprice competition, with their additional costs to consumers, are reinforced by resale price maintenance, which forbids price competition on branded items among dealers or retailers. The rationale for fair trading is that the manufacturer needs to set retail prices in order to protect his brand name, his product differences, and his investment in advertising. From the dealer's point of view, resale price maintenance forbids unfair price cutting, or sales below costs. Sales below invoice cost, or the price paid by the dealer, are prohibited by other laws governing unfair competition. Resale-price-maintenance contracts protect the dealer's margin, therefore, and bar prices below full

[1] A few well-known firms, whose brand names are synonyms for products, have never advertised, presumably because any increase in sales would reflect an expanded total demand, benefiting their competitors.

[2] J. K. Galbraith, *American Capitalism*, Houghton Mifflin Company, Boston, 1952.

cost, including the expenses of doing business as a dealer. But such expenses vary with the type of services offered, so that fair-trade contracts lead to nonprice competition at the dealer's level in terms of varying services.

The costs of resale price maintenance to the consumer are twofold. If dealers could cut prices and increase sales without a costly merchandising effort, the increased volume of production might lower costs and prices further. Resale price maintenance forbids this process. Quite aside from this, the legislation, and especially the nonsigner clause, narrows the areas of price competition and therefore increases prices paid by consumers. The consumer loses the simple and measurable variable of price and must deal with the complex area of varying products and services. The dealer lacks freedom of action to lower prices if he chooses this form of competition.

Resale price maintenance has produced other significant results. Many contracts result from dealers' pressure, particularly those with high costs, to secure a generous margin, but the manufacturers do not always object to other dealers selling below the list price. Such sales, although violations, increase the total sales of the manufacturer. Fair-trade prices, therefore, vary in the extent to which they are observed.

The existence of fair trading has, in many cases, stimulated the production and sale of competing items which are not fair-traded. Many private brands of appliances or drugs can be sold because consumers are familiar with a similar article which is nationally advertised at a listed price. The dealer can thus encourage consumers to buy the private brand or non-fair-traded make by pointing out the similarity in quality and the difference in price between the two items.

At the same time, other factors have influenced the growth of nonprice competition, and the abolition of resale price maintenance would not necessarily produce widespread price wars or a generally lower level of prices. Some manufacturers using resale price maintenance have found it increasingly difficult to police their dealers; in such cases, undoubtedly price competition would spread, following the end of a contract. Other contracts are uniformly observed, and prices and margins might well remain stable even if resale contracts vanished, because of the tendencies to stable prices we have already examined. Some manufacturers find their list prices observed without using resale-price-maintenance contracts, and other incentives, including selected distribution and cooperative manufacturer-dealer advertising, exist to maintain prices.

The fair-trade lobby has presented data showing that prices in states where resale price maintenance is illegal tend to be higher than in states where fair-trade contracts are in force. To conclude from such evidence that resale price maintenance generally lowers the prices paid by consumers begs the question. Prices offered by dealers depend on their costs as well as on the type and extent of competition in the market. Cosmetics and drugs return a generous margin to supermarkets, whose costs run substantially lower than those of the small independent druggists, who first secured resale-price-maintenance contracts. It may be that the supermarkets are thus enabled to offer slightly lower prices on the rest of their stock. But cost savings on the fair-traded items themselves cannot be passed on to the consumer, whose range of choice is thus narrowed. Nor can dealers who sell only fair-traded goods pass on any cost savings which may accrue. In so far as resale price maintenance reduces price competition costs to the consumer are probably increased.

CONSUMER CREDIT

We turn now to the role of consumer credit in the purchasing process and to the trade practices and institutions which have developed some $28 billion of outstanding consumer credit in the present-day United States economy. There are two main types of credit: firms use production credit in business enterprises which produce income to pay the debt, and households use consumer credit to acquire goods and services which provide satisfaction but not income to pay the debt. It has long been customary to analyze short- and intermediate-term consumer credit separately from long-term credit, represented by home mortgages. Statistics on consumer credit are published by the Federal Reserve Board from two sources of data, the accounting records of institutions holding credit and the survey of consumer finances reporting the debts owed by households. Data from the second source were included in previous chapters.

Our present interest, therefore, is in credit used to pay for consumption goods and services or used to refinance debt originally incurred for this purpose. We may distinguish loans, or the advance of funds, from the advance of goods and services, but since people rarely borrow money in order to save it (in the strictest sense of not spending it), both forms lead to consumption of goods and services. We may also distinguish installment from noninstallment credit and may analyze their different effects on household income and expenditure. Figure 20-1 illustrates various forms of credit and gives the definitions used by the Federal Reserve Board.

Deferred payment, as a part of the purchasing process, may be merely a convenience to the consumer or a prerequisite to his purchase. The

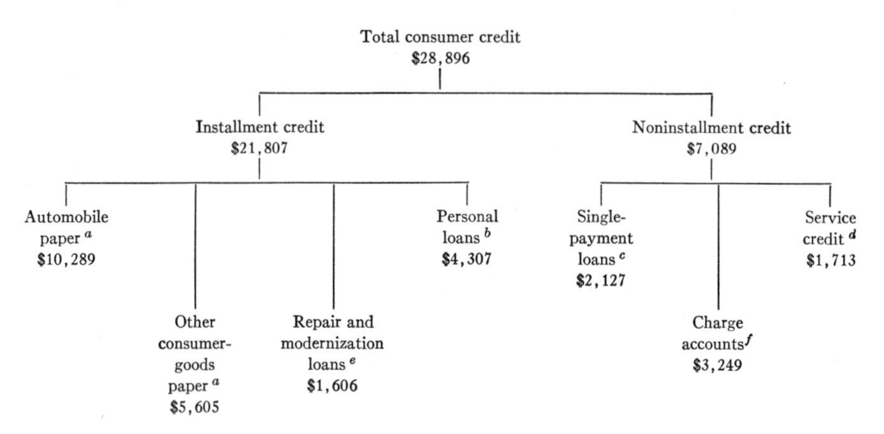

[a] Automobile paper and other consumer-goods paper represent credit extended for the purchase of these goods and secured by the items purchased. Such credit may be extended by a retail dealer or arranged by him with a financial institution, or it may be loaned directly by a financial institution. It includes credit on purchases by individuals of automobiles and other consumer goods which may be used in part for business purposes.

[b] Personal loans include all installment loans not covered previously made by financial institutions, for consolidation of consumer debt, payment of extraordinary expenses, taxes, or insurance premiums. Some of these loans are used to purchase consumer goods, but are not included in previous categories unless they are secured by the goods purchased.

[c] Single-payment loans are scheduled to be repaid in one payment, held chiefly by commercial banks, and used for short-term needs such as taxes or insurance premiums.

[d] Service credit is the amount owed by individuals for professional services, including doctors, hospitals, and so forth, and for purchases from service industries, including utilities, education, and transportation.

[e] Repair and modernization loans are used to finance major alterations and additions to homes, as well as the purchase of home equipment. The figure relates to the loans held by financial institutions; credit extended by retail outlets is included in "other consumer-goods paper."

[f] Charge accounts are the outstanding balances owed to retail dealers for purchases of consumption goods by individuals.

FIG. 20-1. Short- and intermediate-term consumer credit, Dec. 31, 1953 (in millions of dollars).

familiar charge accounts, including those of retail stores and public utilities, illustrate the first case; installment credit for automobiles and other consumer durables, the second.

The types of charge accounts offered by retailers vary widely and form a part of nonprice competition. When the retailer extends credit, he incurs additional costs, for bookkeeping and billing, for credit investigation, for collection and loss on bad accounts, and finally for the working capital involved. Many business systems have been developed in an effort to reduce these costs, for example, the plate or card to identify customers and record charge transactions for many stores. Since World War II, commercial banks have originated a charge service for small retailers which credits the store's account with its receivables, leaving the bank to bill and collect from charge customers. Despite these gains in efficiency, credit costs remain and are passed on to the consumer in prices. Generally speaking, the retailers' price is the same whether the consumer uses the charge services or not, although discounts for cash payment on major items do exist. But for the most part the consumer must buy from different stores in order to buy goods where the differences in these credit services are reflected in prices.

The convenience of periodic billing by telephone, electricity, and other utility companies has probably never been questioned by consumers who have used coin meters. The latter alternative increases the cost to consumers and is not widely used. Other types of service credit, particularly medical bills, frequently reflect unexpected expenditures and cannot be analyzed separately from the whole problem of medical or health services in the consumption pattern.[3]

Installment sales, chiefly of automobiles, remain as the outstanding component of consumer credit. Automobile paper has increased since 1939 from about 21 per cent of the total consumer credit outstanding to 35 per cent in 1953, as more households have spent more in buying cars. Over the same period, charge accounts have declined from about 20 per cent to 11 per cent of the total, service credit has taken about the same share (6 to 7 per cent), and other consumer-goods paper has declined slightly from 22 per cent to 19 per cent.

Many consumers have insufficient income to pay the full purchase price of major purchases, and fractional payment by installment buying has come to be an accepted part of consumption patterns. It not only provides the consumer with goods and services sooner than he might otherwise acquire them, but in many cases savings accrue as payments are completed.[4] Consumption spending in other areas is of course influenced by the commitment of future income to a schedule of repayments.

The consumer obtains, then, real services, but again these vary among different institutions. Credit for major consumer-goods purchases may be extended by the retailer's installment plan, arranged by the retailer with a financial institution, or extended directly by the lending institution.

[3] See Chaps. 10 and 12 for details on this category of spending.

[4] Cf. Chaps. 12 and 15.

Once the credit contract is signed, it may be held by the retailer or sold by him to other financial institutions. There have developed, therefore, specialists in the various stages of credit, of whom the sales finance companies serving retailers are perhaps the most important. Credit arrangements (and their costs to consumers) can vary in terms of the down payment required, the time period for payments, and the terms of payment. This kind of credit is secured by the commodity purchased, and the consumer must also pay the costs of insurance to protect the seller's equity in the merchandise. The prices of the commodities may reflect part or all of these varying services.

Commercial banks and other financial institutions, including credit unions, pawnbrokers, small loan companies, and savings and loan associations, also make loans which are not secured by the goods purchased. Other forms of collateral, including savings accounts, securities, or life insurance policies, may be used. Such loans are of course paid for with interest, and rates are now subject to regulation in most states.

CONCLUSIONS

Nonprice competition confronts the consumer with a number of alternative purchasing methods, some reflected in price differentials and others not so reflected. Consumers may consider maximizing the utility of the purchasing process itself. But because different services represent, to the seller, different ways of doing business, the consumer must usually purchase in different outlets to obtain more or less service. In the next chapter, we shall investigate the growth of retailing and the type and importance of different kinds of retail outlets.

Questions and Points for Discussion

1. How does nonprice competition complicate the problem of consumers' choice?
2. How can advertising or installment credit increase consumer satisfaction? How can it decrease consumer satisfaction?
3. Why might selected distribution be used for pianos? Why not for magazines?
4. What are the costs, to consumers, of the yearly model change in automobiles? Of resale price maintenance on branded drug items?

References

Borden, Neil H.: *Advertising in Our Economy*, Richard D. Irwin, Inc., Homewood, Ill., 1942.

Chamberlin, E. H.: *The Theory of Monopolistic Competition*, Harvard University Press, Cambridge, Mass., 1931.

Editors of *Fortune Magazine: Why Do People Buy?* McGraw-Hill Book Company, Inc., New York, 1953.

Federal Reserve Bulletin, "Short and Intermediate-Term Consumer Credit," current issues.

Scott, James Dacon: "Selected Distribution Defined and Described," in Malcolm P. McNair and Harry L. Hansen, *Readings in Marketing*, McGraw-Hill Book Company, Inc., New York, 1949.

Wales, Hugh G. (ed.): *Changing Perspectives in Marketing*, University of Illinois Press, Urbana, Ill., 1951.

21. *The Consumer and the Retailer*

In a primitive economy, consumption depends chiefly on household production, and as the economy develops, households become less self-sufficient. Specialization and the division of labor increase total output as workers perform one job rather than many and receive money payments for their work rather than the finished goods which they produce. In a fully developed economy, therefore, "consumption" consists chiefly in expenditures out of money income, with household production forming only the relatively minor item of income in kind. Adam Smith noted that at any given time the limits to specialization were set by the boundaries of the market, and the market is limited by the costs of the exchange process. A fully developed economy requires not only money, or a medium of exchange, but also marketing institutions that specialize in the process of exchange.

The functions of marketing have been variously defined: we may recognize the functions of assembling and storing, transporting, buying and selling and, in connection with these operations, the functions of risk taking and financing. Various marketing specialists have developed, combining these functions in different ways, and retailing, or the sale of finished goods to households, is one specialized marketing institution.

In 1950, personal consumption expenditures in the United States totaled $194 billion, and of this $185 billion, or 95 per cent, was paid to business, chiefly to retailers. Some farmers, manufacturers, and wholesalers sell directly to the consumer, but the roadside vegetable stand, the mill outlet, and the distributor's warehouse are less important to the consumer in the market than are retail stores. In this chapter, we shall summarize briefly some historical developments in marketing and analyze the structure and characteristics of the retail market where consumption expenditures are made. But the student of consumption should remember that other marketing agencies—wholesalers, distributors, transportation companies, brokers, and so on—also influence the consumer, his dealings with retailers, and his purchases of goods and services.

THE DEVELOPMENT OF AMERICAN RETAILING

In the colonial economy, the most important marketing function was foreign trade, handled by the shipping merchants who were concentrated in the seaboard cities. Retailing was a side line of such merchants, who were also interested in shipowning, building, real estate, and banking. These functions began to be separated as the economy grew, and some retail stores appeared out of the agglomeration of shipping merchants' business interests.

The seaboard cities were also markets for the craftsmen of the colonial period—the cobbler, cabinetmaker, blacksmith, tailor, and jeweler—who usually made work to order, so that a sale to a specific customer preceded his production. Some of these craftsmen developed manufacturing operations to reach a larger market, and others began to concentrate on retailing, by particular lines of goods.

The inland areas depended on peddlers and trading posts for the consumer goods to supplement household production. At fairs and trading posts, consumers could exchange farm produce for urban supplies, as well as trade some of their goods and services with each other. The peddler traveled in rural areas between the fairs, offering small consumer goods which were easily transportable.

The use of inland waterways gave rise to river towns and the country merchant, who assembled farm produce, either on commission or on his own account, for sale to the seaboard shippers, who provided consumer goods in return. Again, such merchants eventually specialized, becoming millers or brokers or country shippers or retailers. Their diverse operations were duplicated in small towns and villages throughout the country, however, where the general store performed most of the marketing functions appropriate to rural areas isolated from industrial, commercial, or financial centers.

The general country store was an American phenomenon, with few counterparts in other economies where agricultural development took other lines. The store was the sole supplier for the local agricultural producers, providing goods for both farm and household needs, extending credit from one crop year to the next, exchanging farm produce for town goods, and playing a dominant role in the social development of the community.

Retailing began, then, among merchants who were traders rather than suppliers of services to consumers. In the country store, trading frequently meant barter, where farm produce was exchanged directly for household needs, and the owner's profit reflected his skill not only in judging the quality of eggs and butter acquired from the farmer's wife but also in managing his store. In most stores, trading meant bargaining, and different consumers paid different prices. Sales on credit were common practice, owing partly to the scarcity of currency. Where money was available, it included foreign coins and bank notes of diverse origin, further complicating the trading process. Despite the variety of skills required in retailing, it was easy to enter the field, for little capital was needed and much was advanced by wholesale suppliers. Most stores carried a meager inventory, and the common transactions were sales of staple goods carried in bulk. The retailer's function, as it became distinct from wholesaling or importing or other trading interests, was primarily that of distribution, getting what goods were available from producer to consumer and financing consumption expenditure. The concept of retailing as a service function came later.

NINETEENTH-CENTURY INNOVATIONS

By the time of the Civil War, retailing was commonly an independent business. In the latter part of the nineteenth century, a number of innovations occurred which produced specialized retailing functions, including most of the institutions we recognize today; these changes reflected the widening and deepening of the market, necessary to further specialization, which stemmed from the industrial development of the country. As factories increased, they provided new supplies of goods to be marketed and new marketing areas in the expanding towns and cities. The railroads replaced inland waterways and the latter's influence on urbanization and trade. In the seaboard cities, wholesaling assumed new importance as domestic industry flourished and inland markets grew. Retailing, prior to the twentieth century, specialized by developing new forms of organization and new functions in the marketing process.

Large-scale retailing. The first notable division of labor in retailing was the separation of selling from administration. Further specialization took place in a variety of ways, and large-scale retailing developed in the department store, the mail-order house, and the chain store—the three major forms of handling an increased volume of sales.

The owner-manager of an established store whose sales volume increased hired selling assistants first and then a clerk for bookkeeping.

Since employees could not bargain with customers as effectively or consistently as the single proprietor, the one-price system introduced by R. H. Macy and John Wanamaker was quickly adopted, except in the country general store, which still depended on barter. Retailing in towns or cities was specialized by broad lines—groceries, dry goods, hardware, apothecaries, fancy goods, stationery, furniture, and so on—and when such stores expanded, they provided a much wider selection of goods and considerable departmental organization within their field. New lines were added and inventories were stocked in depth as domestic suppliers expanded and transportation became more dependable and less costly. The sales force was assigned to specific lines of goods, and this division of labor eventually produced the buyer, responsible for stocking a line or a department and supervising its sales.

An expanding volume of sales focused retailers' attention on sources of supply and the possibility of a shorter buying route. The large-volume retailer by-passed the jobber and frequently the wholesaler, to purchase directly from manufacturer or importer. Such a process was encouraged, during the latter part of the century, by the expansion of manufacturers and a growing output of mass-produced, standardized goods. Brand names and trade-marks appeared more frequently, as the producer turned out packaged rather than bulk goods, and appeals were made directly to the consumer by advertising the firm's name and product. Both manufacturers and retailers experimented with the wholesaling function, and the distributive route became shorter in many lines. One logical result of such a process was integration of retailing with the manufacturing or importing function, and the latter part of the nineteenth century found many large city stores owning factories or establishing workshops to turn out millinery, shoes, or furniture, while the chain stores imported foods, owned their coffee roasters or bakeries, or were established by manufacturers who took over the retailing function, particularly for shoes, confectionery, sewing machines, and so on.

Along with the experiments in integration came experiments in widening the sphere of retailing, culminating in the department store on one side and the chain store on the other. The department store offers a combination of lines of goods otherwise stocked by separate specialized retailers. The history of R. H. Macy [1] affords probably the best description of a department store's origin and development. Starting with one or two

[1] Ralph M. Hower, *History of Macy's of New York, 1858–1919*, Harvard University Press, Cambridge, Mass., 1943.

lines, such stores added departments, so that in one store the consumer could buy dry goods and hardware, toys and men's furnishings, and a host of other items otherwise stocked by specialized retail outlets. The department store's volume required, of course, further specialization within the organization and combined the buying and selling skills of many experts with the economies of large-scale operations in centralized accounting, financing, and store management. Leased departments, another innovation of the period, enabled stores to expand into new lines and offer a complete department-store stock without incurring all the risks of ownership. The growing urban centers not only provided enough customers for such a store but, in the latter part of the nineteenth century, the interurban transportation to carry the customers and their purchases.

Another means of increasing sales volume was pioneered in this period as chain stores were introduced. The chain consists of many retail outlets under the same management, and chains began in several distinct fields. The oldest existing chain, the Great Atlantic and Pacific Tea Company founded in 1859, was followed by the Grand Union Company, the Kroger Company, the American Stores Company, and many regional chains in the food field. The F. W. Woolworth chain not only pioneered in the field of multiunit operation but also introduced a wholly new area of retailing, the five-and-ten-cent stores, which are technically known as *variety* stores. It was followed by the McCrory Stores Corporation, S. H. Kress and Company, and S. S. Kresge. Chains were beginning in other fields, including drugs, shoes, tobacco, restaurants, and general merchandise. The chain-store system attained its spectacular development, however, in the early years of the twentieth century.

Finally, the same period saw the beginning of still a third form of large-volume selling, in the development of Sears, Roebuck and Company, Montgomery Ward, and other pioneering firms in the mail-order business.[2] While the department stores and chain stores served the expanding urban markets of the country, the mail-order houses tapped the vast rural market which had been almost completely served by general stores in country towns or villages. It is worth pointing out that, despite the rise of industry during the nineteenth century, over half the country's population was in rural areas as late as 1910, and agricultural production fur-

[2] Much of the discussion of mail-order houses in this chapter is based on the outstanding history of Sears, Roebuck and Company, *Catalogues and Counters*, by Boris Emmet and John E. Jueck, University of Chicago Press, Chicago, 1950.

nished between 10 and 15 per cent of the total national income. Specialization in farming meant that household production dwindled as farmers raised cash crops and purchased their clothing, tools, and household needs. The general store financed these purchases from one crop year to the next and stocked an inventory capable of supplying every need but offering little choice or variety. Prices were high, because the storekeeper both bought and sold on long-term credit, because his turnover was low and his buying power limited, and because transportation charges formed a high proportion of the costs of relatively small purchases. The agrarian movement in the latter part of the nineteenth century symbolizes the farmer's discontent with low farm prices and high prices for the goods he purchased. Much of this discontent crystallized into resentment against the "middlemen," and the mail-order-business promise to sidetrack the middleman had a strong appeal for rural consumers.

Montgomery Ward was established in 1872, and Sears, Roebuck and Company, Spiegel, May, Stern Company, and many other mail-order firms were founded in succeeding years. By 1908, Sears was the largest company in the field, with net sales which had grown from $140,000 in 1891 to $41 million in less than twenty years. The mail-order business offered items and prices that were attractive to farm households, and mail-order catalogues offered choice and variety beyond the resources of a general store. By the turn of the century, Sears alone distributed almost 1 million catalogues, billed as *The Consumer's Guide*, and listing thousands of items in twenty-four merchandise lines. Although sales were for cash, a general guaranty of satisfaction was supplemented by many specific warranties and return privileges.

New retailing policies. Such expansion among retail outlets not only reflected a developing economy: it represented aggressive selling and the introduction of new retail policies. Advertising increased, and definite prices were quoted in newspapers and handbills, thus encouraging the general adoption of the one-price system. Sales for cash only were an innovation, publicized widely by some and imitated sporadically by others. Most stores following this policy claimed lower prices as a result. And price wars or spectacular price reductions occurred in both urban markets and the mail-order field.

Window displays, special sales, and promotions were adopted during the period, and Easter became a commercial season about the turn of the century. Some promotional efforts, notably furniture sales during the summer months, helped reduce the seasonality of retail sales. Sales of factory surpluses, seconds, or rejects were promotional efforts for some stores but also gave rise to bargain-basement departments or to separate retail stores specializing in such merchandise. Aggressive selling tactics emphasized the differences between retail outlets, as department stores urged the customer to buy everything under one roof, specialty shops stressed their complete stocks offering a variety of selection, chains advertised their low prices, and the slogan "Send No Money" identified Sears, Roebuck and the mail-order business.

The concept of service to the customer was the outcome of this competitive process with its differentiation among stores. Furnishings and fixtures in retail outlets were improved, some large stores introduced a marble-palace effect copied from France, and the amenities of light, ventilation, elevators, waiting rooms, and store restaurants were publicized to attract customers. Privileges of returning or exchanging goods were widely extended by many stores, and the retailer began to take more responsibility for the quality of his offerings. Advertising copy included more precise definitions and descriptions of the items. Some retailers began to specify their purchases for factory production. Numerous private brands appeared at the turn of the century, and the battle for pure food and drug laws helped to focus attention on the quality first of drugs and foods and then of other items. As consumers' incomes increased over the period, producers and retailers not only offered higher quality goods but also began to emphasize style and fashion. Stores that followed a strictly cash policy experimented with providing the conveniences of a charge account by introducing various forms of customers' deposits, and all these developments led retailing away from trading or mere distribution into the area of service to the consumer.

TWENTIETH-CENTURY DEVELOPMENTS

While the retail institutions and functions discussed above originated prior to 1900, there is no statistical evidence as to the structure of United States retailing prior to the first Census of Distribution in 1930. Local studies suggested that retailing was expanding rapidly, both in sales volume and number of employees, that the rate of business failure was high owing partly to the ease of entry and partly to poor management, and that the department stores, the chains, and the mail-order houses offered a substantial threat to the "independent" store doing a traditional retailing business. The twentieth century saw the development of this threat, with intense price competition, and organized efforts to regulate retail trade, as well as further innovations in the field.

Large-scale retailing. The department store attained its majority during the early years of the new century. The original idea of providing everything a consumer might purchase was fully developed, as lines were expanded, inventories stocked in depth, and constant attention given to sources of supply. Management and administration assumed new importance as the stores sought to consolidate their gains by centralizing policy, limiting the department buyer's independence, and introducing accounting and control methods which helped the store to analyze its operations. Experiments with merchandise and merchandising continued—automobiles were sold on the fifth floor, hairdressing services on the balcony, groceries on the first, and attempts were made to break into the mail-order business.

The chain-store system expanded rapidly during the first three decades of the century, until in 1929 some 22 per cent of total retail sales were made through such outlets. The relative importance of chains varied, however. Chains accounted for only 14 per cent of lumber and hardware sales but for over 33 per cent of the general merchandise business, including drygoods and variety stores. Most chain-store systems grew by opening new stores rather than by acquiring independent outlets. The chain store became familiar to the consumer, offering standardized goods in a convenient location, with ample stocks at low prices. Some cost savings resulted from the cash-and-carry policy of the chains, but a more important development was the chain-store warehouse, which eliminated wholesalers by purchasing from the manufacturer and distributing to the chain's retail outlets. While most chains functioned only as retailers, some were also important manufacturers, particularly in the confectionery and shoe fields.

Various characteristics of the chain-store system appeared in other areas of retailing. Some independent retailers organized voluntary chains. Others set up cooperative purchasing arrangements to give the small stores some of the buying advantages of the chain. Even the large-volume department stores recognized the gains possible by such arrangements, particularly as some of the general-merchandise chains enlarged their stocks and became department stores. In the late twenties, the mail-order houses opened retail stores, offering the consumer both the advantages of the chain system and the complete inventory of the department store.

The mail-order business continued to expand during the first two decades, particularly after parcel post was introduced in 1912. In order to ship more efficiently, branch plants were opened in various regions, and the first retail store was opened by Montgomery Ward in a mail-order plant, followed by others in rapid succession. Although the financial crisis of 1921 probably precipitated the venture of mail-order firms into retail outlets, such a development was inevitable. The urban population continued to expand as a proportion of the total, and the automobile began to reduce the isolation of the rural market. Mail-order volume dropped, as a percentage of total sales, and by 1929 Ward's alone was opening 25 new stores a week—reminiscent of A. and P.'s effort in 1921, when new stores were opened at the rate of 50 a week.

These three important types of retailing expanded in the face of keen opposition. Independent retailers attacked first the department store, then the mail-order house, and then the chain system.

Part of the opposition to these large-volume retailers stemmed from a fear of monopoly and the evils associated with bigness in every industry. Part of it, however, represented the concern of independent retailers about the intense price competition offered by the chains. Hence, the legislation of the period took two forms, one restraining monopoly or bigness and the other supporting small business.

The Sherman antitrust law of 1890 had little application to retailing, but the provisions of the Federal Trade Commission Act and the Clayton Act of 1914 regulated the buying and advertising practices of large retailers by outlawing price discrimination and certain types of exclusive agency arrangements. Pressure also developed against specific forms of large-volume retailing. Aside from a barrage of local publicity campaigns, such pressure produced abortive movements to legislate the new retail institutions out of existence. Prohibitive taxes on department stores were declared unconstitutional early in the century, and the opposition to the mail-order business culminated in unsuccessful efforts to defeat the parcel post law of 1912.

Antichain-store legislation, chiefly in the form of progressively steeper taxes on each outlet operated by a retailer, developed during the 1920s, attacking both the conventional chains and the new retail stores opened by the mail-order houses. In 1931, the Supreme Court declared that chain stores could legally be classified separately from other retailers for tax purposes and that taxes graduated according to the number of stores were not unconstitutional. Following the decision, many state governments adopted such laws, and, by 1941, some 28 states had enacted 60 bills imposing graduated taxes. Local ordinances were also passed, and the fight against chain stores culminated in Representative Patman's "death-sentence" bill, introduced in Congress in 1938. All this warfare against chains precipitated some objective investigations. The legislator could learn the results of the Federal Trade Commission study of chain stores, 1932 to 1934, a Congressional special committee investigation of chain-store practices, 1935–1936, and the hearings on the Patman bill, in 1940. The death-sentence bill was killed in committee in 1940, and the chain stores became a recognized part of the American retailing structure.

The movement to protect small business culminated in resale price maintenance and the Robinson-Patman Act of 1936, which aimed to prevent price competition and to reduce some of the cost advantages of large retailers, by which they were enabled to lower prices. This type of legislation gained much headway during the depression years, when the conventional retailers suffered heavy losses.

By the end of the thirties, the various forms of retailing organization were fairly well stabilized. In terms of organization, specialized stores still dominated retailing. Department and mail-order firms handled over 10 per cent of total retail volume. The country general stores accounted for about 5 per cent of the total, and the rest was sold by specialized stores, of which the largest group was food stores and the next largest dealers in automobiles and accessories (including filling stations). In terms of ownership, over 73 per cent of all retail sales were made by independent stores, and over 90 per cent of sales in the automobile, hardware, jewelry, and furniture fields. Chain stores sold 90 per cent of all the variety merchandise and dominated retailing of shoes, automobile accessories, groceries, cigars, drugs, and food. Other institutions, including company stores, state liquor stores, house-to-house canvassing, and consumers' cooperatives, were also well established, although none of them accounted for more than 1 per cent of total sales. The cooperative movement developed first in the marketing of agricultural products, and only during the depression did consumers' retail cooperatives become significant. Petroleum associations were next in importance in the cooperative movement, which was characterized by small stores located in rural areas.

New retailing functions. Developments in retailing since the thirties have been less organizational than functional. Profound changes in the economy supported the innovations of supermarkets, shopping centers, discount houses and manufacturers' attempts at direct distribution. One influence was the automobile; the second, the willingness of consumers to take over some of the functions of conventional retailing.

The supermarkets originated in the grocery fields and were largely independently owned at first, although the chains rapidly adopted the techniques.[3] The original appeal of the supermarket, born during depression years, was low prices. These reflected cost savings from self-service and a large volume obtained by combining all food lines in one store. Consumers appreciated the wide variety of offerings and the convenience of one-stop shopping. Self-selection spread to other lines of merchandise, particularly after the war. The supermarkets added nonfood lines, including liquor, drugs, household hardware, and even shoes and clothing accessories. Many variety chains adopted self-service and self-selection for items more commonly appearing in department stores and specialty shops.

Supermarkets were first opened in abandoned warehouses or other low-cost locations and offered abundant parking space. The advantages to consumers in driving to one place for a majority of their purchases supported the growth of the shopping center, a postwar development reflecting the drift of families to the suburb and the decline of big city stores. The shopping center varies from the block of stores put up in a new housing development to the huge areas located on through ways, designed to attract consumers from neighboring suburban areas. Shopping centers include department stores, which decentralized by opening branches since the war, and chain-store outlets as well as specialty shops. The centers offer the consumer new services of convenience—shopping at night, playgrounds for children, restaurants, theaters, banking facilities, and service establishments such as dry cleaners and beauty parlors.

These developments have meant that consumers now perform many of the functions of the retailers of 1870. Self-selection has replaced service in many lines, the consumer's liquid assets replace the retailer's working capital when cash sales outweigh credit, and the homeowner's automobile provides physical transportation for the goods. The habit of buying food once a week or less reflects not only the increase in household mechanical refrigeration but also a shift of storage functions from retailers to consumers. The rise of the discount house reflects other retailing functions which have been dropped or shifted to the consumer.

[3] The Super Market Institute defines its subject as a completely departmentalized food store with at least the grocery department full self-service and with a minimum sales volume of $500,000 a year. In 1939, sales in supermarkets accounted for 9 per cent of the total sales of grocery and combination stores; in 1948, for 25 per cent. In 1939, the average sales per store were smaller for the chain outlets, but, by 1948, chain-store supermarkets had an average sales volume exceeding that of the independents.

Discount houses owe their existence to resale price maintenance and to manufacturers' advertising of list prices, particularly in the field of home appliances, radios, and TV. Because consumers are familiar with established retail prices, discount houses can advertise prices below list, or at a discount. Although cut prices have appeared sporadically in automobiles, drugs and liquor and during local price wars, the term *discount house* refers to an established way of doing business. Few reliable statistics exist on the volume of sales of such outlets, and their selling practices vary widely. For the most part, discount houses offer the consumer considerable price reductions at the expense of a wide selection of goods, a convenient store location or shopping comfort, installation or maintenance service, credit terms, return privileges, or assistance in selection. In such cases, the consumer forgoes one or more services to gain a lower price made possible by the retailer's cost saving. Other discount houses, however, offer all the usual shopping services and rely on a large volume of sales to lower their operating cost margin so that prices can be cut. For example, Masters, Inc., a firm operating discount houses in three cities, offers conventional retailing services and reports on a volume of almost $20 million annually and operating costs of only 11.20 per cent, whereas an average markup of 35 to 50 per cent is provided by the list prices for appliances and hardware.

Discounting has two major implications for retailing, one in the field of resale price maintenance, and the other in the extent to which retailing functions can be further realigned. The department store, the chain store, the mail-order house, and the supermarket have all preceded the discount-house innovation of obtaining lower prices by increasing sales volume. Since all these institutions have found a place in the retailing structure, presumably the discount house can be accommodated as well, increasing the choices available to consumers by providing still another type of outlet with another combination of retailing functions. Retailers whose higher costs and prices reflect, not inefficient management, but additional services will presumably survive, depending on the consumer demand for these services.

To a considerable extent, however, the discount house depends upon conventional retailers and their services, particularly those of display and demonstration, information, and persuasion. Both department stores and specialty shops incur costs in offering a wide selection of merchandise, an inventory stocked in depth, and the assistance of knowledgeable sales personnel. These costs represent a loss when customers shop the conventional stores and subsequently purchase from discount houses. Such costs are particularly important when new products are introduced and the retailer has to "sell" the consumer in order to create demand. Early sales of color television were confined to the small conventional retailer, who incurred the costs of salesmanship; sales of the newly introduced room air conditioners dropped during 1953, despite widespread price cutting, because of an absence of selling effort. The discount house also benefits from the repair and maintenance service offered by conventional retailers, whose service departments are generally justified on the grounds of increasing product sales. In some cases, costs of these services are now borne by the manufacturer or the consumer himself. When the combination of manufacturer's advertising and neighborhood persuasion convinces the consumer to buy a clock radio, no great need exists for a retail margin high enough to cover sales expense. Where repair services can be performed more efficiently by specialists, retailers and consumers alike benefit.

But the realignment of all these functions among manufacturers, retailers of different types, and consumers can take place logically only when retailers are permitted to offer varying combinations of services at varying prices. And, under present resale-price-maintenance legislation, this freedom is not available to many retailers. Department stores complain that manufacturers do not police the discount houses for illegal price cutting. The discount houses benefit from the services offered by the higher-price stores, which are not free to change their method of operation and lower their prices in violation of fair-trade contracts. And to the extent that the discount house is able to gain a large volume because other stores are offering the services of consumer information and persuasion, the costs of retailing are not distributed to those consumers who benefit. The consumer cannot, therefore, have a realistic choice between discount houses and retailers offering other services until price-maintenance legislation is revised, providing for consistent application to all stores, or until it is abolished.

The reader will recognize other innovations in distribution which, for lack of space, cannot be detailed here. Among these may be mentioned coin-vending machines, direct selling by means of clubs (most important in the book field), door-to-door canvassing, and direct mail distribution from manufacturers. All these innovations provide a wide variety of retailing services and in many cases have shortened the distributive route, with consequent cost savings to the consumer. None of the innovations described in this chapter has swept the retailing field, and in view of the variety of consumer preferences and tastes in our economy it is doubtful if one form of retailing could ever come to monopolize the field. Experiment will undoubtedly continue and different ways of performing the basic retailing functions be provided. But the functions must be performed, and neither consumer nor manufacturer can realistically hope to achieve the cost savings of specialists in the retail field.

THE STRUCTURE OF PRESENT-DAY RETAILING

In 1948 some 1,800,000 retail stores were enumerated by the Census of Distribution, or 1 store for every 83 people in the United States. Total sales during 1948 amounted to $130 billion. About 14 per cent of the labor force worked in retail stores, either as employees or as owner-managers. In terms of national-income concepts, retailing in 1948 provided $300 billion, or 13 per cent, of the total national income. Over half this sum was paid out in the form of wages, but $9 billion represented income from unincorporated enterprises, and about $3 billion was income to corporations.

These statistics demonstrate that retailing plays a major part in our economy and that its development reflects substantial economic changes. A well-known thesis of economic development states that, as a country's national income increases, more of it will originate in distribution and service industries. Certainly retailing, as one such industry, has accounted for a larger share of the national income in the United States over the years, and retail workers form an increasing proportion of the total labor force. But the structure of retailing, rather than its absolute size, makes a peculiar contribution to the economy. In 1948, some 67,000 retail stores, or about 4 per cent of the total, made over 42 per cent of the total sales, with an annual volume each of over $300,000. But there were almost 400,000 stores each of which sold less than $10,000 annually, and all these accounted for less than 2 per cent of total sales.

Retailing is typically, therefore, a field of small enterprises. Further evidence of this phenomenon is to be found in the high proportion of unincorporated retail businesses. Some 88 per cent of all retail firms are unincorporated. Or, stated differently, only 12 per cent of all retail firms are corporations, the average sales of which are almost ten times those of unincorporated retail outlets. It is also the case that one out of five proprietors of unincorporated enterprises are retailers—the highest proportion outside of agriculture. These facts reflect the ease of entry into retailing. And that more skill and experience are needed in retailing is apparent from the high rate of business turnover in the field. Thus, of 400,000 new businesses established in 1948, 143,000 were retail stores, and, of 9,000 business failures in 1949, over 4,000 were retailers.

Our interest throughout this chapter has been on the retailing institutions that have developed a large volume of sales. This for two reasons: first, the innovations we have described have markedly changed the character of retailing as a marketing process, and, second, large-volume stores sell most of what consumers buy. Efficiencies of scale in retailing have led to lower prices and to a variation in services for the consumer in the market. Many small stores exist only by paying less than competitive returns to the owner who provides both labor and capital.

We may summarize the contemporary picture of retailing by analyzing the share of the market serviced by the different types of retailers we have distinguished. In 1948, mail-order houses accounted for 1 per cent of total sales, stores operating two or three units accounted for 7 per cent, larger chain stores operating four or more units for 22 per cent, and single-unit retail stores for the remaining 70 per cent of total sales. These proportions have changed only fractionally since 1929, and as we have noted, innovations since then have been in a realignment of marketing functions rather than in organization.

The costs of retailing to the consumer depend on two factors, efficiency and the services demanded by the consumer. We have already seen that the retailer's costs (and hence margins and prices) depend on the services he performs for the customer, as well as on his volume of sales. Sales volume has increased, in the types of retailing we have described, by providing some services at the expense of others. The variety of selection offered in a shopping center is a service to the consumer; the time and transportation required to get there are a cost to the consumer. The ease and speed of self-selection in a supermarket are a service to the busy housewife with a full schedule; the lack of a friendly salesclerk to choose a good roast or a ripe melon is a cost to the new housekeeper seeking advice. More important, however, is the point made earlier—different combinations of services must be offered by different retail stores, for the consumer cannot specify both the type of service and the product he wishes to buy with it.

There are inevitable costs in distributing goods to the consumer. Some of the functions of distribution may be most efficiently performed by manufacturers, some by wholesalers or brokers, some by retailers, and some by consumers. But as long as we value the freedom of consumer's choice, we must recognize that it conflicts with any pure concept of efficiency. If consumers are to have the opportunity of choosing different kinds of marketing institutions, the costs of supporting those various institutions must be paid. As consumers, we can look for lower retailing costs, first, from an increase in the efficiency of individual stores, second, from the services we can forego to gain other services or the efficiencies of scale due to large volume, and, finally, from the extent to which we are willing to accept standardized distribution methods, without the variety of offerings by a variety of retailing institutions. The American economy of mass production depends on standardized goods and a homogeneous consumption pattern. It may be, therefore, that distribution methods will also become an area of standardization and interchangeable parts, or it may be that the tastes and preferences involved in consumer purchasing methods will remain heterogeneous, requiring a varied distribution system to satisfy them.

Questions and Points for Discussion

1. Trace the influence of changing transportation methods on the development of retailing.
2. Explain the significant innovations of the mail-order house, department store, and chain store. What effect did each of these have on consumption patterns?
3. What functions of nineteenth-century retailing are now shared with manufacturers?
4. Look up the Census of Distribution data on retail sales by kind of business. How does this compare with data in the National Income Supplement on consumption expenditures by categories?
5. Discuss the relative importance, in your marketing area, of shopping centers, department stores, chain stores, specialized stores, and discount houses.

References

Clewett, Richard M. (ed.): *Marketing Channels*, Richard D. Irwin, Inc., Homewood, Ill., 1954, chaps. 1–3.

Emmett, Boris, and John E. Jueck: *Catalogues and Counters*, University of Chicago Press, Chicago, 1950.

Hower, Ralph M.: *History of Macy's of New York, 1858–1919*, Harvard University Press, Cambridge, Mass., 1943.

Lewis, W. A.: "Competition in Retail Trade," *Economica*, vol. 12, pp. 202–234, 1945.

U.S. Bureau of the Census: *United States Census of Business*, 1948, and current edition.

Williamson, Harold F.: *The Growth of the American Economy*, Prentice-Hall, Inc., New York, 1951, especially chaps. 3, 12, 15, 26, 40, and 45.

22. *The Consumer Information Problem*

We characterize our economy as one where choice is relatively free, and one where consumer choice is decisive. It is the choices of consumers which have shaped consumption patterns and led to the development of products and marketing institutions. Consumer choice, channeled back to producers, determines how the resources of an economy are used. Total consumer demand creates a large part of national income, and the implications of consumer choice reach far into the economy—to give a retailer his best August sales figures, an independent chemical firm the hope of survival, a bus conductor new employment in a factory, or an investor new stock to buy in an expanding concern.

Choices depend, of course, on a knowledge of the alternatives. Hence, the pattern of consumer choice is shaped not only by the alternatives which exist but also by the information available to the consumer about these alternatives. One objective of this chapter is to examine the sources of available information which influence consumer choices.

Aside from setting limits to consumer choice, the information available to consumers influences competition. Competition exists only where the seller faces potential buyers who have other opportunities for purchase. Competition requires, thus, not only the presence of other sellers but also knowledge, on the buyers' part, that such sellers exist. An informed buyer knows what sellers offer commodities which satisfy his demand, how these offerings compare in quality, and how they compare in price. Such buyers are needed to make for effective competition among sellers in the market. The second objective of this chapter, therefore, is to look at the information available to the consumer in his role as catalyst of competition—is he the kind of informed buyer who makes for effective competition?

INFORMATION AND EFFICIENCY

This volume has focused upon the decision-making process in the household and upon the allocation of income among lines of expenditures in households. The economy is affected by the *aggregate* choices of consumers, the 4 million households which buy automobiles, the 2,000 households which patronize a local supermarket, and the consumption spending of all the households taken together. The choice problem remains, however, one for the individual consuming unit, and this individual unit cannot, acting independently, acquire in an efficient manner the information which it needs to make choices. This is the consumer information problem. The question then arises: "Why does this problem exist? Why cannot the consuming unit acting alone acquire sufficient information for choosing readily and efficiently?"

We can think of two possible approaches for the consumer seeking to inform himself. Either he must become sufficiently expert to understand what a product is, and hence predict the satisfaction it will give him, or he must test the product and find out, through experience, what utility it has.

The first approach—to understand the nature of a product and predict its quality in performance—becomes increasingly difficult with increasingly complex production and products. To analyze the structure of plastic dishes, synthetic textiles, molded plywood furniture, lemonade mix, or shampoo, for example, would require proficiency in more fields of technical knowledge, as well as more laboratory equipment, than any one consumer could possess. Appliances, of course, have long been a mystery to the typical household—hence, the trend to more automatic and foolproof products appears in everything from cameras to cars, precisely because the consumer cannot understand the workings of the machinery with which he is surrounded. So this approach is in reality closed to the typical consuming unit.

The second approach, that of testing, is beyond the means of the individual consumer. The only way he can obtain products for testing is to buy them. Hence, his firsthand knowledge of a product comes with his experience of using it after purchase. If consumers are truly to satisfy their preferences, this type of information is essential. The consumer's taste tells him whether or not to buy a new brand of olives, but only after he has eaten them. The consumer chooses a mattress in terms of comfort, among other things, but the final information on this point comes from several nights' sleep on the mattress in question. Only after the family has experienced the offerings and tribulations of television can it be accurately located on a preference map. Experience with a specific item not only shapes the consumer's preferences and tastes but allows him to choose in these terms, and any other type of information runs a poor second to the facts of experience in use.

The inability to get experience, or to make tests prior to consuming, is obviously important in certain areas, particularly where purchases are infrequently made. If the reaction to olives is one of distaste, the consumer can alter his food-buying pattern at small cost. But where there is no experience from successive purchases, such a reaction can be extremely costly. Houses and home furnishings are examples of such products, and consumption expenditures which involve time as well as money are typically made without the benefit of firsthand experience. The summer at camp, the years at college, the trip abroad, the Broadway first night, or the vacation drive to Yosemite cannot, by their very nature, be repeated. Thus, this approach, too, is closed to the typical consumer, especially for the expensive "one-shot" purchases.

The large firm which buys large quantities for use in production can afford to test the performance quality of its purchases and to become an informed buyer of certain items. If sheet metal or potash or cotton thread is a large part of his total cost, sufficient saving can result from informed buying to pay for testing and quality-control services. Furthermore, the firm may be a sufficiently large buyer to specify its needs to the supplier. But even the large firm does not test all its purchases—only those where cost savings are probable. Comparable savings to the household consumer do not exist, because no item looms large enough in his budget to warrant a costly test of its performance qualities.

Finally, these obstacles to the consumer's efforts to inform himself are multiplied by the fact that the individual household buys a multitude of different goods and services in many different markets. Purchasing, or even using the things bought, is not the only function in life for the household. *There is, therefore, not enough time to learn of all the possible alternatives before forming a preference or making a choice.* And the consumer cannot, unaided, become an informed buyer aware of the potential competition in every market situation.

This, then, is the nature of the consumer information problem: the typical consuming unit lacks the time and resources to become adequately informed with respect to the potentialities and the limitations of all the alternatives. Hence, the consumer turns to outside sources of information. Some of his knowledge comes from organized sources, some information is thrust upon consumers, and much more becomes available to the consumer who seeks it.

INFORMATION AND PREFERENCES

In previous chapters, we have discussed the influences of taste and preference on consumption patterns, and we have noted the social influences or pressures which form consumer tastes and preferences. Rather than leave this topic, as some economists have suggested, to the sociologists and psychologists, we prefer to consider some of its implications in the economic sphere.

We have already touched upon advertising and its costs and effects on habits and tastes. Sellers play a major role in informing consumers about the existing alternatives by advertising their products and by providing displays, labeling, and explanation or persuasion. But consumers themselves provide information which may support or destroy this sellers' effort. Buyers and users of a product provide a better display medium than any which the seller can devise, and information from a consumer carries the priceless ingredient of a report on experience in use, which can be far more persuasive than a seller's appeal. The information provided by consumers not only demonstrates many possible alternatives but to some extent dictates the choice among alternatives. It is probably safe to say that most preferences exist without a consideration of all the alternatives because society has already decided among them. This is certainly true of broad categories of expenditure such as housing, food, clothing, household operation, and so on, where we eat and wear and use what we do without thought of the possible alternatives.

The information problem becomes acute, we believe, when new preferences are formed and consumer habits are changed. *The constant stream of new and altered goods and services makes the problem of considering available alternatives a continuous occupation.* When new products are introduced, advertising can play a valuable and informative role, calling attention to new products and new developments in familiar products. Sellers must tell what the product is and how it is used and suggest its purchase as a specific alternative. In a technologically minded society like ours, innovations are news, worth reporting for their own sake, and so information is provided by the amount of publicity given to the development. Again we find, however, that consumers themselves provide the decisive information on the new products. Those consumers who are innovators publicize their latest experiments, and information about the new product or service spreads rapidly. Statistics on sales of new products illustrate the point that information originating with consumers is a necessary supplement to sellers' advertising. Nylon hose, detergents, dacron shirts, and television were introduced with sizable advertising campaigns, but major sales increases occurred as satisfied consumers spread the word. It appears, therefore, that some relatively few purchasers have a disproportionate effect on total consumption preferences, and this phenomenon bears further investigation.

In societies with sharp class divisions, the formation of taste has been accepted as one of the functions of the upper classes, and consumer preferences were thought to trickle downward from the aristocracy to the masses. In the American economy, new products are not designed for the select wealthy few whose tastes and preferences will determine what reproductions become available en masse. Instead, innovations are aimed at an enormous market of middle- or upper-income consumers. Yet, within this market, there seem to exist a select few whose tastes and preferences trickle outward, and these *innovating consumers* may be called the aristocracy of today's taste development. What makes them innovate, why they are accepted as arbiters of taste, where they are located, and how their functions are performed remain the newest of unanswered questions about consumption patterns.

INFORMATION FOR COMPETITION

In order to be an informed buyer whose choices enable competition to function, the consumer must be able to compare the offerings of different sellers. A full comparison requires a knowledge of the various characteristics of the product, of its availability, of its price, and of the terms of sale. Information on all these points is normally proffered by the seller, but the consumer can turn to other sources for amplification.

Guides to buying, or product and price information which helps consumers choose, are of two kinds. A general explanation of quality, performance, and characteristics in a given field of consumption enables the consumer to evaluate more fully the specific products from which he chooses. Recommended buys of a specific product or brand, on the other hand, provide the consumer with a choice he may adopt.

The first type of information is offered by government agencies, trade associations, some university and research organizations, and radio, newspaper, and other publicity articles. The consumer can learn about cuts of meat, the meaning of thread count in sheets, how to launder synthetic textiles, and the various characteristics of electric irons from such sources. Many such offerings include information useful not only in making consumption expenditures but also in using the goods and services purchased —information useful in the home-management branch of consumption, where the good or service selected is *used* to provide consumers with utility or satisfaction.

Of particular note are the publications of the Federal government, which provide an abundance of information to the consumer. The Bureau of Human Nutrition and Home Economics publishes a wide range of bulletins on many different products, as do other branches of the Department of Agriculture. Standards for purchasing established by many governmental agencies provide information on products ranging from galvanized-iron pails to roofing materials. The Department of Health, Education and Welfare, the Office of Education, the Fish and Wildlife Service, and many other agencies publish regular or intermittent bulletins dealing with specific products or services.

Similar general information about goods or services and their uses provides much of the content of so-called women's magazines and of more specialized periodicals given over to housing, or landscaping, or hobbies of one kind or another. All these guides to consumption purchases resemble, in a sense, the columns of literary and theatrical reviews, which have a much longer history but the same major objectives—that of describing the products available as a guide to consumer choice. Such information requires more or less evaluation on the part of the individual consumer. In some cases, he is better able to look for certain signs of quality—well-marbled beef, a tag indicating the percentage of wool content or inspection by the underwriters, whether bureau drawers are joined by glue or screws, and whether a pitcher will pour sirup without dripping. For the most part, he is expected to evaluate the various characteristics of a product *in terms of his own set of preferences or value system* and to use the information in making his own choice.

Other buying guides go further toward recommending a choice for the consumer, and typical of these are the bulletins of Consumers Union and Consumers' Research. These two organizations are estimated to reach an audience of about 5 per cent of all spending units, with a buying power of about $15 billion annually.[1] The two organizations confine their reports, however, to relatively few products, which are revised periodically. Electrical appliances of all kinds, household equipment from glue to can openers, drugs and cosmetics, staple food products such as canned goods, cake mixes, and processed cheese, and some textile products including sheets, men's socks, and nylon hosiery are typical, with more information given on automobiles than on any other single article. The agencies buy products for testing and analyze the structure and performance of individual brands. On the basis of objective, technical investigation, the products are then rated not acceptable, acceptable, or best buy. While it is possible, therefore, for the consumer to accept the choice of such a rating, it is also possible for him to use the information in determining his own choice.

The integrity of the product-rating agencies has been attacked on many varied grounds, but always unsuccessfully. As important as the honesty or competence of these agencies in providing consumer information is the ability of the consumer to assess the kind of information they provide. The ratings cannot be accepted blindly. Because of small-scale organization, neither Consumers Union nor Consumers' Research can test every product immediately after every revision, and the rating of last year's dishwasher or detergent may not apply to this year's product. This complicates the problem for new products—where consumers are seeking information and producers are redesigning and developing to "get the bugs out." A different problem is the variation in quality or performance between individual items. The consumer who thinks in terms of standardized mass production and interchangeable parts sometimes forgets that one jar of X's mayonnaise can be different in color, texture, or taste from another jar of the same product. As a result of factory variations, the individual consumer's experience with a product may differ materially from the rating. Finally, there are characteristics of consumption expenditure not considered in the product rating. The availability and quality of repair and maintenance service for appliances can be a major consideration, as can the availability of retail outlets handling the recommended brands. It should be noted, however, that neither Consumers' Research nor Consumers Union suggest that it is their role to solve the problem of consumer's choice. They simply sell a service—the service of providing guides to buying.

[1] E. R. Been and J. S. Ewing, "Business Appraises Consumer Testing Agencies," *Harvard Business Review*, March–April, 1954.

Aside from product ratings, these publications include articles giving the more general type of information discussed previously—what to look for in home construction and in buying eggs and fish, how to apply insecticides and artificial respiration, and so on.

It seems clear that such general, factual discussion of products and prices most fully meets the needs of consumers for information relevant to their choices. No system of rating can correspond to every schedule of consumer preference, although it may be a valuable guide to choice. Furthermore, there is at present no organization with sufficient resources to test and rate even a majority of consumer goods and services, aside from revising such ratings in the light of product changes. But it seems likely that most consumers could profit from a more thorough search of the general information available with respect to most categories of purchases. The following check list suggests a number of specific queries, any or all of which may seem more important to one expenditure than to another:

1. Product analysis:
   a. What is the product (or service); of what is it made; how is it to be used?
   b. How is the product designed; is it of pleasing appearance or easy to use? This should include an appraisal of containers or packages for some goods, of handles and corners on others.
   c. What is the efficiency of the product in performance; how well does it do its job?
   d. How durable is it; how long does it last?
   e. What are the dangers or inconveniences in its use?
2. Supplements to the product:
   a. What other goods or services does the product require, and must these be purchased, or are they available to the consumer? This should include a consideration of storage space.
   b. Will the consumer need training or skill to use the product?
   c. What home maintenance and care does the product require; what skilled repair services will it need?
3. Expenditure analysis:
   a. What does the product cost, and does the price vary by retail outlets?
   b. What are the charges for credit, or various means of payment?
   c. Are there installation or accessory charges?
   d. What are the supplementary expenditures for goods or services used with the product?

e. Will the product have any resale or scrap value?

f. What does the expenditure mean in terms of the consumer's income, or that part of it available for the purchase? Does the expenditure mean commitment of future income?

g. What recourse does the consumer have if he is dissatisfied? Can the product be returned or the purchase price refunded?

If complete and reliable answers to all these questions are found, the consumer will probably be fully informed with respect to his choice problem. His purchase will represent a valid preference among alternatives, and a valid part of the competitive process. Hence, it is likely that the consumer will benefit more from information programs making such facts available than from unreliable advertising claims or oversimplified grading programs.

Questions and Points for Discussion

1. Why is consumer information necessary to competition?
2. What influences the choices of an uninformed buyer?
3. Should government assume more responsibility for providing consumer information? How?
4. Look up the information provided by Consumers Union or Consumers' Research on a product which is important to your consumption pattern. What other factors would you consider in making a purchase?
5. Of the questions on the check list on page 417, which would you try to answer before buying (*a*) an automobile; (*b*) a house, (*c*) an electric ironer; (*d*) a permanent wave; (*e*) a pair of shoes; (*f*) a new brand of canned corn?
6. Where would you find information to answer the questions chosen in the problem above?

References

Annual Cumulative Bulletin, Consumers' Research, Inc., Washington, N.J., 1955.

Coles, Jessie V.: *Standards and Labels for Consumers' Goods,* The Ronald Press Company, New York, 1949.

Consumers' Research Bulletin, Consumers' Research, Inc., Washington, N.J., recent issues.

Consumers Union of the United States, Inc.: *Consumer Reports Buying Guide*, current issue.

Newsletter, Miami University, Council on Consumer Information, Oxford, Ohio, recent issues.

Reid, Margaret G.: *Consumers and the Market*, F. S. Crofts & Co., New York, 1938, chap. 22.

Scitovsky, Tibor: *Welfare and Competition*, Richard D. Irwin, Inc., Homewood, Ill., 1951, chaps. 2, 28.

23. Government Programs and the Consumer

Our final view of the consumer in the market must include some analysis of the influence of government upon this market. Government policies affect consumer incomes, the products and prices involved in consumption, and the choices made by consumers.

GOVERNMENT AND CONSUMER INCOMES

Government programs have affected consumer incomes directly by providing social insurance benefits, direct relief to the indigent, and military pensions and allowances. Such payments amounted in 1953 to about $13 billion, or 5 per cent of total personal income. Less direct, but with considerable influence on consumer incomes, are government policies establishing minimum wages in many industries and income payments in agriculture.

Social insurance benefits enable most income earners in our economy to provide for future income. To the consumer, the Old Age and Survivor's Insurance program and the Railroad Retirement Act resemble private insurance, since contributions are made out of current earnings to provide for future benefits to the contributor at his retirement or to his survivors. Because the Federal government administers the plan, however, the resemblance to private insurance is superficial. Income payments are not based on contributions made, and the rules for determining either OASI taxes or OASI benefits can be and have been changed to meet changing situations. Most notable, the consumer has no choice with respect to the program: if he is "covered" by the law, his contributions are mandatory. As of March, 1954, some 46 million workers were insured. Monthly benefits of $3 billion were being paid to about 4 million families. About three-fourths of these received payments to retired workers, and the rest were surviving dependents.

The Federal government has also provided for insurance against unemployment, which enables consumer income to be maintained when production declines. Neither an individual worker, a firm, or even a private insurance company can insure against the risk of unemployment, since widespread unemployment means an economic decline affecting business in general.

The Social Security Act of 1935 imposed a tax on employers which could be offset by tax payments to the state for unemployment insurance, and employment security programs were inaugurated by all the states shortly thereafter. The contributions from employers are used to pay benefits to maintain the incomes of unemployed workers under certain broad rules laid down in the Social Security Act. Administered by the several states, unemployment compensation programs vary in their coverage, the amount of payroll taxes paid by employers, the eligibility requirements for benefits, and the amount of benefits. In 1953, some 37 million workers were covered. The programs paid about $1 billion to 1 million beneficiaries (weekly average). The average weekly payment of $23.58 compensated for about 43 million weeks of unemployment.

Current payments to veterans consist chiefly of compensation and pensions to veterans and their dependents, as the readjustment benefits provided by the so-called G.I. Bill of Rights declined rapidly after their postwar peak. Such payments provided income, in 1951, to some 3 million persons.

Income received from these programs represents past contributions in some form by the participants involved. The programs of direct relief, administered now by state and local agencies, differ from social insurance and military benefits by providing income on the sole test of need.

Direct relief, or public assistance, goes to support dependent children, older people, and the blind and totally disabled who are in need of income. In determining need, local agencies consider the income and resources of the consumers involved, but the standards for minimum incomes vary considerably by communities. About 2½ million old people received assistance; some 2 million consumers, including children and parents, received aid to dependent children; and about ½ million received income under programs of general assistance or aid to the blind or disabled. Some $2.4 billion was paid to consumers on this basis in 1953, much of the money being furnished by Federal grants-in-aid to the local governments involved.

All these payments, the social insurance benefits, payments under the veterans' programs, and public assistance, are called *transfer* payments. While the funds are paid out by government, they come from taxes which transfer income from the taxpayers to the income recipients. Income, earned from current production, is transferred to people who have not supplied any current productive services. Total transfer payments are shown in detail in Table 23-1.

Table 23-1. Amount and Number of Recipients, Government Transfer Payments, 1953

	Amount (000,000 omitted)	Number (000 omitted)
Total transfer payments	$13,801	
Federal government:		
Old Age and Survivor's Insurance benefits	2,979	1,419
State unemployment insurance benefits	954	812.1 *
Railroad retirement insurance benefits	515	527
Railroad unemployment insurance benefits	46	40
Federal civilian pensions	395	282
Government life insurance benefits	718	
Military pension, disability, and retirement payments	2,720	1,273.2
Adjusted compensation benefits *	1	
Mustering-out and terminal-leave payments	352	
Readjustment program benefits	499	
Other	481	
State and local governments:		
Government pensions	560	
Cash sickness compensation	50	
Special types of public assistance	2,207	4,928
General assistance	150	
Other	158	

* Average weekly number.

While these figures represent direct government payments to some consumers, other consumer income is supported and maintained by government action. Chief of these are the minimum-wage laws of state and Federal governments.

The Fair Labor Standards Act provides, for workers engaged in interstate commerce, an hourly wage of at least $0.75, and payment of at least time and one-half for work over 40 hours a week. Supplementing this Federal regulation are the minimum-wage laws of the several states. Thirty such laws provide for minimum wages for women and minors, and seven extend the standards to men. Most states appoint commissions to establish minimum rates in different occupations. Another labor law in force in many states requires employers to pay wages at regular intervals, usually every two weeks, and forbids wage deductions to pay fines or debts incurred by the workers.

Although workers' incomes depend on employment opportunities as well as prevailing wage rates, the minimum-wage laws have helped to maintain a high level of consumer income. The laws providing for regular wage payments mean that workers have greater freedom and choice in disposing of their incomes. It is estimated that about 21 million workers are protected by minimum-wage laws.

The various farm support programs represent another approach to the maintenance of consumer incomes. The money cost of Federal programs concerned with supporting farm prices and incomes has varied substantially from year to year, from $324 million in 1938 to $2,268 million in 1946, for example. All these expenditures by the Federal government were not received by farmers, however; administration costs are included in these sums, and the full price increase in many support programs has not always been passed along to farmers. But it is clear that large sums have been paid out to support farm incomes over the years.

These farm support programs are criticized for a variety of reasons: (1) their continuous cost to the Federal government; (2) the fact that the Federal government must often accumulate surplus stocks by supporting farm prices above free market levels; (3) the conflict between the widely held beliefs concerning the merits of a free-enterprise system and governmental intervention and production controls in agriculture. But government programs to support and raise farm incomes continue in effect, and the majority of farmers seem to approve of them in one form or another. Hence, it would appear that such programs will be with us for some time to come.

Low farm incomes in agriculture take two principal forms. The incomes of commercial farmers fall drastically when farm prices go to pieces as they did in the 1930s and as they have shown a tendency to do since 1953. These farm price gyrations are not responsible for the low incomes received by subsistence, or part-time, farmers, who are relatively poor because they operate less efficiently, with productive units of an inadequate size. The various price and income support programs of the past have been directed toward the income problems of commercial farmers. The very small producer operating an inadequately sized unit is the forgotten man in our national economy. We have no specific income support programs designed to fit the needs of these farm people.

The government policies influencing income have a common objective of reducing poverty, or of supporting needy consumers at some kind of minimum level. Government has only recently assumed the obligation of maintaining consumer income, and much dispute and confusion surround both this goal and methods of reaching it. The definition of poverty, or need, remains relative, and the amount of assistance which government can provide is not unlimited. Some observers deplore the loss of rugged individualism, thrift, and independence they see in social security measures. Others applaud the built-in stability given to total consumer income by these measures and the sense of security enjoyed by individuals and families.

Perhaps the greatest confusion in these programs arises from the ambiguity of their objectives. The student of consumption can see consumer income as the problem common to all forms of social insurance, relief, and minimum-wage or price laws. But these regulations are not unified in an explicit policy of establishing a floor for family income. Relief for certain groups—the blind, dependent children, the disabled—has always been more socially acceptable than a program of general relief to all whose incomes are below some standard. Payments to veterans involve emotional reactions to war service and sacrifice; minimum-wage and price laws involve questions of production and employment. A clear-cut statement is still lacking as to the extent of poverty itself which will be tolerated in our economy.

GOVERNMENT REGULATIONS IN THE MARKET

Government influences consumption out of income by taxing consumers and by regulating producers and sellers. Although taxes obviously reduce consumer income, we can also think of taxes as paying for various goods and services provided by government. We have already seen that most consumers are required to provide for Old Age and Survivor's Insurance. In the following chapter, we shall examine other goods and services provided by government, turning now to the regulations which affect the consumer in the market.

Food and drugs. Consumers who spend $65 billion per year for food make choices from products which have been processed, inspected, packaged, labeled, and advertised under local, state, and Federal regulations of wide scope. At the local level, health and sanitary regulations control the conditions on the premises and the health and cleanliness of employees. Local ordinances range from requiring employees to have the X-ray test for tuberculosis to forbidding dogs or the use of tobacco in food stores. Local and state regulations provide for periodic inspection or checking of the weights and measures used, and official standards for these rest with the Federal Bureau of Standards in the Department of Commerce. Sanitary regulations also apply to many food-processing industries, with meat and milk especially regulated and inspected to prevent the spread of disease.

Standards applying to canned and processed foods are promulgated by the Pure Food and Drug Administration and the Department of Agriculture. To quote the FDA, these standards provide for the most part "for accurate labeling by name so that the consumer can make his own choice . . . and that [products of different identity] can be marketed under properly descriptive names." [1] While such regulations prohibit the sale of foods not meeting United States standards, their chief effect is to keep such products "safe, pure, and truthfully labelled." Standards of identity list the ingredients which must be present in the food in proper proportions and allow other ingredients to be added at the producer's option. Other standards specify the amount of food to be contained in any package.

For meat moving in interstate trade, the Meat Inspection Act provides continuous inspection of slaughtering, and meat cuts are stamped to show government grades for certain meats, as well as inspection. Finally, the consumer buying food is protected from false and misleading advertising by the Federal Trade Commission, which requires, for example, that the exact proportions of ingredients be listed in advertising.

Sanitary and health regulations are a vital problem in regard to drugs, cosmetics, and therapeutic devices, for which similar standards have been devised by the Food and Drug Administration, and unwarranted advertising claims outlawed by the FTC. Both agencies rely heavily on the cooperation of producers and sellers, in establishing standards, agreeing on fair claims, and abiding by the regulations which exist. With rapid advances in the development of "wonder drugs" and special ingredients,

[1] *Annual Report,* Food and Drug Administration, 1951.

the cooperation of producers is essential. Normally, food or drug additives are thoroughly tested by chemical producers or food processors before seeking the approval of the FDA, and the number of sellers operating in ignorance or willful violation of the law is small. The FDA does, however, seize food or drugs which are contaminated or toxic, and the FTC can issue cease and desist orders or instigate civil penalty suits against violators of its orders.

Housing. The most important regulations covering housing are local ordinances on zoning and building codes. By segregating residential, commercial, and industrial areas, zoning laws provide the privacy, light, fresh air, and freedom from noise or odors which local residents consider necessary to their homes. Acreage or street-frontage requirements go further to prevent crowded houses or dangerous traffic. Many communities rely on planning boards or commissions to lay out the future development of their localities, so as to provide roads, schools, parks, and homes in proper proportion.

Building codes and inspection rest upon the powers of the local government to protect the health and safety of the inhabitants. Sanitary regulations prescribe specifications for plumbing and refuse-disposal equipment, and fire hazards are outlawed by regulations and inspection of wiring and electrical equipment. Beyond these, the building code may specify the kinds of materials and dimensions for certain structures, provisions for ventilation and fire escapes, and other characteristics of housing.

The Federal Housing Administration has also had a considerable impact on housing through the inspection and valuation programs which are part of its home-finance procedure. The agency insures home mortgages which meet certain specifications, and both the financial characteristics of the mortgage and the technical features of construction are subject to close investigation. Recently, the agency revised its technical work to improve the assurance that consumers get what they are paying for in a newly built or existing home.

Other consumer goods. Governmental regulation of apparel goods has to do chiefly with proper labeling of fiber content and is administered by the Federal Trade Commission. Three specific acts provide special areas of responsibility, the Wool Products Labeling Act, the Fur Products Labeling Act, and the Flammable Fabrics Act. The last prohibits the sale of fabrics or garments whose synthetic-fiber content is dangerously flammable; the other two specify information which must be included on a tag or label. The agency inspects products and their manufacture to ensure compliance with these measures.

The Federal Trade Commission's general responsibility to prevent unfair competition and deceptive acts and practices has affected almost all kinds of consumer goods and services. Firms have been forbidden to represent themselves as colleges or Federal placement bureaus, forbidden to claim a false therapeutic benefit from hair tonic, cigarettes, or patent medicines, ordered to disclose actual prices or interest rates in various time-payment plans, and dissuaded from disparaging or imitating a competitor's trade name or product.

The Commission makes some general investigations, but most of its actions result from complaints, usually made by competitive firms who are at a disadvantage. After investigation, the Commission may issue a cease and desist order against the unfair-trade practice, or it may determine that no unfair practice exists. Where the order is violated, the Commission may instigate a civil suit, but most of its orders do not reach a court review. Much of the Commission's work is carried on in cooperation with industry, particularly through the Trade Practices Conferences. Here a group of trade representatives meets with officials to determine the rules of fair-trade practices within the industry. The Commission sometimes recognizes these rules as legally binding, and frequently the industry members agree to adhere, voluntarily, to other rules. In recent years, many of these conferences have reduced the number of conflicting and misleading claims in advertising.

Services. Consumption expenditures on services include many areas where government regulations protect the consumer and affect his choice. Table 23-2 shows total consumption expenditures, in 1954, on various types of services, roughly classified by the kind of regulation which exists.

The whole field of public utilities is generally subject to government regulation. Both the services offered and the rates charged by firms supplying electricity, gas, water, transportation, and communication are regulated in the public interest. Government grants such companies a monopoly within a given area to gain the economies of large-scale operation and supervises these operations to be sure that consumers gain from the economies of scale. Regulation of interstate transportation is the responsibility of the Interstate Commerce Commission; state and local commissions grant franchises to local transportation firms, approve their routes and services, and regulate the fares charged. Similar supervision is given by local, state,

Table 23-2. Consumption Expenditures on Personal Services
(In millions of dollars)

Unregulated services:	
Repair and cleaning	$9,846
Personal care	1,175
Domestic service	3,051
Entertainment	5,518
Regulated and/or government-operated:	
Public utilities:	
Electricity	2,692
Gas	1,550
Water	715
Telephone, telegraph	2,640
Intercity transportation	1,189
Local transportation	2,171
Personal business:	
Financial services	5,886
Debt interest	2,817
Legal services	1,004
Medical care and death expense:	
Professional services	4,420
Hospitals and sanitariums	2,602
Medical care and hospital insurance	887
Funeral and burial expense	1,168
Education, religious and welfare activities	5,440

SOURCE: U.S. Department of Commerce, *National Income Supplement to the Survey of Current Business*, 1954, Table 30.

or Federal government agencies to the telephone and telegraph companies. The Federal Communications Commission exercises control over radio and television stations as well. Regulating agencies supervise most of the firms supplying household utilities such as water and power.

Aside from regulating business in this field, government also operates many utilities. Municipal waterworks, bus systems, and electricity supply departments are typical examples. Thus, of approximately 4,000 electric utility supply systems in 1950, over 1,500, producing one-fifth of the total kilowatt-hours, were publicly owned, most of them by municipal authorities. A most significant aspect of government-operated services has been the work of the Rural Electrification Administration and the Tennessee Valley Authority in making electricity available to more consumers.

The field of medical and health expenditures is again closely supervised by government. The work of the Food and Drug Administration has already been mentioned. Physicians, nurses, and pharmacists are licensed by local and state authority, which provides the assurance that standards of training have been met in these professions. Again, many health services are provided by governments, including the inspection and supervisory activities of local public health administrators, and clinics and hospitals operated by municipal, county, or state authority. Thus, while the expenditures in Table 23-2 refer to privately supported hospitals, such institutions provided less than one-third of all the beds available in the country, while state and local hospitals provided over half. Further activities of government in this field are urged, less to protect consumers from existing services than to extend the range of health services to more consumers.

Finally, the expenditures made by consumers in the area of personal business go to institutions which are closely supervised by government in the interests of the economy as a whole. Fees for legal services are paid to experts who are licensed after state examination to be sure that professional standards are met. Some of the interest paid on debt is determined by small-loan laws existing in many states.

All public savings institutions are licensed and examined by some government agency, to provide the protection of conservative business practices for consumers who accumulate deposits or borrow money. Banks, insurance companies, building and loan funds, small-loan companies, and other agencies operate under detailed rules governing the amount of capital and the way investments are made. The Securities and Exchange Commission requires that complete information on stocks and bonds be available to the consumer-investor. Beyond this, the Federal government provides other means of saving, through United States savings bonds and the postal savings plan.

Perhaps the most widespread protection of consumer savings is given by the Federal Deposit Insurance Corporation and the Federal Savings and Loan Insurance Corporation, inaugurated during the thirties. These two agencies provide for the insurance of individual deposits in the event of bank failure. Like many other agencies, however, their work in preventing consumer loss has been highly effective.

CONCLUSIONS

Although government regulations have a far-reaching influence on consumer goods and services, no single policy of consumer protection guides all agencies. Many laws, including that establishing the Federal Trade Commission and the local building codes, were passed to protect business more than the consumer. Few actions by government regulatory agencies stem from consumer complaints, and while technical, legal, and business experts serve on the staffs of these agencies, there are few consumer representatives. For the most part, government regulations serve to provide information to the consumer and to prohibit substandard goods and services—with the minimum standards variously interpreted.

As the previous chapter suggested, such a restricted sphere of government action probably serves best to enhance the consumer's freedom of choice. But government regulations, like consumer choice, are also hampered by the facts of technological change and limited resources. None of the agencies mentioned in this chapter have sufficient funds or manpower to carry out all their responsibilities. New products and advertising campaigns cannot be immediately reviewed by the FDA and FTC. Changes in materials and consumer wants have outmoded many local building codes. Savings and loan companies and insurance companies are pressing for revision of some of the rules governing their investments. The extent to which government should supply services, in such fields as public utilities and health, is hotly debated. In the following chapter, we shall examine in more detail the government services to consumers.

The service of protection to consumers—by maintaining consumer income and regulating products, prices, and trade practices—seems to suffer most from a lack of recognized objective and from insufficient resources. There are few opportunities for consumers to obtain protective action from any of the regulatory agencies—largely because their work is technical and consumers lack the knowledge and resources to prepare a formal complaint. One obvious remedy would be to have experts representing the ultimate consumer serve in such agencies—but such consumer divisions have been formed in the past, in agencies like NRA or OPA, with little effect on the programs dealing with business. A more useful approach, therefore, might be to consolidate the interests of any agency by declaring consumer protection to be the chief objective and by deriving programs to meet this goal.

The next great weakness—a lack of resources for all consumer protection programs—stems again from the failure to recognize the common objective of these programs. Funds are not appropriated, in our governmental scheme, for causes which lack a formulated goal and a powerful backing. While it is true that most regulatory agencies find that violators number a small minority in any field, much more could be done for the cooperating firms in any case with more manpower and more equipment. With the limited resources currently available, government protection has done a limited job of preventing the more flagrant abuses and providing somewhat more complete information to the consumer. With an increase in resources, the performance of this task could be greatly improved.

Questions and Points for Discussion

1. Since 1930, how have transfer payments changed as a proportion of total personal income?
2. What future changes do you expect in the number of consumers receiving government income support? In the amount of income received?
3. Explain how social insurance resembles and differs from private insurance.
4. Argue for and against the establishment of an executive agency, to be known as the Department of Consumer Interest, with an executive officer of cabinet rank.
5. In the past year's report of the Federal Trade Commission, analyze the number of cases handled by the type of violation. Explain how consumers were affected.
6. Give a report on one food standard established by the Food and Drug Administration. How does this affect consumption?
7. Get a copy of your local building code. Do the rules allow construction of housing below the minimum described in the Bureau of Labor Statistics standards discussed in Chapter 13?

References

Annual Report, Federal Housing Administration.
Annual Report, Federal Trade Commission.
Annual Report, Food and Drug Administration, 1951, and most recent issue.
Burns, Eveline: *The American Social Security System*, Houghton Mifflin Company, Boston, 1949.
Social Security Bulletin, current issues.

PART FIVE

The Consumer outside the Market

To this point, the focus of the inquiry has been on the decision making of individual consuming units. We have presented a theoretical explanation of consumer behavior, a record of consumer expenditure behavior, and an analysis of consumer action in the market—but all have focused on the individual consuming unit as the decision-making unit. Even where the policies and actions of business firms and government have been considered, they have been discussed from the point of view of their impact on the decision making of individual consuming units. And this is as it should be, for the dominant decision-making unit on the consumption side in our society is the individual consuming unit or household.

But we do make collective decisions, often through government but not in all cases, which have a bearing on consumption. Choice decisions with respect to the kinds and quantities of goods and services consumed are often made collectively (e.g., police protection, public school systems). And many more decisions of a collective type are made with reference to rules of conduct or regulations which have an influence on the behavior of individual consuming units (e.g., licensing of physicians, resale price maintenance, Federal milk-marketing orders). Part V, therefore, will be devoted to these group aspects of consumption. Chapter 24 will be concerned exclusively with collective consumption—its extent and its nature. Chapter 25 will lastly ask, and provide some answers to, the question: "What kind of economic policy do consumers want?"

24. *Collective Consumption*

The first point to be settled in this discussion of collective consumption is: "What do we mean by group, or collective, consumption?" [1] To answer this question, we must go back to the concept of consumption developed in Chapter 1. It will be recalled that the consumption process includes three parts: (1) the selection of a particular set of goods and services; (2) the "using up" of that set of goods and services; (3) the production of satisfaction or utility, for the consumer, as goods and services are used up. And, with a few exceptions, the exposition to this point has assumed that this tripartite process takes place within individual consuming units.

But all three phases of the consumption process can and do take place among groups. A group of consuming units can select a specific combination of goods and services (e.g., make choice decisions). A group of consuming units can use up a given combination of goods and services (e.g., a public park, police service). And each consuming unit in the group presumably receives some satisfaction (not necessarily the same amount of satisfaction) from the using up of the goods and services involved. The concept of group, or collective, consumption is thus made clear; it refers to the consumption process where a group of consuming units is involved rather than a single unit.

THE NATURE AND FORM OF COLLECTIVE CONSUMPTION

Collective consumption always occurs and can only occur through some form of group organization. Some form of group organization is required (1) to provide a vehicle through which choice decisions may be made jointly and (2) to regulate the using up of goods and services, hence the distribution of satisfaction among the consuming units involved. In other words, if collective consumption is to take place, a means must be found for converting the views of the individual consuming units involved into

[1] The terms *group* and *collective* will be used interchangeably in this chapter.

group decisions with respect to the kinds and quantities of goods and services to be consumed and for distributing among the individual consuming units involved the satisfaction-producing qualities of the goods and services selected.

Collective consumption occurs under two major types of organization, (1) governments and (2) voluntary associations. The principal distinction between the two is that the authority of organized governments rests in part at least on the use of police powers, whereas the authority of voluntary associations rests entirely on persuasion. We shall now inquire into the nature of collective consumption under these two organizational forms.

Organized government. It will be recognized at once that forms of governmental organization vary widely within the United States. We have organized governments at three levels—Federal, state, and local—and governmental forms vary widely at each of these levels. Thus, in using the term *organized government*, it is clear that we do not have in mind some specific form of governmental organization. On the contrary, we recognize that governmental organization assumes many and varied forms. And the kinds and quantities of goods and services consumed collectively vary with the level and form of governmental organization.

Numerous and varied types of collective consumption occur under the Federal government of the United States. The citizenry of this organized government have, for example, made decisions which result in collective consumption in whole or in part in such areas as:

1. Military protection (i.e., a policing service for the nation)
2. Provision of roads and waterways
3. Medical service for veterans
4. Care of the needy (e.g., aged, unemployed)
5. Educational services

The central governments of countries less democratic in form and fact (e.g., Iran and Spain) probably are involved in fewer areas of collective consumption and to a lesser degree than the Federal government of the United States, whereas the central governments of countries more inclined toward the welfare state (e.g., the United Kingdom and Norway) are probably involved in more areas of collective consumption and to a greater degree than the Federal government of the United States.

Collective consumption under state governments in the United States is common in the following areas:

1. Roads
2. Education

3. Public welfare
4. Care of criminals and the mentally deficient
5. Parks

The quality and quantity of resources employed to provide the facilities and services consumed collectively vary greatly among states. Some states build many and good roads, other states build few and poor ones, and so with educational services, mental institutions, and the care of the needy.[2] In other words, the citizenry of some states *choose* to devote such resources as are necessary to provide high-quality and adequate road and educational systems for group use, and others do not.

Individuals consume collectively a wide range of services and facilities under local governments. The following areas are commonly involved:

1. Education
2. Parks and playgrounds
3. Public health services
4. Streets and traffic controls
5. Water and sewer systems
6. Police protection
7. Fire protection

More services are consumed collectively under some local governments (e.g., a library system, a zoo, an orchestra), but these are less common. And again the quality of services and facilities varies greatly among localities. It is generally accepted in the United States that the services and facilities listed above will be consumed collectively, but the decision makers (i.e., voters, elected representatives, and administrators) exhibit a wide range of choices with respect to the quality and quantity of resources employed to provide these services.

Voluntary associations. Some form of group organization is indispensable to collective consumption, but it need not take the form of government. The collective consumption of goods and services takes place through many and varied voluntary associations. Church congregations are an important case in point. It is common practice for a congregation to decide under the rule and laws of the church involved to build a new church building, or purchase an organ, or hire a custodian, and use up the facilities or service as a group to yield satisfaction to the individual members. And this, of course, is exactly what we mean by group, or col-

[2] For a good discussion of these variations by states see Alvin H. Hansen and Harvey S. Perloff, *State and Local Finance in the National Economy*, W. W. Norton & Company, New York, 1944, chaps. 2, 5–7.

lective, consumption. Going beyond individual church congregations, it is also common for religious sects to establish schools, colleges, and social clubs for the joint use of their members. Again this is group consumption: choice decisions are involved, the using up of facilities is involved, and the creation of satisfaction is involved.

Religious organizations are one of the more important forms of non-governmental organizations through which collective consumption occurs, but by no means the only form. A parent-teacher association providing a public school with a public-address system is an illustration of collective consumption. A group of businessmen coming together on a voluntary basis to form, construct, and maintain a golf club with all the necessary facilities is an illustration of collective consumption. A neighborhood group coming together to build an ice-skating rink or a basketball court on a vacant lot is also an illustration of collective consumption. Our social structure is permeated with such forms of voluntary group consumption, ranging in magnitude from a city-wide parochial school system to two neighbors going together to purchase and use a power lawn mower.

On some occasions, the group consumption activities of voluntary associations assume a more formal and binding form. The consumption of insurance protection through a mutual insurance company will be formalized by contracts between the group organization and participating consuming units, stating the rights and obligations of all parties concerned. The same is true in the case of the establishment of a community road or alley designed for joint use. In other words, it is not uncommon for voluntary associations to require participating consumer units to enter into a contract with the organization, stating in detail the responsibilities and obligations of all parties. Thus, voluntary associations sometimes make use of the law, and indirectly the police power of the state, to effect their purposes.

We have not mentioned consumer purchasing cooperatives in connection with collective consumption, since this form of group action would seem not to satisfy the first criterion of collective consumption. *Decision making with respect to the choice of goods and services remains with the individual consuming unit purchasing through a cooperative.* The cooperative grocery or drygoods store is a form of business organization; it is concerned with producing form, or place or time utility. The fact that group action is involved, and group action by consuming units, does not mean that the action involved is consumption. The activities of a consumer cooperative are productive acts, hence not collective consumption by our definition.

THE EXTENT OF COLLECTIVE CONSUMPTION IN THE UNITED STATES

In measuring the extent of collective consumption in the United States, we shall follow the classification laid down in the previous section and present measures of collective consumption undertaken, first, through *organized governments* and, second, through *voluntary associations*. And our criteria for including a group activity under collective consumption, or excluding it, stems directly from our definition of collective consumption. An activity is included if (1) the choice of goods or services, or the choice of resources used to provide the goods and services, is made jointly by participants of the group; (2) the goods and services provided are "used up" by the participants of the group; and (3) satisfaction is provided, or produced, for all participants of the group or for that part of the group designated in the original decision making. Thus, for example, the provision and use of a public school system clearly fall under the heading of collective consumption. On the other hand, the provision and use of a playground for all the children in a community by some one public-spirited citizen do not fall under the heading of collective consumption, since only one person is involved in the decision making. In sum, a group activity must involve all three phases of the consumption process to be included under collective consumption.

Less clear with respect to proper classification, but more important from the viewpoint of the over-all magnitude of collective consumption in the United States, is the item national defense. Is this collective consumption or something else? In terms of the *purpose* of national defense, the activity may be logically classed as collective consumption, but specific defense activities would seem to be distantly removed from conventional consumption activities. The construction of a battle cruiser or an army camp looks a good deal more like a production activity than a consumption one.

The question just posed with respect to the proper classification of defense or military activities suggests an important aspect of all group consumption. Group, or collective, consumption very often comes into existence where the item to be consumed cannot be purchased at the local shopping center—where the good or service is not readily divisible. Howard R. Bowen makes the following useful observations on this point: [3]

Economic goods are of two types: individual goods and social goods. The two types are similar in that each serves the needs of human beings and each is produced only through the use of scarce resources. They differ, however, in the character of their demand. Individual goods are characterized by *divisibility*. They can be divided into small units over which particular persons can be given exclusive possession (e.g., carrots, sewing machines, barber services). Such goods are amenable to individual demand and to free consumer choice. The amount consumed by any individual can be adjusted to his particular tastes. Social goods, on the other hand, are not divisible into units that can be the unique possession of individuals. Rather, they tend to become part of the general environment—available to all persons within that environment (e.g., education, protection against foreign enemies, beautification of the landscape, flood control). Consequently, these goods cannot easily be sold to individual consumers and the quantities available to different individuals cannot be adjusted according to their respective tastes. The amount of the good must be set by a single decision applicable jointly to all persons. Social goods, therefore, are subject to collective or political rather than individual demand.

Social goods, produced to satisfy a collective demand and consumed collectively, tend to be produced for an occasion or situation and according to the specifications of that occasion or situation. Thus, production activities and consumption activities are commonly intertwined at the group level; in fact, the magnitude of a group consumption activity is often measured by the production efforts involved. In other words, instead of production being carried on by individual firms and consumption by individual households, these activities are commonly merged at the group level so that they become two different sides of the same thing. But where a group activity grows out of the *want* for some type of good or service by a group of consuming units and the decision to acquire that type of good or service is made jointly, we shall define that group activity to be collective consumption.

Collective consumption through government. The expenditures made by governments to provide consuming units with satisfaction-producing services and facilities is our best, and only practical, measure of collective consumption through government. The expenditure data in Table 24-1, classified by type of service or facility provided consumers by govern-

[3] "The Interpretation of Voting in the Allocation of Economic Resources," *Quarterly Journal of Economics*, vol. 58, p. 27, November, 1943.

Table 24-1. Combined Federal, State, and Local Expenditures, Classified as Collective Consumption, Doubtful, and Other, United States, for Selected Years

(In millions of dollars)

Item	1890	1929	1946	1948
Collective consumption items:				
Transportation and communications	$ 92.0	$ 2,115.5	$ 2,426	$ 3,414
Housing services	.....	....	137	19
Educational services	146.5	2,458.9	3,324	4,621
Social security, welfare, and health	68.5	*	4,493	5,759
Regulation and protection	57.6	846.1	1,170	1,517
Veterans' benefits	112.7	559.1	4,573	7,205
Subtotal	$477.3	$ 5,979.6	$16,123	$22,535
Doubtful items:				
National defense	$ 51.6	$ 681.8	$44,950	$10,085
International relations and foreign assistance	1.7	13.5	998	4,779
General government	81.9	808.4	1,642	2,285
Subtotal	$135.2	$ 1,503.7	$47,590	$17,149
Other items:				
Interest on debt	$ 82.8	$ 1,479.6	$ 5,207	$ 5,706
Resource development	3.8	198.8	1,226	1,944
Miscellaneous and unclassified	147.7	411.5	658	1,674
Subtotal	$234.3	$ 2,089.9	$ 7,091	$ 9,324
Total expenditures for all purposes at all levels of government	$846.7	$10,741.6 †	$70,804	$49,008

* Data not available by this category for 1929.

† Unexplained discrepancy between total and subtotals.

SOURCE: R. A. Musgrave and J. M. Culbertson, "The Growth of Public Expenditures in the United States, 1890–1948," *National Tax Journal*, June, 1953, appendix Table IV.

ments *at all levels,* thus yield a quantitative description of the growth and range of collective consumption through organized governments. The expenditure data in the table are listed under three principal headings: "Collective consumption items," "Doubtful items," and "Other items." The "collective consumption" grouping includes those services and facilities which we tend conventionally to associate with consumption (e.g., the use of educational facilities, housing services). The "doubtful" grouping includes items which conventionally are not deemed as consumption, but the services provided by the items in this grouping are in the larger sense of the term consumed (e.g., the service of national defense). The "other" grouping includes items which grow out of group decisions but which are not concerned with the provision of consumer satisfaction, except perhaps in some indirect way.

The student can make his decision with respect to the appropriateness of including the doubtful items in the aggregate of collective consumption expenditures. But he should observe that, if they are not included, collective consumption expenditures of all governments approximate one-half of the total expenditures of all governments in the nonwar years of 1890, 1929, and 1948. If they are included, collective consumption expenditures of all governments run in the neighborhood of three-quarters of the total expenditures of all governments for the years 1890, 1929, and 1948. In other words, depending upon the criteria of classification used, one-half to three-quarters of the activities of all governments in the United States represent collective consumption.

Looking at Table 24-1 in more detail, we observe some interesting developments. Expenditures for transportation and communications and education increased some 55 per cent and 40 per cent per year, respectively, between 1890 and 1929, but only about 3 per cent and 4 per cent per year, respectively, between 1929 and 1948. The rate of expenditure increase is decidedly lower in the second period. On the other hand, for several items, the rapid rate of increase in the period 1890 to 1929 is sustained or becomes more rapid in the second period. The percentage increases per year are as shown in the accompanying table. All along the line, collective consumption expenditures have increased, but the rates of increase differ importantly.

	1890–1929	*1929–1948*
Veterans' benefits.......	10%	63%
National defense........	31	73
International relations and foreign assistance	18	1753

More perspective on the growth and extent of collective consumption expenditures of governments at all levels is gained from Table 24-2, where the collective consumption expenditures of governments at all levels are expressed as a percentage of the Net National Product. It will be observed that the percentage of the Net National Product consumed collectively through organized governments is relatively small—the total of all items

Table 24-2. *Collective Consumption at All Levels of Government as a Percentage of Net National Product, United States, Selected Years*

Item	1890	1929	1948
Nondoubtful items..........	4.3	6.3	9.3
Doubtful items..............	1.2	1.6	7.1
Total....................	5.5	7.9	16.4
Total expenditures for all purposes at all levels of government.............	7.7	11.0	20.3

(nondoubtful and doubtful) rising to 16 per cent in 1948. Thus, the proportion of goods and services consumed collectively through organized governments in peacetime has at no time reached one-fifth of the total, *but since* 1890 *it has been an increasing proportion.*

Collective consumption expenditures by level of government are given in Table 24-3 for the year 1952. Thus, not only the extent of collective consumption by category of consumption may be viewed in the table, but also the points or levels of government where the various areas of collective consumption occur. For example, we observe that all expenditures for, hence consumption of, postal service occur at the Federal level; on the other hand, practically all expenditures for fire and police protection occur at the local level. Further, we observe that expenditure data by category of consumption are given in more detail in Table 24-3 than in Table 24-1. In Table 24-3, expenditure information is given for the various welfare services (e.g., health, hospitals, care of the aged) provided at different levels of government, rather than one over-all figure. In short, Table 24-3 provides a descriptive picture—a snapshot—of all collective consumption taking place through governments in the United States in 1952.

It should be recognized at this point, however, that the expenditure data in Table 24-3 cannot be compared directly with Table 24-1. The accounting of expenditures is done differently in the two tables. We say that the expenditure data in Table 24-3 are on a gross basis; this means that the expenditures noted in Table 24-3 represent the *total* expenditures made in providing the service or facility *regardless of the source of revenue.*

Table 24-3. *Gross Expenditures of Federal, State, and Local Governments, Classified as Collective Consumption, Doubtful, and Other, United States, 1952*

(In millions of dollars)

	Federal	State	Local	Total
Collective consumption items:				
Postal service	$ 2,612	......	......	$ 2,612
Roads and highways	64	$ 2,556	$ 2,094	4,714
Other transportation	713	43	189	945
Housing	106	4	765	875
Education	1,280	1,494	6,824	9,598
Public welfare	42	1,410	1,378	2,830
Health	299	164	276	739
Hospitals	715	968	777	2,460
Sanitation	......	......	992	992
Unemployment compensation	49	971	2	1,022
Old Age and Survivor's Insurance	1,983	......	......	1,983
Police	141	106	833	1,080
Fire protection	......	......	586	586
Veterans' benefits	3,501	142	......	3,643 *
Subtotal	$11,505	$ 7,858	$14,716	$34,079
Doubtful items:				
National defense	$39,990	......	......	$39,990
International relations and foreign assistance	5,189	......	......	5,189
General government	604	$ 361	$ 832	1,797
Subtotal	$45,783	$ 361	$ 832	$46,976
Other items:				
Interest on debt	$ 5,853	$ 144	$ 408	$ 6,405
Resource development †	4,245	539	237	5,021
Miscellaneous and unclassified	3,183	1,164	1,535	5,882
Subtotal	$13,281	$ 1,847	$ 2,180	$17,308
Total gross expenditures of government	$70,569	$10,066	$17,728	$98,363

* This item includes primarily pensions for veterans and life insurance claims; other expenditures specifically for veterans by all levels of government included under other functions are (in millions) $1,394 under education, $31 under public welfare, $151 under health, and $651 under hospitals, or $5,870 in all.

† Includes agriculture and atomic energy program.

SOURCE: Adapted from materials compiled by Arthur M. Borak, University of Minnesota, for use in courses in public finance.

The expenditure item for postal service, for example, represents the total outlay of funds in the provision of this service; in this case, revenues, out of which these expenditures were paid, were raised primarily from the sale of stamps and only incidentally from taxes. In other words, the total amount, or gross amount, of funds expended in the provision of services or facilities is reported in Table 24-3.

The expenditure data of Table 24-1 are *net* in a peculiar sense. The expenditures reported are those expenditures made out of revenues from taxation plus whatever budget deficits may have been involved. Thus, the transportation and communications item at the Federal level in Table 24-1 includes only the deficit incurred by the Postal Department in the years in question—nothing for the expenditures paid out of receipts from the sale of stamps (the major source of revenue). In other words, the collective consumption expenditures reported in Table 24-1 include only those expenditures paid out of tax revenues or borrowings that were expected to be repaid from tax revenues.

Traditionally, expenditures of government have been accounted for and reported on the basis used in Table 24-1. But, since 1951, the reporting of government expenditures has shifted to a gross basis. And this latter method of accounting is more realistic for our purposes. We want measures of collective consumption undertaken through government regardless of the means of financing, and this the gross expenditure data provide. Our definition of collective consumption does not turn on the method of financing; a wide variety of methods or combinations of methods of financing could be employed—all forms of taxation, all forms of borrowing, payments in accordance with benefits received, and so on. There are many and difficult problems to be resolved in this field of public finance, but we shall leave them to students of public finance. Our concern here is to obtain an appropriate measure of collective consumption undertaken through governments. Hence, the totals and subtotals of Table 24-3 yield useful measures of the kinds and quantities of services and facilities consumed collectively at different levels of government.

Collective consumption through voluntary associations. We cannot present a comprehensive quantitative description of the collective consumption taking place through voluntary associations. Expenditure data are not compiled in a form which will permit such an aggregation. But it should prove useful to present a listing of the classes of voluntary associations involved in collective consumption, with estimates of magnitudes where possible.

Such a list would include the following:

1. Informal neighborhood groups, consuming such limited services and facilities as a boundary fence, or a power snow remover, or a car pool

2. Community service groups such as a parent-teacher association, providing playground equipment for the use of neighborhood children, or the Rotarians or Kiwanians, sponsoring a pageant or local music group

3. Religious groups, providing churches, schools, and summer camps

4. Fraternal organizations, providing care for the aged, hospital facilities, and burial services

5. Formal clubs, operating a living facility or golf club, or sponsoring an activities program for young people

6. Business groups such as mutual insurance companies and credit unions

Perhaps the consumption activities of every type of voluntary association are not included in the above six classes, but not many would seem to be left out. Again we find groups providing services or facilities for their members in those areas where the individual consumer cannot drop into a store and purchase a ready-made, handy item. Groups commonly form around, and collective consumption commonly occurs in, those services or facilities which must be developed or produced for the occasion, but which require the use of resources beyond the usual control of a single consuming unit.

We get one measure of religious services consumed collectively from the breakdown of national income data. Expenditures by religious bodies to meet the current operating costs of churches, plus estimated depreciation charges, are given in Table 24-4. Collective consumption for this type of service amounts to somewhat less than 1 per cent of the Net National Product. Several important consumption activities which take place through religious groups are, however, not included in the estimates presented in Table 24-4. Secular educational services provided by religious groups are not included; neither are such items as food costs of "potluck" suppers or summer-camp activities. A complete accounting of the goods, services, and facilities consumed collectively through religious groups might well be double the estimates presented in Table 24-4.

More comprehensive and detailed estimates of collective consumption occurring through voluntary associations must wait on empirical studies that focus on such groups. To date, most income-expenditure studies have implicitly assumed that the household is the key decision-making unit in consumption and have ignored the decision-making processes of groups.

Table 24-4. *Expenditures by Religious Bodies in the Operation of Churches, United States, Selected Years*

Item	1929	1940	1950	1952
Expenditures, in millions of dollars..................	$912	$662	$1,125	$1,296
Expenditures as a per cent of Net National Product..	0.9	0.7	0.4	0.4

HOW COLLECTIVE DECISIONS ARE MADE

Numerous analyses have been developed which purport to "explain" how group decisions are made, although none concentrate on the decision problem of consumer groups. Duncan Black, for example, develops a rationale of group decision making in terms of *preferences* which is comparable in many respects to the indifference approach for the single individual or consuming unit.[4] Black assumes that each member of a group can and does rank motions (or choices) in a definite order of preference. Where each member's preference curve for different motions (or choices) is single-peaked, or $\bigwedge$-shaped, the group or committee can always arrive at a unique solution (i.e., pass one motion, choose one particular item). This follows from the fact that, where each member of a group ranks each motion, or item, among which a choice must be made in a way such that one motion, or item, is preferred to all others (i.e., the preference curve of the individual is single-peaked), one motion, or item, must always get at least a simple majority of favorable votes, or choices.[5] But this explanation does not seem to "explain" very much; it seems to tell us little more than if each member of a committee or group has a $\bigwedge$-shaped preference schedule, and somehow we know the preference schedule for each member of the group, then we can predict which motion will win or which item will be selected by the group.

Using very different analytical methods, involving very different modes

[4] "On the Rationale of Group Decision-making," *Journal of Political Economy*, February, 1948, pp. 23–24.

[5] For proof of this generalization see Black, *op. cit.*, pp. 26–29.

of thought, John R. Commons spent a lifetime studying collective action.[6] It was the thesis of Commons that this is an age of collective action; he held that most of the more important decisions in the twentieth century are made by groups. Thus, it was his method to study the historical development of groups, the decision-making process of those groups, and the types of control effected by those groups over individual decision making. And to the group processes concerned with the control of individual action he gave the name *institutions*. But useful as the Commons type of analysis may be in providing a perspective of social processes and in understanding the decision making of *some particular* group, it does not lead to generalizations with respect to the nature of group decision making. We do not get from his analyses a clear picture of how group decisions are made.

Since a generally accepted general theory of group decision making does not seem to exist, and since, further, little or no work has been done in the way of adapting existing theories to the problem of choice decisions by consumer groups, we shall not try to present a general theory of group decision making in the consumption area. We shall, however, make some general, but incomplete,[7] observations which may provide some insights into the nature of the decision-making processes involved.

Within organized governments. In a certain broad sense, individuals help make group decisions when they vote for candidates in political elections. At least they can register their protest against past decisions of an elected representative by voting for his opponent. But decisions on specific issues are not generally made by the electorate at large, constitutional amendments and referendums being the principal exceptions. Decisions on issues leading to the enactment of laws, which require the compliance of all members of society, are customarily made by elected representatives in legislatures. True, the decisions of legislatures are influ-

[6] See *The Economics of Collective Action*, The Macmillan Company, New York, 1950, or his more penetrating and difficult volume *Institutional Economics*, The Macmillan Company, New York, 1934.

[7] Many points near and dear to the hearts of political theorists are not touched upon in the following section, but perhaps the most important omission is that concerning the role of the administrative branch of the government in decision making. The roles played by the Chief Executive, the program administrator, the technical expert are not mentioned, and they are of increasing importance in the decision making of modern governments. Persons interested in these aspects may want to see *Policy and Administration* by Paul Appleby, University of Alabama Press, University, Ala., 1949.

enced by the administration, the judiciary, interest groups, and influential individuals. But at least many, if not most, decisions are reached through the deliberations and actions of legislatures. Thus, we shall limit our discussion to decision making in this agency of government. In other words, we shall observe the decision-making process of individuals comprising an organized government at the point at which they commonly make decisions—namely, among their representatives in legislatures.

Decisions are made—in our case, choices with respect to goods, services, and facilities to be used jointly—in legislative branches of governments in the United States through a process described by John C. Calhoun as the Doctrine of the Concurrent Majority. Calhoun and, more recently, John Fischer [8] have observed that legislatures in the United States are not composed of well-disciplined parties with thought out positions on each issue. Our legislatures are composed of numerous and diverse interest groups, each representing a different and particular interest (e.g., potato growers, prohibitionists, silver producers, advocates of the advancement of Negroes, World Federalists, etc.). And no one of these groups typically is strong enough to impose its will on all others (i.e., pass a piece of legislation by itself). Thus, the central problem in American politics is that of finding a way to bind together the diverse and conflicting minority groups so that they can take action—make a decision (e.g., make a decision to provide veterans with hospital benefits, build a system of superhighways).

The binding together of a majority on an issue from among the diverse and conflicting groups is accomplished through conciliation, compromise, and endless "horse trading." If one interest group is to win the passage of a piece of legislation, say providing for the serving of hot lunches in all public schools, it will necessarily be forced to give up those features which are most objectionable to other groups, say a free-lunch feature, and then perhaps stand ready to vote favorably on an irrigation project for the arid West and a continuance of tariff protection on manufactured textile products. *This is the way a concurrent majority is obtained; this is the way a decision is reached on one issue.* But once the issue is settled, the majority melts away, and the whole process must be repeated on the next issue, and so on. And, of course, the elements of a majority on one issue will differ from those on the next.

In the process of forming a majority to effect a decision on a particular issue, two unwritten rules are generally observed. First, if the vital in-

[8] "Unwritten Rules of American Politics," *Harper's Magazine*, November, 1948.

terest of a particular group is jeopardized, it may veto the action of the majority. In the Senate of the United States, this veto power is lodged in the filibuster, where a minority is permitted to talk a piece of legislation to death. In other words, outside of emergency periods, the majority will tolerate the view of the minority on issues crucial to the latter's well-being. This unwritten rule makes life tolerable for the minority, helps avoid decisions that lead to civil disobedience and war.

The second unwritten rule is that the minority interest will not use its veto power indiscriminately. It must make every effort to find a compromise on each issue, using its veto power only as a last resort. For if any group wields this veto weapon recklessly or irresponsibly, the other factions or interest groups will turn on that group and remove or destroy the interest which it seeks to maintain. In other words, the majority tolerates the interest of the minority, and the use of the veto power to protect that interest, only to the extent that the majority believes that the interest of the minority is vital—crucial—to the position of the latter.

The formation of a majority from among many, diverse, and conflicting interest groups on a particular issue can take place only through compromise, conciliation, and "horse trading." But bargaining and compromise do not take place easily in the open and usually do not have a fresh, healthy appearance when they do. Thus, the forming of coalitions typically does not take place in legislative halls; coalitions are formed in committee rooms, cloakrooms, and "smoke-filled" rooms out of the public eye. Speeches for home consumption are delivered in the legislative halls, but the aggregating of sufficient votes to carry an issue (or defeat it) is done in committee.

Now the question may be asked: "What has all this got to do with economics? Is not the foregoing discussion concerned with politics, not economics?" Our first answer must be that the foregoing discussion has been concerned with politics—the art of legislative politics in the United States. But politics does not take place in a vacuum. It is always concerned with an issue or a problem, and very often that issue or problem is an economic one. We learned in an earlier section of this chapter that one-half to three-quarters of the expenditures of governments at all levels in the United States is made to provide consuming units with goods, services, and facilities (i.e., may be defined as collective consumption). Thus, we see that a major portion of the decisions of governments are concerned with the kinds and quantities of goods, services, and facilities to provide consuming units. And the foregoing discussion of politics was presented to shed some light *on how these choice decisions are made in organized governments.*

Within voluntary associations. The decision-making process in voluntary associations differs markedly from that in organized governments. This is true, in part at least, because the composition of voluntary associations tends to be more homogeneous than that of organized governments. The voluntary association is less afflicted by diverse and conflicting interests; the membership of a voluntary association is likely to have similar goals and similar interests. This is the basis of their coming together in the first place. Thus, much of the reconciliation of conflicting interests through compromise and "horse trading" which must take place in the legislative bodies of governments to achieve a majority, hence make a decision, is absent in the decision making of voluntary associations.

But the voluntary associations have their troubles, too. The work in voluntary associations—the going to meetings, the preparing of reports, the conducting of a program, the carrying out of an activity—is typically done in part or whole by volunteer workers. And where the work of an organization is carried on by unpaid volunteer workers, that work tends to devolve on a faithful few. Those who have been members of a church or a club or a service group will recall how most members are always too busy to help out with the program of the organization, and on each new project the same faithful few—those who truly believe in the purposes of the association—end up carrying the work load. Now, those individuals who do the work—those who organize a church supper, or those who sponsor a carnival to finance the purchase of playground equipment, or those who organize a drive to raise funds to build a community hospital —are the ones confronted with problems, hence the ones who are forced to make decisions. It is generally the case in voluntary associations, especially the more informal ones, that the nonworking members are willing to let the working members take the lead in the decision making of the organization. So long as the rank-and-file members feel that the working members are selfless individuals working for the purposes of the organization, they are willing either to accept the recommendations of the working members or to give them a completely free hand. Thus, the selfless few, who do the work of the group, tend to make the decisions for the group.

The above generalization probably becomes less true as voluntary associations become larger and more formal in organization. The more inclusive the voluntary association becomes, the less homogeneous the composition of the membership. In this context, special-interest groups and conflicting-interest groups develop, and the membership is less willing to let the decision-making function slip into the hands of the working few. Where the membership of a voluntary association is large and the interests of the membership are diverse, the organization must formalize its decision-making procedures. And, within the confines of these procedural rules, we find the same informal processes of compromise, conciliation, and "horse trading" developing that we observed for the decision-making bodies of government. And the cause is the same. The growth of special and conflicting interests, where the voluntary association is large and inclusive, requires bargaining and compromise to form a majority, hence reach a decision.

THE LOGICAL BASES OF COLLECTIVE CONSUMPTION

In thinking back over the kinds and quantities of goods and services that are consumed collectively, either through government or through voluntary organizations, it is clear that most of these items are not sold in convenient units at local shopping centers. The single consuming unit does not customarily purchase in retail establishments at the time of the need for the service so many units of road service or police protection or education or national defense. It does not because it cannot; customarily, these services are not for sale in this form. The single consuming unit customarily joins with other consuming units, either through government or through voluntary associations, to acquire the kinds and quantities of these services that they decide they need; then they use these services jointly.

Now, the important question is: "Why are not these services, which are customarily consumed collectively, produced privately and sold to individual consuming units as each has need for them? Why, for example, are not road systems and educational systems customarily produced by private firms and units of road service and educational service sold to consumers as they want them?" It was fairly common early in our national history for private companies to build a road or a bridge and sell units of the service in the form of tolls. Educational service is not uncommonly offered for sale by private schools at the primary and secondary levels, and private institutions at the collegiate level are an accepted part of our higher educational system. And the family that wants additional police protection can hire that service from private agencies. So we have had experience, in some cases considerable experience, with individual purchases of these services. The question thus remains: "Why have we come to depend largely upon a collective form of consumption in certain consumption lines?"

Efficiency in providing service. One justification for, as well as an explanation of, the tendency toward collective consumption in certain lines (e.g., roads, public parks) is to be found in the gains in efficiency from this form of consumption as compared with private consumption.[9] If, for example, each individual using the road system were required to pay at the time of use for each unit of road service consumed, our road system would be cluttered up with tollhouses and tollhouse attendants. To collect from each user of the road system, pay stations would have to be located at each principal intersection, and the user would have to stop at each of these stations to pay or be checked off in some fashion. Such a procedure would lead to a serious wastage of time by all users of the road system. And the money costs of maintaining toll stations at each principal intersection would be exorbitant.

Thus, we see, where consumers of a service have ready access to the service at many points in time and space, that a policy aimed at selling units of that service at the time of use leads to an inefficient type of operation. Inconvenience to the consumer and high operating costs make private consumption undesirable where ready access to the service prevails. Efficiency is to be gained by having the group decide what kind of road system or park system we are to have and how it is to be financed and then permitting each consuming unit to use the facility free of charge within the rules governing its use.

Extra-buyer benefits. A second justification for collective consumption in certain lines (e.g., education, police protection, sanitation) is to be found in the benefits that accrue to others from an adequate level of consumption by each individual in those lines. The consumption of education benefits others besides the persons being educated: an educated electorate is basic to the maintenance of a democracy; high productivity resulting from complex technical skills rests, in turn, on a literate working force; technological advancements, hence new and better products for everyone, grow out of the advanced training of young men and women; the writing of a powerful novel for the enjoyment of many results from the educa-

[9] This and later paragraphs benefit from the discussion of "The Role of Government Expenditure," chap. 10 of *Economics of Public Finance*, by O. H. Brownlee and Edward D. Allen, Prentice-Hall, Inc., New York, 1954.

tion of some yet unknown person; and so on. All these are examples of extra benefits that accrue to society from the education of particular individuals. Thus, we call these benefits *extra-buyer benefits*, for satisfaction from the consumption of education accrues to persons other than the one purchasing the education.

Police protection illustrates another form of this extra-benefit principle. If one community does not maintain adequate police protection and it becomes a haven for criminals, this circumstance increases the cost of police protection in other areas. Thus, the cost of police protection in any one area may be reduced by adequate protection in all areas. Similarly with sanitation: the practice of poor sanitation in one area places an extra burden on neighboring areas.

Thus, in those lines of consumption where (1) others seriously suffer from the failure of certain persons to consume adequately or (2) others benefit materially from adequate consumption by the relevant persons, the community or society generally specifies the level of consumption for all and by law or convention or both forces everyone to consume at that level or above. This is what we do in such lines as education, public health, police and fire protection, and national defense. And the justification for this form of collective consumption rests in the extra benefits realized or extra costs avoided by members of the group taking the action.

Minimum standards of consumption. A third justification for collective consumption in certain lines (e.g., food, housing, medicine) is to be found in the necessity of maintaining a minimum standard of consumption in these lines. It is clearly demonstrable that the failure of consumers to achieve a minimum standard of consumption in such lines as food, housing, and medicine results in an increased incidence of disease, retarded physical development, and lowered physical activity. Where this underconsumption results from old age, physical handicaps, or catastrophes (e.g., death of the principal income earner, a flood), most of us feel an obligation to aid, or give assistance to, the persons in need. Basically, we do believe that we are our "brother's keeper." And the minimum standards of consumption suggest the levels at which consumption needs to be maintained.

Holding these beliefs and having a growing body of knowledge with respect to consumption standards, communities acting through their representative governments have in recent decades decided what kinds and quantities of goods and services should be made available to disadvantaged members of the community, and under what conditions. In other words, the community determines what kind of welfare program it is to have and, in doing so, makes decisions with respect to the kinds and quantities of goods and services to be used by consumers coming under the welfare program. And since the community makes the choice decisions, we call the process collective consumption. The justification for the community making these kinds of decisions rests on the following line of reasoning: (1) minimum standards of consumption can be formulated with reasonable objectivity in certain lines; (2) where these standards of consumption are not met, human failure results; hence, (3) the community should protect individuals from this form of failure by helping all members of the community achieve the minimum standards.

The more common justifications of collective consumption presented above, which in fact become explanations for the tendency toward more collective consumption, refer most directly to that consumption occurring through governments. The latter two reasons for, or justifications of, collective consumption through governments are also relevant with respect to voluntary associations. The extra-benefit argument and the consumption-minima argument provide, respectively, the rationale for a voluntary association (1) purchasing playground equipment for the use of all children in a neighborhood and (2) establishing and maintaining a home for the aged. In fact, the success of a program of collective consumption undertaken by voluntary association rests entirely upon the persuasiveness of these two arguments. The voluntary association by definition is denied the use of force—police power. Hence, any group consumption activity undertaken by it can succeed only to the extent that members believe that (1) persons other than those immediately consuming the service or facility benefit (i.e., there are extra-buyer benefits) and (2) they have an obligation to help other members of society realize a decent standard of living.

Questions and Points for Discussion

1. What do we mean by group, or collective, consumption? Develop a full but concise definition.

2. What types or forms of collective consumption typically occur at different levels of government in the United States?

3. Describe the dollar magnitude of collective consumption undertaken through governments in the United States: in the aggregate, by type of service provided, by level of government.

4. Is collective consumption increasing or decreasing in the United States? What percentage of the Net National Product of the United States is consumed collectively?

5. Do we have a generally accepted general theory of group decision making? If so, describe it. If not, why not?

6. What justifications are commonly advanced for collective consumption? Describe each, and give your appraisal of each.

References

Arrow, Kenneth J.: *Social Choice and Individual Values*, Cowles Commission Monograph 12, John Wiley & Sons, Inc., New York, 1951.

Black, Duncan: "On the Rationale of Group Decision-making," *Journal of Political Economy*, February, 1948.

Brownlee, O. H., and Edward D. Allen: *Economics of Public Finance*, Prentice-Hall, Inc., New York, 1954, chap. 10.

Commons, John R.: *The Economics of Collective Action*, The Macmillan Company, New York, 1950.

Musgrave, R. A., and J. M. Culbertson: "The Growth of Public Expenditures in the United States," *National Tax Journal*, June, 1953.

25. *Economic Policy and the Consumer*

To this point, we have not discussed economic policy as it relates to consumption. We have not said what the consumer *ought* to want or *ought* to decide or *ought* to do. And very little has been said with respect to how the economy *ought* to operate to contribute to the well-being of consumers. In fact, the policy-connoting verbs *ought* and *should* have been used sparingly, and purposely so. The hope has been that, as knowledge and understanding are acquired with respect to how the economy operates, and the role of the consumer in the economy, the individual can and will make progressively wiser decisions on all policy questions relating to consumption.

It is perhaps of some advantage, however, for students of economics to get the views of their teachers and authors on policy, for several reasons. First, the student gains perspective for appraising the work of a speaker or writer if he knows the views of the person involved on important policy questions. Second, it is helpful in formulating a position on a policy question to know how others have approached the problem and dealt with it. Third, the views of the party concerned, the authors in this case, on certain issues might turn out to be useful and valuable. In any event, we shall devote the few remaining pages of this volume to a consideration of certain courses of action that might be taken on certain questions relating to consumption (i.e., policy).

It will come as a disappointment to some and a relief to others to discover that the authors have no clear-cut program of action to offer consumers. They do not know, except possibly with respect to the minimum level of consumption in some of the more basic items, what goods and services family units ought to be consuming. They have no pet institutions or practices to offer consumers which would solve most or all of their ills. In short, they have no specific policy proposals to make. And this complicates the problem of discussing policy; it is easier, far easier, to be *for* something.

But there are policy questions, having a bearing on consumer well-being, that we can study with profit. Questions concerning over-all social goals are continuously being debated and decided by society: whether more personal security is desirable, for example. And the implications for consumer well-being of pursuing such a policy objective might well be considered in a discussion of economic policy for consumers. Then, there are the more prosaic questions concerning means, or methods, of achieving the generally accepted social goals to be decided: whether, for example, public grades and standards are more desirable than private grades and product differentiation. In the interests of brevity, we shall limit this discussion of policy to questions of the latter type. Given the generally accepted social goals of the 1950s, we shall consider (1) those areas where the choice of means for achieving a social goal has important implications for consumer well-being and (2) what the implications of certain alternative courses of action may be. And it should be recognized that the conclusions of the authors with respect to the implications of a particular course of action amount in fact to a policy suggestion. It is important to remember, however, that these conclusions amount to *suggestions*—suggestions which are not necessarily all-inclusive and which are relevant only in the context of the generally accepted social goals of the 1950s.

THE POLICY PROBLEM

It is probably incorrect to think in terms of some one course of action which best fits the needs of all consumers in all respects, hence might be described as *the* policy for consumers. This is true for a number of reasons. First, consumption is only one among numerous activities in which the individual may be engaged: he is likely to be engaged in some sort of productive activity, or possibly as a parent, or as a conversationalist, or as a lover, or as something else. Hence, consumption plays a different role for different individuals, depending upon its place in the activities schedule of the whole man. Certainly, we cannot and should not equate the concept of a consumer with the whole man.

Second, individuals in their part-time role of consumers are not a homogeneous lot. The diversity that we observe among individuals with respect to interests, personal goals, and cultural and physical backgrounds also applies to these individuals as consumers. These differences among individuals lead to differences in spending and saving habits, differences in the allocation of income among major categories of consumption, and differences with respect to particular goods and services consumed. In short, the choice decisions of consumers vary widely in society, as do the modes of thought and action in arriving at those choice decisions. Hence, it is inappropriate to conceive of consumers as a group of homogeneous individuals with similar interests and aspirations. And the quest for a policy for consumers, in the sense of fitting most or all of the needs of most or all consumers, would seem to be a waste of time. We can and do have policies with respect to the consumption of whisky and milk, hours of work, and the use of land. But we do not have a consumption policy, just as we do not have a production policy. Neither production nor consumption is sufficiently homogeneous to require or permit the formulation of *a* policy.

But, within reason (i.e., taking into account long-run consequences as well as the short run, the rules and mores of society, and some consideration of the other fellow), all consuming units do seek to maximize the satisfaction of the members composing them. This is a generally accepted form of behavior in Western democratic societies: each consuming unit is expected to live in a way that maximizes the well-being, material and otherwise, of each individual in it. Thus, consuming units generally share this common experience and seek to achieve this common goal.

We can, however, agree on the general acceptance of this maximization goal by members of society without making any real headway on the problem of what to study or discuss as consumption policy. The practical problem remains: "How is the general maximizing goal to be translated into specific, or concrete, policy questions admitting of answers?" Our analysis in Part II pointed up the difficulties involved in prescribing a specific pattern of consumption to maximize the satisfaction of all consuming units or, for that matter, any one unit. We cannot at this point in answer to the question: "What bill of goods and services will maximize the satisfaction of consuming unit A?" say that consuming unit A should save some given percentage of its income, or cease going to "movies," or substitute milk for coffee, and so on. The policy pursued by each consuming unit with respect to the allocation of its limited income (and possibly time) can only be determined by the consuming unit involved, *where we accept the general social goal of satisfaction maximization for the individual, but where the individual's utility functions are not known or cannot be known.*

The above conclusion with respect to a specific policy question is essentially negative, but it does suggest one thing, namely, how to select specific questions for discussion that have a bearing on the maximization of the consumer satisfaction. We shall select for consideration specific policy questions that are suggested by, or emerge from, previous analyses in this volume. From our experience with decision-making problems of consumers, where the social goal of satisfaction maximization is assumed, we shall select the more important questions concerning the means of realizing that goal for discussion. In other words, our study to this point becomes the guide for translating the general goal, satisfaction maximization, into specific policy questions, the implications of which we shall consider here.

POLICY QUESTIONS FOR CONSIDERATION

Increased consumer information. By this we mean: "Would the dissemination of more information more widely among consumers concerning the characteristics and performances of products customarily consumed be desirable?" We shall not, however, concern ourselves with whether this line of action should be executed by private or public institutions; perhaps a division of responsibility is in order. Stated more precisely the question then is: "Should consumers generally increase their expenditures (either in direct payments or in taxes) to become better informed concerning the characteristics and performances of products in the market?"

In general terms, it would seem that, if increased consumer information helped consumers to select the items which satisfied their wants at a lower net cost, then more information would be desirable. In this circumstance, more information would increase the satisfaction received by consumers in their choices of goods and services from any given income.

There is considerable evidence which suggests that consumers would be importantly benefited from more information. The wide difference to be found in the prices of similar items sold under different brand names in drugs, textiles, and household appliances suggests that more and better information in these areas would aid consumers to improve their choices (i.e., obtain a bill of goods that satisfies their wants at a lower cost). The misinformation, half information, and appeal to emotions common to much advertising suggest that more factual information would be helpful to the consumer. Finally, efficient choices can be made only where information concerning alternatives is complete: the consumer cannot possibly select a bill of goods and services that maximizes his satisfaction where he does not know of the existence of important product substitutes.

And this is most important in a country such as the United States, where the consumer is confronted with such varied and diverse product and service substitutes.

Too much information concerning minor items can, of course, become burdensome, and too active decision making on minor items can become irksome. Furthermore, we would not want to pursue a policy of disseminating consumer information that costs more than the gains resulting from a more efficient selection of goods and services. And the point where increasing costs of disseminating information become equal to the gains in total satisfaction received cannot be determined with exactness. But the authors would be inclined to guess that consumers generally in the United States fall far short of that point. In other words, the pursuit of a general policy designed to increase information concerning the characteristics and performance of goods and services customarily consumed would increase the total satisfaction of most consuming units.

Increased governmental inspection and regulation of goods and services. By this we mean: "Would more governmental inspection and regulation of goods and services be desirable?" Governmental agencies at various levels in the United States commonly inspect and regulate the processing and handling of water, foods, and drugs, also the provision of certain technical services (i.e., medical services), and to a lesser degree such items as housing, securities, and sellers' claims on any product. Where the consumption of a product is indispensable to the well-being of consumers and consumers are unable readily to test the product for required qualities or characteristics (i.e., fluid milk, drugs), it seems appropriate to have some public agency inspect and test the product involved. Indeed, there would seem to be no other way to protect consumers against the fraudulent activities, or possibly ignorance, of a few sellers.

Whether this type of regulatory work should be intensified in existing lines and extended to other lines is an open question. Or perhaps, more accurately stated, the question does not admit of a general answer. It may be the sanitary ordinances with respect to milk are too severe in some communities or perhaps in most communities, and the sanitary regulations with respect to public eating places are too lax in some communities or perhaps most communities. These, however, are questions of fact that cannot be determined in this short discussion of policy. They can be determined only by individual investigations of the product or service for the communities involved.

In this policy area, then, we are unable to reach any general conclusions as to the desirability of more inspection and regulatory work. In the main, the question can be resolved only through empirical investigations, and these by local communities. It is important to recognize, however, that each community must have some agency for reviewing existing regulatory work and considering the desirability of extending regulation and control to some new product or service. Further, the more dissemination of information that occurs concerning the characteristics and performance of products and services, the less reliance that need be placed on regulatory actions. And this would seem to be desirable, since regulations that are policed through widespread consumer action are generally more effective than those policed by a few government officers.

Maintaining and increasing competition. By this we mean: "Would more widespread and more effective action to maintain and increase competition be desirable?" Competition takes two principal forms, price competition and product competition, and the consumer has an important stake in both forms. The former permits the consumer to purchase more products with the same amount of funds and the latter to purchase a better product with the same amount of funds. And either leads to increased consumer satisfaction. The practical question is: "How is this competition to be maintained and enhanced?"

Traditionally, we have relied on the enforcement of the Sherman Act, and later antitrust acts,[1] to maintain competition. In broad terms, these acts make any type of restrictive agreement or arrangement among firms illegal, but the application of this principle to particular restrictive agreements or arrangements is determined by the courts as cases arise. This particular policy has two important weaknesses. First, the maintenance of competition is made to depend upon the taking and the winning of a court action. Court actions are costly in terms of both time and money; hence, this type of action is employed only in the more important or dramatic instances. Second, lack of competition, or monopoly, under the Sherman Act is made to depend upon proof of collusion, and overt collusion is sometimes difficult to prove.

What is more important, lack of competition can and does take other forms. Bigness influences competition: there is little or no competition where one firm occupies 90 to 100 per cent of the market. But the antitrust laws and court decisions are ambiguous on this point. The absence of competition among rivals often takes the form of a nonaggressive, live-

[1] The Clayton Act of 1914 and the Federal Trade Commission Act of the same year.

and-let-live policy by the rivals, and where this is the case, a spirit of competition cannot be revived or induced by court action. The problem is not one simply of breaking up or restraining collusive action: it is one of instilling an attitude—a willingness to compete—in some instances, and the establishment of a sufficient number of firms in others.

There are numerous courses of action besides the antitrust approach leading to more rather than less competition in the economy that might be pursued if we are really serious about increasing competition. Those to be discussed here are designed to force competition where court actions are powerless. These courses of action include:

1. *Government aids to getting started in business.* This approach might involve assistance in financing, assistance in organization and management, and assistance with the technical aspects of production. The objective of increased competition is achieved through this approach by encouraging the entry of new firms in old and established commodity lines.

2. *The establishment of government-owned, yardstick plants.* This approach involves the construction and possible operation of efficient plants in monopolized areas. In areas of nonaggressive competition this form of action can strike fire and revive the competitive spirit: for example, the provision of electric power in rural areas through government-sponsored cooperatives in the 1940s awakened private power companies as nothing else could. Perhaps more of this in fields heavily monopolized (e.g., medicine, television) would bring to the consumer some of the blessings of competition—lower prices, more efficient service, and better-quality products.

3. *Government research and development in nonagricultural lines as well as in agriculture.* This approach would involve the operation or subsidization by government of experiment stations to develop new products and production methods. Under this approach, the fruits of research and development would be available, in part at least, to the small producer as well as the large corporation, hence strengthen the competitive position of the small firm relative to the large one.

4. *The development of Federal controls over incorporation procedures.* This approach would require all firms operating in interstate commerce to incorporate (i.e., organize) under the same rules and in the public eye. Rigorous action here could reduce and perhaps eliminate interlocking directorates and corporate mergers made with the sole aim of obtaining a stronger monopoly position in the market. This line of action would help counteract the continued trend toward bigness.

How far any one of these, or all four of these, courses of action should be pursued is open to debate. Certainly, the pursuit of any one of these, or all four of these, courses of action should not be to establish competition for its own sake. We are not interested in competition for its own sake; we are interested in competition for the benefits to consumers that are supposed to flow from this form of economic organization. The criteria for appraising the consequences of the pursuit of these various competitive policies can then be stated as follows: (1) Do they contribute to production efficiency? (2) Do they contribute to the passing along to the consumer the gains realized from increased efficiency? (3) Will they contribute to a continued improvement of the products involved? In general terms, it would seem that a pursuit of the courses of action outlined above would satisfy these criteria. But the best-intended governmental actions sometimes yield unhappy and unexpected results. Thus, a wise competitive policy should involve a continuous appraisal of any specific action program in the light of the above criteria.

Establishment of consumption minima. By this we mean: "Would the establishment of a program of action designed to assist consumers achieve certain defined minimum levels of consumption be desirable?" Minimum standards of consumption have been slowly developing over the past several decades. The question is: "Should this process be speeded up, first, in formulating the minima and, second, in effecting them?" The answer to this question would seem to turn on two considerations: first, the extent to which consumption falls below realistically determined minima and, second, the extent to which the social philosophy is accepted that the stronger members of society should help the weaker or indigent members of society.

With respect to the first consideration, it would appear that there is much underconsumption (i.e., consumption falling below realistically determined minima) in medicine, housing, and activities for teen-age groups. Underconsumption in food and education in the United States remains acute in a relatively few instances, but the problem is no longer widespread. In physical terms, a problem may be said to exist in certain consumption lines and situations.

With respect to the second consideration, there is little to be said. One either believes that he should help the weaker, indigent, members of society to realize some minimum standard of consumption, or he does not. The consideration is an ethical one; and conclusions with respect to ethics may not be deduced from logic. They are based on the individual's value system, which is acquired from experience over time.

But, for those individuals who hold the view that society should assume the responsibility of caring for, or guarding the welfare of, its weaker members, the realization of minimum standards of consumption becomes a desirable policy. It becomes an effective course of action for eradicating consumption deficiencies.

Fiscal policy and consumer incomes. By this we mean: "Should the fiscal operations of the Federal government be managed with the goal of maintaining stable money incomes at a high, or full, level of employment?" In an economy where government does not play an active role, the volume of employment and the level of money incomes of those employed are determined by the interrelations of the three aggregates, consumption, saving, and investment. In modern-day economies where governments do play an active role, the fiscal operations of governments (i.e., the collection and disbursement of funds by governments) also influence the volume of employment and level of money incomes. To illustrate this proposition, let us consider three cases out of an infinite number of possible situations; and let us assume that each of these cases starts from a full employment situation.

Situation 1. The government increases its expenditures for defense purposes. It increases taxes by the amount of the increased expenditures, pursuing a "pay as you go" policy. Consumer spending is reduced by the amount of the taxes, so that aggregate saving is unchanged. Total investment also holds constant. In this case, *aggregate expenditures* do not increase, and employment and money incomes do not change. Aggregate expenditures composed of total consumer expenditures, total investment, and total government expenditures do not change; hence, prices and incomes do not change.

Situation 2. Government increases its expenditures for defense purposes. But, in this case, it does not increase taxes by the full amount of the defense expenditure (a budget deficit is created). Consumer expenditures are reduced, but not by the full amount of the defense expenditure. Savings may be assumed to hold constant, but private investment increases in the favorable economic climate. In this situation, aggregate expenditures increase owing to (*a*) the government expenditures financed through borrowing (the amount of the budget deficit) and (*b*) the increased private investment financed out of private loans. This is the familiar case of a wartime inflation. Money incomes and the price level rise through the injection of purchasing power created through the expansion of credit.

Situation 3. Government decides to pay off debt by banks. It increases taxes to accomplish this purpose. Consumption is reduced by the amount of the increased taxes. Savings may be assumed to hold constant. Private business investment declines in the unfavorable economic climate. In this case, *aggregate expenditures* decrease owing to (*a*) the debt-repayment policy of the government and (*b*) the decline in private investment. Here we have a deflation originating with the government's decision to run a budget surplus for the purpose of reducing the public debt.

Each one of the above cases could be elaborated upon in the way of tracing the consequences of the initiating fiscal action or in the way of developing the possible interrelations with monetary policy, wage policy, foreign-trade policy, and so on. But these ramifications are beyond the scope of this discussion. The important point to be made from the above cases is that *governmental fiscal operations have a direct effect on aggregate expenditures and aggregate expenditures in turn have a direct effect on the volume of employment and level of money incomes.* And the concern of consuming units with this problem is obvious: the employment status and money incomes of the income earners of consuming units determine in large measure the level and patterns of expenditure of those consuming units.

Bearing in mind that the fiscal operations of government have a direct effect on aggregate expenditures and aggregate expenditures have a direct effect on employment and money incomes, (1) we do not want government to ignore these relations and take fiscal actions which lead to either inflation on one hand or unemployment on the other, and (2) we do want government to take those fiscal actions, in so far as it is possible, which counteract inflation on one hand and unemployment on the other. In general terms, this means that we want the fiscal actions of the government in periods of unemployment to contribute to an expansion of aggregate expenditures and in periods of inflation to contribute to a contraction in aggregate expenditures. More specifically, this means that government should seek to run a budget deficit in periods of unemployment and a budget surplus in periods of inflation. Such a fiscal policy is known as a *countercyclical* policy, and its purpose is that of maintaining aggregate expenditures at a level which generates full employment. In this view, the fiscal operations of government represent a giant balancing wheel for the economy—pouring purchasing power into the economy in periods of deflation and drawing purchasing power out in periods of inflation—the ultimate goal being more stable and more certain consumer incomes.

An active household expenditure policy. By this we mean: "Should consuming units generally spend more time and effort weighing and appraising expenditure alternatives, experimenting with new products and practices, and adjusting to new situations?" In a dynamic society such as ours, the answer to this policy question would seem to be "yes." Where commodity prices are continually changing, new products and services are coming onto the market, money incomes are changing, and tastes and preferences are being molded and changed, a consuming unit cannot expect to maximize the satisfactions of its members, or in vector-analysis terms maintain a high disbursement efficiency, *from a static expenditure policy*. Utility maximization by consuming units in a dynamic world requires a continuous and conscious adjustment in the allocation of expenditures to the dynamic elements of that world.

Purchasing by habit or rule of thumb in the case of minor items, such as cigarettes and chewing gum, probably does not lead to serious disbursement inefficiency. And the avoiding of conscious decision making with respect to these minor items may contribute to the easing of psychic tensions. But all of us have had experience, in our own lives and those of acquaintances, with the purchasing of food and clothing items by habit and larger consumer items by arbitrary rule. And it is in this area of consumer expenditures that disbursement inefficiencies develop. Those consumers who do not make conscious choices and experiment in the areas of food, clothing, household furnishing, and durable goods cannot expect to maximize their satisfactions in the dynamic world in which we live.

Here, then, we encounter another application of the equimarginal principle. How much time and energy should decision makers in the household pull away from their role of parents, or citizens of the community, or income earners, and so on, to expand and intensify the process of choosing or selecting goods and services used in living? Obviously, there is no single answer to this problem for all households. Each household must allocate those limiting factors, time and energy, among the various activities of the household as best suits the preferences and values of its members. But if consuming units generally were cognizant of the potentialities for increasing their total well-being (i.e., total satisfaction) from adopting and maintaining an open-minded, inquiring, innovating attitude in their selection and acquisition of goods and services used in living, we might see considerably more time and effort devoted to decision making in this area.

In a certain sense, we are saying that a wise purchasing policy for consumers is superior to an inept one. But, in a more profound sense, we are saying that a wise purchasing policy in a dynamic world requires conscious and continued deliberation, a willingness to explore and experiment, and finally active adjustment in consumer purchasing patterns.

CONSUMER PARTICIPATION IN POLICY FORMATION

No major consumer movement has ever developed in the United States, and there are no prospects that one will develop in the foreseeable future. This failure, if we are to call it that, stems from the heterogeneity of consumers with respect to values, goals, and practices—also, because the individual has other roles to play besides that of a consumer. And in the United States the role of the producer has and continues to be emphasized. But this does not mean that the individual cannot or should not participate in and help influence the formation of policies that have a bearing on consumption. The consumption activities of each individual constitute an important part of his total activity; hence, the individual has a vital interest in consumption and will on occasions want to join with others with similar interests to take a stand on issues relating to consumption. In other words, many, if not most, *individuals* are not interested in participating in a consumer movement which focuses on every issue from the viewpoint of the consumer, but they are interested from time to time in influencing existing or potential courses of action relating to consumption.

The question is: "How may individuals from time to time participate in and influence the formation of policies relating to consumption?" Different observers of social action would no doubt give different answers to this question, but the authors would suggest the following: Producer groups organized around a particular product or activity will not in general be interested in questions relating to consumption. Except in the insurance field, consumer groups are unimportant or nonexistent. Therefore, the individual interested in participating in and influencing the formation of policies relating to consumption must turn to and work through general purpose groups: parent-teacher associations, the League of Women Voters, businessmen's service clubs, political action groups, and political parties.

Most individuals will not have joined one of these general purpose groups for their stand on some policy issue relating to consumption. The typical individual will have joined one of these groups in an effort to be a good citizen—to help make his community or society a better place in which to live. These are the individuals who provide the mortar which binds communities and societies together. Now, it is among these socially minded persons working in general purpose groups that policy positions with respect to consumption are commonly taken, hence an influence on consumption policy is exerted. And it is among the members of these general purpose groups that the individual seeking to influence consumption policy will find friends and allies.

Policy formation is not an easy task. A particular policy (i.e., a particular course of action) in an important field involving an important issue will be formed and executed only through the hard work of those most concerned. Thus, we may not expect any one of the policy lines discussed in the previous section to take concrete form and be carried out in an automatic fashion. The realization of any one will depend on the efforts of interested individuals. But, in this case, interested individuals have few or no well-organized consumer groups through which to work. Thus, the fate of these policies along with others related to consumption depends in large measure upon the efforts of existing general purpose organizations. These are the organizations which in the past have championed policies designed to increase the satisfaction of consumers, and these are the organizations with which individuals interested in consumer policies must expect to work in the future.

Questions and Points for Discussion

1. What difficulties are encountered in formulating a single, inclusive policy for consumers?

2. Make a list of policy issues, or questions, important to consumers. How does your list differ from that presented in this chapter? What do you think gives rise to this difference?

3. Do you agree with the authors with respect to the minor role played by consumer organizations in the United States? If so, what is the explanation for this failure of consumer organizations to develop and flourish in the United States?

References

The Economic Report of the President submitted to the Congress annually.

"Economics for Consumers," published regularly in *Consumer Reports*, Consumers Union of the United States, Inc.

Norris, Ruby Turner: *The Theory of Consumer's Demand*, Yale University Press, New Haven, Conn., 1941, chap. X.

Waite, Warren C., and Ralph Cassady: *The Consumer and the Economic Order*, 2d ed., McGraw-Hill Book Company, Inc., 1949, chap. XXI.

Index